TRANSACTIONS OF THE
ROYAL HISTORICAL SOCIETY

FIFTH SERIES

VOLUME 24

LONDON
OFFICES OF THE ROYAL HISTORICAL SOCIETY
UNIVERSITY COLLEGE LONDON, GOWER ST., W.C.1
1974

ISBN 0 901050 22 9

Made and Printed in Great Britain by Butler & Tanner Ltd, Frome and London

CONTENTS

TRANSACTIONS OF THE
ROYAL HISTORICAL SOCIETY

THE PROBLEM OF PAPAL POWER IN THE ECCLESIOLOGY OF ST BERNARD[1]

By J. W. Gray, M.A., F.R.Hist.S.

READ 9 FEBRUARY 1973

BORN in 1090, dying in 1153, Bernard Abbot of Clairvaux lived through the aftermath of that great ideological upheaval which is generally (though rather misleadingly) known as the 'Investiture Contest'. As he played a leading part in the religious life and ecclesiastical politics of his age it is not surprising that his massive output of sermons, treatises and letters should have given rise to an even more massive output of historiographical comment and interpretation. It is equally understandable that modern Bernardine studies should have tended to concentrate on the question of Bernard's attitude to the basic ideas of the eleventh-century reform movement—and, in particular, to the expression which was given to these by Gregory VII during his stormy pontificate. Yet, as Dr Kennan has recently pointed out, so far from providing a clear answer to this question these studies confront us with a 'bewildering garden . . . from which a student can pluck an interpretation of Bernard's . . . theory as Gregorian, anti-Gregorian, . . . proto-protestant or any one of a variety of other hues'.[2] Can order be brought into this chaos, or do these various interpretations reflect an inherent ambiguity in Bernard's own thought?

As far as the relationship between the spiritual and temporal powers is concerned, Dr Kennan's 'Review of scholarship' shows clearly enough that at least one school of thought—that which sees Bernard as a consistent 'Gregorian' or 'exponent of the

[1] The following abbreviations are used in footnotes: *PL = Patrologia Latina*, ed. J. P. Migne; C = *Sancti Bernardi Opera*, edd. J. Leclercq *et al.* (Rome, 1957–). The numeration of Bernard's letters refers to *PL* 182.

[2] E. Kennan, 'The *"De consideratione"* of St Bernard of Clairvaux and the papacy in the mid-twelfth century: a review of scholarship', *Traditio*, 23 (1967), p. 73.

hierocratic theme'[3]—is too dependent on selective quotation and too neglectful of historical context to survive scholarly criticism intact.[4] When we bear in mind that the 'Gregorian' passages in Bernard's letters can be balanced by others (for example, in the letters which he wrote to Conrad of Germany) which stress the co-equality of the two powers under God,[5] and that the much-quoted 'two swords' passage in the *De Consideratione papae* occurs in the context of the Roman republican revolt, not of 'right order in the world at large',[6] we may well be inclined to agree with Mgr Jacqueline's comment that 'Bernard est plus orienté vers la solution des cas concrets que vers la constitution d'une théorie générale abstraite',[7] and to accept Dr Kennan's suggestion that his views on this subject tend to reflect the atmosphere of a post-concordatory era in which the argument about the relationship between the two powers had been *de facto* resolved by compromise.[8]

But the argument which had been reopened by the eleventh-century reformers was not of course solely concerned with this relationship. By the time when the conflict between Gregory VII and Henry IV began, the papacy was already at odds with important sections of the episcopate over the question of the exemption of Cluniac houses from diocesan jurisdiction,[9] and of the twenty-seven theses of the *Dictatus papae* nine were concerned with the claim of papal primacy in a strictly ecclesiastical sense, and fourteen with the assertion of papal authority *vis-à-vis* the episcopate.[10] This ecclesiastical side of the Gregorian programme has been aptly described as an attempt to 'substitute a disciplined, objectively ordered administrative mechanism for the informal, traditional, or patrimonial organization which had directed the social life of the Church hitherto',[11] and its centralizing tendency was most clearly revealed in the fourth and twenty-fourth theses of the *Dictatus,* which asserted the authority of papal legates over

---

[3] W. Ullmann, *The growth of papal government in the middle ages* (London, 1955), pp. 426–37.

[4] E. Kennan, *art. cit.*, pp. 94–111.

[5] *Epp.* clxxxiii, ccxliv, 1; see also the 'dualist' argument addressed to Henry of Sens, quoted on p. 9 below.

[6] E. Kennan, *op. cit.*, pp. 101–5.

[7] B. Jacqueline, *Papauté et épiscopat selon St Bernard de Clairvaux* (Paris, 1963), p. 2.

[8] E. Kennan, *art. cit.*, p. 107.

[9] H. E. J. Cowdrey, *The Cluniacs and the Gregorian reform* (Oxford, 1970), chapter II.

[10] *PL* 148, cols 407–8.

[11] H. V. White, 'The Gregorian ideal and St Bernard of Clairvaux', *Journal of the history of ideas,* 21 (1960), pp. 324–5.

the episcopate and provided for the by-passing of inferior ecclesiastical courts by direct appeals to Rome.[12] The first formal and public opposition to it came from the *Reichskirche* bishops assembled at Worms in 1076, and though the Worms sentence[13] is perhaps best known for its repudiation of Gregory's claim to be a valid pope,[14] the terms in which it rejected his views on church government are of much greater historical significance. Addressing Gregory, the signatories declared that 'you have taken from the bishops . . . all that power which is known to have been conferred on them through the grace of the Holy Spirit . . . for you assert that if any sin of one of our parishioners comes to your notice, even if only by rumour, none of us has any further power to bind or loose the party involved', and added that the effect of such action was to 'distend all the limbs of the Church which before your times led a quiet and tranquil life, according to the admonition of the Apostle', and to 'shake into pitiable disorder the whole strength of the Apostolic institution, and that most comely distribution of the limbs of Christ which the Doctor of the Gentiles so often commends and teaches'.[15]

Rather surprisingly, this important text appears in only one of the many useful general collections of medieval texts in translation which have appeared in recent years,[16] and Dr Ullmann has briefly dismissed it with the comment that 'constructive criticism was not the strength of the episcopal resistance'.[17] Yet, as Dr Ullmann has also pointed out, the bishops' attack on the programme of the *Dictatus* did contain a 'material point';[18] indeed, as they went on to suggest by their reference to Gregory's defiance of 'sacred learning', it was firmly based in Scripture and patristic tradition. Christ's commission of the binding and loosing powers to his disciples (which Matthew's gospel reports separately from his similar commission to St Peter) had been interpreted by SS Cyprian, Jerome and Ambrose as implying the directly divine origin of the apostolic role of bishops and their consequent apostolic co-equality with popes, and this view had been given wide

---

[12] *Quod legatus ejus omnibus episcopis praesit in concilio, etiam inferioris gradus . . . ; quod illius praecepto et licentia subjectis liceat accusare.*

[13] *Monumenta Germaniae Historica*, edd. G. H. Pertz *et al.*, *Legum IV, Constitutiones I*, pp. 106–8.

[14] The sentence was not (*pace* Ullmann, *op. cit.*, p. 350) a 'deposition', but a declaration of the legal invalidity of Gregory's election process.

[15] Translation taken from *Imperial lives and letters of the eleventh century*, edd. T. E. Mommsen and K. F. Morrison (New York, 1962), p. 148.

[16] *Documents of the Christian Church*, ed. H. S. Bettenson (2nd edn, Oxford, 1963), is the exception.

[17] Ullmann, *op. cit.*, p. 349. [18] *Ibid.*

currency by a Pseudo-Isidorean decretal which stated that 'the priestly order began with Peter, because to him was first given pontifical status (*pontificatus*) in the Church of Christ . . . but the rest of the apostles received honour and power with him in equal association (*pari consortio*) and wished him to be their chief (*principem*)';[19] moreover, the idea of the Church as a divinely ordained living organism, or 'Body of Christ', was a commonplace of early medieval ecclesiology which rested on interpretations of a number of New Testament texts by St Augustine and Gregory I (among others).[20] How was the papal *principatus* to be interpreted, and where did the effective headship of the 'Body' reside? The classic texts of the pre-Gregorian period, from the much-quoted Gelasian letter to the Pseudo-Isidorean collection, were open to differing interpretations which may perhaps for the sake of brevity be described as 'episcopal' and 'papal'—the former placing the headship in Christ, ascribing a 'primacy of honour' to the papacy, and stressing the theme of apostolic co-equality, and the latter transferring the headship to the papacy and expounding the papal *principatus* in a strictly juridical and governmental sense.[21] The significance of the Gregorian programme lay in the fact that it restated the papal view of these texts with unprecedented rigour, but (as Dr Ullmann has noted) the earlier canonical collections had to be purged of 'episcopal bias' before they could be used to support it,[22] and the Worms sentence was a sharp reminder of the existence of an alternative tradition. Though the bishops' opposition to Gregory's policies can be said to have been 'unconstructive' in the sense that it simply contradicted them, and though it was no doubt partly motivated by self-interest and temporary subservience to royal power, it derived great strength and staying-power from its roots in this tradition. Moreover, far from being resolved by compromise, this ecclesiastical side of the argument was complicated and exacerbated during Bernard's lifetime by—to name only three twelfth-century developments—the claims of primates to intermediate status in

---

[19] *PL* 130, col. 72B–C; for the patristic tradition see M. J. Wilks, *The problem of sovereignty in the later middle ages* (Cambridge, 1963), p. 349.
[20] For a useful summary see *Dict. de Théol. Catholique, ad v.* 'Eglise', pp. 2150–53.
[21] See the texts assembled by Gratian in D. 96, cc. 9–16. Ullmann (*op. cit.*, pp. 180–84) emphasizes the papal bias of Pseudo-Isidore—but *cf.* Fornier and le Bras' comment (quoted *ibid.*, p. 182 n. 8) that 'on a dit bien à tort que l'idée dominante d'Isidore était l'exaltation de l'autorité du Saint-Siège. Ce qui est vrai est qu'il poursuit avant tout la restoration de l'indépendance, de l'autorité et du prestige de l'épiscopat.'
[22] Ullmann, *ibid.*, p. 294.

the hierarchical system, the proliferation of new monastic orders, and the development of canonical jurisprudence and papal jurisdiction; meanwhile, the Pseudo-Isidorean reference to apostolic co-equality found its way through the *Decretum* and *Panormia* of Yvo of Chartres into the *Decretum* of Gratian[23] and, as we shall see, discussion of the 'Body' analogy continued inconclusively.

As a leading Cistercian spokesman and active participant in the public life of the Church, Bernard was bound to become involved in, and express views about, the question of 'right order' in a strictly ecclesiastical sense. Were his views on this subject 'Gregorian'? In attempting to answer this question it is important to remember at the outset that he brought to the argument all those literary skills which educated churchmen of his age had inherited from the classical world through the Fathers, encyclo-paedists, and text-book writers of the early medieval period—and prominent among these was the persuasive art of rhetoric. As Dom Leclercq has pointed out, literary exaggeration was a character-istic feature of the rhetorical tradition,[24] and it can be as clearly seen in the condemnatory parts of Bernard's arguments as in his *exordia* or introductory passages, which were designed to make the recipients more 'benevolent, attentive, and docile'.[25] More-over, in approaching the vast range of Bernard's comment on the subject of church government we must bear in mind that its reliability as a guide to his considered views may vary according to circumstance: it seems likely that the occasional references to this topic which occur in his sermons will be least affected by rhetorical distortion, since the sermons were primarily concerned with moral and spiritual issues;[26] on the other hand the treatises, which dealt at greater length with problems of ecclesiastical dis-cipline in which the recipients were themselves involved, may well be influenced by Bernard's sensitivity to the likely views and interests of those to whom he was writing; finally, the letters, which tend to reflect his immediate (and sometimes highly

[23] *PL* 161, cols 321B and 1149A; Gratian, D. 21, c. 2.

[24] J. Leclercq (tr. K. Misrahi), *The love of learning and the desire for God* (New York, 1961), pp. 146–48. See also *ibid.*, pp. 215–20, 317–18, for the rhetorical tradition in general, and Bernard as representative of it.

[25] I take this definition of the *exordium* from Alcuin's *Dialogus de Rhetorica* (*PL* 101, cols 929–30), which is a paraphrase of Isidore's *Etymologiae*, ii, 7 (*PL* 82, col. 128A).

[26] *Cf.* Leclercq's comment (*op cit.*, pp. 326–27) that Bernard's ability to 'achieve, in a period when rhetoric holds sway, a perfect literary mortification which mirrors his own detachment' is most noticeable in his more purely spiritual and mystical writings.

emotional, not to say irascible) reactions to particular events and individuals, should perhaps be regarded as the least reliable source of all. The inevitably very small sample of Bernard's opinions which follows has been selected with these considerations in mind—beginning with the sermons, going on to three treatises in which he discussed the nature and limitations of abbatial, episcopal, and papal power respectively, and only referring incidentally to the letters.

One of Bernard's most important contributions to twelfth-century religious thought was his development of the idea of the Church as the 'Bride' rather than the 'Body' of Christ, and he expounded this theme at length in the series of sermons on the Canticles which he preached to the inmates of Clairvaux between 1135 and 1148.[27] Like all his sermons these strike a predominantly subjective and spiritual note, but they are also both indirectly and directly relevant to the question of church government. In the first place, whatever extra dimension the 'Bride' theme may have added to the congregation's awareness of the spiritual significance of the Church, it did not necessarily imply any new view about its constitution; whether as 'Head' or as 'Bridegroom' the figure of Christ is seen as predominant; whether as 'Body' or 'Bride' the Church is seen as a divinely created organism or living whole—so that the conservative deductions of the Worms sentence could follow as naturally from either theme. Did Bernard make such deductions? To answer this question we must turn to those passages in the sermons where the subjective note is briefly replaced by comments on the structure of church government in the world. Here Bernard certainly stresses the importance of *discretio*, or the preservation of a proper relationship between the various parts of the hierarchical structure, as the basis of order and unity in the Church, reminding his congregation that 'when no-one is content with the office assigned to him, but all attend to everything indiscriminately, there will be no unity, but rather confusion'[28]—but it is a remarkable fact that his description and discussion of the relationship between the parts includes no reference to papal power. For Bernard the preacher it is abbots and bishops who, as rulers of the regular and secular Church respectively (*christiani . . . utriusque ordinis principes*), 'strongly control it by just laws' lest it collapse into ruin,[29] and it is of bishops that

[27] For the general significance of the Canticles in medieval religious thought, and particular textual and stylistic questions relating to Bernard's sermons, see Leclercq, *ibid.*, pp. 106–8, 208–14, C I, pp. xv–lxv, and C II, pp. ix–xxxiii.

[28] *Serm. in Cant.* xlix, 5 (C ii, p. 76).

[29] *Serm. in Cant.* xlvi, 2 (*ibid.*, pp. 56–57).

he speaks when he says (here quoting a much-used text from Matthew's Gospel) that their divinely ordained authority is in no way dependent on their individual qualities;[30] conversely, the only reference to the Petrine 'power of the keys' which we find in these sermons occurs in a purely moral and spiritual context, in which Peter is seen as a guide to Christ and the true Christian life.[31] Nor do Bernard's other sermons alter the impression left by those which he preached on the Canticles; preaching, for example, to a Cistercian General Chapter on the 'three orders of the Church' he finds in Noah the prototype of the 'first order' of 'rulers of the Church', among whom he includes the abbots in his audience[32]–and though his sermons in honour of SS Peter and Paul contain one reference to the Petrine commission, this too is given a purely moral and spiritual interpretation.[33]

As far as the abbatial 'rulers of the Church' are concerned, the fullest exposition of Bernard's views on church government is to be found in the *De Praecepto et dispensatione*.[34] This treatise is closely related (both in its actual text and in the structure of parts of its argument) to a long letter which Peter the Venerable of Cluny wrote to Bernard in defence of Cluniac observance of the Benedictine Rule against Cistercian criticisms.[35] Although the uncertain date of both works makes it impossible to give a firm answer to the question whether Bernard influenced Peter or *vice versa*, their interdependence provides us with a good opportunity to compare the views of the two authors. On most points these coincide: both agree that the dispensing power of abbots does not extend to the alteration of immutable divine laws;[36] both agree, nevertheless, that obedience is due even to evil abbots because their authority is divinely ordained (here using the text from Matthew's Gospel which Bernard was later to use in his sermon on the Canticles);[37] but their accounts of the relationship between abbatial authority and other parts of the hierarchical system are different. Whereas Bernard simply says that abbots derive their powers from 'the rules of SS Basil, Augustine and Benedict, the authentic canons, and any other ecclesiastical institutions of fit authority',[38] and

[30] *Serm. in Cant.* lxvi, (*ibid.*, p. 186).
[31] *Serm. in Cant.* lxix, 4–5 (*ibid.* pp. 204–5).
[32] *Serm. ad Abbat.*, 1 (C v, pp. 288–89).
[33] *Serm. in Sollemn. Apost.* (*ibid.*, pp. 189–90).
[34] C iii pp. 253–94. Textual questions are discussed *ibid.*, pp. 244–50.
[35] *PL* 189, cols 112–59.
[36] *Loc. cit.*, pp. 257–58, and *loc. cit.*, cols 148A–B.
[37] *Ibid.*, pp. 275–76, and *ibid.*, col. 153C.
[38] *Ibid.*, p. 256.

makes no reference at all to the question of papal power, Peter devotes a long and somewhat tortuous passage to this very point. According to Peter:

> . . . although the Roman chief priests (*praesules*) have greater power than other fathers of the Church—although, that is, they have authority over the whole Church—yet these we are defending have equal power in the sense that, as the Roman chief priests preside over the whole Church, and other pontiffs (*pontifices*) over individual churches, so these monks rule their subjects in all things with equal power and authority. For although the Roman chief priest may correct the errors of others by his special authority, nevertheless these others have complete power over their own subjects, and equal authority in giving orders so long as they do not err.[39]

Why then did Bernard fail to mention the question of papal power, not only in his sermons but in a treatise which was directly concerned with questions of ecclesiastical law-enforcement and dispensation? Bearing in mind the monastic context of the material we have so far been considering, it seems at least probable that its general tone reflects both the strong tradition and the actual constitution of the Cistercian Order. As Mgr Jacqueline has pointed out, the *Carta Caritatis* with its complex order-structure and sensitivity to the jurisdictional rights of diocesan bishops ran clean contrary not only to the Cluniac system, but to the centralizing principles of the Gregorian programme as well.[40] Moreover, if we turn to the record of Bernard's own participation in disputes about monastic discipline we can find very clear evidence of his opposition to papal intervention in particular cases; in the case of Robert of Châtillon, for example, he appealed from an adverse papal judgment to the judgment of God,[41] and in the case of Adam of Morimond he openly contradicted a papal dispensation by reiterating a sentence of excommunication which had been passed before it was granted.[42]

Do Bernard's views on the episcopal office confirm or modify the impression left by the sermons and the *De praecepto et dispensatione*? For an answer to this question we must turn to the *De moribus et officio episcoporum*, which he composed for Henry, archbishop of Sens,[43] and which incidentally provides a

[39] *Loc. cit.*, col. 153A–B.
[40] Jacqueline, *op. cit.*, pp. 29, 117–19.
[41] *Ep.* i, 7.   [42] *Ep.* vii, 20.
[43] *PL* 182, cols 809–30.

very clear example of his rhetorical technique, in the sense that
its hortatory and critical themes are set within the frame of an
exordium and *conclusio* which contain those parts of the argument most likely to be welcomed by its recipient. So Bernard
begins by referring to the directly divine origin of the episcopal
binding and loosing powers,[44] and ends by describing monastic
exemption from diocesan jurisdiction as resistance to the bishop
in his capacity as 'Vicar of Christ'.[45] Between these points he
devotes most of the treatise to an exposition of the moral and
spiritual qualities most necessary for a bishop, and it is in connection with the last of these—humility—that he refers to the
subject of *discretio*. After reminding Henry of his obligation to
prevent 'the aggrandisement of one church against another'
among his own provincial subjects, on the ground that such
aggrandisement is 'offensive to the Church's Bridegroom',[46] he
also reminds him that he in turn must obey the Pauline injunc-
tion to 'be subject to the higher powers'—driving this point home
by quoting Christ's instruction to his disciples to 'render unto
Caesar the things that are Caesar's, and to God the things that
are God's' and adding: 'if you regularly support Caesar's successor
—that is, the king—in his courts, councils, business, and armies,
is it beneath your dignity to show similar respect to each and
every Vicar of Christ, as has been ordained from ancient times
among the churches?'[47] Though we may note in passing that
Bernard's strongly 'dualist' line of argument at this point fits
rather ill with the notion that he was a thoroughgoing 'hierocrat',
the argument does end with a reminder of the existence of papal
authority. Yet the reminder is vague and general, and it is somewhat weakened by Bernard's ascription of the 'Vicariate of Christ'
to bishops as well as the papacy and, more particularly, by the
fact that it occurs in a context in which he condemns the actual
exercise of papal jurisdiction in particular cases. As we have seen,
elsewhere in the treatise he describes the aggrandisement of
churches and the exemption of monasteries as not merely regret-
table but actually deleterious to the 'Bride of Christ' and the
apostolic function of bishops; yet he also says that aggrandisement
is facilitated by 'Romans . . . who care not how the matter be
settled, but dote on gifts and rewards',[48] and that exemptions are
gained by 'papal privileges obtained at a price'.[49] In asserting, as

[44] . . . *regni coelorum claves Deo auctore vobis traditas suscepistis (loc. cit.,*
col. 812B).

[45] *Ite nunc ergo, resistite Christi Vicario . . . (ibid.,* col. 832C)

[46] *Ibid.*, col. 82A.   [47] *Ibid.*, col. 829B–C.

[48] *Ibid.*, col. 828B.   [49] *Ibid.*, col. 832C.

he does here, that the papacy itself is responsible for disturbing the divinely ordained structure of the Church, he speaks the language of the Worms sentence.

So far Bernard's comments on the subject of church government seem to reinforce the results of a quite different line of investigation—those studies of the politics of the early twelfth-century papal *curia* which have tended to show that Innocent II, whom Bernard strongly supported against Anacletus during the papal schism of the 1130s, was the candidate of an 'anti-Gregorian' party.[50] Yet the schism also produced one of Bernard's most strongly 'Gregorian' utterances on the subject of papal power, in a letter reminding the citizens of Milan that:

> the Apostolic see, by a unique privilege, is endowed with full authority (*plenitudo potestatis*) over all the churches of the world. Anyone who withstands this authority sets his face against the decrees of God. She can, if she judge it expedient, set up new bishops where hitherto there have been none. Of those which already exist she can put down some and raise up others just as she thinks best; so that, if she deem it necessary, she can raise bishops to be archbishops or the reverse. She can summon churchmen, no matter how high and mighty they may be, from the ends of the earth and bring them to her presence, not just once or twice, but as often as she sees fit.[51]

This letter may serve as a sharp reminder of the fact that, however dubious Bernard may have been about 'Gregorian' policies, and however ready he may have been to challenge particular papal decisions when they ran contrary to his own ideas and interests, he was equally capable of exalting the role of the papacy when he felt such a line of argument to be tactically necessary. Here, he was dealing with a dispute about the archbishopric of Milan which severely weakened the Innocentian coalition at a crucial moment in the history of the papal schism, and in the circumstances a 'Gregorian' manifesto no doubt seemed the most likely way of bringing the dissidents to heel.[52] Moreover, exactly the same tactical considerations apply, *mutatis mutandis*, to other letters of a similarly 'Gregorian' character which Bernard was to write during other ecclesiastical crises—for example, the dispute over the election to the archbishopric of York,[53] or the Roman republican revolt.[54] Such rather ephemeral evidence must surely

---

[50] White, *art. cit.*, pp. 334–36.   [51] *Ep.* cxxxi, 2.
[52] For the circumstances of the dispute, and Bernard's part in resolving it, see E. Vacandard, *Vie de St Bernard* (2nd edn, Paris, 1927), pp. 375–90.
[53] *Ep.* ccxxxix.   [54] *Ep.* ccxliii, 3.

be set in the context of Bernard's more carefully considered reflections—and for this reason it is fortunate that the last and longest
of his treatises, which was addressed to the Cistercian Pope
Eugenius III, was mainly devoted to a discussion of the role and
powers of the papacy.

Unlike Bernard's advice to Henry of Sens, the *De consideratione papae* was written in instalments during the very considerable period between Eugenius' accession to the papacy in 1145
and the year of his (and Bernard's) death in 1153;[55] moreover,
its internal structure is very much more complex. But though for
these reasons it may at first sight seem very different from the
earlier work, the general content and much of the actual phrase-
ology of its first four books is so strikingly similar as to suggest
that Bernard may have used his advice to Henry as a model.
De moribus et officio papae would be an appropriate title for
these books, and in them we encounter the familiar components
of a Bernardine argument—the self-abasing preface, the passages
exalting the role and office of the recipient, and the 'hard core' of
exhortation and criticism. The main substance of Bernard's discussion of the role of the papacy in the Church is concentrated
in the second and third books, and it begins with a remarkable
eulogy of Eugenius' power as monarchical ruler of the Church.
This passage has been so frequently quoted, and plays such a
large part in the argument of 'Gregorian' interpreters of Bernard's thought, that it is hardly necessary to repeat it *verbatim*;
suffice it to say that in its exposition of the papal *plenitudo
potestatis*, and in its ascription to the papacy alone of
that 'Vicariate of Christ' which Bernard had previously
ascribed to all bishops, it speaks—even more clearly than the
letter to Milan—the language of the *Dictatus Papae*.[56] But
it is the *exordium*, not the whole of Bernard's argument,
and as we read on we find him first modifying and then con-
tradicting it.

The first stage in this rhetorical counterpoint is reached when
Bernard reminds Eugenius that *plenitudo potestatis* does not after
all mean absolute sovereignty and dominion, but rather the status
of *villicus* or steward of Christ, and proceeds to interpret this role
in purely pastoral terms which are strongly reminiscent of his

[55] C iii, pp. 393–493. Textual questions are discussed *ibid.*, pp. 381–91.
Quotations in the text above are taken (with some modifications) from the
translation by G. Lewis (Oxford, 1908).

[56] *Op. cit.*, Book ii, c. viii, 15–16. Though it is clear from the context that
this passage refers to papal power in the Church only, Ullmann (*op. cit.*, p.
429 and n. 3) follows Alexander III and Innocent III in giving it a wider interpretation. On this point, see Kennan, *op. cit.*, p. 97.

sermons on SS Peter and Paul.[57] However, after placing this
initial emphasis on Eugenius' pastoral role Bernard does turn
to the question of the papacy's jurisdictional powers, and it is at
this point that his argument begins to diverge from that of the
exordium. First, after a long diatribe against the abuse of appeals
to Rome, he reminds Eugenius that direct appeals which by-pass
inferior courts are not only deleterious to ecclesiastical discipline
in practice but invalid in principle, on the ground that 'an appeal
must be from a sentence'[58]—a proposition which exactly corre-
sponds with the objection which the Worms sentence had raised
against papal acceptance of 'mere rumour' and which would, if
adopted in practice, have prevented the whole twelfth-century
development of the 'universal ordinary' jurisdiction of the
papacy.[59] However, this in turn leads to a more drastic stage in
the argument when he comes to the question of exemptions.
Characteristically, he approaches this topic by way of a lurid
account of the disastrous practical consequences of the 'exemption of abbots from bishops, bishops from archbishops, archbishops from primates and patriarchs'; then, after remarking
rather ambiguously to Eugenius 'you do this because you have
the power, but whether you have the right is open to question',[60]
he goes on to state the case against exemptions in a passage which
so clearly echoes the language of the Worms sentence, and so
clearly contradicts the monarchical doctrine of the *exordium*,
that it deserves to be quoted at length:

> You err if you reckon that your apostolic power is not only
> supreme, but the only power ordained of God. If this is your
> opinion you differ from the apostle, who says . . . 'let every
> soul be subject to the higher powers'. He does not say 'to the
> higher power' as if all power belonged to one man, but 'to the
> higher Powers' since it resides in many. Your power, therefore,
> is not the only power from the Lord; there are middle and
> lower powers. And as those whom God hath conjoined are
> not to be put asunder, so those whom God hath subjoined are
> not to be put on a footing of equality. If you cut off a finger,
> attach it to your head, and let it hang side by side with your
> arm, as a hand for the upper parts of the body, you create a

[57] *Ibid.*, Book iii, c. i.

[58] *Iniqua autem omnis appellatio, ad quam iustitiae inopia non coegit.
Appellandum a sententia* (*ibid.*, Book iii, c. ii, 7).

[59] For this aspect of papal jurisdiction, see F. W. Maitland, *Roman canon
law in the Church of England* (London, 1898), chapter III.

[60] *Op. cit.*, Book iii, iv, 14.

monstrosity. Something like this happens if you place the members in the body of Christ otherwise than he himself arranged them.[61]

The fourth book of the *De consideratione papae* is mainly concerned with the relationship of the papacy to its immediate Roman environment, and though Bernard's advice to Eugenius about the management of his *peculiaris populus*[62] and *curia* is of great interest, it is not strictly relevant to the wider question of papal authority in the Church at large. However, no account of Bernard's views on this question would be complete which ignored his reference to papal legates in the fifth chapter of this book, and the rhetorical *conclusio* on the subject of papal power (balancing the *exordium* in the second book) with which it ends. The fifth chapter illustrates the important point that though Bernard was a rigorous critic of the venality and misgovernment of individual legates *a latere* he never raised any objection in principle to the fourth thesis of the *Dictatus*,[63] or lent his support to the strong tide of opposition to it which continued to be a notable feature of ecclesiastical politics throughout his lifetime; in this respect at any rate he can be firmly classified as 'Gregorian'. On the other hand, though the *conclusio* may at first sight seem to be just a repetition in more flowery language of the *exordium*, it is significantly different. Though it contains an impressive list of papal roles—'. . . a rod for the powerful, a hammer for tyrants, the father of kings, the mitigator of laws, the salt of the earth, the light of the world, the priest of the Most High, the vicar of Christ, the Lord's anointed, and lastly the God of Pharaoh'—this list is preceded by the reminder that 'you are not sovereign lord of bishops but one of them', and the papal 'vicariate of Christ' is not here qualified (as it had been in the *exordium*) as 'unique'.[64] Mgr Jacqueline has described this passage as a 'mélange de poésie et de juridisme' in which 'l'éclat des images ne doit jamais nous dissimuler le rigueur et la précision de la doctrine canonique',[65] but though precision and rigour were certainly present in the *exordium* the former seems here to have been replaced by rhetorical poetry, and the latter (in so far as the passage refers to the relationship between the papacy and the 'middle and lower powers') by unresolved tension.

[61] *Ibid.*, Book iii, c. iv, 17.
[62] For the use of this term to describe the Roman people, see Ullmann, *op. cit.*, p. 63.
[63] See n. 12 above.
[64] *Op. cit.*, Book iv, c. vii, 23.
[65] Jacqueline, *op. cit.*, pp. 407–8.

Long before he reached this *conclusio* Bernard had written a passage in the first book of the *De consideratione papae* in which he advised Eugenius not to follow the example of his recent predecessors and offered the first Gregory, not the seventh, as a model.[66] Between the writing of the first and fourth books his relationship both with Eugenius and with the papal curia had sharply deteriorated, for various reasons among which his disastrous involvement in the crusading movement[67] and his unsuccessful attempt to lead an English and 'Gallican' episcopal party against the 'Romans' during the heresy trial of Gilbert of Poitiers[68] are possibly the most important. Consequently, some of the ambiguities and inner contradictions in the later parts of his discussion of papal power may well reflect his growing doubts about his ability to influence papal policy—doubts which he clearly indicates in his prefatory remarks to Eugenius at the beginning of the fourth book, when he says:

> if I knew better . . . how you received what I have already sent, I should proceed to the rest of my work with corresponding confidence or caution, or I might of course stop altogether. But since the distance which separates us renders such knowledge impossible, you must not be surprised if my discourse flows more thinly and ambiguously as I diffidently approach the middle of my subject.[69]

Nevertheless, the overall effect of the later books is to reinforce the hint he had dropped at the outset; in the circumstances, the extent to which they reveal his underlying sympathy with the doctrine of the Worms sentence is surely remarkable.

Dr Southern has vividly described the contrast between 'pre-Gregorian' Rome, to which 'men went . . . not as the centre of ecclesiastical government, but as a source of spiritual power',[70] and the 'post-Gregorian' Rome of the mid-twelfth-century—the governing centre of a system in which 'loose communal ties were drawn together in bonds of strict law, a vague sense of obligation was replaced by an exacting set of rules, and close definition was

---

[66] *Op. cit.*, Book i, c. ix.

[67] Bernard's comments, *ibid.*, Book ii, c. i, show how severely the failure of the second crusade had affected his position—but long before this his recruiting drive in Germany had run contrary to papal policy, which hoped for Conrad's assistance in Italy (see Vacandard, *op. cit.*, ii, p. 308 and n. 3).

[68] The most reliable account of this episode is in John of Salisbury's *Historia pontificalis*, ed. M. Chibnall (2nd edn, London, 1962), pp. 15–23.

[69] *Op. cit.*, Book iv, c. i.

[70] R. W. Southern, *The making of the middle ages* (London, 1953), p. 136.

sought where general principles had formerly sufficed'.[71] Bernard's response to this transformation was to say the least ambiguous, and the unresolved tension which appears in his final reflections on papal power is equally apparent in his attitude to the legal system which developed to support it: on the one hand he recognized its usefulness, and was himself no mean practitioner in the field of canonical jurisdiction and argument;[72] on the other, we find him drawing a sharp contrast between the letter of the canon law and the spirit which ought more properly to be the prime source of order and unity in the Church—variously describing the former as 'the laws of slaves and hirelings' or 'the laws of Justinian', and the latter as 'the law of Christ' or 'the law of God'.[73] Consequently, insofar as the Gregorian programme involved the unqualified acceptance of a fully centralized governmental structure, his attitude to the question of papal power in the Church can be described as 'anti-Gregorian'—and from a strictly logical or jurisprudential point of view it can perhaps also be described as incoherent.

Yet we have only to look again at Bernard's last treatise as a whole to see that to judge his views by such narrow criteria is to misunderstand them. Though *De moribus et officio papae* may well be an appropriate title for its first four books, the fact remains that Bernard himself gave a different title to this treatise —and the terms in which he explained both the title and the general plan of the work to Eugenius show that he regarded his discussion of the place of papal power in church government as only a part of a much larger scheme. According to Bernard, 'consideration' (which he distinguished from action[74]) was similar to contemplation,[75] and its four objects were 'yourself, things below you, things around you, and things above you'.[76] In this scheme the discussion of church government is set within a frame of subjective moral themes on the one hand, and theologically objective or contemplative ones on the other, and though Bernard in fact allowed his discussion of the first 'object of consideration' to alternate with his discussion of the second and third, he devoted the whole of the fifth and final book—which is also the longest—to 'a vision of heaven and speculation about the Divinity'.[77] For him, the first and last 'objects of consideration'

[71] *Ibid.*, p. 151.
[72] Kennan, *art. cit.*, pp. 105–6.
[73] Characteristic examples of this contrast can be found in *Ep.* xi, 5, and *De consideratione papae*, Book i, c. iv.
[74] *Op. cit.*, Book v, c. 1.　　　　[75] *Ibid.*, Book ii, c. 2.
[76] *Ibid.*, Book ii, c. 3.　　　　[77] Kennan, *art. cit.*, p. 114.

were always more important than the intervening ones; as Dr Ullmann has said, 'to rank him among the "political" writers would be some sort of degradation of his objectives'.[78] Moreover, if the weakness of the 'proto-protestant' school of Bernardine interpretation lies in its tendency to concentrate on this more spiritual side of his message to the exclusion of all else, the strength of his ecclesiology lies precisely in his refusal—not his failure—to provide a logically coherent solution to the perennial problem of the right relationship between the moral and spiritual insights which ought to inspire a Church, and the governmental structure which (in an imperfect world) is necessary to preserve and sustain it as an institution.

Nevertheless, the growth of more orderly and more effectively centralized governmental systems was a general trend of the age in which Bernard lived,[79] and, as Dr White has pointed out, 'charismatic ideals provide no rational principle for conferring leadership', and leave room for 'the intrusion of influences which are essentially irrational, unpredictable, and hence destructive of orderly development'.[80] Consequently, during the century after Bernard's death his complex reflections on the subject of papal power in the Church were simplified by selective quotation and interpretation so as to serve the propaganda-requirements of papal monarchy,[81] and by the beginning of the fourteenth century the 'triumphalist' interpreters of the papal 'Vicariate of Christ' had completed the theoretical revolution which began with the *Dictatus papae*.[82] Meanwhile, the trends in church government which Bernard had most strongly opposed turned out to be irreversible; the 'universal ordinary' jurisdiction of the papacy everywhere undermined the ordinary jurisdiction of bishops, the Cistercian Order itself sought and obtained exemption, and Gratian's *Decretum* turned out to be only a foundation for the vast edifice of the *jus novum*. Yet, as the exposition of the doctrine of papal sovereignty in the Church proceeded to its logical conclusion, the gulf between theory and practice steadily widened. In a world in which the actual operations of papal government were *de facto* circumscribed, with the tacit approval of most of the episcopate, by working conventions of a strongly 'dualist' kind, it could be clearly seen that the rearrangement of the

[78] Ullmann, *op. cit.*, p. 426.
[79] Southern, *op. cit.*, pp. 145–46.
[80] White, *art. cit.*, p. 348.
[81] A process which began with Alexander III and Innocent III. See n. 56 above, and Ullmann, *op. cit.*, p. 428 n. 4, p. 430 n. 8, p. 433 nn. 2 and 3.
[82] Wilks, *op. cit.*, chapter II.

'members in the body of Christ' had failed to achieve its ostensible aim of strengthening the Church as a fully coherent and independent institution; moreover, the structural changes of the post-Gregorian era can hardly be said to have done much to foster that true spirituality in the Church which had always been Bernard's main preoccupation. Nevertheless, though the tide of history ran against him in the twelfth and thirteenth centuries it seems to be turning in his favour in the twentieth; as the complexity of his thought is rediscovered, the problem with which he wrestled is once again being generally discussed—and though the form in which he expressed it was ecclesiological, his reflections upon it may perhaps be said to be as relevant, *mutatis mutandis*, to universities as they are to the Church Universal.

The Queen's University, Belfast.

NEW LIGHT ON THE INVISIBLE COLLEGE
THE SOCIAL RELATIONS OF ENGLISH SCIENCE IN THE MID-SEVENTEENTH CENTURY

By Charles Webster, M.A., D.Sc., F.R.Hist.S.

READ 9 MARCH 1973

IT is difficult to compose an account of the development of experimental science in seventeenth-century England without reference to the Invisible College. Indeed its grandiose title has come to be applied almost indiscriminately to any informal group of scientists, and no doubt this popular usage will continue, regardless of the conclusions reached by this or any other specialist paper. But such popular usage should not obscure the relevance of the Invisible College to certain serious historical problems. First, it is necessary to establish the identity of the scientific group which captured the imagination of the nineteen-year-old Robert Boyle. The College not only provided his initiation into science, but also inspired such strong motivation that Boyle became preoccupied with natural philosophy. For the rest of his life science was pursued not so much as a gentlemanly diversion, but in the spirit of a religious mission. Secondly, the Invisible College is relevant to any appreciation of the factors involved in the remarkable expansion of English experimental science which began shortly before the establishment of the Invisible College in 1646. This movement rapidly generated a whole spectrum of informal scientific groups and culminated with the formation of the Royal Society in 1660.

Straightforward identification of the Invisible College is ruled out by the paucity of evidence. The only direct references to the College come from the correspondence of Boyle, who mentioned it by name on only three occasions. From the first reference, contained in a letter to his former tutor Isaac Marcombes in Geneva, it is apparent that the College had been in existence for a short time by October 1646. Boyle provided Marcombes with a brief epitome of the aims of the *'Invisible'* or *'Philosophical College'*.

The other humane studies I apply myself to, are natural philosophy, the mechanics, and husbandry, according to the principles of our new philosophical college, that values no knowledge, but as it hath a tendency to use. And therefore I shall make it one of my suits to you, that you would take the pains to enquire a little more thoroughly into the ways of husbandry, &c. practised in your parts; and when you intend for *England,* to bring along with you what good receipts or choice books of any of these subjects you can procure; which will make you extremely welcome to our *invisible college . . .*[1]

A slightly different perspective is given in a letter to Francis Tallents, fellow of Magdalene College, Cambridge. This letter implies that the meetings of the Invisible College were held in London, providing a disincentive to Boyle's returning to his country home at Stalbridge in Dorset.

. . . the corner-stones of the *invisible,* or (as they term themselves) the *philosophical college,* do now and then honour me with their company, which makes me as sorry for those pressing occasions that urge my departure, as I am at other times angry with that solicitous idleness that I am necessitated to during my stay; men of so capacious and searching spirits, that school-philosophy is but the lowest region of their knowledge; and yet, though ambitious to lead the way to any generous design, of so humble and teachable a genius, as they disdain not to be directed to the meanest, so he can but plead reason for his opinion; persons that endeavour to put narrow-mindedness out of countenance, by the practice of so extensive a charity, that it reaches unto every thing called man, and nothing less than an universal good-will can content it. And indeed they are so apprehensive of the want of good employment, that they take the whole body of mankind for their care.[2]

A final brief reference to the Invisible College comes from a letter to Samuel Hartlib, written in May 1647. Boyle observed:

. . . you interest yourself so much in the *Invisible College,* and that whole society is so highly concerned in all the accidents of your life, that you can send me no intelligence of your own affairs, that does not (at least rationally) assume the nature of *Utopian.*[3]

Apart from the three well-known quotations above, two others probably refer to the Invisible College. The first is contained in

[1] Letter from Boyle to Marcombes, 22 October 1646, *The Works of the Honourable Robert Boyle,* ed. Thomas Birch (London, 1772), i, p. xxxiv. The Hartlib Papers, deposited in Sheffield University Library, cited in this article are used with the kind permission of their owner, Lord Delamere.

[2] Letter from Boyle to Tallents, 20 February 1647; Boyle, *Works,* i, pp. xxxiv–xxxv.

[3] Letter from Boyle to Hartlib, 8 May 1647; Boyle, *Works,* i, p. xl. In the 1744 edition 'rationally' reads 'relationally'.

an early essay, perhaps written in 1646 or 1647. At the point where criticism of authority is discussed, Boyle notes in passing that 'The Experiment of this I have lately seen in those I have had the happiness to be acquainted with of the Philosophicall Colledge: who all confess themselves to be beholding for the better part of their rare & newcoynd notions to a Diligence & Intelligence of their Thoughts'.[4] A further passing reference to the Invisible College comes from a letter to Boyle from his sister Katherine, Lady Ranelagh, probably composed in June 1647, which enclosed a letter 'from one of your own fraternity, who thinks himself in the highest class of your philosophical Society'.[5]

Although this concludes the well-authenticated references to the Invisible College, the letters composed by Boyle during this period abound with comments about college proposals. It has been too readily assumed that the term 'college' invariably denotes the Invisible College. However, close reading of the letters and reference to context indicate that Boyle applied the term to a wide variety of projects. His correspondents would not have been confused by this convention, but subsequent failure to appreciate implicit distinctions of meaning has led to mis-identification of the Invisible College and to much vain theorizing about its intellectual standpoint.

The traditional interpretation of the Invisible College emanates from Boyle's editor, Thomas Birch, whose 'supposition has with the passage of time acquired almost the authority of definitive interpretation'.[6] Birch believed that:

The Invisible College . . . probably refers to that assembly of learned and curious gentlemen, who, after the breaking out of the civil wars, in order to divert themselves from those melancholy scenes, applied themselves to experimental inquiries, and the study of nature, which was then called the new philosophy, and at length gave birth to the Royal Society.[7]

[4] 'Boyle Sermons', Royal Society, Boyle MS, 197, fos. 7v–8r. I am indebted to Professor J. Jacob for pointing out this reference.

[5] Letter from Lady Ranelagh to Boyle, 3 June [no year], Boyle, *Works*, vi, p. 522. Reference to problems over Boyle's Connaught lands suggests 1646 or 1647. In February 1646 Boyle gave Arthur Annesley authority to handle the affairs of his Irish lands; R. E. W. Maddison, *The Life of the Honourable Robert Boyle, F.R.S.* (London, 1969), p. 65. A postscript probably refers to Broghill's membership of the Derby House Committee for Ireland in June 1647.

[6] D. McKie, 'The Origins and Foundation of the Royal Society of London', *Notes and Records of the Royal Society*, xv (1960), p. 21.

[7] Boyle, *Works*, i, p. xlii. This quotation was repeated from the 1744 edition without alteration, but in 1756 he replaced 'probably' by 'seems to be' in *The History of the Royal Society* (London, 1756–60), i, p. 2.

Birch believed that Boyle was referring to association with the celebrated founders of the Royal Society whose weekly scientific meetings could be traced back to 1645.[8] However, Wallis emphatically avoided reference to 'melancholy scenes', this aspect of Birch's explanation being taken from Sprat's Royalist apologia for a later gathering of natural philosophers in Oxford.[9]

Birch's theory has been repeated by the standard histories of the Royal Society, many specialist studies and almost all general works.[10] Most advocates of this theory have assumed that the 'college' references in Boyle's letters refer invariably to the precursor of the Royal Society. Even Turnbull, who has adopted a highly critical attitude to the texts, believes that Boyle refers to the Wallis group in the letters to Marcombes and Tallents. Boyle's recruitment into science appears to have been conducted by a group which had developed a taste for collaborative exercises in experimental science, reflecting a movement which was spreading throughout Europe in the wake of the fertile 'new philosophy' of Galileo, Mersenne and Descartes.[11] Birch represented the Invisible College as a reaction against the parliamentary regime and revolutionary situation in England by fair-minded intellectuals who sought consolation by affiliating with a productive scientific movement.

Identification of the Invisible College with the 1645 group has been strongly disputed on both biographical and textual grounds.[12]

8 John Wallis, *A Defence of the Royal Society* (London, 1678); *idem*, Letter to Dr Thomas Smith printed in *Peter Langtoft's Chronicle*, ed. T. Hearne (Oxford, 1725), i, pp. clxi–clxiv; also in C. J. Scriba, 'The Autobiography of John Wallis, F.R.S.', *Notes and Records of the Royal Society*, xxv (1970), pp. 17–46.

9 Thomas Sprat, *History of the Royal Society* (London, 1667), pp. 57–58.

10 Birch's interpretation is followed by C. R. Weld, *History of the Royal Society* (London, 1848), i, pp. 39–40; R. F. Young, *Comenius in England* (London, 1932), pp. 17, 77; D. Stimson, 'Comenius and the Invisible College', *Isis*, xxiii (1935), pp. 373–88; G. H. Turnbull, 'Samuel Hartlib's influence on the Early History of the Royal Society', *Notes and Records of the Royal Society*, x (1953), pp. 101–30; P. R. Barnett, 'Theodore Haak and the Early Years of the Royal Society', *Annals of Science*, xii (1959), pp. 205–18; *idem*, *Theodore Haak, F.R.S.* (The Hague, 1962), p. 81; R. F. Jones, *Ancients and Moderns*, 2nd edn (Berkeley and Los Angeles, 1961), pp. 177–78.

11 Harcourt Brown, *Scientific Organisations in 17th Century France* (Baltimore, 1934); Barnett, *Theodore Haak*, chapters 4 and 10.

12 R. H. Syfret, 'The Origins of the Royal Society', *Notes and Records of the Royal Society*, v (1947), pp. 75–137; D. McKie, 'Origins and Foundation of the Royal Society'; M. Boas, *Robert Boyle and Seventeenth Century Chemistry* (Cambridge, 1958), pp. 31–33; R. E. W. Maddison, 'Studies in the Life of Robert Boyle, F.R.S. Part VI. The Stalbridge Period, 1645–1655, and the Invisible College', *Notes and Records of the Royal Society*, xviii (1963), pp. 104–24; *idem*, *Life of Boyle*, pp. 67–69.

Boyle's description of the utilitarian and utopian bias of the
Invisible College is not easily reconcilable with Wallis's account
of classic scientific problems under consideration in the 1645 group.
McKie finds it impossible to believe that any precursor of the
Royal Society or the Society itself was involved with 'philanthropic
Utopian topics of universal charity and goodwill to all men'.[13]
Furthermore, there is no evidence to connect Boyle with the members of the 1645 group listed by Wallis until long after the formation of the Invisible College. For instance, the dominant figure,
Wilkins, was not directly acquainted with Boyle until 1653, while,
apart from incidental contacts, Wilkins's associates were not known
to Boyle until after this date. It is also significant that Wallis's
detailed account of scientific meetings in London made no reference to Boyle. Therefore Turnbull's emphatic conclusion that 'In
regard to the origins of the Royal Society it seems that the Invisible
College *was* Dr. Wallis's scientific group of 1645', cannot be
sustained.[14]

An alternative solution was proposed originally in Masson's
monumental *Life of Milton* and more recently in Miss Syfret's long
study of the relation between Comenius, his followers and the
Royal Society.[15] In view of the 'universal, charitable and Utopian'
character of the Invisible College and Boyle's growing intimacy
with Hartlib during 1647, 'it seems far more probable that Boyle's
references to the Invisible College relate to the schemes of Hartlib,
Dury and Comenius for a pansophic college and an Office of
Address in which all their endeavours for the reformation of education, learning and religion were comprehended'. But this alternative hypothesis is not maintained absolutely consistently, since it is
conceded that Wallis and his colleagues were possibly 'included
by Boyle in the Invisible College'.[16] Of course, this extension of
the Invisible College to include Wallis's group exposes this hypothesis to precisely the same objections as the original solution proposed by Birch.

Conflation of the 1645 circle and Hartlib's group into a single
'Invisible College' has recently assisted Frances Yates to unearth
Rosicrucian roots for the Royal Society. A tenuous Rosicrucian
connexion is traced from Comenius and Andreae to the foreigners
Hartlib and Haak and thence to Wallis and his colleagues, the

[13] McKie, *op. cit.*, p. 22.
[14] Turnbull, 'Samuel Hartlib's Influence', p. 129. Italics as in the original.
[15] Syfret, 'Origins of the Royal Society'; D. Masson, *The Life of John Milton*
(London, 1859–94), iii, pp. 662–66. See also Margaret Lewis Bailey, *Milton
and Jakob Boehme* (New York, 1914), pp. 64–72.
[16] Syfret, *op. cit.*, p. 128.

precursors of the Royal Society. Boyle's use of the term Invisible College to describe this extended group is supposed to reflect continuing influence of the Rosicrucian *ludibrium*. 'We have thus here a chain of tradition leading from the Rosicrucian movement to the antecedents of the Royal Society.'[17] This account of formative influences on the precursors of the Royal Society is open to strong objection, but from our point of view Boyle's Invisible College is irrelevant to this issue, since it relates to neither the 1645 group, nor (as will be demonstrated below) to the followers of Comenius.

With the elimination of the 1645 group, a growing body of opinion has inclined to associate the Invisible College with the English followers of Comenius. The recent investigator of the origins of the Royal Society concludes that the Invisible College 'consisted of the founder members of a "philosophical college" which failed to materialise—the Office of Address envisaged by Hartlib'.[18] Ascribing more general Comenian functions to the Invisible College, Shapiro believes that the members 'hoped that through pansophia, a combination of universal knowledge, universal education and universal language, society could be improved and universal peace established'.[19]

This solution is indeed supported by the general resemblance between the views on natural philosophy expressed by the Hartlib circle and those in the Boyle letters referring to the Invisible College. Purver has described the growing sympathy between Boyle and Hartlib which developed during 1647 and 1648. But this does not account for the *origins* of the Invisible College in 1646. Boyle's correspondence suggests that his acquaintance with Hartlib dates from March 1647; the first reference to Boyle in Hartlib's voluminous papers is contained in a letter from John Hall to Hartlib, dated 26 April 1647. The extensive correspondence of Sir Cheney Culpeper, which gives a detailed impression of the day-to-day activity of Hartlib's circle first refers to Boyle in November 1647.[20] Nowhere in Hartlib's papers is there a reference to the Invisible College. Thus the association between Boyle and Hartlib occurred

[17] Frances A. Yates, *The Rosicrucian Enlightenment* (London, 1972), pp. 182–84.

[18] M. Boas, *Robert Boyle and Seventeenth Century Chemistry* (Cambridge, 1958), pp. 5–32. See also C. Hill, *Intellectual Origins of the English Revolution* (Oxford, 1965), pp. 105–6.

[19] M. Purver, *The Royal Society; Concept and Creation* (London, 1967), p. 205; B. J. Shapiro, *John Wilkins 1614–1672. An Intellectual Biography* (Berkeley and Los Angeles, 1969), pp. 26–27.

[20] Boyle, *Works*, i, pp. xxxvii–xxxviii; letter from Hall to Hartlib, 26 April 1647, Sheffield University Library, Hartlib Papers, LX 14. Letter from Culpeper to Hartlib, 10 November 1647, Hartlib Papers XIII.

too late for the latter to be regarded as the projector of the Invisible College.

The only source for speculations about Hartlib's involvement with the Invisible College comes from two letters addressed to him by Boyle in April and May 1647. The first promised support for 'that college, whereof God has made you hitherto the midwife and nurse'. Here Boyle was not referring to his own Invisible College, but to Hartlib's recently announced scheme for a state-endowed Office of Address, which was to be anything but 'invisible'.[21] The Office of Address dominated Hartlib's attention from 1646 onwards and it was quite natural for Boyle and others to refer to this agency as a 'College'.[22] Boyle's second letter referred explicitly to the Office of Address project and its associated literature, but also to an unspecified 'college', which from the context clearly relates to John Hall's projected utopian society, *Leucenia*. Finally this letter contains the third of Boyle's direct references to the Invisible College, which is best seen as a reply to Hartlib's requests for information. Boyle observed that 'you interest yourself so much in the *Invisible College*', reassuring his correspondent that 'the whole society is so highly concerned in all the accidents of your life'.[23] Thus this widely quoted letter does not provide evidence for the identification of the Invisible College with Hartlib's Office of Address. Quite the reverse; it indicates that the College had enjoyed until that time an independent history. After this late initiation into its affairs Hartlib undoubtedly exercised a deep influence on Boyle and his colleagues. Thus he was not the founder, but the liquidator of the Invisible College, providing a stimulus for the College to shed its invisibility in order to assume a more active role in public life.

Each of the above solutions to the Invisible College problem is rendered unacceptable because of incompatibility with basic biographical and textual evidence relating to Boyle. It may be unpalatable to believe that the brilliant young intellectual was collaborating with neither the leading natural philosophers nor the major group of puritan social reformers, but the basic facts of his biography suggest that London possessed yet a third centre of intellectual organization. Perhaps a more durable solution to the problem of the identity of the Invisible College might be produced

[21] Letter from Boyle to Hartlib (undated, but ascribed to April 1647 by Syfret), Boyle, *Works*, i, pp. xlvi–xlvii.

[22] The Office of Address was frequently referred to as a College by Culpeper and Dury; e.g. Letter from Culpeper to Hartlib [March 1646]: 'I cannot take notice of the extensiones of that colledge you have in your mind . . .' Sheffield University Library, Hartlib Papers XIII.

[23] Letter from Boyle to Hartlib, 8 May 1647, Boyle, *Works*, i, p. xl.

if we proceed from the basic facts of Boyle's biography and then consider whether his early associations suggest a tenable basis for a reconstruction of the Invisible College. An important clue on this matter is provided by evidence which suggests that Benjamin Worsley was Boyle's first scientific associate.[24] Indeed Worsley may have been the figure 'who thinks himself in the highest class of your philosophical Society' mentioned in the letter cited above, since this contains a postscript appealing for Boyle to assist Worsley's career by interceding with Broghill, who was a member of a relevant 'committee'.[25]

Particularly important evidence about the association between Worsley and Boyle comes from two letters composed in November 1646 and February 1647, precisely the period from which our first evidence about the Invisible College is derived. In scientific topics selected for discussion, utilitarian bias and social outlook, these letters to Worsley are strikingly consistent with Boyle's descriptions of the Invisible College. It is therefore very likely that they represent an interchange of ideas between two members of the fraternity.

In the first letter Boyle wrote at length about the merits of Worsley's plan for large-scale saltpetre manufacture, after hearing from his sister Katherine of favourable parliamentary response to this project. Such active industrial enterprise was morally excusable if it was not motivated by curiosity or avarice, but by 'the good they may do with it'. For his part Boyle, at his country home in Dorset, adopted the 'grand employment . . . to catechise my gardener and our ploughmen concerning the fundamentals of their profession'. He had already made novel observations and hoped soon to convey information which would further Worsley's 'great design' to publish a discourse *de usu partium* for the 'great world'.[26] In the second letter Boyle developed a theme mentioned in the first, that active correspondence could partly compensate for separation. Again Boyle was in Stalbridge, while Worsley had remained in London. In extravagant terms Boyle begged Worsley to continue his correspondence in order 'to sweeten my unwelcome

[24] Worsley's importance has been pointed out in Maddison, 'Studies in the Life of Boyle . . . The Stalbridge Period', pp. 110–11; *The Life of Robert Boyle*, p. 69. M. Boas also emphasizes the role of Worsley, but within the context of the Hartlib circle; *Robert Boyle and Seventeenth Century Chemistry*, pp. 7–31.

[25] Letter from Lady Ranelagh to Boyle [3 June 1647], Boyle, *Works*, vi, pp. 522–23. See note 5 above.

[26] Letter from Boyle to Worsley [n.d.]; Boyle, *Works*, vi. pp. 40–41. From internal evidence it is clear that the letter was composed shortly after 21 November 1646; see Maddison, *Life of Boyle*, p. 70.

separation from you'. His immediate concern was information about practical chemistry from Worsley's laboratory, pending the arrival of a wagon containing chemical apparatus which would form the nucleus of his own laboratory. He was clearly excited by the prospect of establishing a laboratory and frustrated by delays in the transport of his apparatus. But in spite of initial difficulties chemistry was praised for having cemented their friendship. Intense admiration was expressed for Worsley, whose letters were described using one of Boyle's characteristically cumbersome metaphors, as being 'more fertile in philosophy, than news, as oysters are in pearls, than in rattles'. Boyle recognized that he would be the main beneficiary from the correspondence, but he believed that Worsley would gain in stature, as the brightness of planets reflected the virtues of the sun. In addition, Worsley's free communication of knowledge was morally edifying.[27]

In view of the extremely close relationship between Boyle and Worsley exposed by the above letters, it is reasonable to suppose that they were jointly involved in the formation of the Invisible College, some time in the late summer of 1646. From the tone of the letters it is clear that Worsley, who was eight years older than Boyle, was the senior partner in this enterprise and probably its originator. Worsley's characteristic blend of Baconian utilitarianism, experimental chemistry and ambitious social planning, was highly congenial to Boyle and other members of the puritan intelligentsia. If Worsley was not a dominant member of the Invisible College, it will be necessary to discover some other figure displaying his range of interests and attitude to natural philosophy, who was also active in London in 1646 and intimate with Boyle by the autumn of that year. It is improbable that any candidate will be found who fits the role demanded by the Invisible College as well as Worsley himself.

Boyle's letters convey the impression that Katherine, Lady Ranelagh was intimately concerned with the affairs of the Invisible College. While as a woman she may have been reticent about formal membership, there are numerous testimonies of her forceful participation in religious, political and philosophical debates

[27] Letter from [Boyle] to [Worsley] n.d., Boyle, *Works*, vi, pp. 39–40. For the identification and dating at the end of February 1647, see Maddison, *Life of Boyle*, p. 70. Letter from Boyle to Lady Ranelagh, 6 March 1646/7, Boyle, *Works*, i, pp. xxxvi–xxxvii. Boyle's first exercises in experimental chemistry were destined to failure, a letter composed a few days later to Katherine conveying the news that the centre-piece of his laboratory, the furnace, arrived 'crumbled into as many pieces, as we into sects'. Letter from Boyle to Lady Ranelagh, 6 March 1646/7, Boyle, *Works*, i, pp. xxxvi–xxxvii.

among puritan intellectuals. Even as a young woman, she was venerated by her family and acquaintances alike. In time her reputation became inseparably linked with that of her brother. Hence the funeral eulogy of Burnet also commemorated Katherine as the woman who had 'made the greatest Figure in all the Revolutions of these Kingdomes for above Fifty Years'.[28] Accordingly her role was much more than that of a patroness and clearing house for correspondence. She would certainly have exerted as much influence as a full member and her numerous associates would have provided a clientele for recruitment.

The meetings of enthusiasts of the Invisible College probably centred around Worsley's laboratory and Lady Ranelagh's London home in Pall Mall. Although London was the central location for the fraternity, their careers or country residence would frequently have necessitated reliance on correspondence. The letter of June 1647 from Lady Ranelagh probably represents this mechanism in action. By this means the corporate spirit would be maintained in spite of the 'invisibility' of the fraternity.

Having established the close relationship between Boyle, Worsley and Lady Ranelagh it is now possible to move on to consider whether the social group in which they operated provided a feasible base for the wider Invisible College.

The obvious common denominator between Worsley, Boyle and Lady Ranelagh was their Irish connexion, a factor which among other things probably explains Worsley's early acquaintance with the Boyle family. Katherine, the seventh child of the first earl of Cork, married Arthur Jones, second Viscount Ranelagh, whose family had allied with Cork against Strafford before 1640. Through Jones, Katherine became the sister-in-law of Sir John Clotworthy and the niece of Dorothy Moore (the future wife of John Dury) who was the sister of the planter, Sir Robert King. Dorothy and Katherine established a deeply religious friendship and correspondence. At the outset of the Irish rebellion Katherine was besieged in Athlone Castle for nearly two years, before being allowed safe conduct to England. Once established in London, her home became a focal point for meetings of Irish protestants in exile or on political missions to parliament. Katherine was deeply sympathetic to the parliamentary cause, and pressed for the reconciliation of the King to parliamentary points of view.[29] Besides the Irish element and her immediate family, Katherine's circle rapidly

[28] Gilbert Burnet, *A Sermon Preached at the Funeral of the Honourable Robert Boyle* (London, 1692), p. 33.

[29] Letter from Lady Ranelagh to Sir Edward Hyde, Bodleian Library, Clarendon MS 22, fo. 114.

widened to include such puritan intellectuals as Milton, Sadler, Hartlib and Dury.

When Robert Boyle returned from his European tour with Isaac Marcombes, he gravitated immediately to Katherine's home where:

> with thankfulness to God, acknowledg'd as a seasonable Providence . . . since first in the heat of his youth, it kept him constantly in a Religious family, where he heard many pious discourses, & saw great store [of] pious examples, . . . Besides by this means grew acquainted with several Persons of power & interest in ye Parliamt and their party, wch being then very great, & afterwards the prevailing one, prov'd of good use, & advantage to him . . .[30]

Katherine undertook responsibility for the education of members of her family, entrusting Richard Barry, second earl of Barrimore, and her own son Richard Jones to John Milton. Another tutor involved with the Boyle family was Francis Tallents of Magdalene College, whom Robert Boyle introduced to the Invisible College.[31] Boyle, having completed his formal education, was introduced to parliamentarians and puritan intellectuals. Indeed in Katherine's immediate household Boyle would have encountered her sister-in-law, Margaret, Lady Clotworthy, wife of the prominent presbyterian parliamentarian.

By 1646 Robert Boyle's elder brother, Roger, Lord Broghill, had come to assume a leading role in Irish political and military affairs. In parliament he became identified with the party of Robert Sydney, Lord Lisle, who became Lord Lieutenant in April 1646. This alignment involved Broghill in political manœuvres both in London and Dublin.[32] Lisle's party included Sir William Parsons, Sir John Temple and Arthur Annesley, all of whom were accused of 'Independency' by their major opponent the Lord President. Parsons and Temple were long-standing associates of the earl of Cork, while at this time Arthur Annesley was entrusted by Robert Boyle with the management of his estates in Connaught.

By 1646 Broghill and most members of his family were advocates of a vigorous war policy in Ireland, with the result that they were thrown into alliance with the Independent party against royalist advocates of compromise & as well as the more obvious Catholic enemy. The war policy was seen as the most effective means of

[30] Robert Boyle, Autobiographical fragment, British Museum, Sloane MS 4229, fo. 68; Maddison, *Life of Boyle*, pp. 53–54.
[31] Maddison, *Life of Boyle*, p. 65; *H.M.C.*, *Egmont*, i, pp. 474–75, 491–92.
[32] K. S. Bottigheimer, *English Money and Irish Land: The 'Adventurers' in the Cromwellian Settlement of Ireland* (Oxford, 1971), pp. 91–108.

protecting the planting interest and of preventing the suppression of protestantism. The alignments involving Broghill in 1646 were very largely a continuation of associations which had been formed during opposition to Strafford.[33] Indeed in the impeachment of Strafford a crucial part was played by Clotworthy, whose family ties with both Pym and Ranelagh have been regarded as the basis for the 'connection of the Boyle–Ranelagh–Coote group in Ireland and the puritan party in England'. The result of their efforts was described by Cork—'Earl of Strafford was beheaded on Tower Hill as he well deserved'.[34] The early correspondence of Boyle indicates complete familiarity with the everyday developments in the Irish political situation, particularly during the period of his involvement with the Invisible College.

Worsley was involved with Irish affairs at a modest level. His career began in the service of Strafford, and then, at the outbreak of the rebellion, he became an army physician. But he soon left the army service and entered Trinity College Dublin. After obtaining a degree he returned to England, settling in London under the patronage of Sir John Temple, whose propagandist history of the Irish Rebellion was published in 1646. Subsequently Temple probably played an important part in securing Worsley's preferment in the Irish Civil Service. Temple's growing participation in Anglo-Irish politics was signified by his election to the House of Commons and membership of the Committee for Ireland formed in August 1646. Broghill was also actively involved with this committee, which was effectively dominated by the interests of Lisle's party.[35]

Worsley's first official recognition came in 1647, when the House of Commons decreed that 'Dr Gerard Boate, Mr Benjamin Worsley, and Mr Marmaduke Lynne, be appointed physician, Surgeon-General and Apothecary of the Army in Ireland, and sent to Dublyn'.[36] This may have been the topic under consideration in the letter from Lady Ranelagh to Boyle discussed above.[37] Worsley

[33] H.M.C., Egmont, i, pp. 367–74. In March 1647 Inchiquin pleaded with Lady Ranelagh to intercede with her brother on his behalf; ibid., i, pp. 374–75; H. F. Kearney, Strafford in Ireland, 1633–41 (Manchester, 1959), pp. 10–11; Maddison, Life of Boyle, p. 65. Kathleen Lynch, Roger Boyle (Knoxville, Tenn., 1965), pp. 38–69.

[34] Kearney, op. cit., pp. 199–200; Lismore Papers, ed. A. B. Grosart, v (London, 1886), p. 345.

[35] Bodleian, Clarendon MS 75, fos 300–1: autobiographical letter from Worsley to Lady Clarendon; J. B. Whitmore, Notes and Queries, clxxv (1943), pp. 123–28. H.M.C., Ormonde, ii, pp. 256–57, 284–85—Temple and Sir William Parsons were signatories of letters on behalf of 'Chyrurgian-General' Worsley in 1643. For Temple see Bottigheimer, English Money and Irish Land, pp. 101–8; also D. Underdown, Pride's Purge (Oxford, 1971), pp. 43, 82; D.N.B.

[36] Commons Journals, v, p. 247; 17 July 1647.   [37] p. 21 and n. 5.

and Boate were not able to take up appointments in Ireland immediately, probably because internal dissension in the parliamentarian party reduced the level of military assistance given to Dublin until 1649.

The date of Worsley's earliest acquaintance with Boyle is not known precisely, but it probably occurred at the end of 1645 or beginning of 1646. Worsley's reputation had spread by the autumn of 1645 to Culpeper, whose letters dating from this period expressed growing interest in Sadler, Milton and Worsley, all of whom were by this time involved in Lady Ranelagh's circle. In February 1646 Culpeper conveyed his joint regards to 'that excellent Lady at Westminster' (probably his first indirect reference to Lady Ranelagh), Mr and Mrs Dury and Worsley.[38] It is also apparent from these letters that although Culpeper and Hartlib were generally familiar with Worsley's projects during 1646 their association with him was not intimate. This was probably due partly to personal factors, but also to the fact that while they approached social policy in a similar spirit, experimental science occupied a much higher place in Worsley's programme than in the Office of Address of Hartlib and Dury.[39] While maintaining good relations with Hartlib, Worsley found Boyle a more congenial choice for participation in the Invisible College. Thereafter the Invisible College was announced to scholars who were under the patronage of the Boyle family such as Marcombes and Tallents. Thus the general context for the development of the Invisible College was provided by Lady Ranelagh's circle, reinforced by the Anglo-Irish members of Lisle's party. There is much circumstantial evidence to suggest interaction between the scientific and political groups which crystallized around Lady Ranelagh during 1646.

Two obvious candidates for the Invisible College within the Ranelagh circle are the brothers Gerard and Arnold Boate, both physicians of Dutch origin whose London careers in the 1630s had been punctuated by conflicts with the College of Physicians.[40]

[38] Letters from Culpeper to Hartlib, 31 October and 12 November 1645, 23 February 1646/7, Sheffield University Library, Hartlib Papers XIII.

[39] This difference of emphasis is particularly apparent from the long series of letters on the Office of Address composed by Dury in 1646 and 1647. There is no reference to experimental science or Worsley, Hartlib Papers III.

[40] For Gerard (1604–1650) and Arnold Boate (1606–1653), see *Nieuw Nederlandsch Biographisch Woordenboek*, iv, pp. 211–12; Sir George Clark, *A History of the Royal College of Physicians* (Oxford, 1964–66), i, pp. 262–3, 297. H.M.C., *Ormonde*, ii, pp. 155–56; *Cal. State Paps. Dom., 1649–50*, pp. 66, 588; *Irelands Natural History*, ed. S. Hartlib (London, 1652), sigs. A6r–8r; Bottigheimer, *op. cit.*, p. 177: Boate invested £180, in expectation of a reward of 847 acres. T. C. Barnard, 'The Social Policy of the Commonwealth and Protectorate in Ireland' (Oxford D.Phil. thesis, 1972), pp. 332–5.

Subsequently they became involved with the Boyle family, Worsley and various Anglo-Irish politicians. Arnold settled in Dublin in 1636 where his patients included both Ussher and Strafford. Thereafter for some years his career followed that of Worsley. He joined the army medical corps, as physician-general to the army in Leinster; he then returned to England at about the same time as Worsley, joining his brother in London from May to October 1645, before leaving for Paris. Gerard Boate remained in London and his patients included Robert Boyle and Lady Ranelagh, as well as other members of the Boyle family. One of Robert Boyle's early medical notebooks has entries derived from Worsley and Gerard Boate.[41] Just before the establishment of the Invisible College Gerard Boate began work on a comprehensive natural history of Ireland, based on information collected by his brother, Sir William Parsons and his son Richard Parsons. Involvement of Gerard Boate with Worsley in the Ranelagh circle may have facilitated their joint appointment to the Irish army medical service in 1647. Gerard Boate arrived in Dublin in late 1649, only a few months before his premature death. The Boates display characteristic attributes of the Invisible College, enthusiasm for Baconian natural history, and anti-authoritarianism both in natural philosophy and in medicine. Their first publication, although less radical philosophically than its title suggests, *Philosophia naturalis reformata id est philosophiae Aristotelicae accurata examinatio ac solida confutatio*, was dedicated to Robert Sydney, earl of Leicester, and published in Dublin in 1641. Similar antiperipateticism was probably inherited by Worsley's patron Sir John Temple from his father, the celebrated Ramist, Sir William Temple, Provost of Trinity College Dublin.

In view of the pronounced antiperipateticism of Boyle, Worsley and the Boates, their Invisible College would have undoubtedly attracted the sympathy of Miles Symner, a little-known figure, who was prebendary of Kilmacallan in Connaught from 1634, under the patronage of Sir John King. In 1648 we find Symner writing to his patron's son Sir Robert King, declaring his enthusiasm for 'reall & experimental Learning' and inveighing against the 'ventosities, froth & idle speculations of ye Schooles' which were acceptable for young students, but fatal to university education.[42] There

[41] 'Memorials Philosophical', Royal Society, Boyle Papers XXVIII.

[42] Letter from Symner to King, 24 October 1648; British Museum, Sloane MS 427, fo. 85; Sheffield University Library, Hartlib Papers, XLVII, 6. For Sir William Temple (1555–1627) see W. S. Howell, *Logic & Rhetoric in England 1500–1700* (Princeton, 1956), pp. 194–96, 205–6. Temple's main antiperipatetic work was *A Dissertation concerning the Unipartik Method . . . an Explanation of Some Questions in Physics and Ethics* (London, 1581).

is no direct evidence to connect Symner with the Invisible College in 1646, but it is quite possible that he had been directly in contact with Boate and Worsley in Ireland before that date. Subsequently Symner became chief engineer to the Irish Army, professor of mathematics at Trinity College Dublin, and an active participant in the Irish Survey.[43] Symner reflects Boyle's description of the Invisible College as consisting of 'men of so capacious and searching spirits that school-philosophy is but the lowest region of their knowledge'.

The Anglo-Irish intellectuals associated with the Boyle family provide a much better potential basis for the Invisible College than alternative groups previously put forward. There is nothing in Boyle's early biography to preclude this Irish connexion and it is supported by much circumstantial evidence. I would therefore suggest that the Invisible College was initiated in the summer of 1646 by Worsley and Boyle, as a means to propagate their conception of experimental philosophy among their immediate associates. Initially, active participation came from Lady Ranelagh, Gerard and Arnold Boate, possibly also such figures as Miles Symner or John Sadler.[44] This group was well prepared to receive the ideas developed by Worsley and Boyle. In the Anglo-Irish group they would have found many patrons who were not intimately involved with philosophical, scientific or economic affairs, but who provided encouragement and information. This class includes Broghill, Temple, Sir Robert King, Sir William and Richard Parsons, Sir Charles Coote and Sir John Clotworthy. If the above identification is correct, 'Invisibility' would have been forced on the group by virtue of their unsettled fortunes and obligations outside London. While London provided a focus, it was necessary to maintain communications with Ireland, Stalbridge, Paris and probably the Netherlands.

[43] Symner was the brother-in-law of Henry Jones, bishop of Clogher; H. Cotton, *Fasti Ecclesiae Hibernicae*, iv (Dublin, 1850), pp. 149–50; Barnard *op. cit.*, pp. 339–41 (this author has prepared a longer study on Symner). John Sadler and King were appointed members of the 1653 Committee for the Advancement of Learning, *C.J.*, vii, p. 287; *Acts and Ordinances of the Interregnum*, ed. C. H. Firth and R. S. Rait (London, 1911), ii, pp. 355–57.

[44] John Sadler (1615–1674), a London lawyer and from 1650 Master of Magdalene College, was often mentioned in conjunction with Worsley in letters received by Hartlib in 1647. He became a patron of the Office of Address and served on the 1653 Committees for Law Reform, the Advancement of Learning and tithes. His best-known work is *Rights of the Kingdom* (London, 1649). It is interesting to note that, probably through involvement with Lady Ranelagh, Worsley was brought into contact with Milton. See J. M. French, *The Life Records of John Milton 1639–1651* (New Brunswick, 1950), pp. 9, 10, 183, 214.

Although small in membership and informal in structure the Invisible College evolved a characteristic interpretation of experimental philosophy, which differed strikingly from the 'new philosophy' of the precursors of the Royal Society. The more academic 1645 group were primarily concerned with the classical problems of natural philosophy, while the more practically orientated Invisible College concentrated on the recovery of man's dominion over nature. But it would not have been admitted by the Invisible College that their utilitarian bias was inimical to sound scientific knowledge. Following Bacon, Boyle insisted that the luciferous-fructiferous distinction did not imply that 'Fructiferous Experiments did so merely advantage our interests, as not to promote our knowledge'.[45] 'Trades' were seen as the most productive area for both the systematization of scientific knowledge following the principles of natural history, and for the inductive investigation of nature according to the principles of *Novum Organum*.[46]

Having described the general spirit of the experimental philosophy of the Invisible College, it is necessary to proceed to a consideration of the relationship between its practical and utopian dimensions. Husbandry appears to have provided Boyle's apprenticeship in experimental philosophy and in this search for knowledge he was willing to learn from any class of labourer. In the letter to Tallents Boyle remarked that one of the virtues of the Invisible College was its willingness 'to be directed to the meanest, so he can but plead reason for his opinion'. This sentiment expresses the source of the view developed at great length in the *Usefulnesse of Experimental Natural Philosophy*, that scholars should follow Bacon's advice by abandoning their disdain of manual arts and take advantage of the accumulated experience of artisans to compile exhaustive Histories of Trade and Nature. Quite soon Boyle was instructing his gardeners and husbandmen on the principles of their art, while the letter to Marcombes indicates curiosity about continental practices. Subsequent letters indicate Boyle's interest in such specialist topics as clover husbandry, in line with Bacon's instructions for detailed examination of each aspect of trade.[47] An important sophistication of this natural history concept was due to Gerard Boate. His *Natural History* of Ireland is regarded as a

[45] Boyle, *Usefulnesse of Experimental Natural Philosophy*, 2nd edn (Oxford, 1664), tome ii, pp. 44–45. Boyle follows Bacon, *Novum Organum*, i, aphorism 124. Large sections of the *Usefulnesse* were composed when he was 'scarce above 21 or 22 years old' (A2v); and the rest was completed by 1658.

[46] *Ibid.*, tome ii, 2.

[47] Letters from Hartlib to Boyle, 28 February 1653/4, 8 May 1654, 30 June 1657, Boyle, *Works*, vi, pp. 82, 84, 92.

pioneering attempt to undertake a scientific description of a geographical region. Boate's success was due to various factors, including a Baconian orientation, acquaintance with recent Dutch descriptions of the natural history of Brazil, practical involvement in Irish resettlement, and the selection of a region small enough for comprehensive investigation. Thus he was induced to break with the miscellaneous, antiquarian and anecdotal chorographical tradition, to produce a well-ordered preliminary survey of the economic geography of Ireland.[48] The title page gives an indication of the scope of the first part of this work.[49] He planned two further books, describing the plants, animals and human inhabitants but these were never completed. Topics were covered very unevenly, the greatest attention being paid to mining and metallurgy, description of the ironworks of the earl of Cork and Sir Charles Coote being the most detailed section of the book.[50] This section also probably reflects the growing interest within the Invisible College in refining and metallurgy. Worsley was convinced that the British Isles could yield rich supplies of metals of all kinds. He collected information on recent mining ventures and schemes for exploration and mineworking in various parts of Britain. The potentialities were undoubtedly great, but recent enterprises had been undermined by inadequate technical expertise in dealing with the problem of impurities. This was probably an important factor in persuading him in 1647 that it was necessary to visit Holland where he would have access to Johann Rudolph Glauber, the greatest expert on furnace techniques as well as a fertile contributor to other areas of chemical technology.

From husbandry Boyle turned to the investigation of soil fertility. He agreed with Worsley that plants were nourished by a

---

[48] *Irelands Natural History. Being a true and complete Description of its Situation, Greatness, Shape and Nature: of its Hills, Woods, Heaths, Bogs: Of its fruitfull Parts and profitable Grounds, with the severall way of Manuring and improoving the same. With its Heads or Promontories, Harbours, Roades and Bayes; of its Springs and Fountaines, Brookes, Rivers, Loghs: Of its Metalls, Mineralls, Freastone, Marble, Sea-coale, Turf, and other things that are taken out of the ground. And lastly, of the Nature and temperature of its Air and Season, and what disease it is free from and subject unto. Conducing to the Advancement of Navigation, Husbandry, and other profitable Arts and Professions* (London, 1652). Edited by Hartlib.

[49] F. V. Emery, 'Irish Geography in the Seventeenth Century', *Irish Geography*, ii (1954–58), pp. 263–76. Emery notes of Boate, 'Instead of relying on precedent, the lively versatile minds for which the late seventeenth century is so remarkable, turned to experiment and observation', p. 266. Y. M. Goblet, *La transformation de la Géographie Politique de l'Irlande* (Paris, 1930), regards Boate's work as 'la premiere étude de géographie physique moderne du pays'. i, pp. 147–53.

[50] *Irelands Natural History*, pp. 122–53.

'vegetative salt' generated in the soil. Therefore chemical experiments directed towards an understanding of the process would 'afford very useful Directions to the Husbandman towards the meliorating of his land, both for Corn, Trees, Grass, and consequently Cattel'.[51] It was therefore apparent that husbandry was one of the many trades which required explanation in terms of chemistry, which accordingly appeared to Boyle and his colleagues as a basic science with considerable explanatory potential. Hence his subscription to Worsley's 'great design', which was probably designed to provide a unified description for terrestrial phenomena in chemical terms. This would facilitate the investigation of agriculture, mining or metal-working according to more rational criteria.

Boye's initial enthusiasm for chemistry was undoubtedly stimulated by Worsley's saltpetre project, which epitomized the far-reaching economic consequences which might be derived from relatively simple innovations. Worsley's scheme appeared to offer independence from unreliable exports and relief from the unpopular saltpetre-men, whose digging was a universal cause of complaint, by instituting a simple process for saltpetre manufacture which would guarantee ample supplies of cheap gunpowder. Boyle declared that 'I never found myself in such strong desires for that adored muck, as now, that I see what gallant projects its affluence may promote'.[52] Taking advantage of a scheme which was calculated to provoke widespread interest, Worsley drew attention to the extensive economic consequences of his process.

Worsley's scheme was accompanied with a brief tract explaining the process in simple experimental terms. His aim was to imitate the natural process of the generation of saltpetre by providing materials and conditions suitable for the combination of the fixed and aetherial constituent of the salt. The former was to be provided by chalk, stones, mud or fuller's earth placed in a layer above the more volatile vegetative material, blood and organic remains. Heaps so constituted would mature to produce saltpetre within three to four weeks.[53] Worsley's technical treatise was reinforced by brief tracts outlining the public advantages of his scheme. A typical draft was entitled 'Certain Propositions in the behalfe of the Kingdome Concerning Salt-Peter'. This underlined the abuses of the saltpetre-men, whose methods could be replaced by an indus-

---

[51] *Usefulnesse of Experimental Natural Philosophy*, tome ii, pp. 4–5.
[52] Letter from Boyle to Worsley [*post* 21 November 1646], Boyle, *Works*, vi, p. 40.
[53] 'De Nitro Theses quaedam', Sheffield University Library, Hartlib Papers XXXIX, 1.

trial method which would not only guarantee supplies, but also employ the poor. Saltpetre would also be available for use as a fertilizer, to improve the land, increase crop yields and the capacity to support cattle. So confident was Worsley, that he promised 60lb of saltpetre free for every ton purchased.[54] Boyle echoed Worsley's view that 'enquiries into the Nature of Salt-petre may be of great concernment to husbandry'.[55]

The above documents display Worsley's gifts as a clear-minded scientific expositor and publicist. Worsley's petitions were treated seriously, gaining first the approval of a Committee of Aldermen then the House of Lords in April and November 1646 respectively.[56] News of this success was conveyed by Lady Ranelagh to Boyle. Worsley continued to accumulate information on saltpetre for some time, but no attempt was made to establish his manufacturing process. Hartlib eventually gathered together papers on this subject, commenting sourly that 'Mr. Worsley, that was once so hot upon this subject, both for writing and acting, hath been so much cooled in both respects'.[57] But saltpetre was not so much abandoned as subsumed under Worsley's rapidly expanding economic proposals.

The Invisible College focused on experimental problems which were capable of immediate economic application and incorporation into wider programmes. Interest in agricultural innovation led to collection of data relevant to a general history of husbandry, the plan for a detailed natural history of Ireland and interest in other regional economic surveys. As the author of the introduction to *Irelands Natural History* commented, 'I know nothing more usefull, than to have the knowledg of the Natural History of each Nation advanced & perfected', providing the means to the understanding of 'the Nature & right use of the Creature', which would be revealed during the imminent 'Restauration of all things'.[58] Thus

[54] 'Certain Propositions', Sheffield University Library, Hartlib Papers LXXII 11, three copies; see also LIII, 26.

[55] Boyle, *Usefulnesse*, pp. 5–6.

[56] *Lords Journals*, viii, pp. 573–74; 21 November 1646. 'To the Right Honourable the Lords and Commons assembled in Parliament. The humble Petition of Benjamin Worsley.' With a Certificate signed by members of the Committee of Aldermen, 7 April 1646. An extended version of Worsley's petition is given in 'An Acte for a new way of making Saltpeter', Hartlib Papers LXXII, 11, which mentions Worsley's backers as Sir William Courteen, Francis Joyner and William Hyde.

[57] Letter from Hartlib to Boyle, 5 April 1659; Boyle, *Works*, vi, pp. 116–17. The papers on saltpetre include two letters from Arnold Boate, sent from Paris in 1653, Sheffield University Library, Hartlib Papers XXXIX, 51.

[58] *Irelands Natural History*, sigs. A3r–4r. This section is usually attributed to Hartlib, but this was actually by Dury.

natural history was immediately expanded by the puritan consciousness from a humble investigation into trades, into an instrument to bring about utopian conditions. Hence the recognition by
Boyle that the Invisible College was an expression of 'universal
good-will' which took 'the whole body of mankind' for its care. In
explaining the College to Hartlib, it immediately occurred to him
that any intelligence supplied by Hartlib would be adapted to
utopian purposes.

Boyle was particularly impressed by the demonstration that saltpetre would become the basis for various 'gallant projects'. The
ambitious scale of Worsley's designs may be appreciated from
'Proffits Humbly Presented to this Kingdome', a document undoubtedly composed to reinforce the more straightforward saltpetre petitions. This highly important manifesto outlined five
economic proposals which would benefit the nation, beginning as
one would expect with a brief exposition of the saltpetre design.[59]
The following three short proposals for improvements in manuring, preserving fish and maintaining sheep and their wool in better
condition, were probably in some way related to the utilization of
saltpetre or waste materials derived from its manufacture. These
specific points were designed to create a favourable attitude
towards innovation in preparation for the fifth and longest
proposal which occupied six of the seven pages of the document:

> That whereas there are severall commodities of necessitie and
> pleasure yt wee are forced to fetch out of another countries; some
> with ready money and others with the exchange of our proper
> commodities . . . to the wasteing of the estate of the Kingdome
> Wee humbly offer to make it most evidently appeare That by
> such a well regulated plantation as wee shall clearly and orderly
> describe with such lawes and constituns in it That the most
> yea all of those commodities wee now fetch from those other
> partes, may bee had within our owne dominions.[60]

In support of this proposal for the establishment of American
plantations fulfilling functions closely determined by the British
economy, the author combined well-known arguments in favour
of colonization with ideas on economic diversification which are
particularly associated with Henry Robinson during this period.
With respect to the provision of raw materials and agricultural

---

[59] Sheffield University Library, Hartlib Papers XVII (23). This document is
anonymous, but there can be little doubt that it was composed by Worsley,
possibly in consultation with other members of the Invisible College.

[60] Ibid., fo. 1r–v.

products, Worsley believed that the best prospects lay in the exploitation of the colonies rather than relying on innovations at home. Worsley offered this policy as the foundation for a British challenge to Dutch maritime supremacy; but the full fruits of this enterprise would only be gained if it was associated with a British monopoly of trade from the colonies to Europe.[61] By adoption of the policies of colonial development and regulation of trade, Worsley foresaw a basis for the expansion of trade to other continents; reversal of the drain of bullion, enhancement of the value of English commodities, accumulation of revenues and, finally, British assumption of European supremacy.

The psychological impact on the nation would be considerable:

> The spirits of men will bee more heightned, and their mindes to all generous and greatt actions more fitly disposed, when through these meanes want misery and servitude shall be wholly turned out of doores. And of what conducement to valour & great undertakings the freedome of mens mindes is, Let not only learned Verulam judge, but let ye difference between ye actions and achivments of ye English compared to other Nations, wittnesse.[62]

In the final section of 'Proffits Humbly Presented' Worsley gave an impression of the tasks to which the nation should dedicate itself, once economic buoyancy had been attained.

> If to this wealth and honour thus feasably to bee attained, shall bee annexed a Reformation of laws, and an establishment of rightousnes amoungst us, then to these may wee yet promise to ourselves more glorious thinges as First a Propagation of ye Gospell unto other unknowne partes wherby Gods name and Love to mankind may be more spread and made manifest, 2ndly a Reformation of Education, & soe of all the Unhappinesse hitherto thence springing, by ye setting up and ordaining other kind of schools and teaching. 3rdly Advancement of Learning by men appointed and maintained to keep an Universall Correspondency, by erecting of Threasure Houses for ye Collection of the History of nature, for experiments both Chymicall and Mechanicall & by increasing of choice and public libraries. 4thly endeavoring the Conversion of the Jewes. . . . 5thly the indeavouring an Union and reconciliation throughout all the christian at least all the Protestant Churches.[63]

'Proffits Humbly Presented' and associated documents provide an

[61] Ibid., fo. 2r.　　[62] Ibid., fo. 3r.
[63] Ibid., fo. 4v.

extremely full picture of the intellectual standpoint of the leading member of the Invisible College and throw light on the context in which natural philosophy developed within the Invisible College during 1646. Boyle's letters provide scattered remarks about a group investigating husbandry and experimental chemistry at a practical level, while on the other hand expressing pronounced philanthropic, universalist and utopian aspirations. Worsley's writings enable us to appreciate more fully the relationship between these two planes of activity and also to see that there was no necessary friction between experimental science and ambitious social programmes. The members of the Invisible College were no more unrealistic mystic dreamers than the authors of *New Atlantis* or *Macaria*. Utopian manifestations such as the Invisible College were appropriate to the conditions of 1646, when England appeared to be on the verge of recovery from the initial disruptions of the Civil War. As in 1641 this situation called for programmes for social reconstruction consistent with religious and political aims of the parliamentarians. There was general confidence that defeat of the forces of Babylon signalled movement towards a secure religious settlement or even a millennial Kingdom. Hence there was considerable inducement to develop policies within an ambitious utopian context.

The reconstruction of the Invisible College which has been attempted above contrasts considerably with most previous solutions, both in method of approach and outcome. Solutions to the Invisible College problem discussed in the first part of this paper have been generated according to preconceived notions about the major factors involved in the growth of institutionalized scientific activity in mid-seventeenth-century England. The interpretation stemming from Birch places Boyle, his Invisible College and the Royal Society squarely in the central tradition of the continental mechanical philosophy. English science appeared to be uniformly galvanized into new life by enthusiasm for the experimental problems and conceptual debates originating with Galileo, Descartes and Mersenne. The incentive for English intellectuals to turn their attention to science was supposed to be provided by the positive inducements of the new philosophy and the desire to find refuge from unsavoury developments of the English revolution. The solutions proposed by Syfret and Yates adjust this perspective slightly, to allow Comenian or Rosicrucian pansophist elements to play some small part in the intellectual ancestry of the Royal Society. A rather different point of view emerges once it is recognized that the Invisible College was not connected with the main precursor of the Royal Society. Miss Purver fully acknowledges that

Boyle temporarily aligned with the unsuccessful pansophist ventures of Samuel Hartlib, before returning to the main-stream Baconianism of the early Royal Society. While her interpretations of both the Royal Society and the Comenians are highly questionable, this writer at least recognizes that there was considerable diversity of outlook among the pioneer advocates of the new science in England. The characterization of the Invisible College presented above reinforces this impression of intellectual vigour and diversification in London in the aftermath of the Civil War. But on textual and biographical grounds it is not possible to sustain the reconstructions of the Invisible College produced by historians of science immersed in the conflict over the relative roles of the 'mechanical' and 'hermetic' traditions in the formation of modern science. On the basis of Boyle's biography it is apparent that conventional interpretations of the membership and outlook of the Invisible College are ruled out. It is also clear that Boyle's recruitment into science was not associated with the desire to escape from the uncongenial political situation so graphically described by Sprat and underlined subsequently by writers eager to prove the independent nature of scientific activity. The evidence presented above suggests that the Invisible College was one expression of the debate on religious, political and social affairs within the puritan movement. It is no coincidence that the Levellers, Hartlib's Office of Address and the Invisible College made their appearance simultaneously.

The Invisible College was intimately linked with Anglo-Irish Independents associated with Lady Ranelagh, whose policies were dictated by their dedication to the reconquest, settlement and exploitation of Ireland. The Invisible College and the manifestoes associated with Worsley are accordingly best understood in terms of these policies, which provided an immediate incentive to curiosity about innovations in husbandry and technology, as well as the indirect source for more ambitious designs for exploitation. Aware of the great potentialities for colonization, industrial development and social reconstruction, such puritan intellectuals as the Boates, Worsley and Boyle, were inspired to take these sporadic interests in improvement as the starting-point for a revival of the Baconian programme for the renewal of man's dominion over nature. Bacon's optimistic view of the reconquest of nature, framed in consciously millenarian terms, was ideally suited to the religious and philosophical inclinations of the Invisible College. This association, although short-lived, provides important insight into the factors which caused puritan intellectuals to turn with such conviction to the pursuit of experimental philosophy.

The Invisible College played an important role in the development of Baconianism and the revival of experimental chemistry, contributing important elements to the natural philosophy of Boyle the most influential figure of the pre-Newtonian science. In the short term the members of the Invisible College individually expressed considerable concern over Irish affairs particularly. Hartlib rapidly absorbed the convictions of the Invisible College and he soon became the agent for the completion of the natural history of Ireland, as well as adapting the Office of Address to take account of experimental science and technology. Worsley remained a dominating influence, his greatest energies being reserved for economic policy. His conviction, already developed in 1646, that Baconian enterprise would have adequate opportunity for expression only if colonial trade was subjected to tighter restrictions brought him into alignment with politicians and merchants who favoured control of colonial trade for different reasons. Accordingly, Worsley was allowed to become the exponent of the policies of this group, a factor which probably secured his appointment as Secretary to the Commonwealth Council of Trade, and subsequently earned him an important role in framing and defending the Navigation Act of 1651.[64]

Thus the Invisible College has a degree of general historical interest and relevance to the emergence of the English Baconian tradition which has not been appreciated by conventional history of science, which continues to be dominated by assumptions about the social role of science inherited from Thomas Sprat and Thomas Birch.

Corpus Christi College, Oxford.

[64] For later Irish activities of the members of the Invisible College, see G. H. Turnbull, 'Robert Child', *Publications of the Colonial Society of Massachusetts,* xxxvii (1959), pp. 21–53 and Barnard, *op. cit., passim*; J. P. Cooper, 'Social and Economic Policies under the Commonwealth', in *The Interregnum: The Quest for Settlement, 1646–60,* ed. G. E. Aylmer (London 1972), pp. 133–34. Cooper provides an excellent summary of the various approaches to the origin and significance of the Navigation Act.

GREAT BRITAIN AND THE COMING OF THE PACIFIC WAR, 1939-1941

By Peter Lowe, B.A., Ph.D., F.R.Hist.S.

READ 11 MAY 1973

IN a mood of understandable frustration, the British minister in Bangkok sent a telegram to the head of the Far Eastern department of the Foreign Office in June 1941, referring to the tedious economic discussions he was conducting with the Thai government, saying:

> I am disturbed by the contradictory tone of the telegrams sent to me from His Majesty's Foreign Office ... Some of them breathe that broad and statesmanlike spirit which I have learnt to respect and admire over a period of nearly forty years. Others strike a shrill and petulant note which is new to me ... I have an uneasy feeling that you people in Downing Street live in an ivory tower as regards Thailand ...[1]

The aim of this paper is to examine the formulation of British policy towards the developing Pacific crisis between the outbreak of the European war in September 1939 and the beginning of the co-ordinated Japanese offensives in December 1941. Without doubt it was an extremely difficult period in which to devise a viable policy. The nightmare of the defence chiefs throughout the 1930s—that Great Britain might face simultaneous crises of a grave and demanding nature in Europe, the Mediterranean and the Far East—had become a reality. Inevitably decision-making became more complex in time of war. The Foreign Office had to defer frequently to the views of the chiefs of staff: both the Foreign Office and the chiefs of staff had to come to terms, from May 1940, with the erratic genius of Winston Churchill, who effectively determined the lines of policy approved by the war cabinet. Apart from the inner problems of government departments in London, the external issue was simple and yet not as simple as it at first appeared: when would the United States accept a commitment to resist Japanese expansion? The theme might be succinctly defined as 'Waiting for F.D.R.'

---

[1] Bangkok to Foreign Office (for J. C. Sterndale Bennett), 17 June 1941, F5342/1281/40, F.O. 371/28142. Transcripts/Translations of Crown-copyright records in the Public Record Office, London, appear by permission of the Controller of H.M. Stationery Office.

43

When the European war began, there seemed to be justification for cautious optimism in the Far East. On 23 September Sir Robert Craigie urged from Tokyo that, in the light of the truce between Russia and Japan, marking an end to the bitter fighting on the border between Manchukuo and Mongolia which had continued since May 1939, Britain should offer facilities in Hong Kong for a peace conference to terminate the Sino-Japanese war.[2] Simultaneously the parliamentary under-secretary at the Foreign Office, R. A. Butler, urged a *rapprochement* with Japan. Such a course was, he stated, favoured by Hugh Dalton, the Labour party's principal spokesman on foreign affairs, and by the prominent Conservative back-bencher, Sir John Wardlaw-Milne. Butler observed:

> Russia and Japan are bound to remain enemies, and with our position in India and the East it would pay us to make a return to the Anglo-Japanese alliance possible. It does not appear that there are the makings of a war between America and Japan; the American interests in the Far East are insufficient to justify a major war. I do not believe that it will in the end pay us to keep Japan at arm's length and distrust everything she does for the sake of American opinion. . . .
>
> To sum up, therefore, I would wish to see the position in North China cleared up, including the withdrawal of our garrisons; a 'standing pat' at Shanghai; an improvement of our trading relations with Japan in our mutual interest on a barter basis and as soon as possible, and finally a closer approach to Chiang Kai Shek [*sic*] in order (a) to find out what his mind really is, and (b) if possible to prevent a civil war in China by bringing about a peace settlement in the Far East before it is too late.[3]

Halifax brought the subject before the war cabinet. It was decided on 26 September that Clark Kerr, the ambassador in China, should see Chiang Kai-shek when he visited Chungking in early October and inform him privately of Craigie's proposal: however, it was to be made clear to Chiang that Britain had no wish to persuade him to accept the suggestion contrary to his inclinations.[4] Soon afterwards Halifax decided not to pursue the proposal owing to doubt concerning the Japanese government's attitude.[5] Uneasy

[2] Craigie to Halifax, 23 September 1939, F10533/87/10, F.O. 371/23461.
[3] Minute by R. A. Butler, 22 September 1939, F10710/176/23, F.O. 371/23556.
[4] War cabinet conclusions, 28 (39) 7, 26 September 1939; and 32 (39) 8, 30 September 1939, Cab. 65/1.
[5] War cabinet conclusions, 42 (39) 8, 9 October 1939, Cab. 65/1.

and unsatisfactory as Britain's policy was of giving moral support to China with conspicuously little tangible aid to accompany it, while at the same time voicing disapproval of Japanese policy without allowing it to go too far, there was no alternative. Halifax remarked, in a telegram to Craigie sent on 21 November, that further improvement in relations with Japan was desirable, 'But American support in our present struggle is vital, and it is impossible entirely to ignore the fact that what Japan is doing in East Asia is very closely akin to what Germany has done in Europe.'[6]

Despite the fact that Britain had done little to assist China— paradoxically Germany had initially helped China appreciably and then Russia and the United States lent growing support— Japan bitterly resented Britain's moral support for China. With the looming Japanese threat to Indo-China, the Burma road had become more important as one of the two principal routes for carrying arms and other goods into China, the other being the long overland road from Russia. However, the significance of the tortuous and ill-surfaced road from Lashio to Kunming was in essence symbolical of the Chinese determination to continue the struggle against Japan and of the willingness of various powers to foster that resistance.[7] On 24 June 1940 Craigie reported that he had been handed a memorandum by the vice-minister of foreign affairs requesting the closure of the Burma road and of the Hong Kong frontier.[8] Craigie believed that submission was advisable although he did not, at this stage, consider full-scale war probable in the event of refusal; this should be accompanied by a statement that Britain would expect a strenuous effort to be made by Japan to secure a just, negotiated peace with China.[9] Craigie observed there was a division of opinion between the more bellicose younger officers in the army, who 'have now virtually got out of control' and the senior officers, the former advocating a confrontation over the Burma road.[10] The initial response in the Foreign Office was to oppose closure but to offer concessions in the supply of raw materials to Japan.

The chiefs of staff considered the situation before the war cabinet debated it on 1 July. As was the custom, the matter had

[6] Halifax to Craigie, 21 November 1939, F11946/6457/10, F.O. 371/23534.
[7] Of a total value of £7,028,362 of munitions imported into Rangoon and passed by customs for outward transit to China between 26 March 1939 and 31 March 1940, about £239,000 or 3.4% originated in the British Empire; details communicated by Burma Office to Foreign Office, 29 June 1940, F3529/43/10, F.O. 371/24666.
[8] Craigie to Halifax, 24 June 1940, F3479/43/10, F.O. 371/24666.
[9] Craigie to Halifax, 25 June 1940, ibid.
[10] Craigie to Halifax, 1 July 1940, ibid.

been examined by the joint planning sub-committee, which had prepared an *aide-memoire* to guide the chiefs of staff. The sub-committee opposed the wish of the Foreign Office to keep the road open, for to do so would be to risk war and the danger could not be contemplated. In the sub-committee's view, Britain should endeavour to achieve peace terms acceptable to China.[11] When the chiefs of staff debated the issue, the chief of the imperial general staff, General Sir John Dill, endorsed the report and pressed for the closure of the Burma road as one aspect of a package deal incorporating a broad settlement.[12]

At the war cabinet on 1 July Halifax urged that the Japanese demand should be rejected but, to soften the blow and bearing in mind the views of Australia that great care was necessary in handling Japan, it could be agreed that the volume of traffic using the road be restricted. The colonial secretary, Lord Lloyd, warned of a harsh reaction in Hong Kong and Leopold Amery, the secretary of state for India, vigorously opposed closure. Neville Chamberlain, now lord president of the council, believed that the first priority was to avoid war with Japan. There was some support for an attempt at attaining a comprehensive settlement. Churchill and Attlee expressed general agreement with Halifax.[13] The discussion was adjourned. The Foreign Office still dissented and pressed for keeping the road open, while making additional concessions to Japan. The chiefs of staff pursued it further on 4 July and concluded that 'the War Cabinet should be left in no doubt as to the apprehension which the Chiefs of Staff felt regarding the military necessity of avoiding any steps which might lead to war with Japan ... particularly in the light of the possibility that we might find ourselves in a state of hostilities with France'.[14] When the war cabinet met on 5 July, Halifax restated the opposition of the Foreign Office to closure despite the views of the chiefs of staff. He did not believe that Japan would launch a major offensive but admitted that an attack on Hong Kong was conceivable. However, Craigie and his military attaché in Tokyo held that it would be dangerous to refuse closure. The prime minister stated that, if Britain took a firm stand, the entire burden would fall on her shoulders instead of falling where it rightly belonged—on the shoulders of the United States. 'In the present

[11] 'Policy in the Far East,' *aide memoire* by joint planning sub-committee, 29 June 1940, C.O.S. (40) 506 (J.P.), Cab. 80/14.
[12] Chiefs of staff committee, conclusions 1 July 1940, C.O.S. (40) 202, Cab. 79/5.
[13] War cabinet conclusions, 1 July 1940, 189 (40) 1, Cab. 65/7.
[14] Chiefs of staff committee conclusions, 4 July 1940, C.O.S. (40) 208, Cab. 79/5.

state of affairs he (Churchill) did not think that we ought to incur Japanese hostility for reasons mainly of prestige.'[15] There was general agreement with this conclusion and consideration turned to the most efficacious means of submission. It was felt that the advice of President Roosevelt should be heeded that it was preferable to yield to *force majeure* rather than make an agreement smacking of appeasement as the French had done.

The United States surveyed the crisis with mounting concern but was determined not to intervene. There was much anxiety in the war cabinet at the possible consequences of continued procrastination. Halifax, therefore, instructed Craigie to reach agreement if feasible on restriction of the use of the road rather than closure; if unable to do so, he should accept closure for a three-month period during which Japan would attempt to settle the conflict with China and would work to improve relations with Great Britain.[16] Since Japan insisted on closure and rejected any compromise, Craigie negotiated the surrender. Starting on 18 July 1940 the transit of arms, ammunition, petrol, trucks and railway material was suspended for three months. The importance of the Burma road crisis is that it jolted all departments in Whitehall into a full appreciation of how tenuous the British position was in the Far East.

The consequence was a major review of defence problems in the Far East, the first substantial reassessment since the review in 1937 before the outbreak of the Sino-Japanese war.[17] The weaknesses were starkly revealed. Previous strategy had relied on the ability to despatch a fleet to Singapore when the situation warranted it. There was no likelihood in the foreseeable future of such a fleet being sent owing to the navy being stretched to the limit in the Atlantic and Mediterranean. The principal lessons drawn were that air and land strength must be increased; it would be essential to attempt to hold Malaya itself and not simply Singapore; a serious effort must be made to reach a general settlement with Japan, failing which the aim should be to gain as much time as possible before war started. In addition, it was most desirable to co-ordinate strategy with the Dutch authorities in the

[15] War cabinet conclusions, 5 July 1940, 194 (40) 1, Cab. 65/8. The permanent under-secretary at the Foreign Office, Sir Alexander Cadogan, noted in his diary that Churchill favoured 'surrender' over the Burma road contrary to his own view, see *The Diaries of Sir Alexander Cadogan 1938–1945*, ed. D. Dilks (London, 1971), pp. 310–13, diary entries for 4 July–13 July 1940.
[16] Halifax to Craigie, 11 July 1940, F3568/43/10, F.O. 371/24667.
[17] 'The Situation in the Far East in the Event of Japanese Intervention Against Us', report of the chiefs of staff committee, 31 July 1940, C.O.S. (40) 592 and W.P. (40) 302, Cab. 66/10.

Netherlands East Indies; here the report was less decisive owing
to fundamental disagreement between the General Staff and the
Air Council on the one hand and the Admiralty on the other
hand as to whether a binding commitment to assist the Netherlands East Indies should be undertaken. The first sea lord and
chief of the naval staff, Admiral Sir Dudley Pound, explained on
27 July that it was impossible for the navy to accept any new
commitments unless they were guaranteed by the United States.[18]
So strongly was this view held that the Admiralty was even prepared to envisage the Japanese taking the Netherlands East Indies.
As will be seen later, this issue became a long drawn out and
acrimonious matter in 1941.

Meanwhile the Foreign Office had begun seriously to examine
the possibility of bringing the Sino-Japanese war to an end and
of making concessions to Japan in accordance with the change of
policy determined upon when the decision had been made to close
the Burma road. Sir John Brenan observed that the chiefs of staff,
Craigie and Lothian, plus Australia and, to a lesser extent, the
United States supported the concept of a peace settlement. Brenan
envisaged Japanese recognition of the integrity and independence
of China in return for united economic concessions by the powers;
Japan would undertake to remain neutral in the European war
and to refrain from territorial expansion in any direction. Britain
would offer generous financial assistance and a guaranteed supply
of raw materials to Japan; at the end of the Sino-Japanese war
Britain would surrender her extra-territorial rights in China, as
had been anticipated for over a decade.[19] Sterndale Bennett, the
head of the Far Eastern department, minuted that Brenan had not
gone far enough: a searching appraisal was required.[20] R. A. Butler
reiterated his belief in the need for a settlement:

The 'complete defeat' of Japan can only be brought about by
the enlistment in the war of a first class nation. We should be
unwise to undertake the task and I doubt whether the Russians
or Americans will.

Therefore I think that we should work for as good a settlement in the Far East as we can manage. We & the Americans
have economic weapons against Japan. Under cover of these
we should attempt to secure a modification of the Konoye terms
[of November–December 1938] . . .

To be successful we must be more active with the American

[18] Chiefs of staff committee conclusions, 27 July 1940, C.O.S. (40) 236,
Cab. 79/5.
[19] Memorandum by Brenan, 10 July 1940, F3586/193/61, F.O. 371/24708.
[20] Minute by Sterndale Bennett, 11 July 1940, *ibid.*

Govt. than hitherto.   We cannot have them sniping at us in public while privately telling us that they understand our motives.

I should like to take this line with them:— 'Your & our interests are very similar . . . in the Far East let us try, under cover of our economic weapons, to secure a fair settlement, & to revise our position in China (extraterritoriality etc.). If we look like failing then can we not count on your aid, when the Japs start pouncing on other people's property?'[21]

Further thought was devoted to the subject in late July and early August 1940. However, Anglo-Japanese relations sharply deteriorated following the formation of a new government by Prince Konoye Fumimaro, which proceeded to arrest and maltreat a number of British nationals. The likelihood of a settlement, never bright, receded. The Foreign Office nevertheless consulted other government departments on the terms of a possible future settlement, so as to have the relevant information readily available. The Foreign Office divided the question into the aspects concerning Japan and China directly and the wider issues inseparable from a broad settlement. It was believed that Japan's terms would embrace recognition of Manchukuo; acceptance of the 'New Order'; common opposition to the spread of communism; acceptance of Japanese domination of north China and Inner Mongolia; economic concessions throughout China; and a slow withdrawal of Japanese troops as the settlement was implemented. China's terms were anticipated to be vague but would amount to the full restoration of Chinese independence including the complete withdrawal of Japanese forces. Therefore, it would be difficult to reconcile the two adversaries. Peace could only be realized if other powers offered inducements. As regards a broad settlement, the Foreign Office believed Japan would desire recognition of the 'New Order' and acceptance of racial equality, with particular reference to the United States and the British Dominions; financial assistance to exploit the resources of China; free trade in south-east Asia; guaranteed access to raw materials; and the abolition of the Ottawa tariffs. China would want recognition of her territorial integrity, abolition of extraterritoriality, assistance with her currency and general economic restoration. Numerous difficulties were foreseen in meeting Japan's likely demands, especially where racial equality was involved. Great Britain would expect from Japan undertakings at least to remain neutral in the European struggle and to respect British, Dutch

[21] Minute by R. A. Butler, 23 July 1940, F3633/193/61, F.O. 371/24708.

and American possessions in the Far East and Pacific: from China respect for Britain's particular interests and a promise of participation in the rehabilitation of China.[22] The various other departments consulted were asked to inform the Foreign Office of their conclusions.

The Dominions Office and the Ministry of Economic Warfare expressed considerable doubt as to whether it was in Britain's interest to help to terminate the Sino-Japanese war, thus reverting to the attitude widely held before the Burma road crisis.[23] The most entertaining answer came from the Colonial Office, which stressed the problems inherent in making concessions to Japan but added that if general talks were held, it would like to secure the extension of the lease of the New Territories in the crown colony of Hong Kong.[24] The Foreign Office gloomily concluded that even if the skies brightened east of Singapore the prospects for reaching an acceptable settlement were not encouraging. It should, however, be noted that several prominent figures in public life apparently favoured a settlement, including Lord Hankey, the chancellor of the duchy of Lancaster, Ernest Bevin, the minister of labour, and Sir Walter Citrine, general secretary of the T.U.C.[25] Churchill was profoundly sceptical, advising Halifax to 'go very slow on all this general and equitable peace business between China and Japan'.[26]

The Foreign Office had already reached the provisional decision to recommend reopening the Burma road when the three-month agreement expired in October.[27] The effect on American opinion was the vital aspect. When Lothian and the Australian minister, Casey, saw Cordell Hull on 16 September, Lothian asked him what support would be forthcoming if Britain stood up to Japan and reopened the Burma road. Hull replied that this would depend on the outcome of the 'Battle of Britain': if Britain held out until

[22] Memorandum, 'General Settlement with Japan', enclosed in Foreign Office to Board of Trade, Ministry of Economic Warfare, Colonial Office, Dominions Office, India Office, Burma Office and Petroleum Department, 10 August 1940, *ibid.*

[23] Dominions Office to Foreign Office, 27 August 1940 and Ministry of Economic Warfare to Foreign Office, 2 September 1940, F4108/193/61 F.O. 371/24709.

[24] Colonial Office to Foreign Office, 17 August 1940, F3859/193/61, F.O. 371/24709.

[25] See letter from Lord Sempill to Hankey, 3 June 1941 enclosing notes prepared in September 1940, Hankey papers, Cab. 63/177.

[26] W. S. Churchill, *The Second World War*, ii (5th edition, 1955), p. 571, Churchill to Halifax, 20 July 1940.

[27] Memorandum by Halifax, 'Reopening of the Burma Road', 2 September 1940, W.P. (40) 348, Cab. 66/11.

1941, the United States could adopt a far stronger policy in the Pacific. He implied that the United States would contemplate action which 'might bring United States of America very near to war against Japan'.[28] However, he felt that this would not be to Britain's advantage because it would entail a reduction in supplies to her. He greatly hoped that the Burma road would be reopened. The Foreign Office welcomed Hull's remarks and were inclined to agree that it was not desirable that the United States should go to war with Japan and reduce aid to Britain as a consequence.[29] When the war cabinet examined the position on 2 October, the prime minister 'questioned the statement that it was not in our interests that the United States should be involved in war in the Pacific'.[30] Churchill was interested solely in the moment when the United States would become a full ally, believing that intervention in the Pacific would lead to participation in the European war. The Burma road was reopened on 18 October 1940.

Between October 1940 and April 1941 a series of defence conferences met in Singapore and Washington to exchange views with the Americans and Dutch and to seek improved co-ordination between the various forces in the Far East and Pacific. The first conference met at Singapore in October 1940 as an all-British gathering apart from an American observer. Its report reinforced the pessimism of the chiefs of staff three months earlier. 'Our first and immediate consideration must be to ensure the security of Malaya against direct attack. The Tactical Appreciation shows that the army and air forces in Malaya (including reinforcements now being provided) are, both in numbers and equipment, far below those required in view of the inadequacy of the naval forces available. *This deficiency must obviously be remedied immediately. . . .*'[31] Emphasis was laid on the importance of securing effective Dutch co-operation. In the existing situation it was most improbable that either Malaya or Singapore could be held for other than a brief period. In their commentary on the report, the joint planning staff endorsed a number of the detailed recommendations concerning provision of new aerodromes, extension of aid from India and the need for more discussions with Australia and New Zealand. In general terms, however, the staff concluded, 'We consider . . . that the views of the commanders on the general

[28] Lothian to Halifax, 16 September 1940, F4290/193/61, F.O. 371/24709.
[29] Foreign Office minutes, 20–21 September 1940, *ibid.*
[30] War cabinet conclusions, 2 October 1940, 264 (40) 4, Cab. 65/9.
[31] 'Report of the Singapore Defence Conference, October 1940', 31 October 1940, Cab. 80/24.

defence situation are unduly pessimistic and that they have in
particular tended to over-estimate the minimum air forces necessary for reasonable security.'[32] In their detailed remarks they
stated their opinions more forcefully. The air requirements envisaged at Singapore: 'appear to be entirely divorced from reality.
The Japanese have never fought against a first-class Power in the
air and we have no reason to believe that their operations would
be any more effective than those of the Italians'.[33]

At the end of 1940 preparations were being made for the
'technical conversations' with the United States, scheduled to begin
in Washington in January 1941.[34] In the instructions for the
British delegation, the chiefs of staff stated that the conversations
should be based 'on the hypothesis of a war between Germany,
Italy and Japan on the one hand and the British Empire with our
present Allies and the U.S.A. on the other'.[35] The hypothesis did
not imply a political commitment. Singapore was regarded as
'the key' to the defence of the entire Far East and Pacific.[36] It
was recalled that preliminary consultations had already been held
and from these the principal divergence hinged on differences of
outlook between the British and American navies. The British
naval staff believed that the combined allied forces could combat
Germany, Italy and Japan simultaneously, whereas the United
States naval staff maintained that they could not with confidence
hope to restrain Japan if occupied in the Atlantic and Mediterranean. The British wanted the United States forces to be based
on Singapore whereas the Americans wished to remain at Hawaii.[37]
Churchill, while supporting the instructions, emphasized that,
'It was most important that the attitude to be adopted by our

[32] 'Far East Tactical Appreciation and Report of Singapore Defence Conference, Commentary by the Joint Planning Staff', 1 January 1941, Cab. 79/8.
[33] Ibid.
[34] There was some delay in Whitehall in completing arrangements for the
conversations, to the annoyance of the American military attaché; see The
London Observer: the Journal of General Raymond E. Lee 1940–1941, ed.
J. Leutze (London, 1972), pp. 192–93.
[35] Annex: British–United States Technical Conversations, General Instructions for the United Kingdom Delegation to Washington, 15 December 1940,
Cab. 80/24.
[36] Ibid.
[37] 'British–United States Technical Conversations, Note by the Chiefs of
Staff submitting Draft Instructions for the United Kingdom Delegation to
Washington', 15 December 1940, C.O.S. (40) 1043, Cab. 80/24. Lee, the
American military attaché in London, remarked in his journal that the
secretary of the navy, Colonel Frank Knox, was disturbed at the defeatism
prevalent in the navy, which he attributed to the malign influence of Joseph
Kennedy, the former ambassador in London and now a leading isolationist,
see The London Observer, ed. Leutze, p. 175.

Delegation in the discussions on naval strategy should be one of deference to the views of the United States in all matters concerning the Pacific theatre of war.'[38]

The staff conversations took place in Washington between January and March 1941. In an appreciation of the situation in the Far East, the significance of Singapore as a fundamental constituent of British defence policy was explained. As regards probable Japanese strategy, it was believed that Japan could launch a land and air offensive upon Malaya from Indo-China and Thailand, attack the Netherlands East Indies and probably complete arrangements to attack the Philippines. Japan was estimated to have sufficient strength to carry out all three offensives at once, an accurate forecast in the light of December 1941. The most satisfactory solution would be to base a naval force, including capital ships, at Singapore: because of the heavy British commitment in other theatres, it would be most sensible for this task to be discharged by the United States.[39]

In their rejoinder, the United States staff committee stated that in their opinion if the United States became involved in war with Japan, she would fight Germany and Italy, too; similarly if the United States fought Germany and Italy, she would go to war with Japan if Japan was not then at war with Britain. The staff committee did not think the United States would go to war if Japan occupied Indo-China and Thailand. 'Furthermore, there is serious doubt that the United States would immediately declare war against Japan were that nation to move against Malaya, British Borneo, or the Netherlands East Indies, unless the United States were previously also at war with Germany and Italy.'[40] It was likely that Japan would aim to defeat her opponents one at a time, although a general offensive was feasible. The significant difference from the British appreciation was that they did not accept the concept of Singapore as the mighty fortress that must be held at all costs. 'The general moral effect of the loss of Singapore and the Philippines would be severe. Singapore has been built up in public opinion as a symbol of the power of the British Empire. The eastern Dominions, the Netherlands East Indies and China look upon its security as the guarantee of their

[38] 'British–United States Technical Conversations', *Note by the Secretary*, 19 December 1940, C.O.S. (40) 1052, Cab. 80/24.
[39] 'British–United States Staff Conversation. The Far East Appreciation by the United Kingdom Delegation', 11 February 1941, B.U.S. (J) (41) 13, Cab. 99/5.
[40] 'British–United States Staff Conversations. Statement by the United States Staff Committee: The United States Military Position in the Far East', 19 February 1941, B.U.S. (J) (41) 16, Cab. 99/5.

safety. Its value as a symbol has become so great that its capture
by Japan would be a serious blow. But many severe blows can be
absorbed without leading to final disaster.'[41] While the Washington
talks fostered contacts and mutual appreciation, they did not lead
to the formulation of a carefully co-ordinated strategy against
Japan.

A defence conference was held at Singapore in February 1941
between the British, Dutch and Australians, followed by two
further conferences in April 1941; Americans were present as
observers or participants. It was felt in February that the Japanese
were not in a position to launch simultaneous offensives on
Malaya and the Netherlands East Indies: instead they would con-
solidate their hold on Indo-China, infiltrate Thailand and then
attack Malaya. 'If Japan is certain that the U.S.A. will intervene
to support the N.E.I. or the British Empire, the chances of war
breaking out are reduced to very small proportions.'[42] In April
the statement that Japan was not in a position to attack both
Malaya and the Netherlands East Indies was qualified: it was now
considered that Japan could theoretically do so but in practice
would not owing to her preoccupation in China.[43]

Progress towards securing a unified response among the powers
threatened by Japan was slow, therefore. In the case of the United
States refusal to give a commitment was understandable given
the problems confronting Roosevelt. What is more surprising is
that Britain behaved in a not dissimilar way towards the Netherlands East Indies. Throughout 1941 an interminable debate persisted between the Foreign Office, on the one hand, and the prime
minister and the chiefs of staff, on the other hand. The Foreign
Office maintained that since the Netherlands was allied with
Britain and the Netherlands East Indies was a vital area for the
defence of British interests, an undertaking of mutual support
in the event of Japanese aggression should be entered into. The
prime minister and the chiefs of staff, particularly the first sea
lord, refused to agree to a firm promise of support being given
unless the United States guaranteed support. The Netherlands
government in exile ardently desired an understanding, which
followed logically from the growing bellicosity of Japan and of the
stress on co-operation in the Singapore defence conferences in

[41] *Ibid.*
[42] 'Report of the Anglo–Dutch–Australian Conference', held at Singapore,
22–25 February 1941, Cab. 80/29.
[43] 'Report of the American–Dutch–British Conversations', held at Singapore,
27 April 1941 and 'Report of the British–Dutch Conversations', held at
Singapore, 27 April 1941, C.O.S. (41) 387 and 388, Cab. 80/28.

February and April 1941. The subject was regularly raised in the war cabinet by Anthony Eden, now foreign secretary, and postponed. On 21 July he told the war cabinet:

> that the idea had been dropped of making a public declaration that we should go to the help of the Dutch East Indies if they were attacked by Japan. All that was now proposed was that we should tell the Dutch privately that we would do so, and would inform the United States of what we had done . . .
>
> On the merits of the case, he could not see that, if Japan attacked the Dutch East Indies, we should not go to their aid. He found difficulty in postponing a decision on this matter further, as the Dutch were pressing us to ratify the conversations. The Governments of Australia and New Zealand were in agreement with the course proposed . . .[44]

Churchill once again disagreed:

> As for a Japanese attack on Singapore, he did not believe anything of the sort was contemplated. It might well be that, even if Japan encroached on the Dutch East Indies, the right policy would be that we should not make an immediate declaration of war on Japan. Once war had been declared, Japanese cruisers would attack our sea communications, and none of our shipping would be safe unless heavily protected by convoys. At the present moment we were not in a position to send an adequate fleet to the Far East.[45]

It is remarkable that Churchill was prepared to contemplate Japanese occupation of the Netherlands East Indies, particularly when he himself had cogently pointed out the unacceptable dangers of such a policy to the war cabinet a year before.[46] It was decided, as a compromise, that Eden should inform the Netherlands minister that Britain considered that she had already assumed the responsibility for protecting the East Indies as best

[44] War cabinet conclusions, confidential annex, 21 July 1941, 72 (41) 10, Cab. 65/23.

[45] *Ibid.*

[46] Churchill had then observed: 'that, to his mind, the central facet of the situation, if Japan obtained the mastery of the Netherlands East Indies, was that she would be able to prepare strong positions facing Singapore, including a base for her fleet. If we did not fight, she would be able to prepare these positions in peace, and to use them against us at the moment which suited her best.

If we made it clear that we should fight to preserve the integrity of the Netherlands East Indies, Japan might very well decide against attack . . .' See war cabinet conclusions, confidential annex, 29 July 1940, 214 (40) 7, Cab. 65/14.

she could but that no undertaking could be given on the form that protection would take.[47] The Netherlands government was not satisfied and pressed for the military obligations to be resolved.[48] Discussions continued for months afterwards but no concrete military commitment was extended. Ashley Clarke of the Far Eastern department of the Foreign Office reflected on the situation in appropriately ironic terms:

> The salient points to bear in mind are (1) that we shall have to defend the Dutch East Indies anyway and (2) that the United States can give us no prior guarantee of support although the probability of such support amounts almost to a certainty. We therefore lose nothing by having an unambiguous agreement with the Dutch and we gain nothing by making further appeals to the United States. The reluctance which is felt by the Chiefs of Staff to make a frank agreement with the Dutch seems to me like saying that when invasion comes we will defend Hampshire and of course Devonshire, but we are short of anti-tank guns and will therefore not commit ourselves to defend Dorsetshire unless we get some backing from the President of the United States.[49]

Eden concurred and identified the obstacle, 'It is not only, or even mainly the Chiefs of Staff (C.I.G.S. happens to agree with us) but Admiralty & above all P.M. who take this view . . .'[50] There the matter rested until just before the outbreak of war: an undertaking of military support in unequivocal terms was at last conveyed to the Netherlands government on 5 December after Britain had received a promise of support from the United States. It is a revealing issue in a number of respects, not least for demonstrating the obstinate inflexibility of Churchill and the Admiralty. It damaged relations with the Netherlands government, alienated officials in the East Indies and handicapped effective co-ordination in defence. All to no purpose for, as Cadogan had once minuted, the cynical answer to saying that little help can be given is that there is nothing to lose by promising it therefore.[51]

In the final crisis of 1941 the changing relationship, whereby the immense burden that Great Britain carried was assumed by the United States, reached its climax. In the Far East Roosevelt

[47] Eden to Bland, 1 August 1941, F7214/230/G, F.O. 371/27779
[48] Eden to Bland, 8 August 1941, F7526/230/G, F.O. 371/27780.
[49] Minute by Clarke, 7 November 1941, F11734/4366/61, F.O. 371/27847.
[50] Minute by Eden, 9 November 1941, ibid.
[51] Minute by Cadogan, 6 May 1941, F4128/54/61, F.O. 371/27777.

did not display the decisiveness that accompanied the introduction
of Lend-Lease. Until the eve of Pearl Harbour, he declined to give
Britain a guarantee of support in the event of a Japanese attack
on British possessions. Yet he pursued a tough policy towards
Japan in the economic sphere involving the serious risk, to put it
no higher, of Japan eventually deciding to go to war. The catalyst
came with the Japanese advance into southern Indo-China in
July 1941. Despite initial doubts about provoking conflict in the
Pacific,[52] Roosevelt imposed the drastic freeze on economic relations with Japan including the effective suspension of crucial oil
exports. Within the British government, there were reservations
about going so far; before the American decision was announced,
a more limited form of economic retaliation had been planned.
However, the wider implications of co-operation with the United
States took priority and the war cabinet decided to support the
United States wholeheartedly.[53]

Great Britain was not consulted with any adequacy by the
United States in the protracted discussions with Japan. In one
sense this met the British desire, felt for so long, that the United
States should meet her full responsibilities in the Pacific. However,
it was not satisfactory that Britain should be kept largely ignorant
of developments and much dissatisfaction was voiced in the Foreign
Office. It is of interest to examine the closing stages of the crisis
in late November and early December 1941.[54] By this time the
Konoye government had fallen in Japan; Konoye had made a
genuine attempt to secure agreement with the United States by
removing his foreign minister, Matsuoka, and by offering to meet
Roosevelt for a summit conference.[55] The differences between the
two countries were so great that Hull dissuaded Roosevelt from
seeing Konoye.[56] While still in office, Konoye had accepted fundamental policy decisions in liaison and imperial conferences to
expand south and to go to war with the United States unless

[52] From the Morgenthau Diaries: Years of Urgency 1938–1941, ed. J. M. Blum
(Boston, 1965), p. 377.
[53] War cabinet conclusions, 24 July 1941, 73 (41) 4 and 28 July 1941, 75 (41)
6, Cab. 65/19.
[54] For a fuller discussion of the situation in 1941, see P. Lowe, 'Great
Britain and the Outbreak of War with Japan, 1941', in War and Society:
Historical Essays in Honour and Memory of J. R. Western 1928–71, ed. M. R.
D. Foot (London, 1973).
[55] For a useful brief description of Matsuoka, see Chihiro Hosoya, 'Retro-
gression in Japan's Foreign Policy Decision-Making Process', in Dilemmas of
Growth in Prewar Japan, ed. J. W. Morley (Princeton, 1971), pp. 92–93.
[56] See R. J. C. Butow, 'Backdoor Diplomacy in the Pacific: the Proposal
for a Konoye–Roosevelt Meeting, 1941', Journal of American History, lix
(1972), pp. 48–72.

agreement was quickly attained.[57] His successor as prime minister, General Tojo Hideki, was a resolute advocate of war but agreed that there should be one final attempt to resolve matters peacefully.

The principal obstacles to agreement between Japan, the United States and Great Britain lay in Japan's conflict in China and her membership of the tripartite pact. The special Japanese emissary, Kurusu, proposed a temporary agreement; Hull considered an alternative three-month agreement.[58] The British Foreign Office was at first inclined to give a cautious welcome to the Kurusu mission. Ashley Clarke minuted that 'if the Kurusu suggestion (of possible withdrawal from Indo-China) is genuine there seems to be some ground for a (very cautious) response on the part of the Americans'.[59] Sterndale Bennett agreed: 'We cannot of course rule out the possibility that a piecemeal settlement may merely give the Japanese a breathing space. But to get them really moving in reverse would be a great gain for us.'[60] When more information arrived, it was held that neither Kurusu's proposal nor Hull's contemplated alternative was satisfactory. It was too dangerous to leave loopholes through vague terms and the freezing measures should only be lifted if there was certainty of a significant Japanese retreat.[61] The reactions in Chungking were ferocious. Chiang Kai-shek urgently required aid to bolster his ramshackle regime; he was deeply alarmed at the danger of even a temporary compromise between the United States and Japan. Apprehension had been growing in London for a considerable period over China's ability to continue the struggle and there were rumours of a Japanese offensive in Yunnan to cut the Burma road. Churchill thought that the rumour might be accurate and addressed one of his personal messages to Roosevelt warning that Chiang should not be neglected.[62] In the resulting turmoil in Washington Hull abandoned his own proposal, sent a lengthy

[57] For the relevant documentation, based on notes taken by the Japanese military representatives, see *Japan's Decision For War: Records of the 1941 Policy Conferences*, ed. N. Ike (Stanford, 1967), pp. 77–163. See also A. Iriye, 'The Failure of Military Expansionism', in *Dilemmas of Growth*, ed. Morley, pp. 130–35.

[58] For the text, see *Foreign Relations of the United States* [hereafter cited as *F.R.U.S.*], *1931–1941*, ii, pp. 755–56, and *F.R.U.S. 1941*, iv, pp. 660–64.

[59] Minute by Clarke, 19 November 1941, on Washington to Foreign Office, 18 November 1941, F19475/86/23, F.O. 371/27912.

[60] Minute by Sterndale Bennett, 20 November 1941, *ibid*.

[61] Foreign Office to Washington, 24 November 1941, F12655/86/23, F.O. 371/27912.

[62] Churchill, *The Second World War*, iii, p. 530, Former Naval Person to President Roosevelt, 26 November 1941.

communication to Japan calling for a complete Japanese retreat, including withdrawal from China, and regarded the talks as virtually terminated. He told Halifax that he did not resent Britain's representations, although he thought Churchill had listened uncritically to Chiang. Hull reserved his ire for the generalissimo and for his own colleague, Stimson, who had played a leading part in 'busting' his diplomatic efforts.[63]

All that was clear in London was that the crisis was extremely grave. The uncertainty was precisely where Japan would strike and in what circumstances. The abruptness of the climax seems to have surprised Churchill and the chiefs of staff. It was only a fortnight or so since Churchill had spoken in the war cabinet of the futility of sending more forces to the Far East where they might be inactive for a year and the chief of the air staff had denied that the situation was one of 'extreme danger'.[64] At the end of November Churchill determined to make a renewed effort to obtain a promise of American support: he despatched a personal message to Roosevelt but, from his remarks to the war cabinet, was not sanguine on the answer.[65] At last Roosevelt acted decisively. A discussion took place on 1 December between Roosevelt, Harry Hopkins and Halifax. Hopkins referred to the dangerous impression that 'the Japanese acted while we only sent notes and talked'.[66] Roosevelt concurred and said there must be a clear Anglo-American understanding on the course of action when he received a reply from the Japanese concerning troop movements in Indo-China. He wished to know what Britain would do if the Japanese reply was unsatisfactory or if Japan attacked Thailand outside the Kra isthmus. Halifax commented that the inference was that if Japan moved, there should be a unified response. 'At one point he threw in an aside that in the case of direct attack on ourselves or the Dutch, we should obviously all be together, but he wished to clear up the matters that were less plain.'[67] With regard to the delicate issue of a British advance into Thai territory to take the Kra isthmus, Roosevelt observed that it would be preferable if Thailand

[63] Washington to Foreign Office, 29 November 1941, F12992/86/23, F.O. 371/27913. For the text of Hull's communication to Japan, see *F.R.U.S. 1931–1941*, ii, pp. 768–70.
[64] War cabinet conclusions, confidential annex, 12 November 1941, 112 (41) 1, Cab. 65/24.
[65] War cabinet conclusions, confidential annex, 1 December 1941, 122 (41) 3, Cab. 65/24.
[66] Foreign Office to Washington, 1 December 1941, F13114/86/23, F.O. 371/27913. See also, for a discussion of the last days before the outbreak of war, L. Woodward, *British Foreign Policy In The Second World War*, ii (London, 1971), pp. 165–77.
[67] *Ibid.*

could be persuaded to invite Britain to enter but added that 'strategical necessity' must govern policy. If Britain advanced 'we could certainly count on their support, though it might take a short time, he spoke of a few days, to get things into political shape here'.[68]

In the British reply to Washington, Roosevelt's words were warmly welcomed. The president's promise of support was interpreted as connoting armed support and Britain would accordingly be prepared to implement the preventive operation in the Kra isthmus if 'there were a direct attack or threat of immediate attack on the Kra isthmus'.[69] The Foreign Office added that the Thai prime minister had emphatically stated that the only way to save Thailand from Japanese domination was an unmistakable warning by Britain and the United States. Halifax saw Roosevelt again on 4 December. The president fully confirmed that his previous assurance of support meant armed support, the character of which would have to be determined by the defence chiefs; he agreed that the operation to take the Kra isthmus should be implemented if necessary. Like Churchill, he thought an attack on the Netherlands East Indies was probable and it could be readily presented to American public opinion as a threat to the Philippines.[70] In a further discussion the next day Roosevelt commented on the British proposal that a warning to Japan should embrace an attack on the Burma road, apart from aggression directed against Malaya or the Netherlands East Indies. He could not accept an attack on the Burma road, since this would be part of the Sino-Japanese war which had lasted since 1937. To achieve the political purpose of rallying American opinion, Japanese aggression must be seen as entirely new acts of violence. Otherwise Roosevelt supported the idea of a warning:

> He thinks that if the warning is given by the United States, ourselves and the Dutch, we should act independently all within 24 hours, using different language to mean the same thing . . . He would prefer the United States to get in first. On account of political considerations here, it was important that their action should be based on independent necessities of United States defence and not appear to follow on ourselves . . .[71]

[68] *Ibid.*
[69] Foreign Office to Washington, 3 December 1941, *ibid.*
[70] Washington to Foreign Office, 4 December 1941, F13219/86/23, F.O. 371/27914.
[71] Washington to Foreign Office, 5 December 1941, F13780/86/23, F.O. 371/27914.

War therefore came to British possessions in the Far East and Pacific shortly after the long-awaited promise of American support arrived. The disasters that ensued for Britain were a tragic and yet, in some respects, appropriate concomitant of what one Foreign Office official referred to as our 'fumbling' policy.[72] The Foreign Office appreciated the Japanese menace to some extent but not the full reality. The Foreign Office believed that the imposition of rigorous economic sanctions in July 1941 would bring the crisis to a head ultimately but that there was a chance that Japan might see sense and draw back from the brink. Memories of the policy of appeasement and of the discredit of this policy in the circumstances of 1939–41 haunted the Foreign Office: whatever happened there must be no repetition of Munich. The same outlook characterized policy makers in Washington. There could be no retreat but it might be dangerous to advance. It was difficult to compromise between the two and, if it came to a choice, war had to be accepted. The chiefs of staff, always conscious of weakness, were preoccupied with existing wars in Europe and the Middle East, seriously underestimated Japan and were dominated by Churchill. The Admiralty was the most obdurate in refusing to accept a new commitment in the Far East. While it was understandable enough, the Admiralty did not face up to the full implications of its inflexible attitude. The Air Ministry paid lip-service to the urgent need of improving air strength in Malaya. If Sinclair, the secretary of state for air, and Beaverbrook, the minister of aircraft production, agreed on only one subject, it was that they must resist pressure to send planes out of Europe to theatres where lesser crises existed.[73] In an important discussion in the war cabinet in November 1941 Sinclair seemed confused as to how many aircraft were in the Far East and made a misleading statement.[74] The Air Ministry was sadly mistaken in its confident belief that Japanese aircraft were definitely inferior to those of their opponents. The local defence establishment in Malaya underestimated the Japanese and was too complacent.

As for Winston Churchill, his attitude was a combination of public outspokenness, superficial dismissal of the Japanese threat and effacement when it came to properly co-ordinating defences for the contingency of a Japanese attack. The burdens he carried

[72] Minute by Sterndale Bennett, 5 February 1941, on Craigie to Foreign Office, 3 February 1941, F5401/9/61, F.O. 371/27760.
[73] Sinclair to Beaverbrook, 16 March 1941, and Beaverbrook to Sinclair, 16 March and 11 April 1941, Sinclair papers, Air 19/510.
[74] War cabinet conclusions, confidential annex, 5 November 1941, 109(41)2 Cab. 65/24.

were so great that he could devote little time or reflection to the Pacific. He did not comprehend the resolution and tenacity of Japan. He thought it unlikely that Japan would go to war if American involvement was certain. Even if she did, Japan could be held. All that could be done was to muddle along and hope for the best, the best connoting an eventual American commitment. As was true of most opinion, Churchill exaggerated the power of the United States to block Japanese expansion rapidly. In the midst of the disasters in January 1942, Lord Hankey wrote, 'Either we ought to have avoided the war, or we ought to have prepared for it much better than we did'.[75] The war could not be avoided because the major decisions were taken by Japan and the United States. It is undeniable that Britain should have been better prepared. When it came to appreciating the power and spirit of Japan, the men of Downing street and Whitehall did dwell in an ivory tower.

University of Manchester.

[75] Hankey to Piggott, 26 January 1942, Hankey Papers, Cab. 63/177.

THE QUEST FOR CONCEALED LANDS IN THE REIGN OF ELIZABETH I

The Alexander Prize Essay

By C. J. Kitching, B.A., Ph.D.

READ 8 JUNE 1973

CONCEALMENT has proved one of the most inscrutable aspects of the land market following the English Reformation. It has received only passing reference in standard works on the period,[1] and the gravity of the problem has never been fully appraised by historians, even though the discovery and disposal of concealed property exercised administrators and speculators alike more than any other aspect of the land market for much of the reign of Elizabeth, and consequently left an abundance of documentation.

The Tudors had, from the first, shown themselves anxious to assert ancient feudal rights and to exploit dues and services which had been withheld or allowed to drop,[2] but the 'concealment' problem which preoccupied the nation in the later sixteenth century was almost totally attributable to the dissolutions of the monasteries, chantries and kindred institutions. Such quantities of land were involved in the dissolutions that it was inevitable that, for one reason or another, some of the potential spoil would evade the crown, and even by the end of Elizabeth's reign this problem was far from solved. Indeed, it was worsened by widespread disenchantment at the hours spent in fruitless litigation and wasted clerical effort in attempting to recover concealed lands, at the number of fortunes endangered by the quest, and at the constant prying and meddling in the affairs of innocent bystanders that proved necessary in detecting concealments. The resulting unrest, like the quest itself, has left behind a good deal of documentary

[1] The problem was discussed in J. Strype, *Annals of the Reformation* (Oxford, 1824), II, i, p. 310; III, i, p. 169. More recently, see S. J. Madge, *The Domesday of Crown Lands* (London, 1938); J. Hurstfield, *The Queen's Wards* (London, 1958), p. 34 *et seq.*; and L. Stone, *The Crisis of the Aristocracy* (Oxford, 1965), pp. 415–16. There have been some notable local studies, such as L. P. Wenham, 'The chantries, gilds, obits and lights of Richmond', *Yorkshire Archaeological Journal*, xxxviii (1955), pp. 96, 185, 310.

[2] See J. Hurstfield, 'The revival of feudalism in early Tudor England', *History*, new ser., xxxvii (1952), p. 131, and 'The profits of fiscal feudalism, 1541–1602', *Economic History Review*, 2nd ser., viii (1955–56), p. 53.

evidence, and it is from extensive, though hitherto neglected, sources that the present exploratory essay has been compiled, in an attempt to explain something of the background, the procedure and the implications of concealment hunting, and thus to clear a way for future studies at both regional and national levels.[3]

Granted the speed of the Henrician and Edwardian surveys of church property, the crown had been satisfied with the working accuracy of the results, and became too involved selling off the spoil to expend any great effort in chasing up missing halfpennies and undeclared tenements rumoured to belong to a particular foundation, unless informers proffered evidence or local crown officials discovered enough to warrant a more thorough search.[4] There was no enthusiasm for another nation-wide survey to correct errors in the estimates provided by the original commissioners of the dissolution.

Implicit in the dissolution statutes[5] was the fear that rumours would precede the commissioners and that local conspiracies would arise to dispose of tangible assets and maintain silence on intangible ones. Concealment was easiest during the Edwardian dissolutions, because whilst the monastic commissioners had been able to visit every religious house, the chantry commissioners, faced with endowments in every parish, had to be more selective in their visits, and called only at specified centres in each county, demanding the attendance there of the clergy and representatives of the laity of each parish, who were to bring accounts of all suspect foundations. Records of the endowment of chantries, gilds, obits and lights were at best rough and ready,[6] yet the excusable errors of calculation in the declarations made to the commissioners were easily surpassed by the calculated errors of a determined parish.

---

[3] Unless otherwise stated all references are to documents in the Public Record Office. Crown copyright material is quoted by permission of the Controller of H.M.S.O. The principal sources are: E 178 (Exchequer Special Commissions); E 134 (Depositions); E 302 (Augmentations, Particulars for Concealments); E 315 (Augmentations Miscellaneous Books); DL 44 (Duchy of Lancaster Special Commissions); C 66 (Patent Rolls); SP 12 and SP 14 (State Papers Domestic, Elizabeth and James I).

[4] There were many local enquiries. See, for example, E 301/43, E 301/108 (supplements to chantry certificates); and E 117/10/11. Also R. Somerville, *History of the Duchy of Lancaster*, i (London, 1953), p. 297. Among the more curious instances is a grant of lands confessed as a result of Latimer's preaching, see W. C. Richardson, *History of the Court of Augmentations* (Baton Rouge, 1961), p. 167.

[5] Statutes 27 Hen. VIII c. 28; 31 Hen. VIII c. 13; 37 Hen. VIII c. 4 and 1 Edw. VI c. 14.

[6] There were some honourable exceptions; see, for example, K. L. Wood-Legh, *A Small Household of the Fifteenth Century* (Manchester, 1956).

Robert Harde was one of the four men of Langar, Nottingham-shire, chosen in 1548 to attend at Southwell to reveal his parish's endowments. On returning to his village he was met in the alehouse by one Richard Brothewell who asked him, 'Harde, what have you done concerning our chantry land?' The reply was sharp, 'Hold your peace! You may not call it chantry land.' Brothewell later declared that he 'did perceive that by means of the . . . bailiffs and chief farmers . . . it was meant to be concealed and kept back'.[7]

Such local exchanges must have been frequent, though the evidence is rarely so damning. Vestments, images, books, church fittings and other movable objects disappeared in large numbers, though there were some enquiries in areas where the suspected tally was unusually high.[8] Endowments of masses and prayers were easier to conceal, at least in part, since there were scarcely any accurate account books and few save the priest and the donor knew the exact sums involved. But there were many loose-tongued parish-ioners who might disclose the existence of a foundation without knowing its value, and for this reason deliberate concealment could never be lightly undertaken.[9]

Any property which belonged in perpetuity to the dissolved foundations should have passed to the crown, and anything which they held for a term of lives or years still to run was the crown's for that same term. Yet fluctuations in yearly revenue, and defective accounting, meant that there were numerous technical inaccuracies in the books drawn up by the commissioners at the dissolutions. Furthermore, the crown's own officers often failed to read the accounts thoroughly, and thereby let slip some of the property to which the crown was strictly entitled. Much of the supposed 'concealment', therefore, was wholly inadvertent as far as the tenants and owners of the foundations were concerned. In addition there was a tendency for the local collectors to write off in their books each year sums which they could not gather in because the alleged debtors were destitute or had fled, or for a variety of other reasons.[10] Such book-keeping concealments were regarded as long-term problems by Henry VIII and Edward VI, but at length under Mary, William Berners and Thomas Mildmay called in all royal revenue collectors and examined their accounts and their

---

[7] E 178/2927.

[8] For example, E 315/115, fos. 2, 11; E 315/123, fo. 151.

[9] The names of informers rarely come to light unless they were granted some of the property as a reward or gave information before a commission.

[10] See, for example, *The Inventories of Church Goods, for the Counties of York, Durham, and Northumberland*, ed. W. Page (Surtees Soc., xcvii, 1897) p. 118.

explanations for arrears.[11] This was a massive project which un-earthed a good deal of laxity in the administration and was still incomplete when Elizabeth came to the throne. The longer the discrepancies in the accounts remained unsettled, the greater became the conviction that most concealment was the fault of these local officers, an idea subsequently embodied in a licence of 1571 permitting Henry Middlemore to search crown records concerning forfeit property, and to note those discrepancies which 'are happened by the fraudulent practices and acts of sundry collectors . . . by false certificate made that the said duties were desperate or detained.'[12]

The scrutiny of the accounts by Berners and Mildmay was almost certainly the major impulse behind a new enthusiasm, already manifest under Mary, for rooting out concealments. Elizabeth inevitably sold some good crown lands in the early years of her reign and gave away others as rewards to her courtiers, but she became increasingly anxious not to break further into the reserves than necessary, and from the mid-1560s until 1589 she persevered without regular sales of land.[13] Concealments could hardly be regarded in the same light. As long as they remained undetected they were of no benefit to the crown. Once discovered they would become an asset which the queen might use to satisfy faithful servants, or the land-market at large, without drawing upon the good lands.

The crown itself, then, had every reason to uncover conceal-ments, yet the initiative came from the courtiers seeking lands, and the first evidence that their persuasive voices had won through is tantalizing. With no hint as to how the lands were recovered, the Patent Rolls record six grants of concealed lands to Sir George Howard, master of the royal armoury (and one of the pioneers of the hunt under Mary), between July 1559 and April 1561.[14] Sir Edward Warner, Lieutenant of the Tower, received two such patents.[15] In May 1560 Thomas Paynell obtained a licence to search at his own expense for concealments to the yearly value of £26. 13. 4 in reward for his services to four successive sovereigns, but again there is no indication of the means whereby he detected

[11] *Calendar of the Patent Rolls* (hereafter cited as *CPR*), *Mary*, iii, p. 25. The findings are mainly in E 117 (Church Goods).

[12] C 66/1071, m. 22. Spelling has been modernized in all quotations.

[13] For the later sales see R. B. Outhwaite, 'Who bought crown lands . . . 1589–1603?', *Bulletin of the Institute of Historical Research*, xliv (1971), p. 18.

[14] *CPR*, *Eliz.*, i, pp. 87, 307, 395, 427 and ii, pp. 10, 160. The lands amounted to a yearly value of £65, and a separate record seems to have been kept, SP 12/12, no. 60. See also *CPR*, *Mary*, iv, p. 411.

[15] *CPR*, *Eliz.*, iii, pp. 104, 329, totalling less than £30 p.a.

the lands. Evidently the operation was none too easy, since most of the items included in the resulting patents were valued at only a few pence each, and it therefore took many such discoveries to make up any reasonable total. Paynell died before he had found all the lands to which he was entitled, and his executors became seriously indebted trying to finish the business.[16] Cecily Pickarell, widow of one of the Protector Somerset's stewards, obtained a similar set of patents in recompense for a loan by her husband to Somerset that had never been repaid.[17]

The patents build up a curious picture. At a time when good crown lands were being sold and given away, several persons close to the court either volunteered or were persuaded to look for, on the face of it, a most uninspiring collection of concealed properties scattered in each grant through a dozen or more counties. Certainly, they would have placed the subsequent disposal of the lands in the hands of agents, for the patentees themselves could not conceivably have administered such widely scattered and insignificant holdings, which can only indicate that they expected high profits when selling off their gains. Evidently each patentee had applied for warrants permitting him to search for concealed lands, though none has yet come to light. The costs of any such enquiry were borne by the searcher, and whilst some discoveries undoubtedly arose from informations received by the crown, the majority were derived through the complex process of suing out from the Exchequer or Duchy of Lancaster special commissions of enquiry in which the parishes of a selected area were required to report whether they knew of any concealed property. Two early returns, from Shropshire and Northamptonshire for the year 4 Elizabeth, provide evidence of this general trawl for concealments, and not simply an attempt to investigate items reported by informers.[18] The constables, churchwardens or other sworn men enquired among their neighbours[19] and returned their findings on slips of paper to the commissioners. It is hardly surprising that such enquiries produced a substantial crop of negative returns, and only occasional discoveries, for the method used was no better than that employed in the original dissolution surveys.[20] But the searchers were unde-

[16] *Ibid.*, ii, p. 159; iii, p. 52; v, pp. 236–38.
[17] *Ibid.*, ii, pp. 257, 554, 566.   [18] E 302/1/12; E 315/168.
[19] E 315/168, no. 32; also, for Lancashire, E 315/170, no. 8.
[20] Typical was the return for Middleton Scriven, Salop.: 'We have nothing that is demanded by your books', E 302/1/12, fo. 101c. In later returns only the digests of positive findings generally survive. There is other scattered evidence of the hunt, and in one case a gardener at Hampton Court managed to force the clergy of Berkshire to produce their glebe accounts: *CPR, Eliz.*, iii, p. 477 and SP 12/42, nos. 44–46.

terred, and by the end of the 1560s licences to seek concealments as a reward for service were well established. Early recipients included Edward Cary, groom of the Privy Chamber, Hugh Councell, and John Farnham, gentleman-pensioner—all men of, or close to, the court.[21]

When applicants were set on discovering lands worth over £20 p.a. their enterprise began to smack of big business, their chance of receiving the lands as a gift was largely overridden by the crown's concern to preserve its estates, and an alternative means of disposal had to be found, such as granting the lands in fee-farm. Nevertheless, the aspiring courtiers and crown servants still came forward.

Peter Grey, probably the escheator in Buckinghamshire of that name, ideally placed to handle lands, obtained a licence to search for concealments up to a total yearly value of £100 to be held in fee-farm, with the assurance of co-operation from the law officers when he applied for commissions of enquiry, and with the guaranteed right to look for further lands should any of his original complement subsequently prove not to have been concealed and his profits be thereby diminished.[22] Edward Dyer, the young courtier and poet trying to make a name for himself under the patronage of Leicester, entered the hunt in 1574 for lands to the value of one hundred marks per year in fee-farm, a very modest undertaking by comparison with his later ventures in this field which will be related below.[23] But for the present Dyer's efforts were far overshadowed by those of Thomas, Lord Wentworth, who had obtained the largest fee-farm grant, in July 1570, authorizing him and his heirs to search for concealments to the yearly value of £200. Wentworth received special authorization from Cecil to nominate his own men for the commissions of enquiry pursuant to his discoveries, presenting lists of candidates to the clerks preparing the commissions in the Exchequer and Duchy of Lancaster. This measure of encouragement to private enterprise in the detection of concealments is a sure indication of the crown's desire to solve the problem without undertaking any overall national survey, centrally financed. There is ample evidence in the Patent Rolls that Wentworth and his son obtained the lands only piecemeal over the next decade through the work of many agents and nominees.[24] They en-

---

21 *CPR, Eliz.*, iii, pp. 80, 393; iv, pp. 225–27; v, p. 38. There are many subsequent references to Farnham, e.g. C 66/1158, m. 44; C 66/1163, m. 23; C 66/1144, m. 28.   22 C 66/1181, m. 15; C 66/1198, m. 34; C 66/1328, m. 31.

23 C 66/1117, m. 4. On Dyer, see R. M. Sargent, *At the Court of Queen Elizabeth* (London, 1935).

24 *CPR, Eliz.*, v, p. 15. There are many subsequent patents, e.g. *Ibid.*, pp. 227, 273, 341, 397 and later rolls: C 66/1219, m. 28; C 66/1251, m. 30, etc. For the warrant see E 178/3191. The legal problems are discussed below.

countered both financial and legal difficulties in the process, while the crown made a modest yearly sum from the revived rents of the lands.

A third development, once the idea of concealment hunting became widely accepted, was the increasing number of prospective patentees who offered to *buy* concealed lands, their influence at court presumably being insufficient to put them among the favoured few who obtained the lands as a gift or in fee-farm. They came from much the same milieu: Sir John Perrot, Sir William Drury; John Marsh, William Gryce and Robert Holmes ('the queen's servants'); George Darcy, Robert Bowes and Edward Grimston: all with long records of service.[25] The crown made a major concession by selling the lands at the very favourable rate of ten or twelve years' purchase, which reflects an appreciation of the costs and hazards facing the searchers and also shows in what low regard these scattered fragments were held by the surveyors. These sales continued after the official commissions for sale of crown lands had been terminated. It is clear that they were regarded as exceptions, and that therefore the land market was not as quiescent between the official sales as has often been supposed, yet these were not attractive properties and few were authorized to search for them. The total crown revenue from these special sales before 1580 was certainly well over £3,000 but probably less than £5,000. The exact sum cannot readily be calculated, at least until the *Calendar of the Patent Rolls* has progressed sufficiently for all the grants to be certainly identified. Over some fifteen years this is a modest sum, but the scattered nature of the lands ensured that the quest achieved a notoriety out of all proportion to its returns. A more significant income was derived from the fee-farm grants just instanced, and from the scores of small leases, granted without the fuss of formal commissions, to tenants and others who declared local concealments.[26]

By the early 1570s everyone had seen the potential in concealment-hunting, and patents were issued for the detection of a whole range of neglected dues and services despite growing public

[25] The references so far printed are *CPR, Eliz.*, iii, pp. 62, 453; iv, pp. 51, 162, 352; v, pp. 271, 334, 371, but there are other examples on later rolls, see C 66/1096, m. 1; C 66/1097, m. 7; C 66/1121, m. 2; C 66/1127, m. 30; C 66/1138, m. 15; C 66/1170, m. 3; C 66/1183, m. 12; C 66/1288, m. 16. The list of recipients given in the text is probably almost complete, though more may come to light with further knowledge of the later rolls.

[26] Only the larger leases appear on the Patent Rolls; see, for example, *CPR, Eliz.*, iii, nos. 2106, 2114, 2154, 2166, 2273, 2655, 2810, 2880. No quantitative assessment could be given without identifying all the Particulars for Leases relating to concealed plots.

protest.[27] The crown sought to control detection of lands by restricting patents to those close to the court, but could not vouch for their agents in the field. Positive encouragement was given to Middlemore to search the records for technical concealments,[28] and at the same time, in May 1571, Henry Knyvett was licensed for five years to search all records of the Exchequer for concealment, to pay for copies needed by way of proof, and then to sue out the usual commissions to enquire before a local jury whether he was correct.[29] If successful he was to be entitled to half the arrears due, and a 31-year lease of the property at full rent but without any entry fine.

Record searching became a standard feature of concealment grants, and evidently officers of the Exchequer were also hard at work in the cause, for in the Trinity term of the same year Peter Osborne, the Lord Treasurer's Remembrancer, handed into the King's Remembrancer's office a book of concealments of reserved rents and tenths on grants of Henry VIII. He was awarded the right to one-third of the arrears.[30]

By 1572, protests against the repeated inquisitions of conceal-ment commissioners and against local attempts to by-pass the full machinery of commissions and returns, were sufficiently alarming for the crown to embark on a series of restrictive measures.[31] In February a proclamation halted all commissions and authorized their revocation by *supersedeas* from the Exchequer. Persons with specific grievances were urged to raise the matter at their next local assizes. It was added, however, that the crown fully intended to continue hunting concealments through future patents issued to trusted subjects, and this proclamation seems to have been only a mild palliative with no lasting effect.[32] Again in March 1573 the Law Officers were ordered to ratify no more books of conceal-ments,[33] but the patents soon proceeded. In 1575 the well-known grant authorizing Henry Townsend of Lincoln's Inn and William

[27] Strype, *Annals,* II, i, p. 313; *CPR, Eliz.,* v, no. 194, *et seq.*

[28] See above, n. 12.

[29] C 66/1074, m. 41. Charges of ½ mark for searching and 4d. per line copied were a forminable deterrent; see M. McKisack, *Medieval History in the Tudor Age* (Oxford, 1971), pp. 93-94.

[30] Three years later he was authorized to tackle the records of Edward's reign: see Exchequer Entry Books of Decrees and Orders, E 123/4 (insert between fos. 179 and 180), E 123/5, fo. 158.

[31] The problem of informers was repeatedly discussed in Parliament and was the subject of more than one statute, see Hurstfield, *The Queen's Wards,* p. 42, and statutes 18 Eliz., c. 5 and 31 Eliz., c. 5.

[32] *Tudor Royal Proclamations,* ed. P. L. Hughes and J. F. Larkin, ii (London, 1969), no. 584.

[33] *Acts of the Privy Council, 1571-1575,* p. 211.

Walter to enquire concerning concealed wardships and other feudal dues was issued.[34]

The note of caution was sounded yet again in an Order of the Exchequer in the Easter Term 1577 that

> no commission should be made to enquire of concealed lands but only by depositions and oaths of a Jury of the county where the lands lie.[35]

Some of the abuses connected with concealment-hunting will be discussed below, but the repeated expression of official doubts surely indicates that the nettle had not been fully grasped, and that the crown was too committed to the venture to withdraw completely.

Greater hopes were engendered by another proclamation, in December 1579, prohibiting all further quests for concealments without express permission, cancelling all commissions already at work and urging the speedy termination of cases pending in Chancery and the Exchequer where patentees were seeking to prove their rights to concealed lands.[36] This certainly put an end to the sale of concealed lands, but it was in other respects an empty gesture, side-stepped by new schemes presented to the Court and the Exchequer for handling concealments without again stirring up a hornets' nest.[37] In October 1581, less than two years after the proclamation, approval was given for a virtual monopoly of the concealment market to Edward Stafford, gentleman-pensioner (soon to be knighted and to serve as ambassador to France). The plan incorporated to his advantage many facets of the earlier commissions already described. The patent[38] was to run for seven years, during which time Stafford was to be entitled to claim in fee-farm for 60 years any lands he might prove concealed. He had the right to search any relevant records in the presence of their custodians, but was to bear the cost of copies made. He was to receive property where the crown's title was, after his labours, still in doubt, and the general tenor of the opposition can be seen from a further clause that if any transaction were challenged as affecting the livelihood of a parson, preacher, scholar or poor man it was to be suspended until a ruling had been received from the Exchequer or Duchy Court.

[34] C 66/1136, m. 42. See Hurstfield, *The Queen's Wards*, pp. 39–40, 86–87 and references there cited.

[35] Peter Grey, whose warrant to search antedated this order, was given a dispensation, E 178/3191, no. 4.

[36] *Tudor Royal Proclamations*, ii, no. 644.

[37] British Museum, Lansdowne MS. 47/23, fo. 50.

[38] C 66/1208, m. 26.

Any safeguard intended by this monopoly situation was swiftly subverted by Stafford's contracting-out his patent within a month to one Leycolt who brought in the notorious William Tipper as a partner. Tipper, having already stirred up international controversy by obtaining a patent to find compulsory lodgings for foreign merchants in England, was far down the list of those who might have maintained a respectable image for the concealment quest. It may have been through Sir Christopher Hatton that Tipper was introduced to Edward Dyer, who re-enters the story in May 1585 as recipient of some lands detected under this patent, and who spent the next two years trying to buy out Stafford and his sub-contractors, forging a business link with Tipper that was to last for twenty years.[39] Dyer's petition was successful, but he suffered from the ever worsening public relations of concealment enquiries, and from his own poor record of unsettled debts to the crown, by having important restrictions incorporated in the patent (for instance, the exclusion of university and cathedral lands), and by being compelled to place substantial recognisances with the Exchequer as security. Five years of searching for concealments and two subsequent renewals of the patent thanks to the intervention of Robert Cecil on his behalf only drove Dyer further into debt and postponed the reckoning which was finally wreaked on his estate after his death in 1607.[40] Concealments, it seems, were as unprofitable as his other speculative hobby, alchemy, but Dyer and Tipper became infamous for their far-reaching exploration of the concealment market, and Tipper himself seems to have made a comfortable profit. Their total turnover was estimated at around £30,000 by 1607, and it was on sums such as these that the many hopeful suitors for concealment patents[41] set theirs hearts, though they would have been well advised to contemplate the costs and public hatred that were the inevitable by-products of the search.

Stafford and Dyer did not quite have a monopoly down to the end of the century, for in August 1583 Sir James Croft, controller of the household, successfully mooted a slightly different proposal for solving the problem.[42] He and his agents were permitted to

[39] He also ran into legal difficulties with Stafford, see SP 12/159, no. 37; SP 12/149, no. 24; SP 12/159, nos. 38–43; SP 12/157, no. 87; SP 12/190, no. 96 and E. St. J. Brooks, *Sir Christopher Hatton* (London, 1946), p. 222.

[40] C 66/1270, m. 7; Brooks, *Sir Christopher Hatton*, p. 228; Sargent, *At the Court of Queen Elizabeth*, pp. 132–140; L. M. Hill, 'Sir Julius Caesar's Journal', *Bulletin of the Institute of Historical Research*, xlv (1972), pp. 318–19. One Patent Roll, C 66/1310, is entirely taken up with grants to Dyer, and there are many more references.

[41] Hurstfield, *The Queen's Wards*, p. 42.

[42] C 66/1228, m. 11.

search for four years, approaching alleged owners to persuade them to compound for their arrears and thereafter to regularize their tenure under the crown at full rent. The compounding fee went to Croft himself, but where the party refused to pay, Croft was empowered to compound with anyone else for the land. Numerous entries in the Patent Rolls between 1585 and 1587 of grants made at the behest of Croft[43] testify to the frenzied activity of his helpers throughout the country. Once again, popular opinion had been flouted and all pretence of abiding even by the spirit of the 1579 proclamation had been dropped.

In the late 1580s and early 1590s, therefore, there was another wave of protest with its now familiar murmurs of feigned agreement from the Exchequer. Late in 1588 the Lord Treasurer again stressed that no grants could be made without local inquisitions[44] —hardly a definitive and decisive step in the light of previous similar pronouncements. The resumption of the major sale of crown land in 1589 shifted the emphasis in the land market and took some of the steam out of the protest. Croft's compounding had come to an end, but Tipper and Dyer continued to collect fee-farm patents for concealed lands, and Sir Edward Stanley received two gifts of concealed lands he had detected.[45]

A paper dated March 1592 and preserved among the State Papers Domestic tabulated the worst of grievances popularly conceived against concealment-hunting:[46] incumbents were being subjected to litigation or bribed into disclosing their income; the seizure of lands formerly given to pious uses was itself a breach of faith with the donors, and led men to spend more on 'their friends and kins-folks' and less on the service of God and learning; it eroded parts of the income of preachers and teachers, and fostered an unhealthy desire for secularization; more general discontent prevailed 'amongst all well affected and moderate minded subjects' because there were long and tedious lawsuits; the hopes engendered by the 1579 proclamation had not been fulfilled; even those who should have profited most came off badly, since the dealers failed to realize their initial dreams from the property, 'by God's secret judgement', and the crown disposed of the lands on too favourable terms . . . and so on.

It will be clear even from the limited survey undertaken above that many of these criticisms were well founded, and that the crown

---

[43] Though not in his name. All the grants passed in the name of agents, though they are registered as promoted by Croft.

[44] B. M., Lansdowne MS 56/39.

[45] C 66/1334, m. 21; C 66/1377, m. 1; B.M., Lansdowne MS 59/29.

[46] SP 12/244, no. 688.

had taken them into account when issuing patents and regulating
the conduct of the operation, though it had at no time strongly
demonstrated its will to control the speculators, and had repeatedly
overlooked even the more notorious abuses for the sake of financial
gain. The proximity of the patentees to the court brought further
discredit. From the first, parishes and patentees, concealers and
commissioners, pitted their wits in a struggle for economic survival.

Some concealment hunters, intrepid enough to tackle the lands
of cathedrals, universities and the city corporations, roused the
storms of protest which became nationally famous and which
generated the lists of grievances such as that just described. The
cause célèbre was undoubtedly that of the city of London where
two of Wentworth's agents, Adams and Woodshawe, resurrected
in the 1580s the long-standing problem of the crown's claims on the
land of companies that had supported religious gilds. Examining
the records, they discovered many more lands concealed and embarked upon an intense legal wrangle in which the Chief Justices
were called on for a ruling, and the companies had to compound
with the patentees.[47]

This, however, was only the most famous of many causes. At
Chester, agents of Peter Grey temporarily obtained many of the
cathedral lands in a patent in 1578 because of a technical flaw in
the Dean's title deeds.[48] Whitgift, when bishop of Worcester, complained to the Lord Treasurer of an attempt to deprive his see of
the manor of Hartlebury in 1579.[49] But so little was achieved
against the 'concealers' that he was again compelled, as archbishop
of Canterbury in 1594, to issue a strong protest to the Lord Keeper
and the Chancellor of the Duchy of Lancaster.[50]

Croft's agents roused the anger of York corporation, which
successfully petitioned the Earl of Huntingdon as Lord President
of the Council of the North to protest about the deviousness of
Croft and his men.[51] Stafford and Dyer arranged for many leases
of concealed cathedral and college lands to be undertaken under

[47] J. Stow, *Survey . . . of London,* ii (6th edition, London, 1754), pp. 336–342.
C 66/1219, m. 28; B.M., Lansdowne MS 38 *passim.* The incident is taken up
in the histories of many of the city companies.
[48] R. V. H. Burne, 'Chester Cathedral in the reigns of Mary and Elizabeth',
*Journal of the Chester and North Wales Architectl., Archaeol., and Hist.
Society,* xxxviii (1951), pp. 91–92. But the problem here was part of a wider
dispute over the fee-farm of the cathedral lands.
[49] J. Strype, *The Life and Acts of John Whitgift* (Oxford, 1822), i, p. 171.
[50] *Ibid.,* ii, pp. 196—98.
[51] Claire Cross, *The Puritan Earl* (London, 1966), p. 173; *York Civic Records,*
viii (Yorks. Rec. Ser., cxix, 1953), pp. 78–79, 87, 120. The corporations of
Beverley and Hull also became involved in similar transactions: C 66/1254
m. 1; C 66/1293, m. 7.

the chapters' very noses, and inevitably added to the clamour of protest. The bishop of Lincoln complained about the activities of Stafford's men in his diocese, proceeding on their own authority to ask parishioners and clergy a whole set of questions, many of which had nothing whatever to do with concealments.[52] At Norwich, only the intervention of Coke as Attorney General finally overruled the loss of the bishop's lands to some 'concealers' on another verbal technicality. As as result of this case, a statute was passed to protect the church from such crafty devices.[53] The spoil, it seems, was not as paltry as the early patents might have led us to suppose.

The courts, however, did not turn a blind eye to the ambitions of the searchers, and they balanced equitably their desire on the one hand to detect and punish fraudulent dealings and on the other to defend the rights of tenants and interpret the law generally in their favour if in doubt. For example, a commission sitting at Worcester on 9 June 1563 discovered several concealments in the county, and the tenants were cited to appear in the Exchequer in the Trinity term of the next year. On examining the documents produced against them, the tenants submitted that two lines had been erased at the foot of the inquisition and words superimposed,

> which seemeth not to be presented by any Jury but put in by some sinister means and practice after the Jury had given their verdict.[54]

The judges agreed and the case was dismissed.[55]

There were some cases where allegations of concealment were actually disproved. Cecily Pickarell lost part of a claim to arrears in 1572 because one tenant was able to produce deeds demonstrating that an endowment included in her patent had been only for the term of a chaplain's life, and could not therefore have come to the crown in perpetuity.[56] About 1590 a grant of the lands of Christ's college, Brecon, to Tipper was challenged because the

---

[52] Strype, *Annals*, III, i, pp. 161–69. He was stopped by a *supersedeas* from the Exchequer.

[53] 35 Eliz., c. 3 and 39 Eliz., c. 22. These are discussed in Strype, *Whitgift*, i, p. 173, and particularly in E. Coke, *Institutes*, iv (London, 1797), pp. 76, 256 and *Reports* (London, 1635), iii, p. 72 *et seq.*

[54] SP 12/146, no. 128.

[55] E 123/1A, fo. 53ᵛ, 58ʳ; E 178/2474. In one case the failure of the commissioners to sign and seal their return invalidated their findings: E 123/4, fos. 99ᵛ–100, and in another the failure to state explicitly that the lands had once been used superstitiously invalidated the suit: E 123/4 fo. 288.

[56] E 123/4, fo. 222ᵛ–223.

college had not been dissolved by Henry VIII and had openly paid first fruits ever since, so its lands could not be concealed as the plaintiff alleged.[57]

Even if concealment were provable the patentee could not enjoy his grant in respect of disputed properties until cases arising had concluded in his favour.[58] Knyvett, Middlemore and Wentworth all pursued the Earl of Hertford unsuccessfully (and Wentworth even petitioned the queen to intervene on his behalf) to force the surrender of lands worth £80 p.a. allegedly concealed by Hertford.[59] At the very least it was often necessary to obtain injunctions to evict recalcitrant tenants from concealed lands.[60]

All such litigation was costly and time-consuming, and if there were also administrative delays in drawing up the patents and issuing them, the profitability of the exercise to the patentee was already in jeopardy. Sir John Perrot wrote to Walsingham in June 1575 urging the speedy issue of a grant because

> I have made divers assurances for parts of the lands therein to be passed, and appointed payment of the money, being loath now to live in debt.[61]

It was not unknown for tenant or patentee to resort to fraud in the attempt to defend his own interests. In 1570 Hugh Lyon complained in the Exchequer that tenants of some concealed lands of which he had obtained a lease in the previous year had now got together with the steward of the manor and 'had great talk', arranging a meeting at which, 'being simple men', they planned to declare the lands were not, after all, concealed. The Exchequer insisted that it alone had authority to conduct any reappraisals, and Lyon's rights stood.[62] By contrast, two agents working for Cecily Pickarell seem to have stated that lands had been declared before a commission when in fact no such commission had been issued, and her patent was invalidated in that respect.[63]

These few examples are enough to indicate that almost everyone licensed to search for concealments was compelled at some stage to resort to litigation. The final Elizabethan remedy was a

---

[57] *Hist. MSS., Cssn. Reports, Salisbury*, xiii, pp. 397–398.

[58] For example, E 123/4, fo. 196: an order banning the grant of property occupied by Thomas Norwood, until concealment was proved.

[59] SP 15/19, no. 50; SP 12/75, no. 28; E 123/4, fo. 178ᵛ. *Hist. Mss. Cssn. Reports, Salisbury*, xi, pp. 206–207.

[60] For example, E 123/5, fo. 109, by Thomas Miller, an agent of Middlemore.

[61] SP 12/103, no. 64.

[62] E 123/4, fo. 90.

[63] *CPR, Eliz.*, iii, p. 250.

proclamation of 14 January 1600 which acknowledged that many landholders

> have been of late years greatly vexed, sued and put to intolerable charges by colour of letters patent which are found for the most part to be void in law.[64]

A body of Commissioners to compound for Defective Titles was established, resurrecting the technique of Croft fifteen years earlier. Landowners could effectively insure against any defects for a fixed compounding sum, so that in future 'no person be enforced or drawn to discover the imperfection or imbecility of any their estates or interests'. The rules governing the disposal of concealments were once again set down, under the sign manual, for the benefit of the commissioners.[65]

But this greatly worsened the situation again by whetting the appetite of a new generation of concealment-hunters,[66] and under James I the same ambiguous attitude of the crown prevailed. Attempts were made in the king's general pardon at his coronation and in a proclamation of 1609 to check concealment-hunting[67] but each new stoppage brought laments from those about to take out patents on their discoveries, and the crown was prevailed upon to dispense with each new set of restrictions.[68] There is every suggestion that ever greater sums were being made by the few who persevered in the hunt. But it was not until 1624 that Parliament pressed the matter as a grievance and passed an Act prohibiting the detection of defective titles over 60 years old.[69] Legislation was long overdue: only such a measure could enable the parishes to rest content and reduce the pressure on the law courts. Concealment, of course, continued. Indeed, it was once again to become a burning issue during the Interregnum and after the Restoration when the Royalists' estates were the object of investigation. But

[64] *Tudor Royal Proclamations*, iii, no. 202; C 66/1529, m. 14d.

[65] SP 12/275, no. 128.

[66] See, for example, the complaints of Edward Seymour in *Hist. Mss. Cssn. Reports, Salisbury*, xi, pp. 206–207.

[67] Stow, *Survey . . . of London*, p. 342 et seq. *Cal. State Papers Dom., 1603–1610*, p. 505.

[68] SP 14/35, no. 38. Hugh Hurleston, principal clerk in the alienations office, was said to have discovered under Elizabeth concealments worth £25,000 but was thwarted in his attempt to claim them by James's pardon, *cf.* SP 14/44, no. 83 and SP 14/68, no. 126. The whole question of concealments was under review, however; see SP 14/89, no. 113, 123, and *Cal. State Papers Dom., 1623–25*, pp. 6, 32.

[69] 21 Jac. I, c. 2. Described by Coke (*Institutes*, iv, p. 76) as giving a 'plenary salve for the whole mischief'.

interest in the old monastic and chantry lands had by then been superseded.

From first to last, therefore, the crown saved itself the expense of undertaking another national survey of dissolved church property, and cast the burden on to private enterprise, though well within the confines of the court. That the searchers were numerous enough to maintain the quest uninterrupted throughout Elizabeth's reign and into the next speaks volumes for the desperate last hopes of courtiers beset by problems of debt, and for the business ambitions of the dealers in the land market, who were the only ones to make any real profit from the transactions apart from the crown itself, which continued to derive a steady income from revived rents. But the nation at large, the law courts and finally Parliament itself were thoroughly sickened by the encouragement given to informers and profiteers, the volume of tedious business produced, and the repeated failure of the crown to stand by its best resolutions and control the situation. Those who deliberately contrived conceal-ment in the bygone days of the dissolutions little thought that their action would prove such a lasting concern.*

Public Record Office.

* Some of the points raised in this essay are treated further at a regional level in C. J. Kitching, 'Studies in the redistribution of collegiate and chantry property in the diocese and county of York at the dissolution' (unpublished Durham Ph.D. thesis, 1970), pp. 237–268.

TWO MODELS OF PUBLIC OPINION: BACON'S 'NEW LOGIC' AND DIOTIMA'S 'TALE OF LOVE'

The Prothero Lecture

By Professor Samuel H. Beer, A.B., B.A., Ph.D., F.R.Hist.S.

READ AT THE SOCIETY'S CONFERENCE
17 SEPTEMBER 1973

IT is appropriate that an American should address himself to the subject of public opinion. For, in terms of quantity, Americans have made the subject peculiarly their own.[1] They have also invested it with characteristically American concerns. Most of the work done on the subject in the United States is oriented by a certain theoretical approach. This approach is democratic and rationalist. Both aspects create problems. In this paper I wish to play down the democratic problem, viz., how many of the voters are capable of thinking sensibly about public policy, and emphasize rather the difficulties that arise from modern rationalism. Here I take a different tack from most historians of the concept of public opinion, who, taking note of the origin of the term in the mid-eighteenth century, stress its connection with the rise of representative government and democratic theory.[2]

To direct attention to rationalist presuppositions will also help bring out important contrasts with the view of public opinion that

---

[1] A recent bibliography on mass communications lists 3,000 titles, selected from a total of some 10,000, which, judging by the select list, were virtually all produced in the United States during a period of twenty-two years. To be sure, not all these titles were concerned with public opinion in its political aspect. See Donald A. Hansen and J. H. Parsons, *Mass Communications: A Research Bibliography* (Santa Barbara, 1968)

[2] For the history of the concept of public opinion, I have found particularly useful Hans Speier, 'The Historical Development of Public Opinion', *American Journal of Sociology*, lv (1950), pp. 376–88; Paul A. Palmer, 'The Concept of Public Opinion in Political Theory', in *Essays in History and Political Theory in Honor of Charles Howard McIlwain* (Cambridge, Mass., 1936), pp. 230–57; Wilhelm Bauer, 'Public Opinion', in the *Encyclopedia of the Social Sciences* (New York, 1930–35); Wilhelm Bauer, *Die oeffentliche Meinung in der Weltgeschichte* (Potsdam, 1930); Ferdinand Toennies, *Kritik der oeffentlichen Meinung* (Berlin, 1922). esp. ch. VIII, 'Die oeffentliche Meinung als Faktor des Staatsleben'. Palmer gives other references which can be supplemented with those in W. Phillips Davison and Avery Leiserson, 'Public Opinion' in the *International Encyclopedia of Social Sciences* (1968).

one can find in the classical tradition. Again I differ from the usual history which neglects the discontinuity introduced by modernity. I want to sharpen this discontinuity because I mean to take seriously the classical tradition, from which derive certain current trends in the study of public opinion that promise to reduce the problems created by modern rationalism.

After sketching two models, one modernist, and derived from Francis Bacon's 'new logic'; the other classical, and derived from Diotima's speech in *The Symposium*, I shall turn to the American discussion, stressing certain new trends and concluding with an illustration of this new approach in the form of a short case study from the administration of Franklin Roosevelt.

First, however, I should like to make clear the rationalist presuppositions of the model of opinion formation which has so greatly influenced thinking on public opinion in the United States. I can do that in four propositions, which are sometimes stated as norms, sometimes as matters of fact and sometimes as hypotheses to be tested, and each of which has found champions to support it and opponents to attack it. Stated analytically, the theory holds that bodies of people can be found such that their opinions on public matters will be rational, unified, autonomous and instrumental.

Foremost is the hypothesis of rationality. This means that in arriving at their opinions and in discussing them with others, people are informed, logical and dispassionate. The last word needs comment. It means that, although people may be deeply committed to certain ends, the way in which they assess reality, choose their means and expound their positions is not swayed by emotion.

The hypothesis of unity means that the many opinions of the people will tend towards agreement. Sometimes the theorist finds this unity of opinion at a level of belief and values underlying apparent differences; sometimes it is located in a convergence of opinions over time. In any case pluralism does not have the last word.

The hypothesis of autonomy emphasizes the independence of the process of opinion formation. This means especially independence of authority, certainly of government and usually also of any elite or political leader, so that the initiative in making decisions can come from the reasoning people.

Finally, the hypothesis of instrumentalism signifies that the process of opinion formation and its product are means to some end, not ends in themselves. People go to all the trouble of getting, having and sharing ideas about public affairs because of the effect these ideas have upon government policy and similar matters.

Bacon's new logic and his model of public opinion

One of the first statements, if not the very first statement, of this model of opinion formation can be found in the work of Francis Bacon.

In that great vision of technocracy, the *New Atlantis,* Bacon sketches his view of the ideal polity.[3] In this polity, which he calls the kingdom of Bensalem, there are three sorts of power: royal, paternal and scientific. The royal power is shadowy and almost functionless. For the everyday life of citizens, the crucial power is paternal. Members of the state are grouped in extended families, each headed by its patriarch or Tirsan, whose authority is supported by massive ritual and deferential norms. The power that leads to change and progress, however, is lodged in the scientific elite of the House of Salomon. This power consists in knowledge, more precisely, scientific knowledge. Few in number, although supported by many assistants and operating through a vast apparatus of laboratories above and below ground, the fellows of Salomon's House devote themselves to a life of scientific research from which flow the abundant health and material prosperity of the kingdom. They do not rule by command, but, having decided which new discoveries and inventions are to be made public, communicate this new knowledge to the citizens at large. In effect, however, their purpose dictates the purpose of the whole polity, as Bacon indicates when he puts into the mouth of one of the fellows that brazen manifesto of modernity:

> The End of our Foundation is the knowledge of causes and secret motions of things; and the enlarging of the bounds of Human Empire, to the effecting of all things possible.[4]

For the student of public opinion not the least interesting aspect of this presumed utopia is the system of propaganda by which patriarchal authority is sustained. All the idols of Bacon's rhetoric— the idols of the tribe, the cave, the market-place and the theatre— are unblushingly exploited to win obedience for the Tirsan. Opinion formation among the scientific elite of Salomon's House, however, occurs in a quite different way. Bacon speaks of their 'consultations' to decide such matters as what direction to give to their investigations and which new discoveries and inventions to make public or reveal to the state, but he is vague on the procedure.[5] As one writer has observed, Bacon seemed to presume 'a certain unanimity'

---

[3] The text will be found in *The Works of Francis Bacon,* ed. James Spedding, Robert L. Ellis and Douglas D. Heath (new ed., London, 1870–72), iii, pp. 119–66.

[4] *Ibid.,* p. 156.   [5] *Ibid.,* p. 165.

among the fellows because under this scientific regime 'there is such precision in political things that the wisest men will agree'.[6] Why this tendency to unity of opinion could be presumed appears if we examine how Bacon expects his new logic to work.[7]

The new logic was empirical in that it confined knowledge to propositions that could be tested by experience; conceptual in that it aimed at universally valid laws; dispassionate in that emotion was excluded from any influence on inquiry; and positivist in that all recognition was withdrawn from final causes. Its style excluded figures of speech, poetic connotation and moral exhortation. Altogether, and apart from the exaggerations of Bacon's inductivism, his new logic characterized with remarkable fidelity what came to be recognized as the method of modern science.

But the new logic was not merely a method for the lone inquirer. Bacon was acutely aware of the social relations of scientists with one another and in order to deal with this problem derived from his method of inquiry an appropriate method of scientific communication. He called it the Initiative Method because it would not merely communicate the conclusions of inquiry, but also initiate the listener into the steps by which the conclusions had been reached.[8] This method made possible 'progression' in the sciences, since by means of it one person could 'transplant [knowledge] into another mind just as it grew in his own'[9]—a nice recognition of the need for inter-subjective replicability in scientific method. Moreover, the initiative method invited examination and criticism, since it forced the communicator 'to lay open his weakness' and incited the receiver 'to try his strength'.[10] In this manner science could progress, passing on its gains and correcting its errors. Bacon's new logic in short was not only a method of inquiry, but also a method of communication, of opinion formation and of rational self-regulation.

From this perspective one may better understand why the royal authority has so little function in Bensalem. Between the frictionless traditionalism of the world of the Tirsan and the frictionless rationalism of Salomon's House, there is no ground for politics or government. Bensalem will have an intellectual history consisting of the progress of science. It will have a social history consisting of the impact of science. It will, however, have no political history. The state has withered away.

[6] Howard B. White, *Peace Among the Willows: the Political Philosophy of Francis Bacon* (The Hague, 1968), p. 233.

[7] The principal work in which Bacon discussed his 'new logic' is the *Novum Organum*, first published in Latin in 1620. Translation in *Works*, iv, pp. 39–248.

[8] *Works*, iv, pp. 449–50.

[9] *Ibid.*, p. 449.   [10] *Ibid.*, p. 449.

The classical view of opinion formation

In Bacon's new logic, that paradigm of modernity, I find a very early statement, if not the origin, of the rationalist model of opinion formation. To put the theory in this context highlights its profound contrasts with what ancient and medieval writers thought about the subject. For if one takes the terms 'opinion' and 'public opinion' broadly, it is accurate to say that writers in the classical tradition did have systematic ideas on the subject and it is instructive to examine them.

One contrast is a very different conception of ends and means. While for Bacon what men think was valuable overwhelmingly as an instrument, for the older writers it had value in itself. For Bacon the only kind of thought worth having was scientific knowledge and its value lay in its power over the external world of nature and society. Human empire was the end and the justification. For the earlier writers the purpose of political organization and indeed of all other activity, social and individual, was the pursuit of a certain moral or spiritual condition—for the ancients, virtue, for the medieval Christian, faith. Not the external world, but the internal world of thought and feeling was the place where value was realized.

Given the intrinsic importance of this inner realm, the state was obliged to assume responsibility for its guidance. For Aristotle the end of the state was not security or wealth, but the good life. Knowledge of the good could be achieved through philosophy, that supposed knowledge of final causes which it was Bacon's first object to banish from the realm of science. As practical wisdom, such knowledge should govern the state. In its light the education of the young was to be regulated strictly and in great detail. Nor did the legislator forgo his concern for the promotion of virtue in his governance of adults.[11] The idea of a free market-place of ideas was as unthinkable as the idea of a free economy.

But the suggestion most helpful for my inquiry that can be gleaned from the classical tradition relates to the manner in which opinions are formed and develop from one stage to another. In particular, the classical tradition allots to the imagination a role that the Baconian method excludes.

'Imagination', wrote Bacon, 'hardly produces sciences; poesy (which . . . was referred to imagination) being to be accounted rather as a pleasure or play of wit than a science.'[12] As the source of the devices of non-rational persuasion, however, imagination

[11] See, for instance, his discussion of private property in Book ii of *The Politics. Aristotle's Politics*, trans. B. Jowett (Oxford, 1905), pp. 62–63.

[12] *Works*, iv, p. 406.

could be mastered by scientific method. Accordingly Bacon devoted almost as much attention to his rhetoric[13]—whose 'duty and office' is *to apply Reason to Imagination* for the better moving of the will'[14]—as he did to his 'new logic'. Verse is banished from the rank of arts and sciences. Poetic knowledge is a contradiction in terms. Intellectual progress consists solely in the accumulation of a knowledge of more and more facts and universally valid laws of science. Bacon's method was indeed a 'dry light'.[15] But all else was propaganda.

Among ancient writers one can find a view of intellectual progress which gives a far greater and I should say more realistic estimation of the role of imagination. The classic passage is Diotima's 'tale of love' as reported by Socrates in *The Symposium*,[16] but I should say that all ancient and medieval philosophers who shared the 'great chain of being' outlook—and according to Lovejoy few after Plato did not[17]—took some such view. In this dialogue and especially this rhapsodic passage, I, along with aesthetes over the centuries, find a masterly depiction of the power and significance of expressive symbolism.

Thought and feeling are intimately united. Intellectual progress is impelled by emotion—the Eros. Indeed, the process of intellectual progress is as much the development of desire as of knowledge. Far from the appetites being taken as given, fixed and quite separate from reason, as in Bacon's scheme, they are seen as developing in unison with knowledge. To progress in mind is also to grow in virtue. Dispassionate opinion would be a contradiction in terms.

Central to this 'odyssey of the psyche', to use Stanley Rosen's phrase,[18] is the conception of the mind as constantly in motion. Its movement is not mere flux, but is purposive, passing from stage to stage. The mode of passage is neither deductive, nor inductive, but aesthetic, the mind grasping the future by means of

[13] For Bacon's theory of rhetoric see *The Advancement of Learning* (1605) and its expanded Latin translation, *De augmentis scientarum* (1623). The former will be found in *Works*, iii, pp. 253–491, and the latter in an English version in *Works*, iv, pp. 273–468. For what I say on Bacon's rhetoric I am much indebted to Karl R. Wallace, *Francis Bacon on Communication and Rhetoric* (Chapel Hill, 1943).

[14] *The Advancement of Learning, Works*, iii, p. 409.

[15] *Works*, p. 57.

[16] This passage comes at pp. 572–82 in *The Dialogues of Plato*; trans. B. Jowett (3rd edn., Oxford, 1892), i. But the whole dialogue is relevant to my discussion. I am much indebted to Stanley Rosen, *Plato's Symposium* (New Haven and London, 1968).

[17] Arthur O. Lovejoy, *The Great Chain of Being: a Study of the History of an Idea* (Cambridge, Mass., 1957), esp. chs. ii and iii.

[18] Rosen, *Plato's Symposium*, p. 6.

symbols of anticipation that are essentially poetic. In the Neo-Platonic writings, these symbols become the 'similitudes' by which men perceive how the various levels of being are related to one another and the temporal order is rendered, in the famous phrase of the *Timaeus*, 'a moving image of eternity'.[19] But we modern students of opinion need not accept this explanation in order to appreciate the extraordinary realism of Plato's account of the ever restless psyche, striving, complex, acting and reacting at different levels, often in conflict with itself, moved by symbols that unite both thought and feeling, its clarities of idea and norm surrounded, supported and transformed by metaphor.

The fortunes of the rationalist model in the U.S.A.

From the two radically divergent approaches of modern and of classical rationalism, one can construct two quite different models of what public opinion is, how it is formed and what it does in the state. When one looks at the concepts of public opinion that have informed academic study and popular discussion in the United States, the Baconian influence is overwhelming. At an early date a view that was modernist, rationalist and democratic took root. One can trace the basic ideas in the fierce polemic over popular sovereignty before the Revolution. It was, however, among the Progressives who manned the great movement for reform in the years before the First World War that the faith in public opinion reached its peak. This faith was not merely a belief in the people as the source of authority and as the basis of representation. It was rather an ideal of government by public opinion in as direct, continuous and detailed a manner as possible.

Precisely because Abbot Lawrence Lowell, professor of Government at Harvard and later its President, was a moderate man, his book *Public Opinion and Popular Government*, published in 1913, is indicative of the extent to which this notion of government by public opinion had won acceptance. President Lowell specifies that for 'a real public opinion' to arise, 'the bulk of the people must be in a position to determine of their own knowledge, or by weighing evidence, a substantial part of the facts required for a rational decision'.[20] He mentions limitations. Some matters require such expert knowledge that the public can govern only indirectly. Moreover, there must be a considerable agreement regarding the means and ends of government among the mass of the people—he calls it consensus—or the minority will not feel morally constrained to

[19] *Dialogues*, iii, p. 456.
[20] A. Lawrence Lowell, *Public Opinion and Popular Government* (New York, 1913), p. 24.

accept the decisions of the majority. Yet, as he continues his analysis, it is clear that in spite of these qualifications, he believes there is a wide sphere of government action which can and should be controlled directly by opinions that arise autonomously among the citizens, tend to converge in one coherent view shared by a large number, and are substantially based on factual knowledge and rational understanding. In his conception, such opinions were not simply vague and general feelings. Even with regard to such a technical matter as the granting of public franchises, for instance, he held that the people might well have 'a decided opinion' of 'the general principles' that ought to govern the question.[21]

Complementary to this view of public opinion is his conception of the role of political leaders. He found that few try 'to carry into effect a personal policy of their own on any large scale by leading and educating the community'.[22] Their principal function arises from the need for some mechanism to bring together the proponents of various opinions so that they can combine to carry out a common policy. What was required, he said, in phrases that became conventional in American political science, was 'a species of brokerage, and one of the functions of politicians is that of brokers'.[23] The modest role that Lowell attributed to leadership is a measure of the large autonomy he attributed to public opinion.

At first glance, Walter Lippmann's *Public Opinion*, that brilliant product of postwar disillusionment published in 1922, seems to be diametrically opposed to the optimistic rationalism of Lowell and the Progressives. When one asks *what* Lippmann thinks might be found by the historian or political scientist looking for public opinion, he seems to live in another world from the Mr Lowell who could declare that power founded upon popular opinion is 'noble'.[24] Stating the democratic and rationalist theory with his usual lucidity, and with his usual scholarship tracing it back to the eighteenth century, Lippmann argued that the theory could have applied to the small communities of an earlier day, but that in the era of 'the Great Society'[25]—he was profoundly influenced in diagnosis and remedy by his friend Graham Wallas—the old model could no longer correspond to reality.

Men do indeed have opinions about the vast unseen environ-

21 *Ibid.*, pp. 51–52.   22 *Ibid.*, p. 62.
23 *Ibid.*, p. 62.   24 *Ibid.*, p. 26.
25 Walter Lippmann, *Public Opinion* (New York, 1922), pp. 25, 50, 370. The reference is, of course, to Graham Wallas, *The Great Society: A Psychological Analysis* (New York, 1914).

ment beyond their personal and local lives, but for most these opinions are mere 'stereotypes', mere pictures in their heads,[26] which a host of causes, psychological and social, render ridiculously unreliable as a basis for public policy. When any unity is introduced into this 'chaos of individualism and warring sects',[27] it is surely not the product of an automatic process of rational self-regulation. It is rather a purely emotive and intellectually vacuous unity, manufactured by political leaders. Some of Lippmann's most interesting pages are devoted to examples of how political leaders have used verbal symbols to bring together in support of the leader and his cause persons and groups with quite incompatible interests and aims. 'In the symbol', says Lippmann, 'emotion is discharged at a common target, and the idiosyncrasy of real ideas blotted out.'[28] In short there is no common idea, no common goal, but only common emotion aroused by the symbol. As there was no rationality in the process, Lippmann saw little hope for progress in the product. Given the new means of mass communication and the new knowledge of mass psychology, he found that the possibilities of propaganda—a word just coming into vogue[29]—had created a revolution in the practice of democracy.

In seeking a remedy, far from deserting the Baconian model, Lippmann returned to a more faithful imitation of the original vision of technocracy. For the kind of knowledge on which public policy can be based, he looked to the expert. His hope was that governments and private groups would increasingly be guided by scientists—not only natural scientists but also, he emphasizes, social scientists. It was such 'organized intelligence'[30] that would make the complex and invisible environment intelligible to those who make decisions in the Great Society.

For the management of the masses, Lippmann did not, however, propose some new form of the feast of Tirsan. He asked rather that the rank and file of the inexpert should impose upon themselves a kind of self-denying ordinance in favour of rule by experts. The legitimate role of public opinion, he said, is primarily to insist on procedures which ensure that expert opinions have been consulted. Otherwise, the ordinary citizen should restrict himself to

[26] *Ibid.*, ch. vi and *passim*.
[27] *Ibid.*, p. 235.
[28] *Ibid.*, p. 234.
[29] 'A word has appeared', wrote the young Harold Lasswell in 1927, 'which has come to have an ominous clang in many minds—Propaganda'. *Propaganda Technique in the World War* (New York, 1927), p. 2.
[30] *Ibid.*, part viii.

retrospective judgments on public policy, specifically—and this is also in the spirit of Bensalem—'whether it is producing a cer-tain minimum of health, of decent housing, of material necessities, of education, of freedom, of pleasures, of beauty . . .'[31]

Lippmann presents a threefold typology of public opinion. First is the public opinion of the spontaneous and rational demo-cracy of the rural township of early America. Second is the chaos and unreason that he finds around him after World War I in which, encouraged by the deceptive myth of government by public opinion, the few exploit the many by their mastery of meaning-less and emotion-laden symbolism. Third is his own hope for a cool and self-restrained public that rejects the promissory rhetoric of politicians in favour of the progressive fruits of technocracy. Although rejecting the faith that Lowell accepted, Lippmann no less accepted the Baconian conception of rationality on which that faith depended.

Scientific and humanistic approaches

For political scientists Lippmann's gloomy conclusions and the tension they set up with the old democratic and rationalist faith defined the problem of public opinion for many years and still today are a useful statement of the important questions. While Lippmann wrote, however, a revolution in the method of study-ing public opinion was being prepared. Market research by adver-tising and public relations firms was showing how the distribution of opinions—or information, or preferences, or attitudes—among a large population could be ascertained by questioning a scientifi-cally selected sample. Transferred to the study of political opinions, the new approach produced its best-known embodiment in the polls of Gallup, Harris and their many imitators. While the data of these polls have proved useful to scholarly study, social scientists also developed their own more sophisticated methods of conduct-ing and analysing surveys.

The output of research using the new methods has been prodi-gious, but I can briefly summarize the trend of their findings that bear on the topic of this paper. First, in what one authority has recently called 'the most dramatic change in general communica-tions theory in forty years', the old fear of the overwhelming power of propaganda and mass advertising has been reversed.[32] 'The idea of a passive audience', according to this same writer,

[31] *Ibid.*, p. 313.
[32] Wilbur Schramm, 'The Nature of Communication between Humans,' in *The Process and Effects of Mass Communication*, ed. Wilbur Schramm and Donald F. Roberts (rev. edn., Urbana, 1971), p. 8.

has been abandoned in favour of 'the concept of a highly active, highly selective audience, manipulating rather than being manipulated by a message—a full partner in the communication process'.[33] With regard to the central question of rationality among voters, my late colleague V. O. Key Jr., could say as recently as 1966 in a book on this subject, that 'the perverse and unorthodox argument of this little book is that voters are not fools'.[34] A flood of recent work, however, has developed and supported his position with a wealth of detail.[35] The radical pluralism that once seemed to threaten the coherence of democratic government has also been qualified by findings that voters tend to cluster in large aggregates united on ideological lines, so much so that one writer sees the possible foundation for 'a responsible two party system'.[36]

While the sense of these studies in recent years has been to qualify Lippmann's conclusions, this does not mean that they have come full circle back to Lowell. A major trend has been a new emphasis upon leadership. While the dangers of manipulation seem much less, little evidence supports the old notion of a public that spontaneously generates issues and aligns its powers. The rise in ideological clustering that has been found in elections of the 1960s, for instance, has appeared in great degree as a function of the manner in which candidates and campaigns presented the alternatives. Again, to quote Key, 'the people's verdict can be no more than a selective reflection from among the alternatives and outlooks presented to them'.[37] Hence, as he put the matter negatively but pungently, 'fed a steady diet of buncombe, the people may come to expect and to respond with highest predictability to buncombe'.[38]

No less important than these recent views of the origin, character and consequences of public opinion is the growing sophistication in the methods of survey research. While typology not methodology is my subject, it is necessary at least to mention these changes in method because how you try to find something is intimately

---

[33] *Ibid.*, p. 8.
[34] *The Responsible Electorate: Rationality in Presidential Voting 1936–1960* (Cambridge, Mass., 1966), p. 7.
[35] See, for example, Gerald M. Pomper, 'From Confusion to Clarity: Issues and American Voters, 1956–1968', *American Political Science Review*, lxvi (June, 1972), pp. 415–27. In his comment on Pomper's article, John H. Kessel lists some thirty recent books, articles and papers showing the influence of issues on voting; *loc. cit.*, p. 459n.
[36] Pomper, 'From Confusion to Clarity', p. 426.
[37] Key, *The Responsible Electorate*, p. 2.
[38] *Ibid.*, p. 7.

related to what you think you will find. An authority sums up the change:

> ... human communication seemed a simpler thing in 1952 than in 1970. At that time we felt we had a fairly adequate comprehension of the process and its social uses. We counted on S–R [stimulus–response] psychology, when the intervening variables were properly defined, to explain most of the effects. The study of audiences in terms of social categories promised to explain most of the variance in response to communication. The tools of content analysis, interviews and sample surveys promised to give a good idea of what was getting through [to the recipient].[39]

Experience, however, has obliged researchers to use more complicated models. In particular these authors stress the complexity of 'the intervening steps between communication stimulus and response' and 'the importance of the psychological processes that might be triggered by present and stored perceptions of social relationships and role patterns'.[40]

One consequence of this appreciation of the greater complexity and depth of the psyche was a shift in interviewing technique. The original type of questionnaire used in surveys offered the respondent fixed alternatives from which to choose. This type of interview is satisfactory if the respondent frames the alternatives in the same way as the questioner. But if he has a different or more complex or more ambivalent way of categorizing the material of politics, this type of questionnaire will suppress his idiosyncrasies and indeed, as one recent author has said, 'allow respondents the convenient option of not taking the exercise seriously'.[41] In coping with this sort of problem researchers have used more flexible techniques, such as the prolonged, open-ended interview in which the questioner steers the conversation around to the topics of interest to his inquiry, but tries to avoid imposing his categories upon the respondents. Once the data from these interviews have been assembled, the task of content analysis, performed by coders, is to discern the relevant patterns in the data.

Needless to say, while such methods of interviewing and interpreting data constitute a fuller recognition of the complexity of the subject matter, viz., the human mind, they require a correspondingly high degree of sensitivity among interviewers and coders. It seems to me that such inquiries should exploit the resources

---

[39] Schramm, 'The Nature of Communication between Humans', pp. 6–7.
[40] *Ibid.*, p. 11.
[41] Robert D. Putnam, *The Beliefs of Politicians: Ideology, Conflict and Democracy in Britain and Italy* (New Haven and London, 1973), p. 18.

of humanistic studies, which typically have been concerned with the ambiguous feelings and symbolic references that lie beneath the surface of human utterance.

For social scientists are not the only people concerned with public opinion. In recent years, some of the most illuminating perspectives on the ideas that affect politics and government have come from intellectual historians like Perry Miller, Henry Nash Smith and Leo Marx.[42] These three happen to belong to what is rather solemnly called the American Studies Movement—indeed Miller is more founder than member—whose characteristic innovation has been to bring the methods of literary criticism into fields normally reserved for the historian. Speaking of the 'penetration in depth' that this method makes possible, one historian has said of Henry Nash Smith's *Virgin Land: The American West as Symbol and Myth* (1950):

> In writing the history of symbols and myth, Smith and his successors broke out of the rationalistic view of man that had earlier dominated the study of American intellectual history. Since symbols are dramatic figures rather than purely decorative ideas, they can express paradoxical or ambivalent meanings. By rendering all ideas in pictorial terms, they serve to accommodate conflicting values and to bridge the various levels of rational discourse.[43]

This approach to the role of ideas in history owes much to the influence of certain philosophers and literary critics. I should emphasize Alfred North Whitehead, Suzanne Langer, Kenneth Burke and Rene Wellek. Ultimately, of course, it has its roots in the classical tradition.

The acceptance speech of 1936

I should like to conclude with an illustration of how this approach can be used by the political scientist or historian interested in what public opinion is and does during times of political upheaval. I shall look at a speech that Franklin Delano Roosevelt delivered in 1936 at the height of the New Deal. It is a speech of whose manner of composition I have some personal knowledge. At that time, fresh and green from Oxford, I was working for a young

---

[42] Miller, *The New England Mind* (Cambridge, Mass., 1939–53); Henry Nash Smith, *Virgin Land: The American West as Symbol and Myth* (Cambridge, Mass., 1950); Leo Marx, *The Machine in the Garden: Technology and the Pastoral Ideal in America* (London, 1964).

[43] John Higham, *Writing American History: Essays on Modern Scholarship* (Bloomington and London, 1970), p. 68.

braintruster, Thomas G. Corcoran, then entering on his period of greatest influence. Among his many functions Corcoran would help the President with drafts for speeches on which he would at times let me try my hand. Nothing of mine survived in the final draft of this speech, but I did learn something of how the President worked.

If one begins with the hypotheses suggested by a reading of Lowell or Lippmann, the inadequacies of the Baconian approach for understanding what was really going on during the New Deal readily appear. It is wholly uninstructive to hypothesize that the majority that swept Roosevelt into the White House in 1932 entertained a view of the general principles, or even the vaguest outline of the general principles, that were later embodied in the programmes and policies of the New Deal. Nor did Mr Roosevelt have in mind such principles or programmes. One of the more familiar and well-founded criticisms of his regime was that his decisions expressed no ideology, no philosophy, hardly even an orderly outlook on public affairs.

At the same time, Roosevelt was not a mere broker, acting simply to facilitate exchange and combination in the political market-place. Thanks to his leadership a coalition was elicited from the American electorate that dominated politics for the next generation. Laying the base for a new Democratic party mainly in the cities of the North, Roosevelt added to traditional elements, such as the South and certain big city machines, new strength from organized labour, farmers, recent immigrants, Negroes, old people and intellectuals. It was a coalition which neither Roosevelt nor anyone else planned or even foresaw, but which came into existence in step with the various programmes of the New Deal. Typically for each of the constituent groups there was a programme or set of programmes that not only favoured the interests of the group, but also often defined those interests in a way not previously conceived by the group and its spokesmen. I should not wish to underestimate the contribution of experts to the programmes of the New Deal. After all, that was when college professors began their trek to Washington. But the main active agents in the politics of this upheaval were, on the one hand, the Presidency and, on the other hand, these many groups, organized and unorganized.

From the interaction of leader and followers there issued not only a powerful and long-lived coalition, but also a coherent pattern of policy. That was not readily seen at the time and observers were hard put to make sense of what Roosevelt was doing. With benefit of hindsight, however, one can see the rationale. The programmes of the New Deal clustered around two main problems, economic concentration and economic insecurity, and their main thrust was towards a new balance of economic power and a higher level of economic security. If not a new social order, a major structural reform in the old social order was achieved. The term New Deal acquired a meaning such that it could be used not only to designate a body of measures adopted in the past but also to identify an order of priorities generating new proposals for the future. Broadly supporting this order of priorities, the Roosevelt coalition displayed a power to sustain and propagate itself, the first and most emphatic demonstration being its victory for Mr Truman in 1948 wholly without benefit of charisma.

In its purpose and in its effects the New Deal coalition constituted a coherent public. In neither respect, however, was it the product of concepts pre-existing in the minds of leader or followers. No more were the policies and politics of the New Deal the creation of the 'cunning of history' in which forces of intellectual and social determinism brought about a rational result without the intervention of conscious political choice. The rhetoric of Roosevelt was causally related to the result. It will help to see the nature of the connection, if we look at the critical speech with which he launched his campaign of 1936.

This was the year when the coalition first showed its characteristic features, as well as its overwhelming electoral power. It was also a climactic time for the characteristic legislation of the New Deal. The National Recovery Administration, the central motor of the first Roosevelt years, had faltered and finally fallen under the ban of the Supreme Court. The wide national support that had been enjoyed by Roosevelt in those early days also was increasingly disrupted, as statute after statute imposed new burdens upon business and visited new benefits upon the clamorous ranks of 'forgotten men'. A crude sort of pressure from the Left built up with the rise of three powerful demagogues, Father Coughlin, the Radio priest, Doc Townsend, champion of old people, and Senator Huey Long, the 'Kingfish', of Louisiana. More lasting in its effects was the drive, encouraged by the Administration and protected by the Wagner Act, to organize trade unions in the mass-production industries, which doubled union membership between 1934 and 1938, and often precipitated violent and bloody conflicts. Against this background Roosevelt's rhetoric became correspondingly harsher and his address to Congress on the state of the union in January 1936 bristled with attacks on 'economic autocracy' and men of 'entrenched greed' who sought 'the restoration of their selfish power'.[44]

[44] *The Public Papers and Addresses of Franklin D. Roosevelt*, ed. Samuel I. Rosenman (New York, 1938–50), v. *The People Approve: 1936*, pp. 8–18.

In late June the Democrats assembled in Philadelphia for their national convention and tumultuously renominated Roosevelt. On a Saturday night at the end of the convention week before a crowd of 100,000 enthusiastic supporters packed into an open stadium at Franklin Field, he delivered his speech of acceptance.[45] The theme, linked to the city where they met, was a presumed parallel between the events of 1936 and 1776. As 1776 had wiped out 'political tyranny', so the task of 1936 was to bring 'economic tyranny' to an end. The hyperbole was swollen even by American standards and the metaphors abrasive. '. . . the privileged princes of these new economic dynasties, thirsting for power . . .' '. . . a new despotism . . .' '. . . this new industrial dictatorship . . .' '. . . the resolute enemy within our gates . . .' With phrases such as these Roosevelt developed the parallel as he lashed his opponents and roused his supporters. He summarized his message in a phrase that became one of the most quoted items in the Rooseveltian demonology: 'economic royalists.' '. . . out of this modern civiliz-ation economic royalists carved new dynasties. New kingdoms were built upon concentration of control over material things . . .' '. . . economic royalists complain that we seek to overthrow the institutions of America. What they really complain of is that we seek to take away their power.' The President was very fond of the phrase—suggested by Stanley High, one of his speechwriters[46]— and rolled it off in great style.

The rhetoric came from the leader, often picking and choosing from themes and imagery suggested by his confidants. But what struck me at the time was the role of the convention. The essence of the story, as I heard it then at secondhand, was that while Roosevelt worked on his speech he was listening by radio to the proceedings of the convention, until, catching the belligerent spirit of the delegates, he cast aside a milder version almost at the last moment and quickly dictated the Franklin Field address. The memoirs of Dr Raymond Moley, who worked directly with the President on the speech, support this notion of a sudden shift to a speech with more 'fire' in it, a shift that did occur after Roosevelt had been listening the previous night to the enthusiastic ovations with which the convention had approved the platform.[47] Judge Rosenman, who also helped with the speech, takes credit for the

[45] *Ibid.*, pp. 230–36.

[46] So says Rosenman, *Working With Roosevelt* (New York, 1952), p. 106. Corcoran, on the other hand, recently assured me that the phrase was coined by William C. Bullitt, who was also helping with Presidential speeches at that time.

[47] Raymond Moley, *After Seven Years* (New York and London, 1939), pp. 347–48; *New York Times*, Sat. 27 June, 1936, p. 9.

more fiery portions and a draft in the Roosevelt Library supports his claim.[48] An additional source, however, is suggested by the transcript of the proceedings which show that at the very start of the convention and long before Roosevelt spoke, the keynote of the acceptance speech had been sounded. In a speech of welcome, on Tuesday, Governor Earle of Pennsylvania, like Roosevelt after him, citing Philadephia as a fitting place to meet because of the parallel between the old struggle for political liberty and the current struggle for economic liberty, developed the analogy in a diatribe that won him a prolonged ovation at the convention and brief mention in the newspapers as a possible Presidential candidate in the future.[49] Corcoran assures me that he has 'no doubt' that Roosevelt, who was listening on and off to the convention, heard the speech of Governor Earle, a very close personal friend. Later in the convention, the theme introduced by Earle was also vigorously exploited by Governor Horner of Illinois and Governor Curley of Massachusetts. In short, the rhetoric of the speech was not the isolated creation of the leader. Its emergence was also shaped by the audience to whom it was addressed.

The expression 'economic royalist', is a metaphor, a compressed way of likening those who control great wealth in the twentieth century with those who exercised royal authority in the eighteenth, but the compression makes it less conceptual, more concrete and far more forceful and evocative. It has the incongruity of metaphor. One cannot frame a clear and distinct idea of an 'economic royalist'. Economic power is not the same as political authority and when one tries to think out quite clearly what the expression means the possibilities are vague and numerous. This very vagueness infects the call to action that is implicit in the term. Surely no worthy son of the Minute Men—and Roosevelt also called up that image—can tolerate the continued existence in America of royalists of any sort. But what is he to do? Eliminate those who control great wealth? Regulate them? Nationalize their industries? Bust up their

---

[48] The Roosevelt Library has eight drafts relating to this speech. One, concerned largely with events abroad, contributed only a few phrases. Another is clearly the 'militant, barefisted' version that Rosenman says he and High composed (*Working with Roosevelt*, p. 105). Four drafts combine the Rosenman–High version with the more conciliatory Moley–Corcoran version, to which both Rosenman (pp. 104–105) and Moley (pp. 344–46) refer, but which is missing from the archive. These four drafts show corrections in Roosevelt's hand and are obviously successive revisions culminating in the draft used at Franklin Field. There is also the Press release of the speech and the stenographic copy made at the time it was delivered.

[49] *Official Report of the Proceedings of the Democratic Convention Held at Philadelphia, Penna., June 23rd to June 27th, inclusive, 1936* (n.d.), pp. 20–25.

trusts? The phrase was vague, but at that moment in history its emotive ambiguity faithfully reflected the moving, half-formed purpose of the New Deal to create a new balance of economic power.

In due course, these ambiguities were cleared up. Once the various programmes were established and working, their meaning as a whole could be perceived. Thus in 1952 a penetrating study by J. K. Galbraith discovered the concept of 'countervailing power' amidst certain of the empirical achievements of the New Deal.[50] Mentioning the Wagner Act, Agricultural Adjustment Act, Wage Hour Act and the Securities and Exchange Commission, Galbraith observed that only this concept made fully comprehensible much of the domestic legislation of the previous twenty years and that of the New Deal in particular. Yet, he continued, although in this sense a matter of great practical importance, the concept of countervailing power had hitherto remained unrecognized in economic and political theory.

It is a long literary distance from Roosevelt's flamboyant speech to the ironic prose of Kenneth Galbraith. But there was a line of development from Roosevelt's rhetoric to the institutions of the New Deal and then to Galbraithian ideology. The rhetoric of the economic royalist speech was a symbol of anticipation of countervailing power. A change of public opinion that seems to be the product of ignorance, confusion and manipulation when viewed from Baconian premises is revealed as creative, consecutive and democratic when looked at from the perspective of the classical tradition. Love not logic was the life of the New Deal.

Harvard University.

[50] John Kenneth Galbraith, *American Capitalism: the Concept of Countervailing Power* (Boston, 1952).

GAMES PEOPLE PLAYED: DRAMA AND RITUAL AS PROPAGANDA IN MEDIEVAL EUROPE

By Professor D. A. Bullough, M.A., F.S.A., F.R.Hist.S.

READ AT THE SOCIETY'S CONFERENCE
18 SEPTEMBER 1973

ON 6 January 1378 King Charles V of France took his place in the centre of the top table at a banquet given in honour of a distinguished guest, his uncle the Emperor Charles IV. The setting in the Palais de la Cité, the company and the menu were appropriately sumptuous. Resplendent hangings covered the wall behind the marble table; the noblest guests sat at five large tables, each raised on its own platform; and divided from them by barriers were other tables with seats for more than 800 knights. The entire company was treated to three elaborate courses, each of ten dishes. Then, from its previous place of concealment at the end of the hall, a massive model of a ship emerged carrying a crowd of armed warriors, among them persons identifiable by their arms as Godfrey of Bouillon and other leaders of the First Crusade, together with Peter the Hermit, looking—we are told—as much like the descriptions of him in the chronicles as possible. Propelled smoothly along the floor by men concealed within, it crossed in front of the top table and was then turned round to face towards the centre. An even more massive structure was next brought forward—this time representing the city of Jerusalem, complete with battlemented walls and towers defended by men dressed as Saracen warriors, with the Temple high in the middle and rising still higher above it a tower on which was another figure in Saracen dress 'crying the Law' in Arabic. The Crusaders then descended from the ship and attacked the city with scaling ladders, from which some were made to fall off, until finally the knights entered the city, tossed the unfortunate defenders over the walls and raised in triumph the banners they had brought with them: after which the dinner finished. The superb whole-page illustration which accompanies the contemporary chronicle-account in a manuscript completed within the next eighteen months or so shows the ship on a reduced scale but with a black-cowled bearded Peter the Hermit urging on the Crusading knights who are duly ascending (or falling off) the

97

ladders while distinctively-helmeted defenders try to keep them out.[1]

The 'play' element in aristocratic and patrician behaviour and its concomitant 'conspicuous waste' are familiar alike to the sociologist and the historian, although perhaps never more manifest or having greater functional importance than in the later medieval and early modern centuries.[2] Restless English knights in the 1230s and 1250s and the self-assertive burgesses of Tournai in 1330–31 organized 'Round Tables' and the jousts to go with them. In September 1331, William Lord Montagu, energetically exploiting his recent services to the English king and their bloody sequel, organized a great tournament in Cheapside, on the eve of which he, Edward and select knights paraded through the streets of London dressed *ad similitudinem Tartarorum*, each leading a lady by a golden chain, before they dispersed to their lodgings *cum tubis et aliis diversis instrumentorum:* in the usage of the day *Tartari* meant 'Mongols', and the costumes worn by Montagu and the rest presumably resembled those shown in fourteenth-century manuscripts of Marco Polo and its derivatives (such as Bib. nat. fr. 2810 or Bodl. Douce 264) with helmets of the type worn by the Saracens in the Paris performance in 1378. In 1343, rather more pointedly (according to two versions of the Chronicle that passes under the name of Adam of Murimuth), knights dressed as the Pope and twelve cardinals exercised their skill at Smithfield for three days after Midsummer.[3] In the middle decades of the fifteenth century

[1] *Chronique des règnes de Jean II et de Charles V*, ed. R. Delachenal, ii (Paris, 1916), pp. 235–42; the illustration (Paris, Bib. nat. MS. fr. 2813, fo. 473ᵛ) *idem*, iv (1920), pl. XLI and (in excellent colour) in the Bibliothèque Nationale exhibition catalogue, *La Librairie de Charles V* (Paris, 1966), pl. VIII. L. H. Loomis, 'Secular dramatics in the Royal Palace, Paris, 1378, 1389, and Chaucer's "Tregetoures",' *Speculum*, xxxiii (1958), pp. 242–55 (repr. L. H. Loomis, *Adventures in the Middle Ages* [New York, 1962], pp. 274–92), esp. 243–47, comprehensively discusses the episode.

[2] It will be obvious that I am here using 'play' in a narrower sense than that of J. Huizinga, *Homo Ludens* (Engl. ed., London, 1949, 1971). For the phenomenon in the fourteenth to seventeenth centuries see, *e.g.*, J. Huizinga, *The Waning of the Middle Ages* (Engl. edn., 1924, 1965), esp. chs. 3–7; S. Anglo, *Spectacle, Pageantry and Early Tudor Policy* (Oxford, 1969). F. Saxl, 'Costumes and festivals of Milanese society under Spanish rule', *Proceedings of the British Academy*, xxiii (1937), pp. 401–56, is unexpectedly disappointing.

[3] N. Denholm-Young, 'The tournament in the thirteenth century', *Studies in Medieval History presented to F. M. Powicke*, ed. R. W. Hunt *et al.* (Oxford, 1948), pp. 253–56 (whose characterization of the 'Round Table' is not entirely satisfactory); H. G. Moke, *Moeurs, usages, Fêtes et solemnités des Belges* (Brussels, ?1863), ii, pp. 173–80; *Annales Paulini* in *Chronicles of the Reigns of Edward I and Edward II*, ed. W. Stubbs, i (Rolls Series, 1882), pp. 345–55; *Adae Murimuth continuatio chronicarum*, ed. E. M. Thompson (Rolls Series,

the court of the dukes of Burgundy and the principal towns in his Flemish territories set new standards of lavishness, although some travellers thought more highly of the public display in Venice where, it was generally agreed, the quality of the courtesans—always a measure of the surplus resources of a governing or leisure class —was without peer in Europe.[4]

The consumption of food and drink is the basic human activity which has the greatest number of ritual acts associated with it. They occur in widely-different contexts, in very varied forms and with quite distinct social functions—the loaf of bread in a Sicilian peasant-household at subsistence level taken from a locked cupboard by the mother, kissed by the children and reverently cut by the father; the *caritas quae in pleno potatur calice* (to use Alcuin's words to the monks of Murbach: and who knew better than he?) in the refectory of a religious community in the central medieval centuries or the well-lubricated common meals of the sub-Alpine 'Communities of the Holy Spirit'; the duties of a chief cook as described in the book of household protocol written by Olivier de la Marche (the greatest of the Burgundian court impresarios) for the English king—sitting on a raised chair and holding a big wooden ladle with which he both ceremoniously tastes the soup and chases and even strikes the scullions;[5] the Army mess-night or College gaudy. Great royal occasions, milestones in the lives of rulers and their families such as coronations, weddings and funerals were ones on which 'play' and the rituals of conviviality submerged their separate if overlapping identities in a complex glorification and re-statement of the prestige and authority of the monarch: Louis the Pious on his accession in 814 cleansing the Frankish court and requiring his illegitimate half-brothers to be his *participes mensae;* Otto the Great in 936 elected by Franks and Saxons,

---

1889), pp. 146, 230, the latter—fuller—version being the source of R. Holinshed, *Chronicles* (London, edn. of 1807), ii, p. 627. See further R. H. Cline, 'The influence of Romances on tournaments of the Middle Ages', *Speculum*, xx (1945), pp. 204–11.

[4] Essential references in H. Kretschmayr, *Geschichte von Venedig*, ii (Gotha, 1920), pp. 483, 656. *Cf.* also Carpaccio's famous and much-discussed painting of '(?) Two Courtesans', Venice, Mus. Civ. Correr, no. 46, with the ample bibliography in *Catalogo della Mostra Vittore Carpaccio, 1963*, ed. P. Zampetti (Venice, 1963), p. 227.

[5] *Monumenta Germaniae Historica, Epistolae*, iv (Hanover, 1895), p. 172; P. Duparc, 'Confréries du Saint-Esprit et communautés d'habitants au Moyen-âge', *Revue Historique de droit Français et étranger*, 4th ser., xxxvi (1958), pp. 349–67; Olivier de la Marche, *Estat de la Maison du duc Charles de Bourgoigne*, ed. M. Beaune and J. d'Arbaumont (Société de l'Histoire de France; Paris, 1888), p. 50.

crowned in the palace-chapel at Aachen and then dining in the hall of the palace with the bishops and other magnates while the four dukes 'waited on them'; Henry VI's Paris coronation banquet in 1432 when the unofficial and often uninspired but prolific court poet Lydgate and the master-cook combined their talents to produce 'Soteltes' for each of the three courses, of which the second was:

> 'Themperour and the kyng that ded is, armed . . . and the kyng that nowe is, knelying before hem with this resoun "Against miscreauntes themperour Sigismound/Hath shewid his myght which is imperial;/Sithen Henry the Vth so noble a knyght was founde/For Cristes cause in actis martial;/Cherissyng the Church Lollardes had a falle . . .".'[6]

What distinguishes the Paris dinner of 1378 from all these other occasions is not so much the dramatic *entremets*, nor even the element of impersonation to the extent of introducing foreign-language speech and re-enactment of a secular historic event of nearly three centuries previously, although these are remarkable enough and the latter (so far as is known) without exact precedent: it is the conscious purpose of the performance. The chronicler says categorically at the beginning of his account that the French king staged the history of Godfrey of Bouillon's capture of Jerusalem because 'it seemed to him that in the presence of the greatest men in Christendom no greater deed could be recalled or held up as an example to men who were best able, ought and should be obliged to undertake such an enterprise in the service of God'. As such it was a failure—unless it had some belated outcome in the recruitment for the ill-starred 'Crusade of Nicopolis' (1396). It raises the question, however, whether there may not have been other circumstances in the Middle Ages in which the dramatic medium, albeit in a less 'realistic' form, was used to influence attitudes if not to persuade the spectators to a specific course of action. Drama with a message, even a political message, is almost as old as drama itself; and however thin the dramatic tradition may have become in the earlier medieval centuries, the combination of impersonation and speech seems to offer an alternative form of communication with a non-reading public to pictorial art and 'symbols of authority', whose use in medieval propaganda—at least to the extent of

---

[6] Nithard, *Histoire des Fils de Louis le Pieux*, ed. P. Lauer (Paris, 1926), p. 6 (I,i); Widukind, *Rerum Gestarum Saxonicarum Libri tres*, ed. G. Waitz *et al.*, rev. ed. (Hanover, 1935), pp. 63–67; *The Minor poems of John Lydgate*, ii, ed. M. N. MacCracken and M. Sherwood (Early English Text Society; Oxford, 1934), pp. 623–24.

expressing basic political or politico-theological concepts—is a commonplace of modern historiography.[7]

Indeed, it would seem potentially even more effective: for the major works of art on the interpretation of whose iconography twentieth-century scholars have lavished so much learning and ingenuity were either well-nigh invisible to all but a few blessed with exceptionally good eyesight or else in the pages of books to which even fewer had any sort of access. Moreover, only the simplest of messages is self-evident when translated into static visual terms. We do not need to share the philosophical premises or theological outlook of Theodulf 'of Orleans' (the profoundest scholar but also the most abrasive of colleagues at Charlemagne's court) to agree with him that the message of the Gospels, the moral imperatives given to mankind, are ultimately expressible only in words and not through pictorial representation. The more complex the range of ideas or sentiments which a single work of art or visual 'programme' seeks to convey, the more certain it is that it will be fully intelligible only to those already familiar with the underlying concepts in some verbal form: in this it is not unlike classical ballet, whose story, in spite of the mimetic element, can generally be 'read' only by those who know it in advance.[8] The use of dramatic performance to transmit ideas and form attitudes only very exceptionally should, therefore, tell us something about the nature of 'public opinion' and the need felt to appeal to it in the pre-printing centuries.

Theatre-drama, the 'stage play', never acquired the religious, social and political importance in the Roman Republic that it had previously had in the Greek city-states. The Empire that succeeded the Republic and accepted Christianity as the state-religion in the fourth century developed or created an impressive range of techniques with which to influence opinion in the capital and elsewhere, including wall-notices, episcopal preaching and processions. However the first Augustus had envisaged his authority and the mean of proclaiming it, later emperors directed their propaganda to the glorification of both their office and their person—the ironical tone of the dying Vespasian's 'I suppose I'm becoming

[7] In the light particularly of A. Grabar's work on Byzantium and its art (*L'Empereur dans l'art byzantin* [Paris, 1936; repr. London 1971], etc.) and of the writings of P. E. Schramm and his 'school' on Western European regalia (especially *Herrschaftszeichen und Staatssymbolik*, 3 vols. [*Mon. Germ. Hist.*, *Schriften*, xiii/1–3; Stuttgart, 1954–57]). A cautionary note on the pre-ninth-century material is sounded by Bullough, '*Imagines regum* and their significance in the Early Medieval West', *Studies in Memory of David Talbot Rice*, ed. G. Robertson and G. Henderson (in the press; ?1974).

[8] *Libri Carolini*, II 30 and *passim*: ed. H. Bastgen (*Mon. Germ. Hist.*, *Concilia*, Suppl., Hanover, 1924), pp. 92–100, etc.

a god' (better documented than the pungent last words recently credited to King George V) would have been lost on most of his successors—to an insistence on a unique and total allegiance which embraced the doctrines of the Christian Church, and to the subordination of all branches of government and administration to the imperial will. Debate in the Senate was all too often replaced by the mindless (which, of course, does not mean purposeless) ritual of repeated acclamation of the emperor and his most important servants, for which Nero had set the tone and imported the first claque: witness the promulgation of the Theodosian Code at Rome in 438 when the senators managed 'Destroyers of informers, destroyers of false charges' and 'Through you we hold our honours, through you our property, through you everything' 28 times each and fourteen other acclamations to a grand total of 352.[9] In Constantinople and other Eastern Mediterranean cities, however, it was in the amphitheatres and circuses that the panoply of an orientalized imperial monarchy was most fully displayed and the greatest number of the emperor's subjects could roar their approval, and occasionally their disapproval, in ritualized form or spontaneously. Here even the triumphs of the individual charioteer, achieved by a mixture of skill, luck and courage, could be transmuted into an imperial triumph, on the principle that every achievement in his presence, or before the portraits which enabled him to be ever-present even when physically absent, had its source in his sacred person.[10]

The ritual celebration of an ever-victorious emperor, paragon of the virtues, maintainer of the frontiers, was also expressed during the early Byzantine period—down to the mid-tenth century and beyond—in the annual court ceremony of $\pi\tilde{\alpha}\iota\zeta\alpha\iota\ \tau o\ \Gamma o\theta\iota\varkappa o\nu$ 'playing the Gothic', which brings us near to and perhaps across the uncertain borderline with dramatic performance *stricto sensu*. During the evening meal on the ninth day of Christmas, a courtier brought forward two pairs of men dressed as Goths—wearing furs, masked to give them a shaggy appearance and carrying a shield and rods. Banging on their shields and uttering 'Gothic' cries, the four figures ran towards the imperial table, circled round their opposite numbers and then returned to the sides of the hall. Here, with others and to an instrumental accompaniment, they sang 'Gothic songs'—which seem in fact to be predominantly Latin with an admixture of Germanic words. After this the other performers chanted the praises of the emperor's success in protecting his people from their enemies, punctuated by mock attacks on them by the

⁹ *Codex Theodosianus*, ed. T. Mommsen (Berlin, 1905): *Gesta Senatus*.
¹⁰ A. Cameron, *Porphyrius the Charioteer* (Oxford, 1973), pp. 23–29.

Goths, until the latter uttered their final yell and ran off.[11] This
extraordinary but lively farrago[12] has been judged by most historians of Byzantine ceremonial as no more than a special form of
acclamation, which indeed it is. It is, however, distinguished from
all other examples of the genre by the element of impersonation or
acting and by the use of foreign-language phrases as well as disguise to give greater colour to this. It presumably originated in the
days when Gothic ambassadors or representatives of the defeated
Ostrogoths and their strange noises were a familiar sight in
Byzantium and then became a fossilized part of the annual cycle
of court ceremonial. As far as we know it was unique, although
the eleventh/twelfth-century paintings of the 'royal staircase' at Sta
Sophia, Kiev (now destroyed but known through copies) imply that
dressing up as Goths—and probably being always defeated except
when fighting animals—was an enduring feature of the mimetic
tradition in the Hippodromes.[13]

Only a small part of the ritual apparatus of sovereignty was taken
over directly by the Germanic kingdoms established in Latin
Romania. Thrones, crowns, *imagines regum*, liturgical *laudes*
established themselves very gradually as permanent features of
Western court-life and the symbolism of royal authority: their
conscious exploitation hardly precedes the ninth century.[14] *Venationes* and the long-distance forerunners of the modern bull-fight
seem to have been held in some of the amphitheatres of southern
Gaul and Spain in the sixth and seventh centuries, but there is
nothing to suggest that these were 'royal occasions'. Flattery, however, was as inevitable a feature of a court as was its counterpart
largesse: without gold-giving, no prestige. Venantius Fortunatus,
who left Italy—he said—because of an eye-complaint which St
Martin could heal although others have thought that he was on
the wrong side in a doctrinal dispute, is a notable witness that at
Frankish courts in the late sixth century this flattery was both
Roman and Germanic and accompanied by musical instruments

[11] Constantine Porphyrogenitus, *De Ceremoniis aulae Byzantinae*, I 92 (83):
ed. J. Vogt, ii (Paris, 1939), pp. 182–85; commentary by C. Kraus, 'Das gotische
Weihnachtsspiel', *Beiträge zur Geschichte der deutschen Sprache u. Literatur*,
xx (1895), pp. 224–57 and by Vogt, ii—*Commentaire* (Paris, 1940), pp. 186–91.
[12] Of which the first performance for presumably nearly nine hundred
years was given in April 1973 at the University of Birmingham.
[13] A. Grabar, 'Les fresques des escaliers à Sainte-Sophie de Kiev', *Seminarium
Kondakovianum*, vii (1935), reprinted in Grabar, *L'Art de la fin de l'Antiquité
et du Moyen Age*, i (Paris, 1968), pp. 251–63.
[14] See p. 101, n. 7 and (for the acclamations of rulers) E. Kantorowicz,
Laudes Regiae: a study in liturgical acclamations and medieval ruler worship
(Berkeley—Los Angeles, 1946).

belonging to the two traditions. The *Beowulf*-poem in the form which it has reached us may, in spite of the monsters and the late Professor Tolkien, have helped to reassure its hearers that the old kingly virtues of pagan times still had their place in a changed society: but it is not likely that either the poet or the *scop* declaiming it thought of themselves as mentors of or propagandists for the kings of their own day.[15] The newcomers brought with them their own rituals associated with feasting, fighting and other archetypal male activities and designed to enhance the prestige of their own leaders and people and to diminish that of others. Two characteristic examples, which sometimes merge with each other are the boasting-match and the slanging-match, familiar to readers of the *Sagas* and to ethnologists and anthropologists of extra-European societies. An earlier Germanic example of the second of these, with an at least partially-historical basis, is recorded by Paul the Deacon: in the course of a banquet at the Gepid royal court in the late 540s in honour of the son of the Lombard king and other *iuvenes* who had accompanied him, the Gepid king's son taunted the Lombards with being 'white-footed mares'—supposedly an allusion to a change in their footwear since entering the imperial service as federates—and stinking, and was equally answered; but the king ensured that it all remained good-natured and that the banquet ended merrily.[16]

The contemporary prestige and posthumous reputation of early medieval kings could be fostered by victory in boasting-matches, real or legendary: the North Welsh Prince Maelgwn (Gildas's *Maglocunus*) was believed to have won supreme authority over his rivals by remaining on the waters of the Dovey estuary, thanks to a cunningly-made floating chair, when others had to retreat before the tide. An inversion of this motif is, of course, the well-known tale of Canute, recorded by Henry of Huntingdon, which prompted Milton to the sour comment that 'to show the small power of kings in respect of God needed no such laborious demonstration as Canute had contrived; unless maybe to shame court flatters who

---

[15] A. Chastagnol, *Le Sénat romain sous le règne d'Odoacre* (Bonn, 1966), pp. 57–63 (for late-Imperial *venationes*); *Mon. Germ. Hist., Epistolae*, iii (Hanover, 1892), p. 668 with P. D. King, *Law and Society in the Visigothic Kingdom* (Cambridge, 1972), p. 202 and esp. n. 3; *Mon Germ. Hist., Auctores Antiquissimi*, iv (Hanover, 1881), pp. 131 (lines 7–8), 162–63 (lines 61–64); L. L. Schücking, 'The ideal of kingship in Beowulf', J. R. L. Tolkien, '*Beowulf* the monsters and the critics', both reprinted in L. E. Nicholson (ed.), *An Anthology of Beowulf Criticism* (Notre Dame, Ind., 1963), pp. 35–49, 51–103.

[16] Paul, *Historia Langobardorum*, I 24: ed. G. Waitz (Hanover, 1878), p. 71; Huizinga, *Homo Ludens*, p. 69; G. P. Bognetti *et al.*, *Sta Maria di Castelseprio* (Milan, 1948), p. 386 n. 37.

would not else be convinced, he needed not have gone wetshod home'. A related phenomenon, which would hardly have pleased Milton more, is the single combat between the leaders of opposing armies, or rather the challenge to such a fight—still frequently cited by historians of the central Middle Ages as evidence of the personal courage or naive recklessness (or both) of the monarchs who were the parties to it. Examples can be found in almost every half-century between 800 and 1550—as late as 1528, if reports that reached Erasmus were correct, the Emperor Charles V challenged François I with due ceremony. But whatever had been the case in the pre-Invasion period, it may be regarded as certain that no royal duel was actually fought in these centuries or was seriously expected to be fought, even though elaborate preparations might be made and although twelfth-century chronicles have a circumstantial account of a single combat between Edmund and Canute.[17] To throw down the challenge and to take it up was as much a part of the game of monarchy and then maintenance of a ruler's prestige as crown-wearings or being a bold huntsman. The royal hunt itself had a strong ritual element—as, indeed, what hunt has not? Nowhere is this more vividly conveyed before the relevant manuscript illumination of the later Middle Ages than in an anonymous court poet's account of how in 799 Charlemagne went out from Paderborn, accompanied by his lavishly-dressed daughters and courtiers, to hunt the wild beasts in the dense woods where *pater adsidue Karolus, venerabilis heros/ Exercere solet gratos per gramina ludos.*[18]

The element of 'play'—in Huizinga's wider use of the term—is, of course, apparent in many aspects of Carolingian court life. In the narrower sense, there are tantalizing references in the texts to *ioculatores, mimi* and (once) *spectacula.* Alcuin feared that the pleasure taken in them by Angilbert, abbot of St Riquier, would

[17] R. Bromwich, *Trioedd Ynys Prydein: the Welsh Triads* (Cardiff, 1961), pp. 439–41; Henry of Huntingdon, *Historia Anglorum*, ed. T. Arnold (Rolls Series, 1879), p. 189; J. Milton, *History of Britain*, in *Works of John Milton* (London, 1738), ii, p. 109; Erasmus, *Opus Epistolarum*, ed. P. S. and H. M. Allen vii (Oxford, 1928), nos 2024, 2059; G. N. Garmonsway, *Canute and his Empire* (London, 1964), pp. 13–14, surprisingly preferring the evidence of Henry of Huntingdon and Walter Map (*De Nugis Curialium*, ed. M. R. James [Oxford, 1914], v 4) to *Encomium Emmae*, ed. A. Campbell (London, 1949), p. 24, *cf.* p. lix, n. 3.

[18] *Mon. Germ. Hist., Poetae*, i (Hanover, 1881), pp. 369–70; new ed. by H. Beumann *et al.*, *Karolus Magnus et Leo Papa: ein Paderborner Epos vom Jahre 799* (Paderborn, 1966), p. 70. *Cf.* K. Lindner, *Die Jagd im frühen Mittelalter* (= Gesch. des deutschen Weidwerks, ii; Berlin, 1940), pp. 385–410, esp. pp. 392–95. For real heroics on an imperial hunt, see *Vita Euthymii patriarchae Cp.*, ed. P. Karlin-Hayter (Brussels, 1970), pp. 2–4.

imperil his immortal soul, although others might have felt that this
was in greater peril from his illicit love for one of Charlemagne's
daughters which became more widely known when he left her
chamber before dawn in snowy weather: which (as the late Bishop
Kirk remarked of the unfortunate Eutyches who fell from an upper
room when overcome by heat and the preaching of Paul) could
happen to a gentleman in a very different set of circumstances. The
linking of *spectacula* with *diabolica figmenta*—forbidden, Alcuin
tells us, by the king—suggests very strongly that the reference is to
pagan displays of the kind condemned in a sermon published by
Wilhelm Levison under the title 'Venus a Man' (evidence not,
alas! of a Carolingian Danny la Rue but of the *wissenschaftliche
Ernst* of a great German scholar): namely, dances in front of or in
churches, in which someone assumed the disguise of a stag or old
woman.[19] It is hardly likely that making fun of the foibles and
failings of individuals known to the audience was left to Theodulf
and others writing in Latin and not exploited by *ioculatores* in
their *cantilenae*, to which Notker of St Gall casually alludes. Saints
may have been expected only to smile, but sinners must have
enjoyed a good hearty laugh. In the mid-twelfth century Gerhoh
of Reichersberg claimed that: 'In the mouth of the laity who fight
for Christ the praise of God is growing, because there is nobody in
the whole Christian realm who dares to sing dirty songs (*turpes
cantilenas*) in public'; on which Professor Colin Morris has drily
observed that in spite of Gerhoh's optimism 'the demand for
dirty songs remained buoyant.[20] It would be rash to suppose that,
whatever may have been the case in the Crusading period, ninth-
and tenth-century *cantilenae* had much 'political' and potentially
propagandist content. But it is a warning against dogmatism in
this ill-documented field that a neumed version (i.e. one marked

[19] *Mon. Germ. Hist., Epistolae,* iv, pp. 183, 290, 381–82, cf. id., p. 542,
W. Levison, *England and the Continent in the Eighth Century* (Oxford, 1946),
pp. 302–14, the section cited in the text uniquely from B. M. MS. Cott. Nero
A.II: but Levison had surprisingly overlooked the presence of the same
portion of the sermon in Karlsruhe, MS *Augienses* cxcvi, fos 190ᵛ–191ᵛ (apparently close to but arranged in a different order from this section of Nero
A.II; cf. the heading *De avaricia* on fol. 189ᵛ) from which it was published
by A. Holder, *Die Handschriften des Landesbibliothek Karlsruhe,* v: *Die
Reichenauer Handschriften, 1* (Leipzig, 1906), pp. 447–48.
[20] *Mon. Germ. Hist., Poetae,* i, pp. 483–89, with D. Schaller, 'Vortrags--u.
Zirkulardichtung am Hof Karls des Grossen', *Mitellateinisches Jahrbuch,* vi
(1970), pp. 20–36; Notker, *Gesta Karoli Magni Imperatoris,* ed. H. Haefele
(Berlin, 1962), p. 45 (I,33), which E. Faral—anxious lest this should be used
as evidence for the pre-history of the Charlemagne epics—pointlessly dismissed
as 'anachronistic'; C. Morris, *Medieval Media* (Inaugural Lecture, University
of Southampton, 1972), p. 7.

for singing) of the remarkable *Versus de bella quae fuit acta Fontaneto* or *Planctus Lotharii* of 841 is among the items in a tenth-century poetic collection from southern France. From the same general area (perhaps specifically from the Toulouse region) early in the next century came the earliest extant illustrations of *ioculatores*—very strikingly, in the margins of a liturgical manuscript: one of them, immediately following a picture of King David, shows a pair of knives in the air immediately above a *ioculator* who has balls in his hands while another figure plays a flute. Later representations of David and his court sometime include a figure juggling with knives or swords as well as the more familiar musicians.[21] *Ludi*, which appear to involve ritualized weapon-play comparable to that of the Byzantine 'Gothic game' (with which they could share a remote common origin) and to be the precursors of late medieval sword-dances or fencing dances characteristic of royal courts and noble households, are alluded to with varying degrees of ambiguity, in East Frankish (German) texts from the late ninth century onwards. An enthusiasm for performances involving weapons, more fitting in a lay magnate, is one of the characteristics of Bishop Gunther of Bamberg deplored by the *scholasticus* Meinhard in a letter of *c.* 1060. Gunther possessed a fine specimen of Byzantine 'triumphal art', a silk tapesty showing figures offering helmet and crown to a horsed emperor. Karl Hauck (who belongs to the post-Wagnerian Romantic school of Germanic scholarship) may therefore be right in taking a further statement of Meinhard's to mean that the bishop himself dressed up as an Amalung—the family of Theodoric the Ostrogoth, the only rival to Charles the Great as an historical German hero; but it is more plausibly understood as asserting that instead of pondering on the Fathers the bishop composed texts about Attila, the Amalungs and that kind of thing (something on the lines of the Latin *Waltharius?* or a forerunner of the vernacular *Niebelungenlied?*) which his actors performed.[22]

[21] *Mon. Germ. Hist.*, *Poetae*, ii, pp. 138–39; but for a much-improved edition see D. Norberg, *Manuel pratique de latin mediéval* (Paris, 1968), pp. 165–68. The ms., B. N. MS lat. 1154, comes from Limoges but was probably not written there. The illustrations of the *loculatores* are in B.N. MS. lat. 1118, fos 104 *et seq.*, on which see H. Steger, *David Rex et Propheta* (Erlanger Beiträge zur Sprach—u. Kunstwissenschaft, vi; Nürnberg, 1961), pp. 204–7 and p. 18; for later mss, see esp. Steger, pp. 207 fos.

[22] K. Hauck, 'Zur Genealogie u. Gestalt des staufischen *Ludus de Antichristo*', *Germanisch—Romanische Monatsschrift*, N.F., ii (1951–52), 11–13; Steger, *op. cit.*, pp. 85–94; *Briefsammlungen der Zeit Heinrichs IV*, ed. C. Erdmann and N. Fickermann (*Mon. Germ. Hist.*, Weimar, 1950), pp. 120–21. The fullest discussion of the 'Gunther silk' is A. Grabar, 'La soie byzantine

It is possible that other patrons of public performance found a different context for weapon-play. The importance of the Old Testament figure of David in forming the Carolingian and post-Carolingian concept of kingship is undeniable: but the creation of visual formulae and iconographic programmes corresponding to the verbal imagery of the texts seems to me to have been seriously antedated. Partly for this reason almost no consideration has been given to the possible interaction between the iconography of David and his court, with its dancers and weapon-players, and court ritual in the eleventh and twelfth centuries, when the visual images proliferate and are at times put in an untraditional, 'realistic' setting. The potential interest of such an inquiry is suggested by the picture in the third volume of the Cîteaux 'Bible of Stephen Harding', from which the figure of King David has several times been reproduced to illustrate English influence on Continental Romanesque art and the figures of the musicians find a place in many histories of musical instruments. The rarely-reproduced whole page shows king and courtiers within a kind of children's cut-out castle with carefully represented doors, battlemented walls and towers which are being vigorously defended by Norman (or perhaps one ought to say Anglo-Norman) knights drawn in meticulous detail with their armour, weapons and banners.[23]

Scholarly discussion of the increasingly-elaborate rituals associated with and designed to enhance monarchy in the central medieval centuries has tended to concentrate on the ceremonial of coronations and crown-wearings. In 'the thousandth year of the English monarchy' it is worth making at least a formal nod of obeisance to the evidence suggesting that in the time of Athelstan and Edgar, England was in this matter as much the giver as the receiver. The *Regularis Concordia,* on the other hand, however much traditional English practice it may have included in its recommended monastic usage, shows the overwhelming impact of recent West Frankish and German experience, among which most —but not all—scholars would include the dramatized *Visitatio Sepulchri.*[24] Ottonian Germany's recourse to Latin drama to ex-

---

de l'évêque Gunther à la cathédrale de Bamberg', *Münchner Jahrbuch der bildenden Kunst,* N.F., vii (1956), reprinted in Grabar, *L'Art de la Fin de l'Antiquité et du Moyen Age,* i, pp. 213–27.

[23] Steger, *op. cit.,* pp. 210–12, the 'Harding-Bible' page reproduced pl. 20. For doubts about the supposed significance of the earlier representations of David in Western art see Bullough, 'Imagines regum' (above, n. 7).

[24] *Regularis Concordia,* ed. T. Symons (Edinburgh–London, 1953), esp. pp. 49–51; and various contributions to the 'Regularis Concordia Millennium' Conference, Leicester, 1970, to be published as *Tenth-Century Studies,* ed. D. Parsons (Chichester, ?1974).

press a particular view of monarchy and its responsibilities was, however, neither anticipated elsewhere nor quickly imitated.

This was one part of the remarkable literary achievement of Hroswitha of Gandersheim, in the years immediately following Otto I's revival of the imperial title at Rome in 962. Gandersheim, one of the communities of nuns whose importance in the social and cultural history of late Carolingian and Ottonian Germany is probably still not fully appreciated, had been founded by Otto's great-grandparents and had had a succession of abbesses drawn from the Saxon ducal, subsequently royal and imperial, family—since the late 950s, Gerberga, daughter of one of the more obstreperous members of the family, Duke Henry of Bavaria. Such a background helps to explain how Gerberga received an early education, apparently in a Bavarian monastery, without any suggestion of impropriety and why, having become abbess of the Saxon house which evidently already possessed an unusually good library, she encouraged Hroswitha (who was older than herself) to exploit to the full the community's resources and the talents as a writer which she had already begun to display. The result, in little more than a decade, was eight *legenda* in metrical verse, six 'dramas' in rhythmical prose and two versified histories, concerned with Otto and with the early history of her house.[25] Hroswitha's own conception of the unity of her work, while recognizing the differences of genre, is clear from her preparation of a 'collected edition' in three books with prefaces to each book. The plays constitute book II: its preface contains the author's famous statement that she proposes to provide a Christian alternative to the pagan frivolities of Terence.[26]

The primary theme of legends and dramas is certainly heroic chastity—the triumphant assertion, with Christ's help, in life or in a martyr's death, of individual purity (usually but not always of a woman) against lasciviousness and brutality. In several of them there is also a secondary theme, which provides a link with the third book. The conflict between the exemplars of good and evil, the characterization—not, of course, in any psychological sense—of the hero are sharpened in two of the legends by their setting: in *Pelagius* the persecutor and potential corrupter is the Moslem

[25] The standard edition is by K. Strecker, *Hroswithae Opera* (Leipzig, 1906, rev. ed. 1930). B. Nagal, *Hrotsvit von Gandersheim* (Stuttgart, 1965) is an admirable introduction to all aspects of Hroswitha's life and work, including a section (pp. 32–34) on the manuscript tradition, all with extensive bibliographical references. See further M. Schütze-Pflugk, *Herrscher- u. Martyrerauffassung bei Hrotsvit von Gandersheim* (Frankfurter Hist. Abh., Bd 1; Wiesbaden, 1972), esp. pp. 1–6, which usefully summarizes recent work on the beginnings of Gandersheim.

[26] *Ed. cit.*, p. 113, lines 6 fos.

ruler of Cordova, whose strictly dishonourable intentions, be it noted, are homosexual ones although he is in no sense treated as a caricature; *Gangolfus* belongs to a lay 'courtly' and noble environment, nominally eighth-century Burgundy. So likewise in the first, longest and most elaborate of the dramas, *Gallicanus,* or more precisely in the first and longer of its two parts. Here the setting is the court of the Emperor Constantine, whose daughter Constantia the successful and highly-favoured general Gallicanus hopes to marry. Since the general is still a heathen while Constantia is already secretly but with her father's consent wedded in perpetual virginity to Christ it seems at first as if she will be the triumphant heroine. But the argument of the play is more complex, and not without ambiguity. If Gallicanus is denied his hoped-for bride, he will decline to lead his armies against the Scyths and the Empire will suffer defeat and disaster. Even Christian emperors cannot ignore 'reasons of state': the senators—behaving, it has been suggested, much as a tenth-century *curia* would have behaved—agree that Gallicanus is indispensable and must be rewarded as generously as he demands. So, after an encounter between father and daughter and a scene in which Gallicanus' two daughters (who enjoy such 'courtly' assets as beauty) decide to follow Constantia's way of life, emperor and general engage in an effectively-constructed, almost riddling, dialogue which ends with an implied promise that Constantia herself will make the final commitment. Gallicanus sets out for battle confident in the pagan gods, his army and himself; but threatened with defeat he is converted to Christianity by two courtiers who have been sent to accompany him, and wins a decisive victory. In the aftermath, as a *miles Christi* who no longer needs weapons of war, he displays a whole range of Christian virtues from mercy to one's enemies (more acceptable in the Ottonian than in the Carolingian period) to personal renunciation of carnal desires.[27]

This particular resolution of the dramatic conflict is not one which would commend itself to a modern playwright, except perhaps one writing for *Moral Re-armament*; and any resemblance between Hroswitha's plays and Berthold Brecht's episodic *Lehrdramen* (a comparison much favoured by some modern critics) manifestly stops short of the morality credited to the ideologically-approved ruler figure in Gallicanus.[28] But the tension that arises

[27] *Ed. cit.,* pp. 117–33; Schütze-Pflugk, *op. cit.,* pp. 42–53, whose analysis is here closely followed.

[28] Nagel, *op. cit.,* pp. 22 f. and the references given there. So far as I can see Brecht himself never refers to Hroswitha in his writings, but his desired characterization of Galileo prompted a comment which could well have been

from the encounter of personal morality with needs of state is a perennial one; and the dramatic form made it easier to expound the contrasting qualities that may be demanded from a Christian ruler and his subjects within the framework of a shared teleology. The second part of the play, which is actually concerned primarily with the events leading to the martyrdom under Julian the Apostate of the former general's two Christian advisers, is less effective and subtle: but even in its recognition that the martyrs *were* disturbers of the *pax civilis* of the Empire (a notion which recurs in a very different literary context in the execution of the Garibaldian *esaltati* in Lampedusa's *Il Gattopardo*), it makes the point that one ruled by a non-Christian emperor is necessarily unhappy.[29] Whether because of its literary qualities or because it was appreciated as 'propaganda' for a distinctively Christian rulerdom as well as for the virtues of renunciation and martydom, it is a fact that *Gallicanus* is the one play in the Hroswitha corpus for which there is known to have been an active manuscript tradition in the twelfth and thirteenth centuries the common source of which was a manuscript into which a simple division into scenes had recently been introduced (to produce an 'acting edition?').[30]

The region from which all these copies come, S.E. Germany and Austria, is also one, although by no means the only one, from which there is unusually full manuscript evidence of dramatizations (in Latin) of episodes from the Old and the New Testaments in these same centuries.[31] The comic element is still modest; and it would certainly be misguided to seek a 'social' content in plays that were conceived as an extension of the liturgy and of homilies and presumably intended in performance to convey something to an audience or congregation ignorant of Latin—even though a Marxist critic might have sharp comments to make on the implied conditioning of the illiterate. I have admittedly sometimes wondered whether the better and eminently actable of two French twelfth-century *Daniel* plays, attributed in the unique British Museum manuscript to the *iuvenes* of Beauvais cathedral, embodied some

---

applied to Gallicanus: performance, he said, 'should not aim at establishing the sympathetic identification and participation of the audience with him; rather, the audience should be helped to achieve a more considering, critical and appraising attitude. *He should be presented as a phenomenon, rather like Richard III, whereby the audience's emotional acceptance is gained through the vitality of this alien manifestation*' (*The Life of Galileo*, Engl. ed. by D. I. Vesey [London 1960, 1963, p. 14]).

[29] *Ed. cit.*, pp. 134–39; Schütze-Pflugk, *op. cit.*, pp. 38–41.

[30] Strecker, *ed. cit.*, pp. v, vii; Nagel, *op. cit.*, pp. 33 f.

[31] K. Young, *The Drama of the Medieval Church*, 2 vols. (Oxford, 1933), passim.

mild form of protest against the establishment of the day: it is, after
all, in the same manuscript as one of the earliest and best texts of
the 'Prose of the Ass', with which indeed it may have a textual
link (which did not escape E. K. Chambers); and we have Alexander
Neckham's strangely modern testimony to what an older generation
thought of the bolshieness and intellectual arrogance of the late-
twelfth-century student.[32] If so, it was markedly more subtle than
the more recent variety. The prophetic aspects of the Book of
Daniel which attracted medieval commentators are ignored; and
if oblique criticism *is* intended (which I doubt) it is certainly of bad
counsellors rather than of arbitrary kingship.

Daniel's own foretelling of the coming of the Lord's Anointed
was one of a number of prophecies, mostly from the Old Testament
but also including a long hexametrical text from the Erythraean
Sibyl, which had been brought together in a fifth-century sermon
to demonstrate the perversity of the Jews. Universally regarded in
the Middle Ages as a work of St Augustine (although its true author
was probably his contemporary Quodvultdeus of Carthage), this
section was widely used as a *lectio* at Matins in the Christmas season.
In the twelfth and thirteenth century the so-called *Ordo Prophet-
arum* received the full dramatic treatment in a number of churches:
a version from Laon gives details of how the impersonation of the
prophets was to be established—Daniel *adolescens, veste splendida
indutus*; Elisabeth *femineo habitu, pregnans*; the Sibyl in feminine
garb, with shaved head, crowned with ivy and with a mad expression *(insanienti simillima)*.[33] Sermon and play have a secure place
in the tradition of medieval anti-Semitism. At least, however, they
remained more or less on the level of simple exegesis of prophecies
of the coming of Christ. In this way they were quite unlike the
unattractive Holy Week ceremony in early eleventh-century
Toulouse of 'Striking the Jew', which we learn about only by chance
because a prominent member of the community was beaten so
badly and his eye damaged that he was taken from the cathedral
dying.[34] Considerably more polemical than the *Ordo* was the

[32] Young, ii, pp. 290–301, from Egerton ms. 2615, of which the best description is still (as Mr D. H. Turner has kindly confirmed) *Catalogue of Additions
to the Manuscript in the British Museum . . . 1882–1887* (London, 1889),
pp. 336–37. For the 'Song of the Ass' see H. C. Greene in *Speculum*, vi (1931),
pp. 534–49; Young, i, p. 551, *cf.* ii, pp. 169, 303. Neckham's criticism is quoted
(from *De naturis rerum?*) by E. Gilson in his Preface to M. D. Chenu, *Nature,
Man and Society in the Twelfth Century* (Chicago, 1968), p. xii.

[33] Young, *op. cit.*, ii, pp. 145–50.

[34] Ademar of Chabannes, *Historiarum libri tres*, III, 52: ed. Waitz, *Mon.
Germ. Hist., Scriptores*, iv (Hanover, 1841), p. 139; *cf.* B. Blumenkranz, *Les
auteurs chrétiens latins de Moyen Âge* (Paris—The Hague, 1963), pp. 251–52.

pseudo-Augustinian (but fifth-century) *De altercatione Synagogae et Ecclesiae* which circulated widely from the eleventh century onwards.[35] I know of no conclusive evidence that it was publicly performed with impersonation of Church and Synagogue. There are several reasons, however, for thinking that it may have been, including the (admittedly late) play in which the dramatized prophecies are followed by a version of the *Altercatio* in which the protagonists are named as 'Augustinus' and 'Archisynagogus', the slight evidence that some of the many—largely unpublished—anti-Jewish poems, typified by a (?)thirteenth-century example in a Basle manuscript with the heading *Versus in obprobium Iudeorum et laudem crucis Christi et Ecclesie* were declaimed in public and the eleventh and twelfth-century evidence from southern France and northern Spain for the separate performance with music of the Sibylline verses.[36]

The independent traditions of religious drama, meaningful play and court ritual temporarily come together in the mid-twelfth century in probably the most elaborate and thematically complex of medieval Latin plays. This is the *Ludus de Antichristo*, extant today only in a Tegernsee manuscript of the late twelfth or early thirteenth century but at one time apparently more widely available.[37] As the title indicates, the *Ludus* is in one of its aspects a contribution to or a reflection of medieval eschatological thinking which I would rate as a more important element in the agonizing of the twelfth-century intellectual and a greater influence on historical and political thought than does, I think, Dr Southern. The place of Antichrist in 'the history of the future'—and indeed there is more than a little SF about this thinking, both in its irrationality and its supra-rationality—had been given its definitive

[35] Migne, *Patrologia Latina*, xlii, cols. 1131–40, new edition by G. Seguí and J. N. Hillgarth in *Boletin de la Sociedad Arqueologia*, xxxi (1954). The *Altercatio aecclesie contra synagogam* in two English twelfth-century manuscripts (one of which subsequently interested both Patrick Young and Selden) is a different text, for which a tenth-century English origin has surprisingly been supposed: B. Blumenkranz in *Revue du Moyen Age Latin*, x (1954), pp. 5–159.

[36] Young, *op. cit.*, ii, pp. 192–93; Basel MS. B. IV 26 (s. xiv; ?German) *inc.* *Leta dei loeto meretrix synagogo valeto*; R. B. Donovan, *The Liturgical Drama in Medieval Spain* (Toronto, 1958), pp. 165–67. See also P. Weber, *Geistliches Schauspiel und Kirchliche Kunst* (Stuttgart, 1894), pp. 24–30, 58–81.

[37] Standard edition by W. Meyer, *Gesammelte Abhandlungen zur mittellateinischen Rythmik*, i (Berlin, 1905), pp. 150–70); an easily accessible text in Young, *op. cit.*, ii, pp. 371–87. For the manuscript, Munich clm. 19411 (predominantly a collection of letters and other texts concerning the recent history of the Empire) see W. Wattenbach in *Neues Archiv*, xvii (1892), pp. 33–47.

literary expression for the central medieval centuries, and beyond that date for the less sophisticated intellects, by the Frenchman Adso in the late tenth century.[38] Adso's *De Antichristo*, however, like the oracles of the Tiburtine Sibyl, lent itself readily to adaptation to local political circumstances; and there seems no good reason for doubting that his work in some version or other was the ultimate source of the *Ludus* from the point—just before half-way —at which Antichrist is brought on. The verbal links between the two texts, however, are not very numerous; and the part attributed to *Synagoga* reflects rather the influence of the *Altercatio*. What gives the *Ludus* its interest and importance as a political-propaganda play is the setting in which the struggles with Antichrist take place and the characterization, especially but not exclusively in its first part, of the earthly protagonists and their relationships.

The principal personages come on to a stage on which have been erected 'the Temple of the Lord' and seven *sedes regales*, of which five are then occupied by the king of Babylonia, the Roman emperor, the French king, the Greek king (sic!) and the king of Jerusalem, while the throne of the *rex Theotonicorum* is probably originally left vacant. Preceded by *Ecclesia* who is supported by Mercy and Justice—here personified on stage, it seems, for the first time—the Pope enters simultaneously with the emperor but does not occupy a throne and remains a 'silent personage' throughout. The emperor declares that according to the writings of historians the whole world was once tributary to Rome and that this dependence is now to be re-established. Legates are dispatched to each of the kings in turn demanding their allegiance; the French king retorts that the evidence of historians favours *his* superiority and an army (*acies*) is sent against him, which brings him captive before the emperor whose superiority he acknowledges in words that are faintly reminiscent of the liturgical *laudes* of a monarch. Karl Hauck has supposed, perhaps with more ingenuity than conviction, that since fights had not previously figured in liturgical drama, in the *Ludus* they were in the form of the centuries-old ritual weapon-play or dances. He may be right, but it should be remembered that the *Gallicanus* includes both a scene of the army assembling and a battle episode, in spite of Hroswitha's disclaimer elsewhere of any familiarity with military matters;[39] and I have already

[38] Ed. by E. Sackur as *Epistola Adsonis ad Gerbergam reginam de ortu et tempore Anti-Christo* in *Sibyllinische Texte und Forschungen* (Halle, 1898), pp. 104–13.

[39] Hauck, *art. cit.*, (n. 21), pp. 17 f.; *Gallicanus* VII 1, 1X 2 (*ed. cit.*, pp. 125, 127); *Gesta Ottonis*, lines 243–46, (*ed. cit.*, p. 238); Schütze-Pflugk, *op. cit.*, pp. 46 f.

hinted that manuscript illustrations of David with men under arms
and *ioculatores* may have had some counterpart in 'performance'.
After the emperor's defeat of the French king, others submit
without a fight, until the king of Babylon forces the emperor
to do battle for Jerusalem—where, following his victory, he
deposits his crown and other insignia before the temple altar,
declaring that Christ alone is the true imperial ruler, after which
he returns to (apparently) the vacant throne of the king of the
Germans.

Now the mood changes. Hypocrites appear and gain the favour of
the laity and the king of Jerusalem. Antichrist comes on, supported
by personifications of Hypocrisy and Heresy, he overcomes the
king of Jerusalem, ascends the throne in the temple, drives out
Ecclesia, and in his turn sends out messengers to demand the submission of all the kings of the earth. The king of the Greeks gives
in easily; so does the French king, seduced by Hypocrisy's gifts and
weakened by his subjects'—presumably intellectual—*subtilitas*;
in contrast, the Germans put up a stout resistance and their king
is only won over by a miraculous raising from the dead, after which,
however, he leads Antichrist's army successfully against the representatives of paganism. When *Synagoga*, through the agency of the
hypocrites, submits to Antichrist, he is temporarily master of the
world. The arrival of Enoch and Elijah mark the beginning of his
downfall, although not before the prophets and a converted *Synagoga* have been put to death. Antichrist dies while expounding his
omnipotence to the assembled kings (not, be it noted, in a massive
battle). *Ecclesia* points the moral, all return to the faith and they
depart praising God.

Antagonistic to the French, scathing towards the Greeks, dismissive to the Pope and laudatory to the Germans, the play's political
standpoint and propagandist tone are unmistakable. But in what
circumstances and when was it conceived and performed? It has
never been doubted that it originated in the lifetime of Frederick
Barbarossa and almost all scholars who have considered it have
inferred that it belongs to the earlier part of the reign, although
hardly before the imperial coronation in 1154. Moreover, it seems
to me perverse, although others have felt differently, to suppose
that Gerhoh of Reichersberg was referring in 1160–62 to different
(lost) plays on the subject of Antichrist.[40] Professor Hauck, building boldly on his hypothesis that the *Ludus* combines some of the

[40] See now P. Classen, *Gerhoch von Reichersberg* (Wiesbaden, 1960), pp. 233 f.
with references to previous literature and (p. 224 n. 47) a list of German poems
of the period on the subject of Antichrist. *Cf.* Young, *op. cit.*, ii, pp. 392—93,
524–25.

secular rituals traditional at major court festivals with Latin religious drama, has suggested that it was originally performed as part
of the coronation ceremonies in 1152 and perhaps repeated during
the next Christmas season; and he had won some unexpected
support. Yet the omission of any reference to the play in Otto
of Freising's comparatively detailed account of the opening months
of Frederick's reign would be more conspicuous if it were established that Otto's own contribution to the *Ludus* was direct and
considerable, and not indirect and modest as has generally been
believed.[41]

The contrast between the younger Otto of the *Chronicon*, with
its apocalyptic view of the course of human history, pessimistic,
indifferent to modern developments in speculative thought, concerned with last things, and the cheerful, optimistic older Otto of
the *Gesta Friderici*, with its pragmatic view of recent events, has
puzzled and continues to puzzle scholars: some have claimed to
find a consistency of outlook in the two works in spite of appear-
ances—the more eagerly in recent years because of the incon-
sistencies of their own commitment. The *Ludus*, however, can be
read as a simpler version of the two histories in reverse order. It
is the work of someone who recognizes the importance of the
historiographi in assertions of political sovereignty. The notion
that the last Roman emperor will lay down his insignia in Jerusalem
is found already in Adso; his return *in sedem antiqui regni sui*,
i.e. of the German kingdom, is not. The closest parallel to the
support given to Antichrist by Hypocrisy and Heresy (not yet at
this date, unlike Mercy and Justice, part of the vocabulary of the
visual arts)[42] is in a passage of the *Chronicon*. Hypocrisy's disdain
for the *seculares praelatos* suggests where the author's own ecclesiastical sympathies lie. Tegernsee was a monastery in the diocese of
Freising which had active links with Bishop Otto at this time and
whose scribes were praised by Frederick himself. Other arguments
could be added. I am not suggesting that Otto had any hand in the
writing of the *Ludus*, merely that he was in some measure its
inspirer and guiding hand; and if it was composed at any time
between 1154–55 and the early months of 1157 it would provide a

[41] Hauck, *art. cit.*, pp. 21–23. According to P. Munz, *Frederick Barbarossa*
(London, 1969), p. 377 n.l, 'Hauck's view is now widely accepted': but compare Classen, *op. cit.*, p. 224 n. 46. *Gesta Friderici I. Imperatoris*, II 1—7
(ed. G. Waitz and B. v. Simson [Hanover, 1912] pp. 102–10) cover March-
October 1152.
[42] So I infer from A. Katzenellenbogen, *Allegories of the Virtues and
Vices in Medieval Art* (Studies of the Warburg Institute, 10; London, 1939),
pp. 27 ff.

convincing intellectual link between Otto's two contrasting works of historiography.[43]

Whether the *Ludus* was ever performed at the court or in the emperor's presence we do not know. It is certainly not excluded: but if Gerhoh is referring to this or a related play, it is equally certain that it was presented in churches. The performance of the *Ludus de Antichristo* (in which the words were in fact sung), of the *Ludus Danielis*, of *Gallicanus* was obviously impossible without the availability of a properly-prepared group of *clerici*. The most serious limitations on these and other Latin plays as potential influencers of opinion are, however, independent of both authorship and circumstances of presentation. An audience of knights, *burgenses* or other laymen might have learned something from the gestures and actions of the protagonists identifiable by their costumes, and even recognized some parallel with one or other of the vernacular 'Antichrist' poems: they would have derived little or nothing from the text of the *Ludus*. There is contemporary evidence that even Frederick himself, who was universally regarded as a man of intelligence and eloquence, was not at home in the Latin language.[44]

The same problem was encountered in circumstances in which we might have expected to find a lay audience capable of understanding Latin, such as the self-governing towns of North and Central Italy. In the second decade of the fourteenth century the Paduan notary and communal councillor Albertino Mussato made a bold attempt to revive classical tragedy as exemplified by Seneca. Prompted by recent political events in his city, he chose as his theme the attempt and ultimate failure of Ezzelino to establish a tyranny in nearby Verona during the middle decades of the thirteenth century. The *Ecerinide* was in purely literary terms a considerable achievement; but if its author had hoped to inspire his fellow-citizens—through reading, one imagines, rather than through stage

---

[43] Typical of the attempts to resolve the apparent contradictions between the two works are J. Spörl, *Grundformen hochmittelalterlicher Geschichtsanschauung* (Berlin, 1937), pp. 47–50 and L. Grill, 'Bildung u. Wissenschaft im Leben Ottos von Freising', *Analecta sacri ordinis Cisterciensis*, xiv (1958), pp. 313–21; cf. Munz, *Frederick Barbarossa*, p. 133 n. 1, where other literature is briefly characterized. The link between the *Ludus* and *Chronica sive Historia de duabus civitatibus*, viii 1, ed. A. Hofmeister (Hanover, 1912), p. 393, was already noted by Meyer, *op. cit.*, i, p. 142. A letter of 1155–56 preserved on a later folio of clm. 19411 (fo. 91ᵛ) shows the bishop inviting the abbot of Tegernsee and two of his community to come to him to give advice and help: A. Weissthanner, 'Regesten . . . Bischofs Otto I', *Analecta, cit.*, p. 204 (nr. 151).

[44] Principal references in Munz, *op. cit.*, p. 41 n. 7. But note Rahewin is

performance—to a more vigorous defence of republican liberties
he was disappointed. The Notaries' Guild, representing the very
element in the towns which is commonly invoked to account for
later medieval Italy's new interest in classical antiquity, asked him
to produce a less highbrow work: *non altum, non tragedium, sed
molle et vulgi intellectioni propinquum.* The response was a tedious epic poem.[45] The continuous history of drama in north-east
Italy begins only a century or so later with comedy in the Paduan
vernacular which had previously been used for poetic composition
by members of the learned professions—plays which are note-
worthy for an incipient realism and a sympathetic understanding
of the problems of the poor *contadino*.[46]

The dichotomy of language runs deep in late medieval attempts
to influence opinion. The substantial enlargement of the circle of
those whose acceptance of a particular policy of government was
needed and sought has as one of its elements the emergence of the
university graduate: this became very clear in the debates over the
Great Schism and the ways of ending it. The astrological manipula-
tions of Italian princely and other courts and the different but
equally questionable pressures put on participants in the Great
Council at Constance are reminders that intellectual appeal was
not the only method of influencing opinion. The most distinguished products of the universities were in no way dismissive of
the rituals associated with monarchical or ducal authority—the
careers and writings of men as different as Jean Gerson, Nicolas
of Clamanges and Nicolas Rolin prove the contrary. Even their
humbler fellows could properly be assumed to be thoroughly at
home in Latin and responsive to the written word or, if they were
gathered in the right place, to the intricately-argued, politically-
slanted sermon. Drama, however, had nothing to add to their
political awareness: Gerson's insistence that the *scolares* of Notre

---

echoing Einhard's hyperbolic *Graecam vero melius intellegere quam pronun-
tiare poterat: Vita Karoli,* c. xxv; and the evidence for the use of an interpreter
is not obviously relevant since Richard of London is referring to Frederick's
difficulties in Armenia.

[45] A. Zardo, *Albertino Mussato* (Padua, 1884), with the corrections and
additions in J. K. Hyde, *Padua in the Age of Dante* (Manchester, 1966),
pp. 165–68, 295–99; Mussato, *Ecerinide,* ed. L. Padrin (Bologna, 1900); Mussato,
De gestis Italicorum post Henricum VII Caesarem in *Rerum Italicarum Scriptores,* ed. L. Muratori, x (Milan, 1727), cols. 687–88.
[46] References to the earliest Paduan vernacular writing in Hyde, *op. cit.,*
pp. 298 f.; for a supposed tradition of *popolaresco* comedy, known now mainly
from the sixteenth-century *mariazi* see A. Mortier, *Ruzzante (1502—44), un
dramaturge populaire de la Renaissance italienne,* 2 vols. (Paris, 1925–26), i,
passim and E. Lovarini, *Studi sul Ruzzante e la letteratura pavana,* ed.
G. Folena (Padua, 1965).

Dame, Paris, were not to be taught 'profane and indecent catches' is to be understood in the most literal sense.[47]

There were, none the less, those whose support was worth having and could be gained only through the vernacular. Not every court had access to a brilliant *spilmann* like Walther von der Vogelweide whose muse was at the service—for suitably generous hospitality or cash—of anyone who seemed likely to end the strife which divided his beloved Germany in the decades after 1197; or even an Adam de la Halle, saying the right things in his musical play but to far too restricted a company.[48] Whoever planned the Parisian entertainment in 1378 had clearly made a sound appreciation of his audience, the medium and its possibilities as an instrument of propaganda. There can be no certainty in the matter but there are strong arguments for the supposition that the inspiration was Philippe de Mézières'. Philippe is a fascinating character who had lived in Paris and around the court, where he became for a time tutor to the young Charles VI, since 1373. An ardent Crusader in his youth and a pilgrim to the Holy Land, he was for ten years (1359–69) chancellor to the king of Cyprus where he wrote the first of his Latin and vernacular works designed to persuade European monarchs and *chevaliers* to sacrifice everything for the liberation of the Holy Land. On his journey back from Cyprus he was responsible for the first performances, at Venice in 1370 and Avignon in 1372, of a *repraesentatio figurata* as part of the newly-introduced 'Feast of the Presentation of the Virgin'. His recommendation to his royal pupil that he should read 'es hystoires authentique . . . de la bataille de Troye' suggests that he may also have been the impresario of an intended court production of the 'Fall of Troy' in 1389, apparently using the same sets as the earlier Crusade play—which, however, was brought to an abrupt end when one of the large tables collapsed and ladies began to faint. He is now generally accepted as the author of both the earliest French (prose) version of the edifying story of Griselda, which he certainly believed to have an historic basis, and of *Le Mystère de Griseldis*, a closely-related verse-drama version, completed in or shortly before 1395. The prologue of the play-text contains the striking statement that the *estoire* will be *fait par personnaiges* because the heart of man is more moved by seeing than reading.

[47] A. Combes, *Jean de Montreuil et la Chancelier Gerson* (Paris, 1942); E. Vansteenberghe, 'Gerson à Bruges', *Revue d'histoire ecclésiastique*, xxxi (1935), pp. 5–52; J. Gerson, *Doctrina pro pueris ecclesiae Parisiensis* in *Opera Omnia*, ed. E. Du Pin (Antwerp, 1706), iv, p. 718.

[48] *Die Lieder Walthers von der Vogelweide*, ed. F. Maurer, 3rd ed. i (Berlin, 1967), and for the context of some of the political songs see *e.g.* T. C. Van Cleve, *The Emperor Frederick II of Hohenstaufen, Immutator mundi* (Oxford, 1972), pp. 32, 77, 84, 99 etc., H. Guy, *Essai sur la vie et les œuvres littéraires*

The continuing interaction between ritualized play and stage drama is exemplified by the hunting scenes with which the *Mystère* begins and in the course of which Marquis Thomas of Saluzzo is persuaded to marry.[49] The rest of the action, of course, is concerned with the (to us unattractive) moral tale of the much-tried Griselda, although in this version her return to high estate is celebrated with a concluding *amoureuse chançonette* and dance. Its relevance to current politics is made clear by Philippe's *Epître* of 1395 to Richard II of England in the last book of which he urged him both to read *le cronique autentique* of Thomas and Griselda and to take a new wife, with arguments very like those used in the earlier scenes of the play. It was Philippe's fervent hope that a marriage between the English king and Charles VI's little daughter Isabelle would lead to peace between the two realms and a triumphant joint crusade against the infidel. The marriage took place without the hoped-for consequences, which is perhaps the fate of much propaganda: and fifteenth-century court impresarios, such as Olivier de la Marche, used their talents differently.[50]

Even vernacular plays, then, were not for the groundlings, who lacked *sensibilité*. The masses were not ordinarily required to support a particular policy, still less to be persuaded of its soundness or rightness. Their adherence was sought simply to the exercise of authority by an individual, a dynasty or a ruling group: and

---

de Adan [sic] *de la Halle* (Paris, 1898), esp. pt. 1 ch. 5 and pt. 2 ch. 7, more recent bibliography conveniently in J. H. Marshall, *The Chansons of Adam de la Halle* (Manchester, 1971), pp. 22–24.

[49] Presumably appearing 'on stage' here for the first time, the hunt scene subsequently became a *topos* of the art-theatre, to be brilliantly apotheosized in the 'Royal Hunt and Storm' scene of Berlioz's *Les Troyens*.

[50] N. Iorga, *Philippe de Mézières, 1327–1405, et la croisade au XIV^c siècle* (Bibl. de l'École des Hautes Études, cx; Paris, 1896) remains the standard biography; additional details in G. W. Coopland (ed.), *Le Songe du vieil pèlerin* (Cambridge, 1969), i, pp. 1–7. The texts relating to the Feast of the Presentation are in Young, *op. cit.*, ii, pp. 472–79, 227–42—the source of a bibliographical curiosity entitled *Philippe de Mézières' description of the Festum Praesentations Beatae Mariae. Translated from the Latin and introduced by an essay on the Birth of Modern Acting by Albert B. Weiner* (New Haven, 1958). The prose *Estoire de Griseldis* of 1384–89 has apparently been edited by B. M. Craig (c. 1954), the verse *Mystère de Griseldis* by M. A. Glomeau (Paris, 1923) and also by B. M. Craig, but I have seen none of these and have been compelled to rely on the summary in G. Frank, *Medieval French Drama* (Oxford, 1954), pp. 156–60; for the authorship of the play see Frank in *Modern Language Notes*, li (1936), pp. 217–22. The full text of the *Epistre* (in four books, the last of which contains the recommendation to read *le cronique autentique*) in a very elegant—presumably Parisian—manuscript of 1395, British Museum, MS. Royal 20 B. VI, is still unpublished: but see now J. J. N. Palmer, *England, France and Christendom* (London, 1972), pp. 186–91, 243 and pl. 1.

this was secured most effectively by the street-crier—although few places were as fortunate as mid-fourteenth-century Florence, with its loyal, lively and independent-minded Antonio Pucci[51]—and by the outdoor pageantry in which drama played an incidental and non-political part. Neither the contemporary public nor we gain enlightenment about French royal policy from the performance of religious plays on the streets in connection with a *grande entrée,* first recorded in 1380, or from the public display of 'three very handsome girls, representing quite naked sirens and one saw their beautiful breasts, which was a very pleasant sight, and they recited little motets and bergerettes' on the occasion of Louis XI's *entrée* into Paris in 1461.[52] Yet the mounting of plays by French urban *confréries* and the elaborate static or mimetic displays in early Tudor and Hapsburg pageantry were a means by which particular economic and social groups could declare their loyalty to the régime and sometimes to suggest the services that the ruler was expected to perform for them.

The relationship of playwrights and their public with the new régimes and with each other was a complex and often ambivalent one: more at ease in the vernacular than in Latin although tinged by Humanistic learning, hopeful of future patronage if not already in the charmed circle, the former were eager to acclaim the legitimacy of the sovereign power while expressing reserves about its policies. The Venetians could not be kept away from the theatre even in times of crisis and in the face of legal prohibition. During the 1520s and 1530s the plays of Ruzzante, which brought Paduan *contadino* comedy into the art-theatre, enabled the patricians to enjoy a vicarious penitence for their oppression of the peasantry in their *terrafirma* dominions.[53] A succession of French plays written for performances on special occasions (such as 'La fête des Rois') in *Collèges* and similar institutions from the 1540s onwards take as their theme Caesar's monarchical aspirations and the opposition to it in oblique—and not so oblique—reference to the problems currently facing the French crown: their dreariness as literature is exceeded only by that of a Munich dissertation in which they are discussed; but the earliest has a modest claim to fame because the fourteen-year-old Montaigne was one of its actors. The 'history'

[51] K. McKenzie, *Antonio Pucci: le Noie* (Princeton–Paris 1931), introduction; K. Speight, '*Vox Populi* in Antonio Pucci', *Italian Studies presented to E. R. Vincent,* ed. C. P. Brand et al. (Cambridge, 1962), pp. 76–91.
[52] G. Guenée and F. Lehoux, *Les Entrées royales Françaises de 1328 à 1515,* pp. 13 f., 56–58 (where, however, the contemporary descriptions of the *entrée* of 1380 do not contain any reference to theatrical performances); Jean de Roye, cited Huizinga, *Waning of the Middle Ages* (ed. of 1965), p. 300.
[53] Mortier and Lovarini, *op. cit.* (n. 45); G. Cozzi in *Renaissance Venice,* ed. J. R. Hale (London, 1973), pp. 330–31.

plays written by Juan de la Cueva for the theatre of Seville in the years 1579–81 were, it has recently been conjectured (although many will remain sceptical), subtly criticizing Philip II's policy towards the Portuguese succession.[54] And there is always Shakespeare. That, however, is somebody else's theme.

Even when there are no linguistic or other barriers to be overcome, purposive drama, Brecht's *Lehrdrama*, drama with a message is rarely more than a gloss on other means of persuasion and influencing opinion; and the response to it is only exceptionally as direct as the guilt-ridden Danish king's to Hamlet's Players. 'For some of us it is performance, for others patronage: they are two sides of the same coin', declares The Player in Tom Stoppard's *Rosencrantz and Guildenstern are Dead*. For yet others, he could have added ('being as there are so many of us'), it is to be the public, the playthings of both performers and their lordly patrons: a medieval Player, *clericus* or lay, would probably have made the same omission. Gerhoh of Reichersberg was aware of *publica opinio*—in the sense of, more or less, commonly-held beliefs (about Antichrist) and these only among the learned. 'The heart of man' may indeed be moved more easily by seeing than by reading. Throughout the centuries, however, the mass of men, whether dubbed subjects, citizens or followers of Christ, have been even more responsive to rituals in which they are at once participants and spectators, which simultaneously provide a powerful sense of identification with an existing or developing social and political order and demand an uncritical acceptance of the aspirations and policies of those in whom authority is vested. We have discovered painfully in recent decades that the agonistic contest between the appeal to intellectual conviction and the arousing of primitive emotions, between rationality and irrationality, which once seemed to have been decided, is still a game in play.[55]

University of St Andrews.

[54] J. Hüther, *Die monarchische Ideologie in den französischen Römerdramen des 16. u. 17. Jahrhunderts* (Munich, 1966), esp. the discussion of Muret's *Caesar*, pp. 9–22: but for more penetrating account of Garnier see G. Jendorf, *Robert Garnier and the themes of political tragedy in the sixteenth century* (Cambridge, 1969); A. Watson, *Juan de la Cueva and the Portuguese Succession* (London, 1971), to which Prof. R. B. Tate drew my attention.
[55] Much of the reading for this paper was done when I was enjoying the support of a N.A.T.O. Fellowship awarded for the study of 'The cultural unity of the West: the Early Medieval basis'. I am grateful to the Appointing Committee and, more especially, to Mr John Vernon of the Political Department of N.A.T.O., Brussels, for their generous help and encouragement.

'PARNELLISM AND CRIME', 1887-90[1]

By Professor F. S. L. Lyons, M.A., Ph.D., Litt.D., F.R.Hist.S.

READ AT THE SOCIETY'S CONFERENCE
18 SEPTEMBER 1973

THE Home Rule crisis of 1885–86 is generally held to mark a watershed in the history of Anglo-Irish relations. This it undoubtedly does, though not necessarily for the reasons commonly advanced. The crisis was certainly important in the sense that it obliged the Liberal and Conservative parties to define their attitudes towards Irish self-government and thus to demonstrate to the Irish nationalist party in the House of Commons that their main hope for the future lay with Mr Gladstone and those Liberals who had remained faithful to him after his declaration in favour of Home Rule. But the course of events during 1886 demonstrated just how far the Irish demand still was from being met. The inadequacies of the Home Rule Bill itself, the split in the Liberal party, the firm negative of the Conservatives, the violence of the Ulster Protestant reaction, the veto of the House of Lords which had not even to be deployed in 1886 but was there for future use when necessary—all these things suggested that Home Rule, if it came at all, would not happen overnight at the waving of any Parnellite wand, but would require years, perhaps decades, of labour before it came within sight of achievement.

When the seal was set upon the repudiation of Home Rule by the Unionist victory in the general election of 1886, it was therefore not surprising that the Irish question should promptly have reverted to type and become again—what indeed it had never ceased to be even at the height of the Home Rule fever—a question concerned less with self-government for a cloudily defined nation than with the desperate efforts of a rural population to survive in a period of falling prices, when even moderate rents seemed extortionate and when failure to pay brought eviction in its train. Since this in turn provoked outrages ranging from intimidation to

[1] This paper attempts to deal mainly with the political aspects and consequences of the accusations made by *The Times* in 1887 against Parnell and his movement. The many technical, and indeed moral, issues raised by the controversy are admirably handled by T. W. Moody, '*The Times* versus Parnell and Co., 1887-90', *Historical Studies*, vi (1968), pp. 147–82.

murder, and since in such circumstances it was notoriously difficult to obtain convictions from Irish juries, the government was faced once more with the familiar predicament of how to combine relief for genuinely distressed farmers with a sternly punitive policy to restore peace to the unsettled countryside. By the autumn of 1886 it was clear that although agrarian crime was less than during the land war of 1879–81, morale in Ireland was low and conditions were ripe for a new wave of organized agitation. This, the 'Plan of Campaign', duly appeared in October and although it was, and remained, a limited operation, the fact that its primary aim was to incite tenants on individual estates to withhold their rents altogether if the landlords refused what the tenants estimated to be a fair rent, decided the government to ignore for the time being the warnings of its own agents and of its Irish critics as to the true gravity of the tenants' plight, and to give priority in 1887 to the passing of the Criminal Law Amendment Act. Called 'permanent' because it did not have to be renewed at intervals, the act gave exceptional powers to the Irish administration, including the right to 'proclaim' whole districts, to conduct trials of certain agrarian offences before courts of summary jurisdiction and to declare specific organizations to be dangerous and therefore liable to prosecution.[2]

This fresh outbreak of a recurrent Irish malady gave an added ferocity to the propaganda war which the Home Rule crisis had already precipitated. It is important to be clear, therefore, that when in March 1887 *The Times* began to publish the series of articles entitled 'Parnellism and Crime', the situation was potentially explosive. On the one hand, there was daily evidence of growing unrest in Ireland; on the other hand, there was the indisputable fact that the Liberal party now in opposition was pledged to Home Rule and was to all intents and purposes in political alliance with the leaders of an Irish party which in the past had been deeply involved in the land war and might again be tarred with the same brush. This last assumption was in fact only partly true, for although the new agitation was led by three prominent members of the party, their chairman, Charles Stewart Parnell, pointedly dissociated himself from it at the outset, insisting that he would countenance nothing which might alienate English opinion and thus weaken the Liberal alliance through which alone Home Rule could be realized.[3] His studied moderation might, however, be

[2] For the genesis of the Plan of Campaign, see F. S. L. Lyons, *John Dillon* (London, 1968), chap. 4; for the government's reaction, see L. P. Curtis, jr., *Coercion and Conciliation in Ireland* (Princeton, 1963), chap. 10.

[3] F. S. L. Lyons, 'John Dillon and the Plan of Campaign, 1886–90', *Irish Historical Studies*, xiv (Sept. 1965), pp. 313–47.

neutralized if it could be shown that the Parnellites had in the past been linked generally with agrarian crime, that they had had contacts with the Invincibles, the secret society which had murdered Lord Frederick Cavendish and T. H. Burke in the Phoenix Park in Dublin in May 1882, and that they derived their funds mainly from American sources tainted with responsibility for the dynamite attacks which had excited English opinion in 1883–84. Consequently, in the first of its articles *The Times* promised that it would prove the Parnellite movement to be 'essentially a foreign conspiracy' and that its chief authors 'have been, and are, in notorious and continuous relations with avowed murderers'. But to discredit Parnell and his party was not just an end in itself; it was the means towards a greater end, to discredit Gladstone and *his* party. This further motive was laid bare in an accompanying second leader. ' Mr Gladstone and his party', it proclaimed, 'are deliberately allying themselves with the paid agents of an organization whose ultimate aim is plunder and whose ultimate sanction is murder, to paralyse the House of Commons and to hand Ireland over to social and financial ruin.'[4]

As propaganda this article, and the two sequels of 10 and 14 March, fell lamentably flat. Consisting as they largely did of a rehash of old speeches and stale newspaper reports, they attracted little attention from anyone and none at all from Parnell. But on the morning of 18 April, the day on which the crucial vote on the second reading of the Criminal Law Amendment Bill was to be taken, *The Times* exploded a bombshell of far higher calibre. Announcing to an astounded public that it possessed documentary evidence 'which has a most serious bearing on the Parnell conspiracy', it broke all its own journalistic precedents by publishing in large facsimile on an inner page what purported to be a letter from Parnell to an unnamed correspondent, dated 15 May 1882, and apologizing for having been obliged, as an act of policy, publicly to condemn the Phoenix Park murders. The body of the letter was clearly not in Parnell's hand (it was later alleged to be in that of his secretary), and his contribution appeared to be limited to the words 'Yours very truly', followed by his signature.[5]

At this point, and for a clearer understanding of the later development of the affair, it is necessary to introduce some new evidence. It has been known since the publication of the relevant volume of *The History of The Times* in 1947 that the original intention was to publish the facsimile letter on 27 January 1887, to coincide with the opening of parliament. This plan miscarried because on the

[4] *The Times*, 7 Mar. 1887.
[5] *The Times*, 18 Apr. 1887.

previous day the eminent lawyer, Sir Henry James, not only gave an unfavourable opinion as to the authenticity, and therefore the effectiveness, of *The Times*'s letters (it ultimately possessed no fewer than eighteen), but revealed that he himself had seen them previously, even mentioning a Dublin journalist, Richard Pigott, as having been concerned in procuring them.[6] What has not previously been known (though often surmised) is that *The Times* notified at least one member of the government, W. H. Smith, First Lord of the Treasury and Leader of the House of Commons, that it had incriminating documents and proposed to use them. On 27 January, the manager of the paper, J. C. Macdonald, wrote to Smith explaining that 'a curious disclosure' at the consultation with Sir Henry James the previous evening 'compelled us at the last moment to postpone the announcement intended to be made this morning'. James, he explained, had pronounced that the letters were inadequate to sustain the case put forward. 'I still feel firmly convinced,' he added, 'that they are perfectly genuine documents and that much may be done to strengthen the weak points in them as evidence available in a court of justice. But more time is indispensable for this and meanwhile we must be silent.'[7]

Furthermore, it is clear from two letters in the archives of *The Times*, written by the Home Secretary, Henry Matthews, probably to Macdonald, that in strengthening 'the weak points', the paper was able to call upon official assistance. First, on 14 February 1887 Matthews supplied *The Times* with certain information about the personnel of the Land League and about where the League's accounts had been kept. 'This', he wrote, 'is all I have gathered as yet in answer to your enquiries. I am expecting further information, which I will communicate to you.' His letter ended with an offer to help in deciding upon the genuineness of the letters if copies could be supplied to him. In his second communication, two months later, Matthews conveyed the welcome news that the Irish Attorney-General had promised to write to the Irish Prison Board to prepare the authorities there for a call from *The Times*'s solicitor, Joseph Soames, for the purpose of inspecting the visiting-books at Kilmainham prison, whence Parnell was presumed to have smuggled out one of the most incriminating letters.[8]

[6] John Walter to J. A. Macdonald, 27 Jan. 1887 (Printing House Square Papers); *The History of The Times, 1884–1912* (London, 1947), p. 48.
[7] J. A. Macdonald to W. H. Smith, 27 Jan. 1887, photostat copy (Printing House Square Papers). So far as can be ascertained the original of this letter has not survived in the papers of W. H. Smith (Hambleden Papers).
[8] Henry Matthews to 'My dear Sir' (if not Macdonald, then probably either John Walter (the proprietor) or George Buckle (the editor)), 14 Feb. and 12 Apr. 1887 (Printing House Square Papers).

The fact that the government was thus early involved with *The Times* in an effort to discredit its political opponents was of course hidden from the general public which had only the disclosures of 'Parnellism and Crime' to go by and which found the facsimile letter of 18 April a shattering revelation. Unionists everywhere were triumphant, Liberals were confused and dismayed, nationalists waited anxiously for their leader to repudiate the letter. Late that night (or rather at 1 o'clock next morning) Parnell did denounce it as 'a villainous and barefaced forgery', but his development of the theme, in a House of Commons which heard him in deep silence, was not impressive. His first thought, he said, had been that a blank sheet with his signature must have fallen into unauthorized hands, but as soon as he saw the facsimile he realized that it was 'an audacious and unblushing fabrication'. ' My writing, its whole character', he explained, 'is entirely different. I unfortunately write a very cramped hand . . . It is in fact a labour and a toil to me to write anything at all. But the signature in question is written by a ready penman who has evidently covered as many leagues of letter paper in his life as I have yards.'[9]

For Parnell's denials to have carried complete conviction he ought, so many people thought, at once to have sued *The Times* for libel. He contemplated doing so, but he seems initially to have been persuaded by his Liberal allies—chiefly by John Morley—that this would be unwise. The ostensible ground for such advice was that an action tried before a London jury would be hazardous, since an unprejudiced hearing could not be guaranteed. It would of course have been open to Parnell to take his action in Dublin, but there too, as Morley did not fail to point out, the argument of prejudice would have applied, though in the opposite direction.[10] There are, however, indications that this advice was not entirely disinterested. Word reached Parnell's vice-chairman, Justin McCarthy, through the Liberal editor of *The Star*, Professor J. Stuart, M.P., that the Liberals were deeply divided. Gladstone, it seems, thought Parnell should ask for a select committee of the House to investigate the charges, but Lord Herschell (perhaps the most formidable Liberal lawyer) dissuaded him and was backed by the Liberal Chief Whip, Arnold Morley. Stuart's own view was revealing. He thought Parnell should not go to law because of the risk that a severe cross-examination might turn up past episodes from which damaging inferences could be drawn. Since the Liberals when in power had themselves freely castigated Parnell

[9] Hansard, H. C. deb., 3rd ser., cccxxviii, cols 1225–32 (18 Apr. 1887).
[10] J. Morley, *The Life of William Ewart Gladstone* (London, 1911 edn.), iii, p. 297 [hereafter cited as *Gladstone*].

between 1880 and 1882, using language not markedly different from that now employed by *The Times*, it was understandable that in 1887 they should shrink from a too close investigation either of their present ally or of what they had formerly said about him.[11]

It seemed, then, as if *The Times* and its readers would have to make do with Parnell's original denunciation of the facsimile letter. Meanwhile, the Criminal Law Amendment Bill proceeded laboriously through committee, its passage orchestrated by fresh instalments of 'Parnellism and Crime' from *The Times*. These, though also at first ignored by Parnell, introduced two new elements into the situation. One was the fact (not, obviously, made public at the time) that the second series of articles, 'Behind the Scenes in America', which sought to establish a connection between the Irish parliamentary leaders and the Irish-American revolutionaries, was written by Robert (later Sir Robert) Anderson, who since 1867 had been adviser to the Home Office in matters relating to Irish political crime and who in 1888 was to be promoted to be head of the Criminal Investigation Department. His employment by *The Times*—with official permission, he later insisted—was a further indication that what outwardly appeared to be a journalistic venture had much wider and more serious ramifications.[12]

The other new development was that a former Irish member, F. H. O'Donnell, believing himself libelled by this second series, brought an action against *The Times*. When the case came on in July 1888 his suit ignominiously collapsed, but only after counsel for *The Times* had seized the opportunity not merely to expand the original charges, but also to introduce fresh evidence, including a number of incriminating letters allegedly written by Parnell and by Patrick Egan, the ex-Treasurer of the Land League.[13] The fact that *The Times* was represented in this action by Sir Richard Webster, the Attorney-General, was not necessarily sinister, since it was then still possible for law officers of the Crown to carry on their private practice simultaneously, but although Webster himself always maintained stoutly that at that time he knew nothing outside his brief, his appearance on behalf of *The Times* could not but suggest an official interest in the proceedings.[14]

[11] J. McCarthy and R. M. Praed, *Our Book of Memories* (London, 1912), pp. 102–3.
[12] R. A. Anderson, *The Lighter Side of my Official Life* (London, 1910), pp. 31–32, 111, 283–86; he disclosed his authorship in an article in *Blackwood's Magazine*, April 1910. For a discussion of his role, see L. Ó Broinn, *The Prime Informer* (London, 1971), chap. 10.
[13] The action is fully reported in *The Times*, 3, 4, 5 and 6 July 1888.
[14] Viscount Alverstone (Sir Richard Webster), *Recollections of Bar and Bench* (London, 1914), p. 143.

This dramatic enlargement of the scope of the charges left
Parnell with no option but to repeat and amplify his denunciation
of all the letters attributed to him. On the day after the O'Donnell
trial had concluded he gave the House of Commons a detailed
analysis of the letters—'in his most frigid manner', as John Morley
observed—and ended with this general comment. 'The great majority of them are palpable forgeries—most undoubted forgeries;
they bear the mark of forgery on their very face. The context of
most of these letters is perfectly absurd. In order to attach any
credence to them you must suppose that I deliberately put myself
in the power of men who had halters round their necks and . . .
that I put myself in the position of being accessory before or after
the fact.'[15] Since there were in fact many on the benches facing
him who were quite ready to suppose this, or worse, Parnell resolved
to ask for a select committee of the House 'to inquire and report as
to the authenticity of the letters affecting Members of this House
read by the Attorney-General at the trial "O'Donnell v Walter and
another" '.[16] His first instinct had been to revert to his original
notion of suing *The Times* himself; this, indeed, he later did in a
Scottish court, but at that critical moment he was once more
strongly influenced by Morley, who repeated with emphasis the
old arguments about the danger of cross-examination.[17] Morley's
own innate caution was doubtless reinforced by a letter he received
from Sir William Harcourt at that very moment.

> If [Harcourt wrote] P. brought an action, and it extended (as
> it must) over the whole ground he would be in the same position
> in point of principle (though of course in a less degree) as
> O'Donnell. He would lead *The Times* in defending itself to
> involve a number of other persons . . . indeed the whole of the
> Land League who would be attacked and have no means of
> defending themselves.
>
> Indeed it is impossible to see how this could be avoided except
> by making any one implicated by *The Times* plaintiffs in the
> suit. *Quod est absurdum.*[18]

These substantial objections to a libel suit did not necessarily
apply to an inquiry by select committee, though such an inquiry
held a different danger, that since a majority of the members of the

[15] Hansard, H. C. deb., 3rd ser., cccxxviii, cols 575–81 (6 July 1888); Morley,
Gladstone, iii, p. 299.
[16] Hansard, *loc. cit.*, cols 712–13, 1101–2 (9 and 12 July 1888).
[17] Morley, *Gladstone,* iii, p. 298.
[18] Sir William Harcourt to John Morley, 6 July 1888 (Harcourt Papers,
Box II/B, 1–4).

committee would be opponents of Home Rule, its findings might be affected by political considerations. But to Parnell, who was now becoming obsessed by the need to clear his name, this was a risk well worth taking. On 9 July he arrived at the House of Commons in, for him, an unusually excited frame of mind, intent upon demanding a select committee. John Morley met him in the lobby and urged him, with specious arguments, to hold back—the new batch of letters contained some obvious forgeries which discredited *The Times*'s case, public opinion was no longer much moved by the affair, the government would almost certainly refuse a select committee and what advantage could there be in demanding something which he knew beforehand would be declined?[19] The effect of such arguments on a man of Parnell's temperament was entirely predictable. Although convinced, as he told Justin McCarthy, 'between his set teeth', that 'the whole opposition bench' was against him, he responded instinctively to McCarthy's advice not to trust his personal honour to the hands of any Englishmen and resolve to press for his select committee.[20]

Not until 12 July did he get an anwer to his request. He was then met with an uncompromising refusal from the Leader of the House, W. H. Smith, who reiterated the view held, he said, by ministers since the previous year, that the proper course for individuals feeling themselves aggrieved was to seek redress in the courts. However, instead of a select committee he offered a commission to be appointed by special act of parliament and consisting wholly or mainly of judges 'to inquire into the allegations made against certain Members of Parliament by the defendants in the recent action of "O'Donnell *v* Walter and another" '.[21] Five days later the terms of the inquiry—which already went far beyond the letters of which Parnell complained—were drastically widened by the insertion of the words 'and other persons' after 'certain Members of Parliament'.[22]

Behind this offer lay a curious history. The previous year, just after the facsimile letter had appeared, two Unionist backbenchers had conceived the idea of summoning the editor of *The Times* to the bar of the House for breach of privilege in publishing an article charging an Irish M.P., John Dillon, with telling a deliberate untruth when he himself, in a speech in the House, had accused *The Times* of falsehood. The confused notion behind this clumsy device

[19] Morley, *Gladstone*, iii, p. 299.
[20] Justin McCarthy to Mrs Campbell Praed, 9 July 1888 (McCarthy and Praed, *Our Book of Memories*, pp. 157–58).
[21] Hansard, H. C. deb., 3rd ser., cccxxviii, cols 1101–2 (12 July 1888).
[22] *Ibid.*, cols 1495–1501 (17 July 1888).

had apparently been the hope that the editor of *The Times*, thus summoned, would defend himself with further revelations about Parnell and his party. When the law officers advised that the article was *not* a breach of privilege, some members of the cabinet, to escape from an embarrassing situation, were prepared there and then to accept an opposition motion for a select committee. They were dissuaded by the Solicitor-General, Sir Edward Clarke, who pointed out to them in no uncertain terms that a select committee would be met at every turn by the editor's refusal to divulge the names of his contributors and informants, that each such refusal would have to be treated as a fresh breach of privilege and that in no time at all the work of the entire session would be disrupted.[23] The episode bordered on farce, but the arguments of 1887 against a select committee remained equally valid in ministers' eyes when Parnell asked for one in 1888. Lord George Hamilton, one of those who had to listen to Sir Edward Clarke's homily, may not have been far wide of the mark when he wrote long afterwards that 'if it had not been for this clumsy and uncalled for interference by two private members in a matter which they did not understand, I do not think the government would have been compelled next year to set up the Parnell Commission'.[24]

Nevertheless, though ministers were set against a select committee, this did not mean that they embraced the alternative of a special commission with any marked enthusiasm. On the contrary, the surviving evidence suggests that they accepted it only under strong extraneous pressure. The pressure, on his own admission, came from Joseph Chamberlain. Writing on 10 July 1888 to the lady who was shortly to become his third wife, Chamberlain explained that his first impulse had been to associate the other leading Liberal Unionist, Lord Hartington, with his manœuvre. 'As usual, I could not make any impression, but then I went to the government and saw W. H. Smith and the Attorney-General. They were much more ready to listen, and I hope and believe that they will (to the great confusion of Mr Parnell and his friends) declare their intention to appoint a Royal Commission . . . I am convinced that this Commission will elicit some astounding facts and if the result

[23] Sir Edward Clarke, *The Story of my Life* (London, 1918), pp. 267–68; Viscount Chilston, *W. H. Smith* (London, 1965), p. 250. There were also, as Lord Randolph Churchill was quick to point out, good constitutional grounds, backed by the authority of Sir T. Erskine May, for arguing that matters which might or should come within the cognizance of the courts of law were not suited to inquiry by select committee; W. S. Churchill, *Lord Randolph Churchill* (London, 2nd edn., 1907), pp. 757–58.

[24] Lord George Hamilton, *Parliamentary Reminiscences and Reflections, 1886–1906* (London, 1916–22), i, pp. 72–74.

is to show that more than one member of the so-called nationalist party has been dabbling in assassination the effect would be prodigious.' A few days later he was able to report in a further letter to his fiancée (17 July) that he had just been talking to Lord Salisbury and had found 'that the government is inclined to take my view and press for the Commission in any case, and whether Mr Parnell accepts it or not . . .'[25]

Chamberlain's motives in intervening become clear enough when we remember that it was the Irish question which had separated him from the main bulk of the Liberal party, that the recent failure of the Round Table Conference with his former Liberal colleagues condemned him to an indefinite term in the political wilderness unless he could make himself useful to the Conservatives, and that he had at his elbow his henchman, Captain W. H. O'Shea, the husband of Parnell's mistress and by this time —whether for that or other reasons—the implacable enemy of Parnell.[26] Yet all this does not fully explain why the government responded as it did to Chamberlain's pressure, even though both the Solicitor-General and the Attorney-General were clearly uneasy about using judges in this way.[27] The answer is no doubt partly the one given by both the law officers, that since Parnell refused to go into court, and since there was strong feeling on both sides of the House that the charges ought to be investigated, the logic of the situation dictated that—a select committee being ruled out for the reasons given earlier—some kind of commission was the only alternative.

If, however, we inquire further as to why some kind of commission became the particular kind of commission the government offered Parnell the reason is to be found not in the realm of legal nicety but in the dust and heat of the political arena. Evidence of the final stages whereby ministers reached their grave decision to enlarge the scope of the inquiry (and thus, arguably, to diminish the importance of the letters should they turn out to be forgeries) is conspicuous by an absence which may not be entirely accidental, but it is clear from the debates in the House of Commons and from

[25] J. L. Garvin, *The Life of Joseph Chamberlain* (London, 1933), ii, pp. 386, 387.

[26] For the motivation of what he calls 'the Chamberlain-O'Shea combination', see H. Harrison, *Parnell, Joseph Chamberlain and Mr Garvin* (London, 1938), chap. 10. The omission from the official history of *The Times* of any reference to Chamberlain led Mr Harrison to draw attention to this and other deficiencies in the account there given, as a result of which *The Times* eventually made honourable amends (*The History of The Times, 1921–1948* (London, 1952), pp. 1145–48; also H. Harrison, *Parnell, Joseph Chamberlain and The Times* (Dublin and Belfast, 1953). [27] Clarke, *The Story of My Life*, p. 274.

other contemporary reactions that the view was widespread that the government had succumbed to the temptation to use its parliamentary majority to create a commission, which, though it might be conducted under impeccably legal procedure, would in effect be what Randolph Churchill called it, 'a revolutionary tribunal for the trial of political offenders'. 'It is not for the government', Lord Randolph insisted, 'in matters of this kind, to initiate extra-contitutional proceedings and methods . . . The fate of the Union', he warned, 'may be determined by the abnormal proceedings of an abnormal tribunal. Prudent politicians would hesitate to go out of their way to play such high stakes as these.'[28]

Since Churchill himself was hardly the most prudent of politicians, ministers were little disposed to listen to Satan rebuking sin. Certainly, W. H. Smith's conduct of the debate in the House of Commons showed an indifference to the effect he was creating which bordered on recklessness. On 16 July he moved to introduce the Members of Parliament (Charges and Allegations) Bill, commonly called the Special Commission Bill, before it had even been printed or before those whom it most affected had any idea of what it contained. A more monstrous proposition, said Parnell, pale with fury, was never made by a minister in Smith's position. 'He, as First Lord of the Treasury, the constitutional representative in this house of a great party, of the government, and of the nation, comes and says to me, this Bill Sykes, "It is for the honourable member to say whether he will take this Bill or not" . . . and he says I am to accept this tribunal without knowing the names of the judges . . or whether their number is to be three, five or seven'.[29]

Inevitably, the ensuing debate was extremely bitter, but it was also largely unreal, partly because it was clear that the government was determined to force the bill through (making ruthless use of the closure in committee for that purpose), but also because it was scarcely less clear that the critics of the commission were divided. They could agree, indeed, on certain points—for example, in trying to pin the government down to specific charges when it was evidently bent on a grand inquisition, in crucifying the Attorney-General for his Jekyll and Hyde role as counsel for *The Times* and law officer for the Crown, or in extracting from the reluctant and embarrassed W. H. Smith an admission that the proprietor of *The*

[28] W. S. Churchill, *Lord Randolph Churchill*, pp. 757–60, citing a memorandum which the author calls 'perhaps the most powerful document he ever penned'; for other contemporary reactions, see Curtis, *Coercion and Conciliation in Ireland*, pp. 280–81.

[29] Hansard, H. C. deb., 3rd ser., cccxxviii, cols 1495–1501 (16 July 1888); Morley, *Gladstone*, iii, p. 301.

Times had visited him, as 'an old friend', while the bill was in preparation.[30] But on the fundamental question of whether or not the bill should be resisted *à l'outrance* there was no common ground even among the Liberals. Sir William Harcourt and John Morley were both for forcing a division on the first and second readings and Harcourt's attack on the Attorney-General was ferocious even by his standards. 'You say', he thundered, 'that this tribunal are [*sic*] not to be bound by technical rules. Is it a technical rule that a man should not know whether he is charged and what he is charged with? Why, that is the fundamental essence, and the first conception of justice; and to have the right hon. gentleman the Home Secretary and the Law Officers of the Crown disparaging that which is the first principle of justice, and denouncing it as a technical rule, is one of the most shocking things I have witnessed in this House. Nothing would shock you; for we know very well that you are racing for blood. What we protest against is that any man, even an Irish Member, should be called upon to plead to a sort of hotchpotch, miscellaneous slander.'[31] The decision, of course, rested with Parnell and he was so set upon proving the letters to be forgeries that he opted for accepting the commission with all its disadvantages. Since Gladstone also accepted it (though with reservations) there was little the Liberals could do but stand aside.[32]

In fact, this suited them well enough. Until the commission either demonstrated or disproved Parnell's involvement with crime, it was common sense not to stress the alliance with him. Harcourt, while writing flippantly to Morley that it would save time and trouble if Smith and Parnell could settle the matter by personal combat 'à là Boulanger', impressed upon Gladstone the more serious point that they must at all costs avoid entering into an arrangement with the government as to the actual appointment of the judges. 'It would make us parties and partners in a concern with which we ought to have nothing to do, besides I do not see how we could act in such a matter without the co-operation of Parnell and to do that seems to me open to every possible objection. I see no safe course for us except to stand aloof altogether and to accept no responsibility in the matter.'[33]

[30] Hansard, H. C. deb., 3rd ser. cccxxix, cols 245–56 and 379–94 (23 and 24 July 1888 respectively); A. G. Gardiner, *The Life of Sir William Harcourt* (London, 1923), ii, p. 71; Chilston, *W. H. Smith*, pp. 280–81.

[31] Hansard, H. C. deb., 3rd ser. cccxxix, cols 364–74 (24 July 1888).

[32] Morley, *Gladstone*, iii, pp. 301–2.

[33] Sir William Harcourt to John Morley, 15 July 1888 (Harcourt Papers, Box IIB/1–4); Sir William Harcourt to W. E. Gladstone, 18 [July] 1888 (British Museum, Add. MS. 44,201, fos. 210–11).

Morley was even more emphatic. Irritated by the fact that Parnell, in the teeth of the best legal advice, still hankered after a libel action against *The Times*, he urged Gladstone to leave the commission severely alone.[34] Gladstone agreed, though feeling that a debt to public justice would be paid if someone less responsible were to place the unsavoury details on record—'so unjust to Parnell and so disgraceful to the government, and to parliament'.[35] But Morley had so little sympathy to spare for the Irish leader that he advised even against contributing to a defence fund for Parnell in a letter which more than any other document sums up the damage the government's action had done to the Liberal-nationalist alliance. Arguing that a subscription would not be popular among Liberals 'until they are more completely satisfied that Parnell's hands are clean', he continued. 'Would not a bad impression be likely if we take action which will look like hurrying to assume P's innocence, before the case has been heard? Parnell at present has no sort of claim on us. He has brought on the whole of this evil business, by his steady disregard of our advice.'[36]

If the Liberals were thus in disarray, the government were in scarcely better shape. True, they had got their special commission and in October 1888 the three appointed judges would begin their inquiry, which, ministers might hope, would churn up enough mud to compensate for the possible deficiencies of the hotly controverted letters. But two major problems loomed ahead. The first was whether or not the Attorney-General ought to represent *The Times* before the commission and so repeat his Jekyll and Hyde performance. Webster himself was very clear that he should not, and wrote both to the Solicitor-General and to Smith arguing agitatedly against his involvement.[37] Smith was inclined to let him off, but Salisbury, to whom he sent a copy of Webster's plea, was made of sterner stuff. By a curious chance, Sir Henry James, second counsel for *The Times*, was staying with the prime minister in France when Webster's letter arrived. James, as we have seen, had long had his doubts about *The Times*'s letters. It is not known whether or not he confided these doubts to Salisbury, but we do know from his irate host that he argued, like Webster, that he would be more use in the House of Commons than in court. Salisbury was equally disgusted by them both. 'The simultaneous refusal of these two men

[34] John Morley to W. E. Gladstone, 10 Aug. 1888 (British Museum, Add. MS. 44,255, fos. 252–55).
[35] W. E. Gladstone to John Morley (copy), 11 Aug. 1888 (*ibid.*, fos. 256–59).
[36] John Morley to W. E. Gladstone, 24 Aug. 1888 (*ibid.*, fos. 264–65).
[37] Sir R. Webster to W. H. Smith, n.d. [Aug. 1888], cited in Curtis, *Coercion and Conciliation in Ireland*, p. 281; Clarke, *The Story of My Life*, pp. 274–75.

to go on', he wrote to Smith, 'will have the worst possible effect. There will be no persuading the outside world that they have not run away from the case because on scrutinizing the evidence they satisfied themselves that the case was bad.'[38] He urged them, there-fore, to stand their ground and although Webster continued for some time to protest that the commission was very different from the O'Donnell case and that it would be said that 'the Government have been conducting the prosecution and no amount of argument will satisfy the public of the contrary', he and James eventually yielded to Salisbury's inexorable pressure.[39]

The second problem confronting ministers was how far they should go in assisting *The Times* to make its case. As Arthur Balfour put it to his uncle: 'It is clearly legitimate for us to make what investigations we please with a view to coming at the truth: but ought we, or ought we not, to communicate the results of our investigations (if any) to *The Times*? If we do not, it may get wasted—if we do shall we not find ourselves in a somewhat embarrassing position?'[40] Salisbury replied, predictably, that while each case should be decided on its merits, if evidence which would fix someone's guilt had come 'naturally' into the government's hands, then 'we shall be fulfilling an obvious and elementary duty in facilitating the proof of it before the commission.'[41]

That term 'naturally' was, however, interpreted with a certain elasticity. It included making available to *The Times*'s solicitors the criminal files of the Irish administration; the interrogation of convicted prisoners; the dispatch to London as witnesses of numerous police constables, district inspectors and magistrates; the testimony in open court of the spy, Henri Le Caron, who had penetrated the inner circle of the American Clan-na-Gael and whose evidence (marshalled by the same Robert Anderson who had used Le Caron's material to write the second series of 'Parnellism and Crime' articles) was deemed so important that Le Caron's cover was 'blown' and he himself put in jeopardy of his life; finally, the full-time employment with official sanction of a former police officer and acting Resident Magistrate, W. H. Joyce, to prepare documents and witnesses on behalf of *The Times*.[42]

[38] L. P. Curtis, *Coercion and Conciliation in Ireland*, p. 282.
[39] Sir R. Webster to Lord Salisbury, 7 Sept. 1888 (Salisbury Papers); Viscount Alverstone, *Recollections of Bar and Bench*, pp. 144–45.
[40] A. J. Balfour to Lord Salisbury, 17 Aug. 1888 (Salisbury Papers).
[41] Lord Salisbury to A. J. Balfour, 22 Aug. 1888, cited in Curtis, *Coercion and Conciliation in Ireland*, p. 284.
[42] These various devices are well summarized in T. W. Moody, (*The Times* versus Parnell and Co., 1887–90), pp. 159–65. Much (though by no means all) of this evidence of government involvement depends on documents collected by Joyce, of which only copies of some remain, and on a memorandum written

All this helped to swell the volume of evidence ponderously deployed by the Attorney-General and it helps to explain why, although the incriminating letters were what had first moved Parnell to action, these were only reached on the fiftieth day of the commission's sitting. When that day at last arrived there then unfolded one of the great set-pieces of Victorian legal history, so famous in its detail and its outcome as to need no retelling here. Briefly, between 14 and 22 February 1889, the court and the world heard from *The Times*'s representatives how they had purchased the letters from E. C. Houston, secretary of the Irish Loyal and Patriotic Union, with totally inadequate precautions to establish their authenticity; from Houston how, with similar gullibility, he had bought them from Richard Pigott, a disreputable Dublin journalist whose other attainments included blackmail and pornography; and, at last, from Pigott himself, in a confession written after he had been exposed in merciless cross-examination by Sir Charles Russell, how he had forged the letters.[43] Pigott's collapse, followed by his flight from London and his suicide in Madrid to escape arrest, was the turning-point in the case. Another year, indeed, was to elapse before the commission issued its report, and that report was to find Parnell and his associates, though innocent of the graver charges of criminal conspiracy against them, guilty of certain others, mainly of 'intimidation' (boycotting) and of alliance with the physical-force party in America. But this was neither unexpected nor novel and Parnell had the effective last word when he observed sedately, 'it is just about what I would have said myself.'[44]

by him in 1910 when he was a disappointed and embittered man (N.L.I. MS 11, 119); these materials form the basis of Ó Broinn, *The Prime Informer*. For the interacting roles of Anderson and Le Caron, see H. Le Caron, *Twenty-five Years in the Secret Service* (9th ed., London, 1893), pp. 60 *et seq*; R. A. Anderson, *Sidelights on the Home Rule Movement*, chap. 15, and *The Lighter Side of my Official Life* (London, 1910), *passim*. The government's resolve to help *The Times* is dealt with in L. P. Curtis, *Coercion and Conciliation in Ireland*, pp. 284–91. A hitherto unpublished letter from Balfour to the Home Secretary (in the J. S. Sandars Papers, Bodleian Library, Oxford), with the request that he would ask Anderson to co-operate with Joyce on all relevant matters is further evidence in the same direction (A. J. Balfour to Henry Matthews, 24 Mar. 1889).

[43] The key event in these transactions—Pigott's ordeal in the witness-box— is documented in *Special Commission Act, 1888, reprint of the short-hand notes of the speeches, proceedings and evidence taken before the commissioners appointed under the above act* (hereafter cited as *Spec. Comm. Proc.*), v, pp. 443–576 (20–22 Feb. 1889).

[44] R. B. O'Brien, *The Life of Charles Stewart Parnell* (2nd edn., London, 1899), ii, p. 233. The judges' findings are in *Report of the Special Commission, 1888* [C 5891], H. C. 1890, xxvii, pp. 477–640.

'An age is the reversal of an age.' The propagandist enterprise upon which *The Times* had so blithely embarked in 1887 had in effect been taken over by the government when, rejecting Parnell's request for a select committee, it had offered him instead the wide-ranging special commission. The battle which was then fought out in court and parliament was essentially a battle for the high ground of public opinion. While the issue was in doubt it was still possible for honest Conservatives and Liberal Unionists to stifle their mis-givings about the means, in contemplation of the exalted end they had in view—to preserve the Empire against a violent and foreign-dominated conspiracy. But with the discrediting of Pigott the deadly allegations inspired by the letters rebounded upon their authors. The Liberals exulted and when Parnell first appeared in the House after the Pigott fiasco Gladstone led them in a standing ovation; Parnell, who knew his Englishmen almost as much as he hated them, totally ignored their plaudits and thus mounted still higher in their esteem. Even those who were normally sceptical about the Liberal-nationalist alliance succumbed, if briefly, to the prevailing hysteria. Thus Harcourt, attending the Eighty Club dinner of March 1889, where Parnell sat down in amity with Lord Spencer, Lord Lieutenant when the Phoenix Park murders had been committed, was moved to report to Gladstone that this was 'a striking event and will have a great effect on the public mind . . . There need now be no further difficulty in the public recognition of our *solidarité* with Parnell in the interest of Home Rule. Co-operation with him was always necessary and it is now authentically avowed. In future they will fling the taunt of "Parnellite" against us in vain'.[45] Parnell for his part reciprocated by stressing then and subsequently the moderation of the Irish demand and by displaying repeatedly the political conservatism towards which, indeed, he had been evolving since 1882.[46]

As for *The Times*-Unionist combination, it was in utter con-fusion. *The Times* itself cringed before Parnell and was glad enough to settle his libel suit by paying him £5,000. This, however, was a mere trifle compared with the total cost of the proceedings, estimated at over £200,000.[47] A piteous plea to the government for financial assistance was rejected as 'impossible and impolitic' and 'The Thunderer' of Printing House Square remained for many years crippled in resources and diminished in reputation.[48] The

[45] Sir W. Harcourt to W. E. Gladstone, 9 Mar. 1889 (British Museum, Add. MS. 44, 201, fos. 216–19), *The Times*, 9 Mar. 1889.

[46] F. S. L. Lyons, 'The Political Ideas of Parnell', in *Historical Journal*, xvi, 4 (1973), pp. 749–75.

[47] *The History of The Times, 1884–1912*, p. 89.

[48] *Ibid.*, p. 89; Curtis, *Coercion and Conciliation in Ireland*, p. 297.

government itself was, if anything, even more deeply embarrassed. Salisbury, it is true, maintained an outward calm, dismissing the Liberal rejoicing as premature and remarking, with a perspicuity events were soon to justify, that 'the fact that a man has forged your signature is not proof that you are possessed of every statesmanlike quality and every personal virtue'.[49] Nevertheless, there remained the thorny problem of how to handle the commission's report when it was finally presented in February 1890. After much wrangling the cabinet decided simply to move a resolution accepting it and thanking the judges for their 'just and impartial' conduct. This led to an intensely bitter debate and although an eloquent amendment by Gladstone demanding justice for the Parnellites was defeated, there were fourteen Unionist abstentions and ministers had to run the gauntlet of a terrible indictment by Randolph Churchill. 'What,' he asked, in a voice hoarse with passion, 'has been the result of this uprootal of constitutional practice? What has been the one result? Pigott! a man, a thing, a reptile, a monster—Pigott!—the bloody, rotten, ghastly foetus—Pigott! Pigott! Pigott!'[50]

Of course, in a longer perspective, we can see that Pigott was not the sole, nor even perhaps the chief, outcome of the strange history of 'Parnellism and Crime'. Three subsequent developments may be traced from these tangled events. First, as a recent historian has convincingly argued, the shock of the crisis so unhinged die-hard conservatism as to make it perceptibly easier for Arthur Balfour as Chief Secretary for Ireland to win sanction for the constructive Irish policies he at once initiated.[51] Secondly, whereas up to the summer of 1888 by-election victories had followed a normal pattern, with the opposition making steady, but not spectacular, headway, henceforward what contemporaries soon learned to call 'the flowing tide' set strongly in favour of the Liberals. Between the special commission and the general election of 1892 Unionists lost some fifteen seats while registering only one gain; their majority, 118 in 1886, had dropped by 1892 to 66.[52] Not all of this, of course, was a consequence of the Pigott fiasco, but some of it undoubtedly was.

Finally, and most important, the triumphant issue of the commission had induced among both Liberals and nationalists a euphoria which was natural but quite unjustified. Hypnotized by Pigott, men easily forgot that the state of Ireland remained highly

---

[49] Speech at Watford, 19 Mar. 1889 (*The Times*, 20 Mar. 1889).

[50] Hansard, H. C. deb., 3rd ser. cccxlii, cols 511–16 (11 Mar. 1890). For this extraordinary outburst, see W. S. Churchill, *Lord Randolph Churchill*, pp. 761–72, 876–79.

[51] Curtis, *Coercion and Conciliation in Ireland*, p. 300.

[52] *Ibid.*, p. 301.

volatile. Worse still, they were encouraged to place Parnell upon a pedestal for which neither his public nor his private life exactly fitted him. Thus, when he himself testified before the commission in April–May 1889, few observers really understood how thin was the ice over which he so serenely skated, and they failed altogether to grasp the feature of his evidence which most strikes the historian —that he was so extraordinarily vague about crucial names and dates and facts that it is only possible to conclude either that he was being deliberately disingenuous, or that he was the fortunate possessor of the most defective memory in the public life of his day.[53]

This was easily overlooked at the time and it did not disturb the most fatal legacy of his victory, which was to foster the legend of his invincibility. When, therefore, Captain O'Shea cited him as co-respondent in the divorce proceedings he instituted against his wife in December 1889, there was a tendency amongst even those who might have known better—stimulated, it must be said, by Parnell's own cryptic utterances—to assume that this too was a plot on the same lines, and perhaps set in motion by some of the same hands, as *The Times*'s attack.[54] Thence it was but a step to argue that the new threat would meet the same fate and that O'Shea would go the way of Pigott. In reality, so totally different were the circumstances that Parnell proved far more vulnerable in the divorce-court than he had ever been before the commission. And thus the avalanche, arrested after Pigott's collapse, began to move again, slowly at first, then with gathering pace, towards the final disaster.

University of Kent at Canterbury.

[53] *Spec. Comm. Proc.*, vii, pp. 1–369, especially pp. 55–110.
[54] F. S. L. Lyons, *The Fall of Parnell, 1890–91* (London, 1960), chap. 2.

THE THEORY AND PRACTICE OF CENSORSHIP IN SIXTEENTH-CENTURY ENGLAND

By D. M. Loades, M.A., Ph.D., F.R.Hist.S.

READ AT THE SOCIETY'S CONFERENCE
18 SEPTEMBER 1973

A student of the sixteenth century is always tempted to represent his period as being one of unprecedented change and new departures. In the case of my present subject the temptation is particularly strong, because printing was a new invention, and the technical problems and opportunities which it presented to governments were also new. Nevertheless it would be most misleading to begin a discussion of Tudor censorship with Sir Thomas More's restrictive proclamation of 1530, or even with the introduction of printing to England in 1476. The concept of society, and of the duties and responsibilities of government, which censorship was to reflect was deeply rooted in the past, and was not fundamentally challenged until the puritan revolution of the seventeenth century.

The image used was that of an organism. Society was a 'body politic', each of whose members existed in a fore-ordained and permanent relationship with the rest. This situation expressed the will of God, and its preservation represented that *pax terrena* which St Augustine had described as the highest achievement of temporal government. To sow discord in society—to set one member against another or any member against the head—was thus not merely a crime but an offence against God. This ideal of harmony, and of unquestioning acquiescence in the will of the ruler and the *status quo*, enjoyed universal currency largely because the attainment fell so far short of the aspiration. All medieval societies were in process of being slowly won from narrow allegiances to wider, from violence to litigation, and from self-help to dependence upon public authority. In this process the concept of the 'body politic' was both an inspiration and a help. Tudor England was still in the throes of this development when the controversial policies of Henry VIII and his children added a new emphasis to the traditional insistence upon the solemn duty of obedience. It would hardly be an exaggeration to say that the whole success of their revolt against the papacy depended upon their ability to persuade their subjects to accept this adaptation of the ancient theory. Tudor propaganda derived much of its effect from deep-rooted fears of lawlessness and strife which owed little to the immediate issues of controversy. The official attitude was well expressed by the Lord Keeper, Sir Nicholas Bacon, in 1567:

> It is given to the Queen's Majesty to understand that divers her subjects by their evil dispositions do sow and spread abroad divers seditious errors and rumours to the derogation and dishonour first of Almighty God in the state of religion established by the laws of this realm, and also to the dishonour of her highness in disproving her lawful right to supremacy amongst her subjects. And this that they do is not done secretly or by stealth, but openly avouched . . . as for example by bringing in and spreading abroad divers seditious books and libels from beyond the seas . . . if such disorders be not redressed by law, then must force and violence reform . . . then you well know that law is put to silence and cannot be executed which should only maintain good order. . . .[1]

Censorship was thus an inevitable consequence, not only of an insecure regime but also of the responsibility which had rested upon the monarchy time out of mind to protect society from its own disruptive instincts, and to defend the people of God against the wily onslaughts of the devil in whatever form he was then supposed to appear.

> bringing in of these books and seditious libels [Bacon continued] maketh mens minds to be at variance one with another, and diversity of minds maketh seditions, seditions bring in tumults, tumults make insurrections and rebellions, insurrections make depopulations and bring in utter ruin and destruction of mens bodies, goods and lands.

The roots of censorship lay far back in the Middle Ages, in two separate but related codes. On the one hand, the law of the church forbade the teaching of heretical doctrine, and in England this law had been reinforced by the early fifteenth-century statutes against Lollardy. In 1408 Convocation had prohibited the reproduction of English translations of the scriptures, unless such translation was specifically authorized, and in 1414 Parliament had confirmed the legal right of ecclesiastical officials to proceed against the makers and writers of heretical books.[2] On the other hand

---

[1] Public Record Office, State Papers Domestic, Elizabeth, vol. 4, no. 52.
[2] D. Wilkins, *Concilia* (London, 1737), iii, p. 317: 2 Henry V, 1, c. 7.

stood the law of treason, and that small group of statutes sometimes collectively known as *Scandalum Magnatum*. Open abuse of the king, whether in speech or writing, was an ancient offence and could be construed as treason under the Act of 1352. For example in 1450 a certain William Dalton of Ipswich was indicted for declaring 'that he would that our sovereign lord the king . . . were as cold at his heart root as the stone under his foot be so we had another king that could better rule this land. . . .'[3] Similarly, defamation of the king's officers and of the 'great men of the realm' was already an offence before the first Statute of Westminster in 1275. The thirty-fourth chapter of that statute provided that anyone who should 'tell or publish any false news or tales whereby discord or occasion of discord or slander may grow between the king and his people, or the great men of the realm . . .' should be imprisoned 'until he hath brought him into the court which was the first deviser of the tale'.[4] It thus became an offence to spread or repeat such gossip as well as to originate it. Two statutes of Richard II repeated the substance of this chapter, adding only that the spreaders of tales whose devisers could not be found were to be punished at the discretion of the Council.[5] These acts remained the basis of the law until the legislation of the Reformation parliament, and were confirmed by statute as late as 1555, when the government of Mary was faced with a fresh upsurge of criticism and hostile comment.[6]

How often this law was invoked we do not know, but the connection between agitation and action was real enough. In 1450 rumours that the court was planning a ferocious revenge for the death of the duke of Suffolk helped to launch the rebellion of Jack Cade. Twenty years later Sir Robert Welles confessed that the Lincolnshire rising of 1470 'was grounded upon this noise raised among the people that the king was coming down with a great power into (the county) where the king's judges should sit and hang and draw great numbers of the commons'—a rumour which Sir Robert himself seems to have invented for the purpose.[7] Recent research has also shown that similar 'tales' played an important part in launching the Pilgrimage of Grace and the Wyatt rebellion of 1554.[8] In the latter year the Council, alarmed by the rising tide

[3] Public Record Office, King's Bench Plea Rolls, KB27/760, r. Rex 3.

[4] 3 Edward I c. 34; *Statutes of the Realm* (London, 1810–28), i, p. 35.

[5] 2 Richard II st. 1 c. 5: 12 Richard II c. 11.

[6] 1 and 2 Philip and Mary c. 3.

[7] 'Chronicle of the rebellion in Lincolnshire, 1470', ed. J. G. Nichols, *Camden Miscellany*, i (London, 1847), p. 22.

[8] M. E. James, 'The Lincolnshire rebellion of 1536', *Past and Present*, 48 (1970), pp. 1–70; D. M. Loades, *Two Tudor Conspiracies* (Cambridge, 1965).

of disaffection, wrote around to the justices of the peace, urging them to renewed efforts because 'vain prophecies and untrue bruits (are) the very foundation of all rebellion'.[9] Recent studies have tended to show that the connection between words and deeds in the mid-sixteenth century was less immediate than many contemporaries feared, and probably less immediate than it had been in the previous century, but it was close enough for alarm and corresponding precautions to be justified. 'In our country', wrote Sir John Mason in 1554, '. . . talking is preparatory to a doing.'[10]

Seditious talk was both a symptom and a cause of disaffection, and was a constant preoccupation of Tudor governments particularly after the royal supremacy had subordinated ecclesiastical jurisdiction to the Crown. The law expanded and became very much more precise. It became treason to call Henry VIII 'schismatic' or 'heretic' as well as 'tyrant', or to reject his various rearrangements of the succession. It became treason to pray that Queen Mary's heart might be turned from Popery, or to call Elizabeth 'bastard' or 'usurper'. Where we have only isolated examples of proceedings against offenders before 1530, after that date we have plentiful material for a study of the law and its enforcement.[11] However, the basis upon which the law rested did not change. Cromwell and Cecil were more diligent and effective administrators than their predecessors, and could use lay and ecclesiastical officials interchangeably, but their reasons for punishing the authors and spreaders of 'lewd and seditious tales' would have been perfectly comprehensible to the framers of the Statute of Westminster.

Censorship was the extension of this principle to the expression of similar sentiments in writing or in print. Consequently the three methods of communication were frequently linked together. A typical example is a statute of 1563 'against fond and fantastical prophecies', which stood in the direct tradition of *Scandalum Magnatum*. This prohibited the 'publishing and setting forth' of such prophecies concerning the queen 'and other noble persons' by 'writing, printing, singing or other open speech or word'.[12] The

---

[9] British Museum, Cotton MSS, Titus B 11, f. 104.

[10] *Calendar of State Papers, Foreign, Edward VI and Mary* (London, 1861), ii, p. 119.

[11] See particularly G. R. Elton, *Policy and Police* (Cambridge, 1972), concerning the activities of Cromwell and his agents.

[12] 5 Elizabeth c. 15. Another interesting case is that of William Oldenall, tried in King's Bench in 1557 for declaring, 'That the Queen's Majesty was baseborn, and that in St Paul's Churchyard a twopenny book might be had which would prove his saying to be true'. Public Record Office, KB27/1184 r. Rex. 12d.

author of a seditious writing, like the originator of a seditious rumour, might, if caught, be proceeded against for misdemeanour, felony or treason according to the seriousness of the offence. Possessors and distributors of such writings, like the spreaders of rumours, normally stood in danger only of the lesser penalties. But, of course, writings were tangible objects, and printed books and pamphlets went through a sophisticated process of production. So although the principles behind censorship and the suppression of seditious speech were the same, and the laws extremely similar, the techniques of enforcement naturally differed.

Printing was first and foremost a business—a group of crafts by which men maintained themselves and their families. This undoubtedly assisted the process of censorship, but it also brought into existence a complex structure of ordinary trade control similar to that which regulated the production of woollen cloth, pins, or any other manufacture.[13] Consequently there were almost from the beginning two distinct but overlapping systems of regulation, and this fact has to some extent confused the study of government attitudes towards the press. For the half-century after its introduction into England, printing was treated simply as a new and ingenious form of manufacture. Edward IV and Henry VII both patronized printers, and the latter appointed the first Royal Stationer.[14] The main bone of contention was the early domination of the trade by aliens, a domination which was expressly permitted by a statute of 1484 which gave aliens full freedom to practise the craft. This freedom was systematically attacked and undermined by the London Stationers, and a series of statutes in 1515, 1523, 1529 and 1534 whittled away and finally abolished the privileges of the foreign printers. The form of all these Acts, even the last, strongly suggests that they were trade measures in which the government was yielding to the demands of the Stationers, rather than security measures initiated by the Crown.

The monopolistic position of the Stationers was strongly consolidated in 1557 by the grant of a royal charter to the Company, and for the remainder of the century the Wardens operated their own licensing system. As we shall see, this was closely related to government censorship, but it was by no means identical with it. Nor was the Crown's direct concern with the press always of a restrictive nature. The continuous sequence of Royal Printers had begun in 1503,[15] and in 1544 Henry VIII had granted the first

[13] H. S. Bennett, *English Books and Readers, 1475–1557* (Cambridge, 1952).
[14] Peter Actors, 'Stationer to the King' from 1485.
[15] The first man to take that title was William Faques. The Royal Printers were the official agents of government propaganda.

patent monopoly, to Grafton and Whitchurch for the printing of service books. Royal patronage of this kind was naturally regarded with suspicion by the Stationers, and the Company tried extremely hard to persuade Elizabeth to give up the granting of patents which diminished its own control. The major part of the correspondence and litigation connected with printing and book-selling in the second half of the sixteenth century relates to the enforcement of the Stationers' own licensing system, or to quarrels between privileged and unprivileged printers. The most celebrated such case is that between the Company and John Wolfe, which provoked a petition from the Wardens to the Privy Council in 1583, and dragged on in Star Chamber for several years before being resolved by compromise. Wolfe's protest touched the prerogative because he challenged the granting of patent monopolies, but there was never any suggestion that the content of his work was seditious.[16]

There would have been a Stationers' Company with exclusive policies, a licensing system and a great deal of litigation even if the Tudors had never evinced any serious interest in the propaganda functions of printing—just as it would have been an offence to write seditious or heretical words had the art of printing never been invented.

Nevertheless, the development of the press did present both church and state with a security problem of unprecedented dimensions. John Foxe put his finger upon the point very accurately when he contrasted the effectiveness of protestant teaching in his own day with the earlier impact of Wycliffe and Huss:

> ... although through might be stopped the mouth of John Huss ... God hath opened the press to preach, whose voice the Pope is never able to stop with all the puissance of his triple crown....[17]

In England the first awareness of this danger dawned with the appearance of early Lutheran tracts, and of Tyndale's English New Testament in the mid-1520s. The ecclesiastical machinery, which had dealt so effectively with Lollard writings in the previous century, was soon seen to be hopelessly inadequate in this new situation. In 1524 Cuthbert Tunstall, the bishop of London, issued the first regulations which recognized the distinctive importance of the new medium. No books were to be imported without episcopal permission, and no new works were to be printed without licence from the same authority. The effect of these orders seems

[16] W. W. Greg, *A Companion to Arber* (Oxford, 1967), pp. 28–29: Public Record Office, State Papers Domestic, Elizabeth, vol. 15 nos. 38–40.

[17] J. Foxe, *Acts and Monuments*, ed. G. Townsend (London, 1844), iii, p. 720.

to have been negligible, and it was not until Sir Thomas More as Lord Chancellor entered the fray in 1530 that any effective action could be taken. A royal proclamation of that year 'for the resisting and withstanding of most damnable heresies sown within this land by the disciples of Luther . . .' condemned fourteen named books and ordered that those possessing them should give them up to the ordinary.[18]

This proclamation did not add anything to the existing law, provide any extra administrative machinery, or decree any secular penalties, but it did mark the first attempt by the Crown to limit and control the production and circulation of books. With More's energy behind it, it also resulted in a period of close co-operation between royal and ecclesiastical officials, which produced a number of arrests during 1531. In December of that year Richard Bayfield, one of the apprehended traffickers, was burnt for heresy.[19] After this, events moved rapidly, and in the crisis of his 'great matter' Henry's concern over the expression of criticism and opposition reached a new level of sensitivity. It cannot be my concern here to deal with the positive side of government propaganda, but this was the period in which Thomas Cromwell enlisted the services of scholars, publicists and printers on a grand scale to defend and explain the king's proceedings. It was also a period in which prosecutions for treasonable and seditious words reached a new level of intensity and effectiveness.[20] By the first Act of Succession it became high treason to 'do or procure to be done by act or deed or word written or printed, anything to the prejudice of the king, against his marriage with Queen Anne. . . .' Also in January 1536 a new proclamation denounced

. . . divers and sundry writings and books, as well imprinted as other in which such writings and books many open and manifest errors and slanders are contained, not only in derogation and diminution of the dignity and authority royal of the king's majesty and of his Imperial Crown, but also directly and expressly against the good and laudable statutes of this realm. . . .[21]

Such works were to be given up within forty days, not to the ordinary but to the Lord Chancellor or Thomas Cromwell. *Scandalum*

---

[18] P. L. Hughes and J. F. Larkin, *Tudor Royal Proclamations*, i (New Haven, Conn., 1964), pp. 181–86: for the date, see Elton, *Policy and Police*, p. 218 n. 5.
[19] D. M. Loades, 'The Press under the Early Tudors', *Transactions of the Cambridge Bibliographical Society*, iv, i (1964) p. 32.
[20] Elton, *Policy and Police*.
[21] *Tudor Royal Proclamations*, i, pp. 235–37.

Magnatum as well as heresy had now brought the printers into
the forefront of controversy.

In spite of this, there was as yet no system of royal licensing.
The phrase 'cum privilegio regali' which appears in a number of
variants in the colophons of numerous works printed from 1518
onwards seems to have signified a form of copyright rather than
an *imprimatur*.[22] Such privileges could be granted by authorities
other than the king, for example the chancellors of the universities,
and were the predecessors of the patents of monopoly which began
to appear in the 1540s. It was not until 1538 that the old system
of episcopal licences was superseded. In November of that year an
important proclamation 'for expelling and avoiding the occasion
of . . . errors and seditious opinions by reason of books imprinted
in the English tongue' laid down fresh regulations for the trade.[23]
No English books were to be imported without the king's special
licence, on pain of imprisonment during pleasure and forfeiture
of goods; and no English book was to be printed within the realm
unless licensed by members of the Privy Council or others
appointed, on pain of imprisonment and fine at the king's discretion. Every duly licensed book was to contain the full effect
of the licence 'plainly declared and expressed in the English tongue'.
Although the bishops retained certain functions, the main burden
of inspection and control had now been assumed by the Crown,
which already bore the burden of punishing breaches in the existing laws.

Thomas Cromwell's campaign against sedition in the 1530s enjoyed, as we know, a considerable measure of success, but seditious
printing was one of his lesser problems. The government brought
off a notable *coup* in confiscating all seven hundred copies of *The
Nun's Book* before they could be distributed, but references to
publishing or distributing undesirable books are few among the
surviving records and punishments. Prevention was better than
cure, and it was no doubt the need to systematize prevention which
led to the introduction of royal licensing. The system seems to
have had some effect. The Council acted against offending or
suspect printers on a number of occasions, and in the early 1540s
clandestine publications began to appear. These were books which
can be shown on typographical evidence to have been printed in

[22] F. S. Siebert, *The Freedom of the Press in England, 1476–1776* (Urbana,
Ill., 1965), pp. 35–36.
[23] *Tudor Royal Proclamations*, i, pp 270–76. It is clear from the original
draft of this proclamation, amended in the king's hand, that many of the
important changes introduced were Henry's own ideas. Elton, *Policy and
Police*, p. 256 n. 1.

England, but which bore colophons ascribing them to Leipzig or Wessel.[24] An underground press was the natural consequence of more stringent official oversight. In 1543 the government intensified its pressure. For the first time specific penalties for unlicensed printing appeared upon the Statute book.

> . . . if any printer, bookbinder, bookseller, or any other persons or persons . . . print or cause to be printed, or utter, sell, give or deliver withint this realm or elsewhere within the king's dominions of any of the books or writings before abolished or prohibited . . .

the offender was to be imprisoned for three months and fined £10 for each book.[25] If he repeated the offence a second time he was liable to forfeiture of goods and perpetual imprisonment. These penalties could be inflicted irrespective of the content of the books concerned, and quite independently of any other penalties which might have been incurred by their authors. This statute therefore clearly marks a new stage in the development of royal policy, a stage perhaps necessitated by the growth of clandestine publishing or perhaps by a decline in the efficiency of less formal conciliar methods after Cromwell's death.

The death of Henry himself in 1547 brought about a relaxation of the treason laws, and a sharp increase in all forms of religious controversy. Somerset and Cranmer, moving cautiously towards a protestant establishment, found themselves caught between two fires. The latter, like other protestant divines, was inclined to see 'truth' as possessing an irresistible persuasive force. By allowing Reformed ideas a much greater liberty of expression, he seems to have hoped to bring about a rapid and peaceful conversion of the country. If such was his hope, it was speedily disappointed, and within a few weeks he found himself denounced with equal vigour by radicals who were disappointed with his caution and conservatives who were disgusted with his heresy. To such traditionalists as Shephen Gardiner, protestantism was the religion of 'liberty', and liberty was the solvent of the whole social order. Damage the fabric of reverence and obedience in one place, he argued, and the whole structure was in danger. '. . . by his reasoning', he wrote in an attack on William Turner, '. . . it were idolatry for the servant to make courtesy to his master, wherein he should bow the knee, or the goodman to kiss his wife; but to kneel and kiss his superior's hand

[24] *Transactions of the Cambridge Bibliographical Society*, iv, i, p. 33 and n.
[25] 34/35 Henry VIII c. 1.

were by him foul and filthy abomination. ...'[26] 'O devilish liberty', wrote the similarly minded Miles Huggarde, 'I would to God Germany might have kept thee still. ...'[27]

Such arguments carried considerable weight and the English protestant leaders shared their opponents' belief in the need for uniformity. In the late 1540s they had had no experience in the formulation of policy, and soon became alarmed and disillusioned by the outburst of preaching and pamphleteering which greeted their early leniency. 'I never saw so little discipline as is nowadays,' lamented Hugh Latimer in 1549, and he was soon preaching that '. . . the wicked preachers . . . the gainsayers' must 'have their mouths stopped'.[28] Consequently the protestant establishment which was set up between 1549 and 1553 was no more tolerant of dissenting opinions than the regime of Henry VIII. It was, however, rather less successful in making its will effective. This was partly because of the inevitable difficulties attendant upon a royal minority, partly because of dissensions within the Council, and partly because impatient radicals like Hooper were valuable allies in combating the immense, if somewhat inert, weight of conservatism. The law was not changed during the reign of Edward VI, and the proclamations for its enforcement did not bring about any significant developments. On 13 August 1549, the sole licensing authority of the Council was reiterated, this aspect of its work being placed in the hands of 'Mr Secretary Peter, Mr Secretary Smith and Mr Cicill, or the one of them. ...'[29] A further proclamation of 1551 concerning the control of imported books, and of plays and interludes, spoke more generally of '. . . writing signed with his Majesty's most gracious hand, or the hands of six of his said Privy Council'.[30] Such evidence as we have for the effectiveness of this control comes mostly from the records of the Council, and is not extensive. A small number of printers and others were interrogated and bound by recognizances not to offend again. In March 1551 William Seth was arrested on a charge of importing popish books, and his examination gives an illuminating glimpse of what was clearly a well-organized smuggling business.[31] At least one London printer, Robert Caly, fled abroad during this period and played a part in producing English catholic propaganda; but the major challenge seems to have come from a great

[26] Gardiner's tract against William Turner; *The Letters of Stephen Gardiner*, ed. J. A. Muller (Cambridge, 1933), p. 480.
[27] Miles Huggarde, *The Displaying of the Protestants* (London, 1556), f. 114ᵛ.
[28] Hugh Latimer, *Sermons*, ed. G. E. Corrie (Parker Society, 1844), p. 132.
[29] *Acts of the Privy Council*, ed. J. Dasent (London, 1890–1907), ii, p. 312.
[30] *Tudor Royal Proclamations*, i, pp. 514–18.
[31] *Historical Manuscripts Commission, Hatfield*, i, pp. 83–84.

increase in the home production of ballads, broadsides and other ephemera, and in this direction the government's censorship efforts very largely failed.

The advent of the catholic Mary in 1553 led to a further aggravation of the problem. From the beginning the printers and stationers of London seem to have included a disproportionate number of protestant sympathizers, and protestant propaganda had a *panache* and an edge lacking in the writings of conservatives. The queen's first reaction was to see the large output of heretical literature simply in terms of gratifying a demand for novelty and scurrility. Her initial proclamation on religious matters denounced the

> printing of false fond books, ballads, rhymes and other lewd treatises in the English tongue concerning doctrine now in question and controversy . . . which books, ballads, rhymes, and treatises are chiefly by the printers and stationers set out to sale to her graces subjects of an evil zeal for lucre and covetousness of vile gain.[32]

The same proclamation also made reference to 'her grace's special licence in writing', but gave no indication as to how this licence was to be bestowed, and threatened simply 'due punishment' according to the order of the existing law for those who should fail to obtain it. It is not clear how Mary's licensing system worked at any stage of her reign. Perhaps the power remained vested in the Privy Council, but more probably it was returned to the church, particularly after Cardinal Pole took up his legatine responsibilities in England at the end of 1554. Significantly, we know very much more about the government's attempts to suppress heretical and seditious literature already in circulation than we do about any system of search and prevention.

It is not my purpose here to discuss the propaganda campaign against Mary. Its general features are sufficiently familiar. Large quantities of protestant polemic, exhortation and spiritual guidance were printed in such places as Strasbourg, Basle and Emden, and smuggled into the country by numbers of bold and determined men and women. Within England, clandestine presses produced some similar works, and also ballads, broadsheets and books of a more frankly political and subversive nature, such as *The copy of a letter sent by John Bradford*, which was a violent and libellous attack upon Philip.[33] Against this attack the government defended itself for the most part by traditional means, proclamations and

---

[32] *Tudor Royal Proclamations*, ii (New Haven and London, 1969), pp. 5–6.
[33] For the consideration of this work see my note in the *Transactions of the Cambridge Bibliographical Society*, iii, ii (1960), pp. 155–60.

Council letters urging officials to do their duty and enforce the law. The law itself was also twice extended. In January 1555 it became a felony to publish slanders against the king and queen which could not be construed as treason, the penalty being the loss of the right hand. Another statute of the same session also made it treason to preach or write against King Philip's title, or to conspire his death by such means.[34] In June of 1555 an index of prohibited authors was proclaimed, and towards the end of the reign, in June 1558, martial law was extended to cover the possession of any heretical or treasonable book, wherever published.[35]

Enforcement, as usual, fell far short of intention. In spite of the revived jurisdiction of the church, special royal commissions were set up 'to inquire concerning all heresies, heretical and seditious books . . . [within a given area] with power to seize all such books and writings . . .', but they do not seem to have been very effective.[36] Fewer than twenty individuals are on record as having been proceeded against for offences of this kind, and the majority of those escaped any serious penalty. John Day, swiftly detected and apprehended in October 1554, escaped from custody and got away to the Continent. Of the six men arrested in March 1557 for producing a number of clandestine books, three were eventually released upon recognizances of £40, one was indicted and almost immediately pardoned, and the other two disappear from the records.[37] William Rydall, William Copland, John Kingston and Thomas Marsh were all censured by the Council, although no worse penalties seem to have been imposed.[38] Probably there were prosecutions at the assizes, which cannot now be traced, but on the surviving evidence the discrepancy between the anxiety displayed and the level of effective action is very marked.

It is against this background that the incorporation of the Stationers' Company in March 1557 should be seen. The Company already had a long history but the grant of a royal charter increased its prestige, and gave it the right, and power, to defend its own monopolistic interests. These interests could readily be made to serve the policy of the Crown. When the Master and Wardens of the newly chartered company were given the right to search out and destroy books which infringed their own regulations, they were also empowered to '. . . make search in any place, shop or

---

[34] 1 and 2 Philip and Mary c. 3: 1 and 2 Philip and Mary c. 10.

[35] *Tudor Royal Proclamations*, ii, p. 90.

[36] *Calendar of the Patent Rolls, Philip and Mary* (London, 1936–39), iii, p. 24.

[37] *Transactions of the Cambridge Bibliographical Society*, iv, i, p. 44.

[38] *Ibid.*, p. 45. All these men were established printers and among the original 97 members of the Chartered company.

building of any printer, binder or seller of books printed contrary
to statute or proclamation, and . . . seize or burn the same'.[39] Thereafter, it is clear that the government depended heavily upon the
co-operation of the Company in controlling subversive publication.
The Wardens were concerned to protect the interests of their
members, and their licensing system overlapped that of the Crown
without being dependent upon it. It was not until after the Star
Chamber decree of 1586 that a record of the government licence
normally accompanied the registration of a new work in the Company's own records.

The well-documented and complex Elizabethan system was thus
built upon a substantial foundation of practical experience, as
well as upon a more general basis of accepted political and social
theory. There is neither space nor need for me here to discuss the
progressive elaboration of those treason laws with which the government protected itself against catholic intrigue and ideology. The
vast majority of those who fell foul of the government for writing,
printing, importing or distributing seditious books did so in the
service of the catholic church. Men like William Carter and Richard
Verstegan were persistent and courageous, and kept the Council in
a perpetual state of anxiety. Indeed the catholics were well served
by their press, which never wholly succumbed to official pressure,
and it was not the fault of its literary agents that the Roman church
failed to recover England for the Counter Reformation. At the
opposite extreme, although upon a much smaller scale, the government also suffered intermittent anxiety about puritan attacks upon
the queen's management of the church. 'Papists and precisians have
one mark to shoot at', wrote Parker in 1573, 'plain disobedience';
and Cecil, who was sympathetic to their cause, observed that 'to
think it a burden of conscience to observe the orders and rites of
the church established by law (is) a matter pernicious to the state
of Government'.[40]

Consequently penalties were inflicted upon the protagonists of
both sides at all levels, from fining and imprisonment to mutila-
tion and death. Against catholic sympathizers and censorship laws
operated mainly at the lower level. William Carter was one of very
few whose treason consisted principally of clandestine printing.[41]
Against some puritans however, such as Stubbs and Penry, seditious

---

[39] *Cal. Pat. Rolls, Philip and Mary*, iii, p. 480.
[40] British Museum, Cotton MSS, Titus B II, f. 249; quoted by Conyers
Read, *Queen Elizabeth and Lord Burghley* (London, 1960), p. 117.
[41] Carter was a persistent offender, but the government had some difficulty
in securing his conviction; Siebert, *The Freedom of the Press in England*,
pp. 89–90.

writing was the only charge. The latter was convicted and hanged for felony in 1593 for writing an open letter to the queen, part of which ran:

> Therefore, Madam, you are not so much an adversary unto us poor men as unto Christ Jesus and the wealth of his kingdom. But, Madam, this much we must needs say. That in all likelihood if the days of your sister Queen Mary and her persecution had continued to this day, that the church of God in England had been far more flourishing than at this day it is.[42]

If his share in the Marprelate publications played any part in persuading the authorities to act against him, it did not appear at his trial.

It is understandable in the circumstances that such 'derogation of the Queen's authority' should be taken seriously, but on the whole the government seems to have been reluctant to take extreme measures. In his explanation for the necessity of censorship laws in 1567, Bacon justified the sharp application of lesser penalties on just these grounds:

> ... when execution thereof ... by touching half a dozen offenders may sufficiently warn half a hundred, I think those laws nor the execution of them may justly be called extreme. . . .[43]

moreover '[when] by whipping a man may escape hanging . . . it were better to be twice whipped than once hanged. . . .' As in the 1530s, it was clearly recognized that prevention was better than cure and Cecil, like Cromwell, was a master in the management of positive propaganda. He was forced, however, by technical developments to excel his predecessor in his painstaking supervision of the press. The Royal Injunctions of 1559 made comprehensive provision for licensing:

> '. . . because there is great abuse in the printers of books, which for covetousness chiefly regard not what they print so they may have gain. . . .'[44]

Licences could be granted by the queen herself, six of her Privy Council, the two archbishops and the bishop who was ordinary of the place of publication, or by any two of them, provided that the ordinary was one. At the same time, to prevent the publication of

---

[42] Public Record Office, King's Bench Plea Rolls, KB27/1325 r. Rex 3.
[43] Public Record Office, State Papers, Domestic, Elizabeth, vol. 44 no. 52.
[44] *Visitation Articles and Injunctions*, ed. W. H. Frere and W. P. M. Kennedy (Alcuin Club, London, 1910), iii, p. 24.

pamphlets, plays or ballads, 'heretical, seditious or unseemly for Christian ears', such works must be licensed by three members of the newly-established ecclesiastical commission. The same commissioners were also made responsible for overseeing all other matters concerning the printing or importation of books, '. . . to which her Majesty straightly commandeth all manner her subjects, and especially the Wardens and Company of Stationers, to be obedient.'[45] These regulations were supplemented in 1566 by a Council decree laying down a scale of penalties for unlicensed printing (irrespective of content), which involved exclusion from the trade, fines and imprisonment. Twenty years later the whole system was drastically simplified by a well-known Star Chamber edict which placed all licensing (except that of law books) in the hands of the archbishop of Canterbury and the bishop of London;[46] and in the closing years of the century those perpetual gadflies the actors and players of interludes were curbed by the evolution of a subsidiary licensing system operated by the Lord Chamberlain and his assistant the Master of the Revels.[47]

The enforcement of these regulations lay first and foremost in the hands of the Stationers' Company, and its registers provide the best evidence for the working of the system.[48] The Company organized weekly searches, and the Court of Assistants destroyed illicit books, defaced illegal type, fined, excluded and occasionally imprisoned offending printers on its own authority. Co-operation with the ecclesiastical commissioners was close, if not always enthusiastic. In 1582 the Company complained of the charges which it had undergone through searching for and suppressing popish books by warrant of the Commission.[49] The commissioners never seem to have hesitated to issue instructions to the Wardens, and these were almost invariably obeyed. From 1588 onwards the licensing function of the archbishop of Canterbury and the bishop of London was regularly delegated to a group of deputies, and the names of these men constantly appear authenticating licences in the Stationers' Register. By the end of the century the appointment of Master Printers was tightly controlled by High Commission,[50]

---

[45] *Ibid.*, p. 25.

[46] Public Record Office, State Papers Domestic, Elizabeth, vol. 190, no. 48.

[47] E. M. Albright, *Dramatic Publication in England, 1580–1640* (New York, 1927).

[48] *A Transcript of the Registers of the Stationers' Company, 1554–1640*, ed. E. Arber (London and Birmingham, 1875–94).

[49] British Museum, Lansdowne MSS, 48/83 f. 195; Greg, *A Companion to Arber*, p. 91.

[50] This was also laid down in the Star Chamber decree of 1586. Siebert, *The Freedom of the Press in England*, p. 70.

and it is probable that that court dealt with a proportion of the more serious offences against the licensing laws.

The part played by Star Chamber is rather less clear. It certainly handled patent and privilege cases, and concerned itself with the issuing of regulations, but does not seem to have dealt with penal offences. In 1593 the pursuivant Richard Topcliffe sent what he described as 'a lewd traiterous book' to Lord Keeper Puckering, commenting that he did not know how soon there might be proceedings 'in Star Chamber or elsewhere',[51] but the jurisdiction of Star Chamber did not extend to treason, and major disciplinary cases seem to have been dealt with exclusively by the courts of Common law. A systematic search of the assize records would probably reveal many such cases. It is well known that John Udall was so handled, and glimpses can be caught of proceedings against more obscure men, such as Robert Sutton of Aylsham, indicted at the Norfolk assizes in 1584 for distributing and defending a book containing the words 'not to be with the pope is to be with Anti-Christ'.[52] It may well be that the bulk of those who disappear from the records after imprisonment and interrogation by the Council were committed to the assizes, but for the moment their fate remains unknown.

The council, of course, bore the overall responsibility for enforcement, and it might use other agents than the Stationers or the Ecclesiastical Commission. Outside London the Lord Lieutenant or justices; inside London the Lord Mayor, as when the latter acted in 1568 to arrest the author of a pamphlet against the duke of Alva. Occasionally the Council even acted directly, as it did in 1570 to suppress William Elderton's ballad *Dr Story's stumbling into England*.

The impression created by a study of Elizabethan censorship is one of great assiduity and relative effectiveness. Techniques of suppression had kept pace with the techniques of sedition, and it is hard to imagine any sixteenth-century government doing better. Yet it was, in an important sense, a barren achievement. With its emphasis upon uniformity and strict repression of criticism, official thinking had not advanced beyond the Lollard laws, and *Scandalum Magnatum*. At the same time political and social developments had created a much more stable and governable community than that which the Tudors had won in 1485. Censorship had played its part in helping to bring this about, but by 1600 the time had come for a more mature and discriminating philosophy, which could take account of informed criticism and comment. When this

---

[51] Public Record Office, State Papers, Domestic, Elizabeth, vol. 244, no. 4.
[52] *Ibid.*, vol. 170, no. 48.

did not happen, the whole concept of the 'body politic' began to seem an oppressive mechanism, and the next generation of critics was driven to seek an alternative image of society. It found it in the puritan 'ship of state', which implied a very different theory of the role of the subject in government.[53]

University of Durham.

[53] For a full examination of the implications of this image, see M. Walzer, *The Revolution of the Saints* (London, 1966).

THE PROGRESSIVE MOVEMENT
IN ENGLAND

By P. F. Clarke, M.A., Ph.D., F.R.Hist.S.

READ 19 OCTOBER 1973

ON the centenary of the birth of C. P. Scott, the political outlook of the *Manchester Guardian* under his editorship was explained thus: 'He, and those who wrote under him, thought always in terms of what he called "the progressive movement". What was important was that those who were agreed on reforming measures should work together to secure them.'[1] In its use of the rather imprecise label 'progressive', in its conception of a reform movement wider than strict party boundaries, in its distinctive flowering in the press—in all these respects the progressive movement of early twentieth-century America gives us some notion of what Scott had in mind. And indeed American historiography can, I believe, suggest valuable lines of analysis which have not been fully applied in England. Perhaps the most obvious would entail giving closer attention to the intellectuals and publicists and asking more searching questions about their role in politics. A few years ago the late Charles Mowat pointed to the broadly similar problems in social policy which Britain and the United States faced at this time; and he commented on how, despite these similarities, the history of social reform in the United States had been written with due attention to the history of ideas: in Britain, by contrast, almost exclusively in terms of political and administrative history.[2] It would not, perhaps, be fair to extend Mowat's observation by saying that in England we purposely write history with the ideas left out.

   Though the title of my paper was intended to prompt some consideration of the more familiar American application of the term, the progressive movement in England should not be regarded as a mere analogue of the American example. Whether the frequent

---

[1] *C. P. Scott, 1846–1932. The Making of the 'Manchester Guardian'* (London, 1946), p. 236 (probably by J. L. Hammond). In this paper I have restricted references to a bare minimum. I am very grateful to Dr J. A. Thompson for his criticism of an earlier draft; and my indebtedness to Mr Stefan Collini, for advising me in general, and in particular for bringing his understanding of L. T. Hobhouse to my aid, surpasses all reasonable limits.

[2] C. L. Mowat, 'Social legislation in Britain and the United States in the early twentieth century: a problem in the history of ideas', *Historical Studies*, vii (1969), pp. 81–82.

British use of the label progressive in the years immediately before
the Great War was stimulated by awareness of the rival progressive
claims of Theodore Roosevelt and Woodrow Wilson is unclear.
The traffic in ideas between England and America, however, was
fully reciprocal. The progressive movement in England in fact came
first. When a new journal, the *Progressive Review*, was established
in London in 1896 it was much concerned, in its internationalist
way, with surveys of 'The Progressive Movement Abroad', and hope-
fully forced William Jennings Bryan's campaign for the presidency
on to this procrustean bed.[3] It is ironic, in view of the later fortunes
of the usage on different sides of the Atlantic, that when the self-
styled English progressives looked for an American progressive
movement they had to invent one.

Who were these men who called themselves progressives? There
is inevitably some difficulty in separating out a special from a more
generalized usage. Belief in progress was a nineteenth-century
Liberal axiom. But by the 1890s men who were not Liberals—the
Webbs for example—could happily be subsumed as progressives.
What seemed important at that time was to emphasize that not all
Liberals were progressive in this sense.

The *Progressive Review* clearly represents one striking appro-
priation of the word. William Clarke, the editor, was a Fabian
Essayist and a journalist on the Liberal *Daily Chronicle*. His
chief collaborators were the Liberal Imperialist Herbert Samuel;
Ramsay MacDonald, then a new recruit to the Independent
Labour Party; the heretical economist J. A. Hobson; and the young
Liberal aristocrat Charles Trevelyan. They saw their review as the
mouthpiece of scientific reformers who were not hidebound by
traditional Liberalism. The Liberal party had done its work. The
Benthamite philosophy and the Manchester economics which had
once given it a theoretical basis were obsolete. Since it seemed
impossible that the party should change its spots, 'we can recognize
no force in the claim of the Liberals to be regarded as the progressive party of the future.'[4] In the field of practical politics, the
progressive usage can probably be traced back to the establishment
of the London County Council in 1889. The Liberal and Conservative parties as such did not contest the council elections; so
the party lines that inevitably emerged were drawn between thinly-
disguised Conservatives who sat as Moderates and thinly-disguised
Liberals who sat as the Reform or Progressist party. Progressists
soon became Progressives.

    [3] See *Progressive Review*, i (1896–97), pp. 75–77.
    [4] *Ibid.*, p. 4; and see Bernard Porter, *Critics of Empire. British Radical
attitudes to colonialism in Africa 1895–1914* (London, 1968), pp. 164–67.

The general currency of the progressive idea owed much to this example. For the L.C.C. Progressives were identified with a definite scheme of municipal socialism. It was this well-publicized programme which prompted Salisbury in 1894 to throw the full weight of the Conservative party against the Progressives, describing the council as 'the place where Collectivist and socialistic experiments are tried.'[5] Now this is to over-rate the novelty of the L.C.C. schemes. Municipal enterprise in London at this time was really rather unremarkable when compared with what had already been undertaken in provincial cities like Birmingham and Manchester. It certainly did not need the Fabians to spearhead the advance, and all recent historians of the Fabian Society unite in deprecating the claim that Sidney Webb inspired the London Progressive Programme. It was London's very backwardness which gave the Progressives their chance. The political capital which they extorted from the situation, however, is the real point; and the fact that both Liberals and Labour men stood under the Progressive banner significantly extended the connotations of the term.

The use of progressive to describe a working alliance between Liberals and Labour brings us to the prevalent Edwardian usage. This paper is not concerned with assessing progressive politics in respect of electoral performance or political influence. But nor does it claim that the full significance of the progressive movement lies in the supposedly advanced political proposals made by a number of journalists, academics, and other professional men. It is the way that their ideas defined the intellectuals' relationship with organized labour which is the crux of the matter; and their view of this relationship forms our central theme.

The problem of how to attract working-class support had been central to the Liberal party's political survival since at least the time of the Second Reform Act. At that time Liberal intellectuals like John Morley had positively welcomed a new kind of division in politics between, as he saw it, 'brains and numbers on the one side, and wealth, rank, vested interest, possession in short, on the other'.[6] For men like Morley, in the Benthamite tradition, the general problem was that of reconciling democracy with the premium on knowledge: of securing some reverence for ideas (and by extension for their begetters) in a democratic scheme of things where numbers would carry the day. One problem was, in effect, to persuade the working man to acquiesce in face of the existing

[5] Quoted in A. G. Gardiner, *John Benn and the Progressive Movement* (London, 1925), p. 212.
[6] D. A. Hamer, *John Morley. Liberal intellectual in politics* (Oxford, 1968), p. 71.

distribution of wealth. For this task no one was better fitted than
Mr Gladstone. The great achievement of Gladstonian populism
was to run a democratic party by keeping class issues out of
politics. Liberal politics characteristically focused on issues of
foreign affairs and other concerns remote from the lives of ordinary
people; yet it was to their judgment on matters like these that
Gladstone made his moral appeals.

The socialist revival of the 1880s and 1890s was an assertion
of a rival conception of politics. On a spectrum running from
Marxism to social reform, there was a common repudiation of
laisser-faire as the guiding precept for the state: indeed socialism
was often used to mean little more than this. This elastic use of
the concept of socialism was paralleled by a more flexible development of the language of Liberalism, which must be attributed to
T. H. Green. Green had recast social ethics so as to make the
criterion of the common good paramount; and in so doing he had
shown that the Gladstonian appeal to conscience could be applied
in an Idealist sense to social and economic problems. How far
Green himself had envisaged a new Liberal agenda of social reform
is doubtful. His writings here are ambivalent.[7] But by making
ethical considerations central he taught a new generation of
Liberals that fatalistic economics were not enough. When men like
L. T. Hobhouse, who acknowledged a debt to Green, confronted
the problems of poverty in the 1880s, it was the moral appeal of
socialism which attracted them. And it is easy to show that, in
responding positively to socialism, they insisted that its collectivist
means should not obscure its ethical ends. Graham Wallas wrote
in 1889 of socialism holding out the prospect of a fuller and richer
life, but added: 'The system of property holding which we call
Socialism is not in itself such a life any more than a good system
of drainage is health, or the invention of printing is knowledge.'[8]
This is the position of Hobhouse in 1893: 'If the change from
individualism to socialism means nothing but an alteration in the
methods of organizing industry it would leave the nation no
happier or better than before.'[9] Similarly with Hobson in 1898:
'A so-called socialism from above, embodying the patronage of an
emperor or of a small enlightened bureaucracy, is not socialism in
any moral sense at all . . .'[10]

This conception of socialism was to be made the basis of a kind
of collectivism which could hoist Liberal individualism with its

---

[7] See Melvin Richter, *The Politics of Conscience. T. H. Green and his age*
(London, 1964), esp. pp. 283, 341–42.
[8] *Fabian Essays in Socialism*, ed. Bernard Shaw (London, 1889), p. 148.
[9] L. T. Hobhouse, *The Labour Movement* (London, 1893), p. 4.
[10] J. A. Hobson, *John Ruskin, Social Reformer* (London, 1898), p. 204.

own petard. In his journalism of the late 1890s, Hobhouse, calling himself a collectivist in a rather self-conscious way, saw old age pensions as an obvious test case in this sense. 'The individualist theory', he wrote in the *Guardian*, 'is that every man and woman— the women are sometimes overlooked—can and should provide for his or her old age out of the margin left by wages over necessary expenditure.'[11] These were the views best articulated by the Charity Organization Society, notably its secretary Charles Loch; and they were supported by the ethical individualism which Bernard Bosanquet derived from the somewhat elusive arguments of T. H. Green himself. This, I think, goes some way towards explaining Hobhouse's particular concern to refute them. Thrift, Hobhouse maintained, was only a contingent virtue and 'to maintain an artificial school of thrift by withholding necessaries that might otherwise be granted is to mistake the means for the end.'[12] Hobhouse was always eager to distinguish means from ends when it came to questions of individualism and collectivism, Liberalism and socialism. Wealth which was socially created ought to meet common needs. Old age pensions gave the workman not benevolence so much as justice. 'It is a method of assigning to him a small fraction of the enormously increased wealth which he helps to create, and which the play of demand and supply in competitive industry will not give him.'[13] Hobhouse urged the Liberals to espouse the heavy taxation of the future increment on land values in and around towns to provide the financial basis for pensions and for housing. As he confided to his editor: 'Practically this union of measures is what I beg to propound to you as the social programme for the party.'[14] These proposals, he wrote in a leader, were 'undoubtedly Socialistic in character in the sense that all Socialists except those who are for immediate barricades would accept them as an instalment of what they want. The principle on which we have based them would also be accepted by many Socialists as a fragment of their belief.'[15] But whether Socialists and Liberals could work together on them was another matter.

Socialism made a moral appeal because of the evils of the existing system. Marxian socialism was acknowledged to contain elements of truth, but its incorrect economic analysis at once vitiated its ethical claims and rendered its cataclysmic strategy irrelevant. For the progressives' critique of Marxism we must start with the Fabians. The Fabians rejected the labour theory of value and hence

[11] Leader, *Manchester Guardian*, 23 February 1899.
[12] *Ibid.*, 25 March 1899.
[13] *Ibid.*, 23 February 1899.
[14] Hobhouse to Scott, 25 February 1899, *Guardian* archives.
[15] Leader, *Manchester Guardian*, 23 February 1899.

the Marxist concept of the surplus as wealth ineluctably extracted from the labourer by the capitalist. Instead they distinguished the presence of various kinds of rent in what they still called surplus value. It is fairly certain that Hobson was indebted to the Fabians in formulating his fundamentally similar theory of distribution.[16] In this, provision for wear and tear was an economic necessity, accounting, in the case of labour, for a subsistence wage. Anything else was some kind of rent. So while Marx had been right to see that surplus value was important, this was not exclusively the product of labour power, nor need labour be denied its share of it. Its distribution represented the economic might of the stronger in every market. Now Hobson agreed with Marx's empirical claim, that the labourer was being exploited under modern capitalism; but he held that this was not a theoretical necessity. Remedies could be found. Trade unions could raise wages if they were strong enough. The state could appropriate that part of the surplus which fulfilled no economic function.[17]

With their theory of the surplus, as representing functionless wealth, the progressives were not only able to point to a fund of wealth which it would be right and expedient to redistribute; they were also able to argue that this kind of reform would not impair the efficiency of the industrial system, since every productive function in it would continue to receive its necessary reward. The flexibility of the economic system was much greater than Marx had supposed. Moreover, if their argument held, it was impossible to envisage a successful form of socialism which did not reward productive functions. Thus, social justice could be approached through properly conceived economic reform; and it was hard to see how it could be achieved more completely on the basis of what Samuel once called 'the unproved theory of State capitalism'.[18]

The growth of collectivism was regarded as a gradual process. This view was sustained by a kind of evolutionary optimism which saw in the modern state—as 'the organized intelligence and will of the community'[19]—a developing aptitude for social control. Though evolution might have resulted in social progress through the working of blind individualism in the past, the real ground for optimism lay with the collectivist future, when progress would be consciously willed. As Wallas put it: 'Collectivism substituted a

[16] See A. M. McBriar, *Fabian Socialism and English Politics, 1884–1918* (Cambridge, 1962), pp. 29–47.
[17] See J. A. Hobson, *The Crisis of Liberalism. New issues of democracy*, ed. P. F. Clarke (Brighton, 1974), pp. xv–xvi.
[18] Herbert Samuel, 'The Independent Labour Party', *Progressive Review*, i (1896–97), p. 256.
[19] (William Clarke), 'Introductory', *Progressive Review*, i (1896–97), p. 6.

direct aiming at the public good for a very hypothetical calculation that the public good might indirectly result from individual and family accumulation.'[20] This vision of the democratic state suggested that the flexibility of the political system was much greater than Marx had supposed. All told, this gave adequate grounds for a principled reformism.

This analysis is in many respects Fabian. The influence of the Fabians was at its height in the early 1890s and at this time many progressives worked closely with the Fabians. They commonly described themselves as collectivists, even as socialists. Yet those most closely identified later with the New Liberalism came to add to the Fabian critique of Marxism, which they shared, a critique of Fabianism. The grounds on which this was based can perhaps be appreciated best in the case of Hobhouse, though much the same would be true of Wallas, Clarke and Hobson. Hobhouse had been very close to the Fabians in the early 1890s; and after he had joined the *Manchester Guardian* Beatrice Webb enthused about it in 1898 as 'practically our organ'.[21] As with so many of the claims confided to her fascinating diary, a measure of scepticism is in order here. Hobhouse was already deprecating the 'temptation to hail any and every extension of State authority, whatever its principle or its object as a triumph for Socialism':[22] which was a clear rebuke to the Fabians. It is significant too that those Fabians whom he hoped to engage for the *Guardian* in 1898, Clarke and Wallas, were the two Fabian Essayists who were moving most decidedly away from the Webbs.

Imperialism was the great polarizing force here. To the New Liberals it manifested the threat to progress from the rising tide of reaction. It was a natural enemy of democracy. The costs of empire, moreover, were seen as a direct financial threat to social reform. It was a recurring theme with men like Hobhouse, Scott, Clarke, Hobson, that jingoism and anti-jingoism was the real dividing line in politics, the test case not only on imperialism but on all policy. Hence the ardour of their opposition to the capitalists' war in South Africa. And this was the test which the Fabians failed. Shaw's tract *Fabianism and the Empire* particularly annoyed Hobhouse, not least as showing that 'to a certain kind of

[20] Quoted in Martin J. Wiener, *Between Two Worlds. The political thought of Graham Wallas* (Oxford, 1971), p. 152.

[21] Beatrice Webb, *Our Partnership,* ed. Barbara Drake and Margaret I. Cole (London, 1948), p. 145. 'Massingham of the *Daily Chronicle* is again our friend: the *Manchester Guardian* and the *Echo* are practically our organs through Leonard Hobhouse and W. M. Crook . . .' (March 1898).

[22] L. T. Hobhouse, 'The ethical basis of collectivism', *International Journal of Ethics*, viii (1898), p. 143.

Socialism the great capitalist presents himself no longer as an enemy, but as an ally'.[23]

Hitherto the operative word in New Liberalism had been 'New'. The expression had first appeared in print in 1889 and it is fairly easy to establish its pedigree over twenty years.[24] Its increasing use in the 1900s to describe proposals which had been advanced in the 1890s in the name of socialism is one indication of a modified stance which amounts almost to a rediscovery of Liberalism. Progressives were led to conclude that 'the teaching of our recent history appears to be not that the older Liberalism is "played out", but that the several elements of its doctrine are more vitally connected than appears on the surface'.[25] In the Boer War it was the old guard— John Morley, Leonard Courtney, and later Campbell-Bannerman —who stood with Labour in opposition to imperialism. Hobhouse's book *Democracy and Reaction* was written in standing recognition of this fact. The alliances of pro-Boer days stuck fast, and there was a unique emotional charge behind the feeling of solidarity on this issue. When Gilbert Murray congratulated J. L. Hammond on the heroic stand of the weekly *Speaker*, he added ironically: 'It is nice to lay up comforting reflections for one's deathbed.'[26] But this is exactly what most of the pro-Boers were prone to do. 'Where were you in 1899?' was their political litmus test. Near the end of his life, in 1930, Scott told Lloyd George: 'I think the best thing the *Manchester Guardian* has done in my time was to oppose the Boer War . . . We were together there.'[27]

This is the context of the separation of the New Liberalism from Fabianism. For on Fabian grounds there was no reason to suppose that the Liberals would be more ready than the Conservatives for the socialistic experiments of Hobhouse's social programme. And the question was of little importance since, either

[23] L. T. Hobhouse, 'Democracy and nationality', *The Speaker*, 11 January 1902, p. 415.

[24] See L. A. Atherley-Jones, 'The New Liberalism', *Nineteenth Century*, xxvi (1889), pp. 186–93; George W. E. Russell, 'The New Liberalism: a response', *ibid.*, pp. 492–99; J. Guinness Rogers, 'The Middle Class and the New Liberalism', *ibid.*, pp. 710–20; R. B. Haldane, 'The New Liberalism', *Progressive Review*, i (1896–97), pp. 133–43; J. A. Hobson, *Confessions of an Economic Heretic* (London, 1938), p. 52. Professor Bentley B. Gilbert's claim (in his edition of C. F. G. Masterman, ed., *The Heart of the Empire* (Brighton, 1973), p. xxxv, n. 8) that the phrase was first used by Massingham in 1909 thus appears invalid.

[25] L. T. Hobhouse, *Democracy and Reaction*, ed. P. F. Clarke (Brighton, 1972), pp. 164–65.

[26] Murray to Hammond, 1 December 1901, Hammond Papers, vol. 30, fo. 4.

[27] Quoted in *The Political Diaries of C. P. Scott 1911–1928*, ed. Trevor Wilson (London, 1970), p. 29.

way, the growth of collectivism would be purely opportunistic—and none the worse for that. In July 1899 we see Hobhouse clearly repudiating this position. 'Our "practical" men', he commented scathingly, 'tell us that it does not matter how you get a reform providing that you get it.' I am sure that he was mentally lecturing the Webbs when he went on to explain that this was fallacious, and primarily so because there was 'all the difference between benevolent officialism setting the world in order from above, and the democratic Collectivism which seeks not to restrict liberty but to fulfil it'.[28]

The Fabians' fatal flaw appeared to him as their illegitimate opportunism—the attempt 'to force progress by packing and managing committees instead of winning the popular assent'.[29] Thus they had fallen prey to the catchwords of efficiency. Beatrice Webb made no bones about regarding elections as useful, not for making decisions, but for eliciting 'the feeling of consent'.[30] The real work was to fall to the expert. This was, as Hobhouse saw it, a distortion of socialism, and he maintained that 'as the "expert" comes to the front, and "efficiency" becomes the watchword of administration, all that was human in Socialism vanishes out of it'.[31] He gave his irony full rein in questioning the credentials of the expert, asking whether he owed his position 'to someone still more highly qualified than himself'.[32] His suspicions in this respect may have had some foundation in view of Beatrice Webb's comment in 1911 that: 'Hitherto Sidney and I have kept ourselves almost exclusively for the work of expert guidance of the expert.'[33] The Fabians had been led through their anti-democratic attitude to a worship of bureaucracy. From the time of the Boer War on, this is the burden of the New Liberals' charge against Fabianism, which, according to Hobson in 1902, relied 'more and more upon the wire-pulling and intriguing capacity of an enlightened few'.[34]

With the return to the older Liberal tradition, we find frequent attempts to demonstrate its essential continuity with modern progressive thought. Cobden was treated with renewed respect. There was altogether a greater emphasis upon establishing the New Liberalism as a legitimate extension from the old.

[28] Leader, *Manchester Guardian*, 7 July 1899.
[29] 'The career of Fabianism', *The Nation*, 30 March 1907, p. 183.
[30] Quoted in G. R. Searle, *The Quest for National Efficiency* (Oxford, 1971), pp. 94–95.
[31] Hobhouse, *Democracy and Reaction*, p. 228.
[32] *Ibid.*, p. 120.
[33] *Our Partnership*, p. 472 (12 March 1911).
[34] J. A. Hobson, 'Ruskin and Democracy', *Contemporary Review*, lxxxi (1902), p. 105.

But just as individualism was an inadequate basis for the modern economy, so it was an inadequate basis for modern democracy. The Benthamite paradigm of the selfish, intelligent, well-informed elector was no more valid than the postulate of economic man. No one did more to demonstrate this than Wallas in *Human Nature in Politics*. At best, the New Liberals expressed confidence that the causes of irrationalism—the control of the press by vested interests was perhaps the chief culprit—could be removed. Their explicit appeals to rational argument and altruism rest on this hope. But this does not, I think, fully explain the confidence which they asserted in the Edwardian period, even in face of apparently discouraging evidence as to why men voted. It was not just the persistence of what Hobhouse termed 'the mob mind' of jingoism: they knew in their hearts that the Liberal and Labour parties owed their success to appeals scarcely more elevated. Here the New Liberals again took refuge in an evolutionary organic view of society as a whole. It was almost as though they imputed to free elections what the classical economists imputed to the free market: an ability to express a natural identification of interests. 'Democracy', Hobson claimed, 'insists that the people as a whole is rational, and that government must express this rationality.'[35]

The New Liberals here sought to reconcile the antagonism between democracy and knowledge which so troubled Liberal individualists by invoking their sociology of politics. Like the Marxists, they accepted that most people would act for most of the time in terms of immediate pressures, but contended that these could in principle be understood in rational terms by the superior intellect of the rational observer. Marxism, of course, claimed a special place for those who understood the historical process, as distinct from those who merely acted as its agents. The New Liberals too were confident that they had cracked the secret of the universe. They understood the social evolutionary process which *makes* popular politics, and this consisted in the increasing ascendancy of an ethical sense in society at large. A relatively unadorned version of this belief can be seen in Hobson's extremely interesting analysis of the results of the January 1910 elections. He put down the strength of Liberalism to the artisan element, to what he called 'associated labour power'; and from this he took heart. For although there had been, as he thought, 'a larger play of rationalism and of conscious individual judgment' than at any previous time—which was, of course, welcome so far as it went—this was less striking than the manifestations of 'the creative instinct of the collective mind seeking to express itself in politics'. And if it moved 'somewhat

[35] Hobson, *John Ruskin,* p. 208.

blindly and unevenly', this was its means of learning 'the art called democracy'.[36]

The New Liberals were optimistic, therefore, about democratic progress. But this view did not promote a passive role, any more than Marxism usually does. The need for thought and action was pressing. The whole point of the New Liberal theory of progress—what Hobhouse called orthogenic evolution—was to assert the importance of mind over matter. The evolutionary problem as it affected social progress was thus transposed from the realm of biology to that of ethics, and this conception of social evolution demanded some element of teleology. In practical terms this meant that progress was assured only if reformers responded to ideas. 'An ideal is as necessary to the reformer as the established fact is to the conservative', wrote Hobhouse.[37] According to Hobson, progress 'must become the conscious expression of the trained and organized will of the people not despising theory as impractical, but using it to furnish economy in action'. And progress was possible because great issues were increasingly settled, not by force, but by 'the supreme court of reason and of morals'.[38]

There is little doubt as to the high place the progressives assigned to ideas within Liberalism. When they wrote of 'Liberalism, whose mastering ideas are intellectual and moral',[39] they were defining it in a manner which exalted their own role. 'The Liberal Party must incessantly be fed with ideas.'[40] This is typical of their *obiter dicta*. In Campbell-Bannerman they detected 'a certain lack of scientific training in the complicated business of modern politics', which led to the reflection that 'the intellectual worker and moral teacher have still much to do to prepare the way for constructive statesmanship'.[41]

When Hammond gave up journalism for a civil service post in 1907, he felt somewhat rueful at leaving the political firing line with 'a long fight for the land' in prospect. But his friend Charles Roden Buxton, who had just been reading Trevelyan's *Garibaldi*, offered the reflection that its author 'had chosen a really usefuller life than the political'. And in 1911 Buxton, after a spell as a Liberal M.P., was writing to the Hammonds again to say: 'I wish I could think that I had spent 4 years of such constant and well-

---

[36] J. A. Hobson, 'The General Election: a sociological interpretation', *Sociological Review*, iii (1910), pp. 116–17.
[37] Hobhouse, 'The ethical basis of collectivism', p. 139.
[38] Hobson, *Crisis of Liberalism*, pp. 132, 182–83.
[39] 'The Government and the party', *The Nation*, 1 June 1907, p. 514.
[40] 'Attractiveness in politics', *The Nation*, 3 August 1907, p. 820.
[41] 'The character of the Prime Minister', *The Nation*, 29 June 1907, p. 653.

directed labour as you have.'[42] Mr and Mrs Hammond had, of
course, meanwhile written a history book. *The Village Labourer*
is not a tract; it does not falsify nor distort the evidence it presents.
The whole point was, as John Morley put it, that it was 'real
history'[43]—real history in the sense that Hobhouse produced real
sociology, or Hobson real economics, or Wallas real political science;
and useful to the cause of progress precisely in so far as this condition was fulfilled. The book was, Hammond was assured, 'a
pushing at the cart which has to be got forward, albeit by the back
wheel, but then again that is the most effective place to push at'.[44]
As the intellectuals sat at their desks, Hobson countering the fallacies
of classical economics, or Wallas wrestling with the problems of
democracy, or Hobhouse exposing the pretensions of Social Darwin-
ism, or Hammond exploring the history of the land question, they
did not suppose themselves to be withdrawn from the real world
of action, but rather to be fighting where the battle was thickest.
They had the sense that it all depended on them.

The New Liberalism professed to be a means of adjusting the
apparently competing claims of collectivism and individualism,
democracy and knowledge, social forces and rational progress. On
this basis it saw room for wide and fruitful co-operation with
Labour as part of a progressive movement. But it is important to
realize that the New Liberalism was not proto-socialist but revision-
ist. Hobhouse wrote in 1911 that 'it is now sufficiently clear to all
parties that the distinctive ideas of Liberalism have a permanent
function'.[45] That this was as true for some of those who called
themselves socialists as for those who called themselves Liberals
can be seen from the case of R. H. Tawney. Tawney wrote in 1912
of 'the stages of thought about social affairs through which I, and
I suppose other people, have passed'. The first stage was that of
individualism—the Charity Organization Society view. This gave
way to theoretical socialism as a general analysis. The third stage,
however, represented a reversion to a view of the state as composed
of individuals, while recognizing that it was only through collective
action that salvation could come. The prevailing social assumptions
were the real corruption and the first priority was to change them.
The Fabians, on the other hand, erred because they wanted to
take short cuts—to trick statesmen into doing what was needful.
Tawney condemns this as strongly as Hobhouse. 'No amount of

[42] Buxton to Hammond, 22 September 1907, Hammond Papers, vol. 16,
fos 76–77; and to Barbara Hammond, 12 November 1911, *ibid.*, fos 157–58.
[43] Morley to Hammond, 29 October 1911, *ibid.*, fos 132–33.
[44] A. M. D. Hughes to Hammond, 25 October 1911, *ibid.*, fos 121–22.
[45] L. T. Hobhouse, *Liberalism* (London, 1911), p. 224.

cleverness will get figs off thistles.'[46] Like the New Liberals, Tawney characterizes the end of socialism in terms of an ethical ideal, resting on a concept of social justice, and a collectivist programme is envisaged as a means to that end.

This crucially affects the relationship between socialism and Liberalism. The New Liberalism can be seen as an attempt to define true socialism as a special case of Liberalism. Admittedly, on a materialist interpretation of history Liberalism is a mere ideology, arising from the economic supremacy of a particular class. (The fact that the bourgeoisie own the means of production is fundamental. Everything else in Liberalism is flapdoodle—tactical concessions to preserve the verisimilitude of the justifying ideology, and therefore to keep the system going to the benefit of the only class who can benefit from it.) Socialism is then the progressive stage, implying the control of the economic structure by a different class, and embodying nothing that was *intrinsic* to Liberalism. But all this depends on a materialist interpretation of a kind which the progressives rejected. Suppose, alternatively, that Liberalism is a system of ideas or values more fundamental than any particular form of economic organization. This, of course, is the view of the New Liberals. 'All that there is, or is to come, in the opening out of the human mind is Liberalism,' is how Hobhouse puts it;[47] while Hobson writes of the 'illimitable character of Liberalism, based on the infinitude of the possibilities of human life'.[48] Its basic tenets are liberty and equality. In the nineteenth century its great and necessary achievement was political democracy. That this was combined with *laisser-faire* economics was, to be sure, not accidental; but it was a subordinate consideration—as the form of economic organization at any time is subordinate to the general ends pursued. By the close of the nineteenth century the urgent tasks of Liberalism were seen to lie in the field of social democracy. It is true enough, therefore, to speak of a Liberal socialism in which Liberalism, far from being superseded, expressed itself as fully as ever.[49]

There was, then, before 1914, nothing in the socialism of Tawney or MacDonald which made a gulf between their political philosophy and the Liberalism of Hobhouse, or Hobson, or Wallas. This

[46] *R. H. Tawney's Commonplace Book*, ed. J. M. Winter and D. M. Joslin (Cambridge, 1972), pp. 45–46 (2 December 1912); *cf.* J. M. Winter, 'R. H. Tawney's early political thought', *Past and Present*, 47 (May 1970), pp. 71–96.

[47] *C. P. Scott, 1846–1946*, p. 84.

[48] *Crisis of Liberalism*, p. 95.

[49] *Cf.* Hobhouse, *Liberalism*, p. 165; Morris Ginsberg, 'The growth of social responsibility', in *Law and Opinion in England in the 20th Century*, ed. Morris Ginsberg (London, 1959), pp. 14–15, 18–19.

I take to be the importance of the progressive movement in the realm of opinion. If we look at the lines of the reform programme which Tawney advocated, we find nothing in the proposals for nationalization and property taxation that the New Liberals did not think of as practical politics; and the spread of socialist opinions among intellectuals before 1914 should not necessarily be taken as marking a breach with Liberalism. In 1911 the Cambridge Union debated the motion: 'That the progressive reorganization of Society on the lines of collectivist Socialism is both inevitable and desirable.' The guest speaker in favour was Sidney Webb; and he was supported by a past president of the Cambridge University Liberal Club, J. M. Keynes.[50] That Keynes should be seen within this progressive framework is a suggestion which I shall develop later.

The identity of interests between the New Liberalism and the Labour party was the main practical implication of the progressive argument. The electoral arrangement between the Liberal and Labour parties was therefore welcomed by all progressives. Liberal historians have castigated this arrangement as a 'disastrous and culpable error' which inevitably led to the ruin of their party by rearing a cuckoo in the nest.[51] It is, of course, quite true that, as things turned out, a record of consistent opposition to Labour would have provided a more secure base for the Liberals as a minority party in the 1920s. This, however, is not the perspective of the Edwardian Liberal revival, when the party was playing for higher stakes. At that time it sought to maintain itself as a party of government, recognizing the legitimacy of working-class aspirations. It could hardly have done this while trying to strangle the Labour party at birth; and those progressives who created the New Liberalism naturally made it the object of their strategy to avoid a choice between bourgeois Liberalism and Labour.

The New Liberals welcomed Labour in parliament as necessary allies. They judged that visionary socialism, in so far as it existed, would be transmuted into social reform. Massingham's *Nation*, regarding the Liberals as 'the practical progressive party' in England, saw socialism as 'partly a competitive and partly a co-operative idea'.[52] It believed that 'sharp limits are set to the progress of a body so largely divorced from middle-class brains and middle-class sympathy as is the Independent Labour Party'. But it

[50] *The Cambridge Union Society Debates, April 1910—March 1911*, ed. Gilbert E. Jackson and Philip Vos (London, 1911), pp. 79–87.
[51] Roy Douglas, *The History of the Liberal Party 1895–1970* (London, 1971), pp. 68–69, 289–90.
[52] 'Attractiveness in politics', *The Nation*, 3 August 1907, p. 820.

was a useful stimulus and 'on the whole, the Liberal party gains more than it loses by contact, even semi-hostile contact, with the younger forces'.[53] There was, after all, nothing vicious in the socialism of the I.L.P., which was undeniably a party of progress; and it was held to occupy 'about the same relation to Liberal politics as the Salvation Army to the regular churches'.[54]

The difficulties in holding the progressive alliance together should not pass unnoticed. The fact that the political parties were themselves coalitions did not help. To this extent, then, the progressives, who felt a real convergent pull towards unity, were subjected to the divergent tactical pressures of party. There must be some doubt, too, as to how far the Labour party really accepted the progressive formula. The progressive argument was that the substantial area of real agreement on policy issues made electoral co-operation necessary. But there are grounds for arguing that the real issue for the Labour party was that of increased representation itself.[55] There were, on the other hand, purely opportunist party pressures working in favour of the progressive alliance, since both Liberals and Labour stood to lose seats to the Conservative party if the entente between them broke down.

The Labour party which emerged as a parliamentary force after 1906 had really been shaped by the trade-union developments of the late 1880s. As Dr Stedman Jones has shown in the case of London, the New Unionism, and especially the great Dock Strike of 1889, separated the organized workers from the residuum.[56] The New Unions thus institutionalized the unskilled workers and improved their wages and employment prospects: but necessarily at the expense of their weaker competitors in the labour market. All organized labour became to this extent 'aristocratic'. Taken in conjunction with the existing limits on the suffrage, this has an important bearing upon the nature of the Labour party, as the mouthpiece of the trade unions and the ally of the Liberal party. By 1910 the electoral strength of Liberalism, at least in industrial conurbations like London and Lancashire where it had most clearly gained ground, had assumed a distinctive class character. As Hobson wrote of the progressive victories in January 1910: 'It is organized labour against the possessing and educated classes, on the one hand,

[53] 'The moral of Jarrow', *The Nation*, 6 July 1907, p. 684.
[54] 'The fear of socialism', *The Nation*, 27 July 1907, p. 788.
[55] See Martin Petter, 'The Progressive Alliance', *History*, lviii (1973), pp. 45–59; R. I. McKibbin, 'James Ramsay MacDonald and the problem of the independence of the Labour party, 1910–1914', *Journal of Modern History*, xlii (1970), pp. 216–35.
[56] Gareth Stedman Jones, *Outcast London. A study in the relationship between classes in Victorian society* (Oxford, 1971), esp. pp. 316–18, 321.

against the public house and unorganized labour, on the other.'[57]

The record of the Liberal Government on welfare legislation, and in particular the associated series of measures running from old age pensions in 1908 to the Budget of 1909 and National Insurance in 1911, should be assessed in this light. Although this was a decisive break with *laisser-faire*, recent studies have shown that some of the older ideas about separating the deserving from the undeserving poor persisted in the provisions for pensions and unemployment benefit.[58] To say that the Liberals might well have turned to Fabian-style labour colonies next[59] is to ignore their firm rejection of the more draconian proposals for Poor Law reform which Mrs Webb so suavely proposed. But the Government did evade action on the Poor Law. And its welfare schemes, especially National Insurance, chiefly benefited the respectable trade-unionized element of the working class: the very men most likely to be on the electoral register.

This takes us some way to understanding the dynamics of the progressive movement, seen as an alliance between the intellectuals and Labour. For what could the Liberal Government offer them? In an illuminating essay, Professor Hobsbawm has stressed the importance to the Fabians of their professional position.[60] To a considerable extent the same can be said of the New Liberals. Though a few could draw on family wealth, they did not countenance the position of the *rentier*. But in criticizing functionless wealth they did not disparage hard-earned salaries. In his 1907 Budget Asquith rewarded 'the laborious middle-classes' by distinguishing between earned and unearned income, and reducing tax rates on

[57] 'The General Election: a sociological interpretation', p. 114. On the socio-economic division in 1910 see Neal Blewett, *The Peers, the Parties and the People. The General Elections of 1910* (London, 1972), esp. pp. 400–1, 404–5, 408–9. Developments in Lancashire are dealt with in P. F. Clarke, *Lancashire and the New Liberalism* (Cambridge, 1971), *passim*; which also argues (pp. 399–400) that the statistical evidence from London printed in Paul Thompson, *Socialists, Liberals and Labour. The struggle for London, 1885–1914* (London, 1967), pp. 299–303, is consistent with growing working-class support for the Liberal party, rather than with the author's contrary interpretation. Dr Blewett's discovery (*op. cit.*, p. 481, n.44) of an important arithmetical error in these statistics now provides a conclusive demonstration, hitherto lacking, that Dr Thompson's inference must be unsound. In areas where Liberalism was traditionally strong, on the other hand, the picture may be different; see Kenneth O. Morgan, 'The New Liberalism and the challenge of Labour: the Welsh experience', *Welsh History Review*, vi (1973), pp. 288–312.

[58] See José Harris, *Unemployment and Politics. A study in English social policy 1886–1914* (Oxford, 1972), esp. pp. 42–43, 349.

[59] Stedman Jones, *Outcast London*, pp. 335–36.

[60] E. J. Hobsbawm, *Labouring Men. Studies in the history of Labour* (London, 1964), for ch. 14, 'The Fabians reconsidered', esp. pp. 257–59, 266–67.

earned income for those receiving less than £2,000 a year. Massingham's *Nation* duly expressed thanks on behalf of 'the man who earns
£500 a year by teaching, or writing, or in business'.[61] The Government was looking after its own here as much as when it established
a new economic security for the organized working class. Moreover,
the progressive alliance gave both groups a new status in government. The trade unions were represented directly in Parliament
by the Labour party which was an independent partner of Liberalism. And the intellectuals achieved a thrilling sense of importance
as the brains behind a great social movement, into the course of
which they had a privileged insight because they saw its development within the terms of their own kind of rationalism.

The New Liberalism lived by ideas. Its conception of a progressive movement rested on the importance assigned to ideas. The
most serious objection that can be mounted against it is that it
ran out of ideas. In considering this charge, we must, I think, go
back to the land. Nothing is so central as this, nor so little understood. The appeal of land reform as a great issue, concentrating
all sections of Liberal opinion, is clear. It was frequently recalled
that Cobden, at the end of his life, had turned the eyes of radicals
towards the land. This side of the land question, which is relatively
familiar, centred on 'the riddle of the village'. It was a refurbish-
ment of the great symbolic crusade of nineteenth-century radical-
ism against feudalism. But with what was described in 1905 as 'the
sensational increase in land values in modern towns', a distinctive
urban problem was coming increasingly to the fore; and, so the
progressives claimed, 'at this point the Liberal tradition and the
Socialist movement converge'.[62] The focus here was on two issues—
the taxation of unearned increment and a public responsibility
for housing.

In dealing with the enclosure movement in *The Village Labourer*,
the Hammonds showed that the conception of absolute property
rights was without antiquity. And whereas an oligarchic House of
Commons could institute whatever it pleased by way of right to
land and life, 'a different kind of House of Commons'[63] could,
by implication, reconsider such matters. *The Village Labourer*
is thus an historical preface to volume I of the report of Lloyd
George's Land Enquiry Committee, dealing with rural land, published in October 1913; and volume II, the urban report, was

[61] 'The significance of the Budget', *The Nation*, 20 April 1907, p. 285.
[62] J. L. Hammond *et al.*, *Towards a Social Policy: or suggestions for constructive reform* (London, 1905), p. 44.
[63] See J. L. Hammond and Barbara Hammond, *The Village Labourer
1760–1832* (London, 1911), p. 47.

published in April 1914, a few months before the Hammonds' companion volume *The Town Labourer* should have appeared. The Land Enquiry Committee was really the prototype for subsequent exercises in Lloyd Georgian policy-making: a 'think tank' of intellectuals whose brains he could pick. Seebohm Rowntree did most of the work.

Perhaps the most striking feature of volume I of *The Land* was the central importance assigned to the proposal for a minimum wage for agricultural workers. This was to draw the obvious moral from the failure of trade unionism and the success of trade boards in other fields where low pay was normal. The idea that a minimum wage should be established on grounds of need alarmed many contemporaries, and only a few years previously would have been regarded as impracticable.[64] The second volume, dealing with urban land, was half as long again as the first (728/498 pp.). By far the largest part of it dealt with the housing problem. It proposed that municipal responsibility be enforced here by direct enactment. But so that the normal family could be decently housed, the committee exceeded its terms of reference and, capitalizing on the Government's acceptance of its agricultural recommendations, proposed a minimum wage for all low-paid wage earners. It asked, too, for a start to be made on site-value rating so that future increases in land values should go to the community which so largely created them. The theme of the land reports was the justice of making the general welfare the first charge on the one indisputably monopolistic factor of production.

Many historians have maintained that the land campaign was in itself testimony that the New Liberalism was not viable, because 'the relevance of the land question to the problems of urban society was now seeming more and more marginal'.[65] It is, of course, true that land taxation, or even nationalization, was the hobby of some staunch upholders of *laisser-faire* capitalism;[66] though the main effect of land agitation had always been to unite the defenders of

[64] See leaders, 'The Land Report', *Manchester Guardian*, 15 October 1913; 'Life in the Towns', *The Times*, 4 April 1914. In 1907 E. G. Hemmerde had used the example of a minimum wage as a self-evident example of 'a law which would bring the industry of the country to a standstill'. (Letter to *Manchester Guardian*, 27 February 1907.) In 1913–14 he signed the land reports.

[65] D. A. Hamer, *Liberal Politics in the Age of Gladstone and Rosebery* (Oxford, 1972), p. 328; *cf.* Harold Perkin, 'Land reform and class conflict in Victorian Britain', in *The Victorians and Social Protest*, ed. J. Butt and I. F. Clarke (Newton Abbot, 1973), esp. pp. 213–14.

[66] *Cf.* Alan J. Lee, 'Franklin Thomasson and the Tribune', *Historical Journal*, xvi (1973), p. 345; Francis Neilson, 'The decay of Liberalism', *American Journal of Economics and Sociology*, iv (1944–5), pp. 281–310.

all kinds of property against it.[67] In characteristic style, Hobhouse thought it would be possible for land reformers like himself to co-operate with land taxers so long as they did not stand in the way of the interventionist side of the programme.[68] Naturally, the New Liberals, as usual, wished to carry as many of the old Liberals with them as possible; but the twist given to the land campaign suggests that it represented rather more than the arcadian fantasies of Lloyd George. Before 1914 it looked as though the problems of inadequate housing, of rising land values in towns, or a minimum wage for the low paid might be the politics of the future.

The First World War brought the first great dissolution of the progressive movement. It helped shake the Liberal party apart. It was a hammer blow to all hopes of rational progress. Like the Boer War, it threw many progressives back upon distinctively Liberal issues, and on these they felt that their Government failed them. This was one important cause of the migration to Labour of men like Roden Buxton, Hobson, E. D. Morel, Arthur Ponsonby, Charles Trevelyan, who had been happy enough with the welfare legislation of the Liberal Government. They changed allegiance not because they thought there was too little socialism in the Liberal party, but because they thought there was more liberalism in the Labour party. Here lies the importance of the Union of Democratic Control as a bond between anti-war progressives of both parties and a bridge from Liberalism to Labour.[69] What is striking about the history of these converts is the absence of any conversion experience. Progressive ideas continued to span the two parties, though now the political alliance between them had irretrievably broken down and the power of Labour was increasing commensurately with the Liberal decline.

Before the war the progressive movement had manifested a common political consciousness shared by Liberals and Labour; and by an ingenious wire-pulling stratagem electoral politics had been brought into congruence with this. But after the war all the tactical pressures made for hostility between Liberals and Labour. Scott learnt in 1917 that Labour had 'already decided to run 350

[67] F. M. L. Thompson, 'Land and politics in England in the nineteenth century', *Trans. Royal Hist. Soc.*, 5th ser., xv (1965), p. 35; Perkin, *loc. cit.*, pp. 181, 208, 210–12.
[68] See the concluding article in his series 'Land and Labour', a parallel exposition of the thinking of the Land Enquiry Committee, *Manchester Guardian*, 10 October 1913.
[69] On this group see Marvin Swartz, *The Union of Democratic Control in British Politics during the First World War* (Oxford, 1971); and Catherine Ann Cline, *Recruits to Labour. The British Labour Party, 1914–1931* (New York, 1963).

candidates of whom 200 should be drawn from the trades unionists and 150 from the intellectuals'.[70] So Labour was to have its own middle-class brains. Scott suspected that they would be the wrong ones. With 'men like Toynbee and Tawney one would feel pretty safe, but I imagine the Webbs are at present chiefly pulling the strings'.[71]

In the 1920s there was no way of translating the measure of agreement between Liberals and Labour into political co-operation. Scott, it is true, played a large part in persuading the Liberal party to put Labour into office in 1924. But it was not a happy or long-lived arrangement. In the General Election which followed its fall, while Labour lost some seats, it was the Liberal party which was routed.

So in November 1924 the ailing Hobhouse and the aged Scott returned to the subject which they had been discussing for thirty years. In response to Scott's familiar contention that the crucial question was the Liberals' relations with Labour, Hobhouse explained that his difficulties with the Liberal party were more fundamental, since he doubted if it any longer stood for anything distinctive. He considered that 'moderate Labour—Labour in office—has on the whole represented essential Liberalism, not without mistakes & defects, but *better* than the organized party since C.B.'s death'. The distinction between 'ordinary Labour' and 'Good Liberal' was obsolete. Apart from the extremists, the real conflict was between progressives and conservatives. It was *party* that got in the way. Two days after writing this Hobhouse added: 'Why not make it our object to maintain principles, define aims, advocate causes, & let party organization adapt itself to these?' And in a further effort before he posted the letter: 'It seems to me that there is possible a distinctive kind of Socialism viz. one based not on the Trade Unions but on the community & social service. The constitution of the Labour party binds it tight to the Trade Unions & their sectional selfishness, a most serious defect. I have once or twice written in the M.G. that the Liberal party might teach Labour true Socialism in the point of view of the community as a whole, but I don't think hitherto they have shown much enthusiasm for this role.'[72]

Now the position Hobhouse was stating here was substantially that of Massingham's successor as the real influence behind the *Nation*, Keynes. Scott had his reservations about 'the arid intellec-

[70] *Scott Diaries*, p. 320 (December 1917).
[71] Scott to Hobhouse, 30 January 1918, *ibid.*, pp. 331–32.
[72] Hobhouse to Scott, 7, 9 and 15 November 1924, *Guardian* archives. Most of the first letter is printed in *Scott Diaries*, p. 468.

tualism of Keynes'.[73] But if the fate of Liberalism were to be staked
primarily on the ability of its intellectuals to formulate policy—
'It will have to come from the body of the party—from people like
yourself,' Scott had told Hobhouse[74]—then Keynes was the man.
Like all the progressives, Keynes had an unshakable faith in the
indispensability of social and political theory. In a famous passage
he asserted that 'the ideas of economists and political philosophers
. . . are more powerful than is commonly understood. Indeed the
world is ruled by little else . . . soon or late, it is ideas, not vested
interests, which are dangerous for good or evil'.[75] The assumption
that ultimately rationality would prevail in the world was basic to
all Liberal intellectuals; it amounted in them to an irrational faith.
'I behave,' Keynes acknowledged, 'as if there really existed some
authority or standard to which I can successfully appeal if I shout
loud enough—perhaps it is some hereditary vestige of a belief in the
efficacy of prayer.'[76] Like Hobhouse, too, Keynes believed that 'the
progressive forces of the country are hopelessly divided between
the Liberal Party and the Labour Party'. But as against joining the
Labour party, the Liberal had the advantage of being able to 'work
out his policies without having to do lip-service to trade-unionist
tyrannies, to the beauties of the class war, or to doctrinaire State
Socialism—in none of which he believes'. It was right and proper
that those Liberals who wanted to die in the last ditch for capitalism—the Alfred Monds, the Winston Churchills—should desert
to the Tories. The Liberals who remained 'should be not less
progressive than Labour, not less open to new ideas', and should
recognize that great changes could not come except with the aid of
Labour in promoting the three political goals of economic efficiency, social justice, and individual liberty.[77] The real root of
Keynes's objection to Labour was that, though there were sophisticated problems of economic policy to confront, 'I do not believe
that the intellectual elements in the Labour party will ever exercise
adequate control.'[78]

It was this belief in the continued place for the Liberal party
in a progressive movement which kept so many intellectuals loyal
to it. Wallas explained in 1928: 'As things are now the Liberals
seem to have more intellectual stuff in them than the Labour

[73] Scott to Hammond, 1 March 1923, Hammond Papers, vol. 34, fo. 283.
[74] Scott to Hobhouse, 19 November 1924, *Scott Diaries*, p. 469.
[75] *The General Theory of Employment, Interest and Money* (1936), in *The Collected Writings of John Maynard Keynes* (London, 1971-), vii, pp. 383–84.
[76] 'My Early Beliefs', (1938), *ibid.*, vol. x, p. 448.
[77] 'Liberalism and Labour', (1926), *ibid.*, vol. ix, pp. 307, 309–10, 310–11.
[78] 'Am I a Liberal?' (1925), *ibid.*, vol. ix, p. 297; and see the previously unpublished remarks at pp. 295–96.

people.'[79] Similarly with Hobhouse's regret at the Liberals' poor representation in the 1929 parliament 'as I think (I know it's blasphemy) they carry more brains to the square inch than Labour, most of whose men are merely dull and terribly afraid of their permanent officials'.[80] And even Hobson, who was influential in the Labour party's economic debates in the 1920s, wrote later that he never felt quite at home there. In his autobiography he expressed the hope that economic democracy would come through what he called 'the rationalization of the Labour Party', apparently meaning its capture by progressive ideas.[81]

With Lloyd George as leader, and the Liberal Summer Schools to feed him with ideas, the Liberal party devoted itself vigorously to policy-making. The Liberal Land Committee produced reports on rural and urban land in 1925 and 1926, and proposed nationalization. The Liberal Industrial Inquiry produced the volume *Britain's Industrial Future,* the famous Liberal Yellow Book, in 1928, and it became the basis of the 1929 election manifesto *We Can Conquer Unemployment.* This sketched out a two-year programme of public works, financed by borrowing, for immediate implementation. It was a frontal attack on the orthodox objections to action generally identified as the 'Treasury View', which it described as 'hoary with antiquity and clothed in the utmost respectability', but which was 'nevertheless completely fallacious'.[82] It is a far more radical document than *Labour's Reply to Lloyd George,* which concentrated on the 'madcap finance' of the Liberal plan. In making a nod towards under-consumption and typifying unemployment as an organic disease, Labour's policy could be called Hobsonian; and nowhere more so than in its inability to grasp the Keynesian insight at the heart of Lloyd George's scheme. 'The essence of his plan', it complained, 'is to spend borrowed money like water during the next year or two . . .'[83]

The election showed that even when the Liberal party spoke with the tongues of men and of angels, it could not win parliamentary seats. During the next two years the Labour Government

[79] Wallas to Walter Lippman, 8 March 1928, quoted in Wiener, *Between Two Worlds,* p. 193.
[80] Hobhouse to Margaret Llewelyn Davies, June 1929, quoted in J. A. Hobson and Morris Ginsberg, *L. T. Hobhouse. His life and work* (London, 1931), p. 67.
[81] See Hobson, *Confessions of an Economic Heretic,* pp. 126, 181.
[82] *We Can Conquer Unemployment. Mr. Lloyd George's Pledge* (London, 1929), pp. 53–54.
[83] *Labour's Reply to Lloyd George. How to Conquer Unemployment,* with a preface by J. Ramsay MacDonald (London, 1929), p. 13; and see Robert Skidelsky, *Politicians and the Slump. The Labour Government of 1929–31* (London, 1967). The relation of Hobson to Keynes is an interesting question on which I hope to write further.

safely covered itself against any charge of spending borrowed money like water. Unemployment mounted. The Liberals counted for nothing. Their prospects plummeted along with the fortunes of the economic system which they had offered to resuscitate. The election of 1929 blighted progressivism; the combination of capitalist failure and a so-called National Government in 1931 buried it. For after this there could be no presumption of a natural connection between progressive ideas and the Liberal party. Most Liberals in parliament initially supported the National Government; many never disentangled themselves subsequently. Ted Scott, who was now editor of the *Manchester Guardian,* gradually swung the paper against the National Government before the 1931 Election. But he considerd that 'politics are getting into an ugly shape and that we shall be driven more and more to take an anti-property line. And that is fatal for a twopenny paper'.[84] 1914 had been the first and 1931 was the second great dissolution of the progressive movement. It was no longer possible to hold all the items of the progressive political faith. Some salvaged one thing, some another. Archibald Sinclair reported in 1933 that 'progressives are more and more beginning to look to the Labour Party as the only possible alternative to the present Government'.[85] This is the way the *Guardian* would have gone but for Ted Scott's death in 1932; 'Good Labour' had always provided the troops and there was no shortage of progressive intellectuals in the party already. Some young men who were heirs to the progressive tradition re-interpreted a straight-line theory of progress in the light of the capitalist crash and became Communists. Some progressives stayed in the Liberal party, the traditional home. Others withdrew from active politics. At all events, the strategy for determining social progress by intellectual endeavour and rational persuasion of the democratic electorate had to be reconsidered. Keynes went off and wrote the *General Theory.* 'This book,' he explained in the preface, 'is chiefly addressed to my fellow economists.'

University College, London.

[84] E. T. Scott to Hammond, 16 November 1931, in David Ayerst, *'Guardian.' Biography of a Newspaper* (London, 1971), p. 473.
[85] Sinclair to Herbert Samuel, 14 October 1933, quoted in Douglas, *History of the Liberal Party,* p. 235.

PRESIDENTIAL ADDRESS

By Professor G. R. Elton, M.A., Ph.D., Litt.D., F.B.A.

TUDOR GOVERNMENT: THE POINTS OF CONTACT

I. PARLIAMENT

READ 23 NOVEMBER 1973

IT is one of the functions of government to preserve in contentment and balance that society which it rules. Some of the tasks involved in that general purpose are familiar enough. Government exists to maintain peace in the nation—to prevent disturbance, punish crime, and generally ensure that people can lead their lives without threats from others. Government must therefore provide the means for resolving disputes peacefully: it must administer justice and be seen to do so. In addition, since no society can ever stand absolutely still, government is charged with the task of reviewing existing relationships—relationships of rights, duties, burdens and privileges—with an eye to supplying reform, that is, changes designed to keep the general balance and contentment from deteriorating. Most discussions of problems of government revolve around these points. Analysis has concerned itself with the machinery available for discharging these tasks, and assessment has concentrated on establishing the degree of success obtained.

However, there is more to it than this. It has long been realized that the so-called realities of government involve further the social structure of the body governed. Government, we know, cannot work unless it obtains obedience and (preferably) consent from the governed and that recognition has led to a good deal of work on the power structure among the governed and its integration into the exercise of power relinquished to the ruler. With respect to the Tudor century, for instance, we have learned something about the way in which power and rule devolved outwards from a monarchy which, however hard it tried to centralize management, still depended greatly on the co-operation of the so-called rulers of the countryside, and we have increasingly come to understand the degree to which the necessary tasks of government continued to be discharged at decentralized points—in local courts and through the often spontaneous action of lesser organs of rule. The vital role of magnates, gentry and municipal oligarchies has of late been much emphasized, to a point where mistakenly low assessments of the power of the centre have unhappily become current. Arising out of this, questions have been asked about the means which help to tie peripheral authority to central; some of the lines of communication among rival interests have been traced; some patronage systems have been analysed. True, we have had rather more calls for this kind of study than performances, and such examples of revealing importance as have appeared have tended to restrict themselves territorially, to concentrate on the land market, and to go easy on the politics; but then, in the conditions set by sixteenth-century evidence, such things as political attitudes (thought, feeling and programmes), or the role and significance of patronage (the pool of favours and advantages on the one hand, the search for them on the other) are more readily apprehended in general terms than documented in working detail.[1] At any rate, we now know that Tudor government depended not only on the activities of rulers both central and local, and on the management of the machinery available, but also on the organization and rivalries of patronage systems constructed around local, familial and political foci which everywhere penetrated the visible politics of the day.

One matter, however, it seems to me, has received little attention: or rather, one particular type of question has not been asked; and since I think that that question (and if possible the answers to it) may bring us a little nearer to understanding why Tudor government remained pretty stable through a difficult century, while instability and collapse attended upon the government of the early Stuarts, it is a question I should like to look at here. Stability is the product of moderate contentment: it is preserved if the operations of government are thought to conduce to order and justice, and if they succeed in taking account of the claims to power entertained by inferior authorities. This last point has, as I have said, been largely seen in terms of local rule and ties of patronage; one element in the system is missing. We know what people wanted and can trace the contacts that put them in the way of getting it, but we have not asked whether the machinery existed to transform ambition and favour into achievement. To be stable, any system needs to include organized means—public structures—to provide for the ambitions at the centre of affairs of

---

[1] An interesting attempt to analyse attitudes in the north has just appeared: M. E. James, 'The Concept of Order and the Northern Rising of 1569', *Past & Present*, 60 (1973), pp. 49 ff.

such persons as can, if those ambitions remain unsatisfied, upset
that stability. The question I want to ask is really very simple:
did Tudor government contain within its formal structure conventional means for the satisfaction of such people? Did it provide
known and accessible instruments which enabled positive interests,
demands and ambitions on the part of the politically powerful
to achieve their ends? Alternatively, did the politically powerful
discover in the machinery of government such means of self-
satisfaction? The question is simple, but the answers, to be reasonably complete, would be very complex indeed, involving, for instance, a full study of all office-holders. All I can hope to do in
this and succeeding lectures is to draw attention to unstudied
problems, or perhaps to a new way of looking at problems studied
often enough before, and to offer some preliminary suggestions.
I also hope that others may feel encouraged to pursue these issues
further.

When we think about the social organization of the sixteenth
century from this point of view—when we ask ourselves whether
the system of government provided obvious organization points
at which the purposes of rulers and ruled (Crown and 'political
nation') came into the sort of contact which could prove fruitful
to the ambitions of those not yet part of the central government—
we are first, and obviously, driven to look at Parliament. Parliament, after all, was thought of as the image of the nation in common
political action, where, to quote Thomas Smith's familiar words
once again, in the making of law the whole realm participates
because 'every Englishman is intended to be there present, either
in person or by procuration and attorney'.[2] The political reality
of this concept needs no further discussion—or should I say that it
ought to need none, though there are still some respected scholars
who have their doubts about it. And yet the evidence has been
accumulating, and continues to accumulate, that the sixteenth
century had a clear understanding of the notion of legislative
sovereignty—of the supreme power to make laws in all respects
that touch the body politic; that it unquestioningly vested that
power in the mixed entity called Parliament—king, Lords and
Commons jointly; and that it was right to treat the operations of
that mixed body as politically genuine rather than prejudged,
constrained or merely formal. It seems to me that memories of
royal claims in the fourteenth and fifteenth centuries, or of the
more explicit monarchic doctrines which appeared in the seventeenth, combine with misleading interpretations of the high executive authority vested in Tudor monarchs to call in doubt the reality

[2] *De Republica Anglorum*, ed. L. Alston (Cambridge, 1906), pp. 48–49.

of what Smith, and many others, regarded as the fundamental commonplace of the English constitution. One man who attended upon that constitution for half a century was quite clear on the point, and since Lord Burghley's opinion has not been often cited it may be worth producing here. He held 'that their Lordships of the Upper House . . . are one member of the Parliament; and also that the Knights, Citizens and Burgesses of this House representing the whole Commons of this Realm are also another Member of the same Parliament; and her Majesty the Head; and that of these three Estates doth consist the whole Body of the Parliament able to make laws'.[3] In addition, he was quoted later as not knowing what the English Parliament could not do in the way of law-making. Full legislative supremacy vested in the image of the nation and politically active there: that was the basis of Tudor government. True, the full doctrine was of recent standing; in the Reformation Parliament, members of both Houses were still troubled to know whether the legislative authority of Parliament extended to the government and order of the church, a severe limitation.[4] The years of that assembly, however, settled the matter and completed the institutional and doctrinal claims of Parliament. I repeat all this only because we are still told at intervals that institutionally Tudor Parliaments were nothing new and politically they marked a decline. The evidence will not support this double scepticism: it points to a novel recognition of the doctrine and an increased political vigour.

As the sovereign maker of laws, Parliament thus stood ideologically central to the problem of political stability; it was potentially at least useful to all who had purposes to serve, whether those purposes were national, sectional or personal, so long as they required innovation and change. On Parliament converged of necessity all ambitions to maintain or to reform the system: it was the chief organ for absorbing and satisfying the demands made upon stability in government. Even rebels regarded it in this light: the Pilgrims of Grace, for instance, while they might denounce alleged recent practices of packing and influencing, nevertheless called for a Parliament after the old and uncorrupted sort to bring peace in the realm.[5] Yet surely to anyone raised in the traditions of English parliamentary scholarship there is something odd about the

---

[3] Simonds D'Ewes, *The Journals of all the Parliaments during the Reign of Queen Elizabeth* (London, 1682), p. 350 (said in 1585).

[4] G. R. Elton, *Reform and Renewal* (Cambridge, 1973), p. 67; and *cf.* ' "The Body of the Whole Realm": Parliament and Representation in Medieval and Tudor England', *Jamestown Essays on Representation* (Jamestown, Va., 1969).

[5] *Letters and Papers of Henry VIII* [hereafter *LP*], xi.1182(2), 1244, 1246.

notion that the institution should be treated as an instrument of
stability. Our historians have traditionally concentrated on conflict
and have studied all meetings of Parliament with an eye to dispute
and opposition. Sir John Neale, to take a very relevant case, found
the main theme of his history of *Elizabeth I and her Parliaments*
in the accumulation of unremitting political differences. The impression he leaves is that meetings of the Elizabethan Parliament
were notable mainly because they set the stage for collisions between
rulers and ruled and gave dissent an opportunity to disrupt the
secret ways of government and policy. If James I came to think
of Parliaments as like to cats that grow cursed with age or complained that his predecessors had saddled him with this tiresome
burr under the tail of the body politic, it was certainly not because
he distrusted stability and saw in Parliament a means for creating
such political stability as might grow from participation in affairs
or from the satisfaction of ambitions. It could be argued that parliamentary conflict only demonstrated the existence of disagreements
which the airing they got there might even help to resolve. Parliaments might be regarded as useful safety-valves in the engine of
government. However, this is a sophistical rather than a sophisticated point: months of quarrelsome debate, so far from removing
the poison of disagreement, tend to increase enmity and 'polariza-
tion'. There is really no sign that in the sixteenth-century disputes
in either house helped to allay conflict, and from the 'nineties the
history of Parliament is one of increasing criticism, increasing
exasperation, increasing failure to restore stability. In any case,
even if Parliaments had helped to release troublesome vapours,
they would still not have been serving as means for satisfying
legitimate aspirations on the part of the governing nation, the role
for which I am trying to cast them. So long as historians of Parliament devote themselves to the description of political disputes
and rival assertions of authority, they are bound to see in Parliament not a means towards stability but an instrument of real or
potential opposition.

Is this preoccupation justified—a preoccupation which (as Neale
did) skates over things done by agreement, or even comes to believe
that agreement could only be the result of pressure from above,
subservience from below?[6] Did people at the time share this view?
It is necessary to enquire what those concerned wanted from
Parliament and why they wanted it at all. In Parliament the nation
(according to contemporary experts) met to deal with its affairs.
This does suggest that in the first place harmony rather than dis-

[6] *Cf.* J. Hurstfield's argument that in the sixteenth century consent only hid
constraint: *Transactions Royal Hist. Soc.*, 4th ser., xvii (1967), pp. 99 ff.

pute was intended, and that a prevalence of opposition and conflict should be treated as a sign that the necessary stability was in danger. The monarch's purposes are reasonably clear. Mostly they called Parliament to get money: Elizabeth was the first ruler of England who let not a single session pass without obtaining supply. They also wanted laws, especially in the revolutionary years between 1532 and 1559 when every session witnessed a full-scale government programme of legislation. Arguably, the Crown had less of an interest thereafter in parliamentary assemblies because, anxious now to hold a line rather than promote reform, it felt less need for continuous further legislation. As is well known, meetings grew much rarer in the second half of the century, though government legislation certainly did not come to an end in 1559. The demands of the struggle with Catholicism saw to that, and even reform, though less intense, did not terminate; not even Elizabeth could make time stand still. However, these practical needs of cash and laws do not fully explain the attitude of Tudor governments to Parliament, at least not after 1529 when all possibility ceased of ruling without the meetings of the estates. Parliaments were wanted because there the great affairs of the nation could be considered, debated and advertised: Parliament was a part of the machinery of government available to active rulers.

In its earlier days, the idea of the image of the body politic called into existence to produce the active co-operation of all its members, was the property of the Crown, even if a century later it became the weapon of an opposition. The conviction behind the royal summons was, for instance, expressed in the circular which instructed sheriffs about their duties in the elections of May 1536. Evidently it was thought desirable to offer some explanation why only a few weeks after the long Reformation Parliament had at last gone home it should be necessary to burden the country again with a Parliament. 'Such matters,' the king was made to say, 'of most high importance have chanced as for the preservation of our honour, the establishment of our succession in the Crown of this our realm . . . have been to us and to all the lords of our Council thought necessary to be discussed and determined in our high court of Parliament to be assembled for that purpose.'[7] These delicate phrases hide the miserable business of the palace revolution which destroyed the Boleyns, and thus far the calling of Parliament seemed necessitated only by the 1534 Act of Succession, now out of date and in need of replacement. But the letter went on to explain that the business was urgent and involved both the public weal and the personal security of the monarch; a matter of high policy,

[7] British Museum, Harl. MS 283, fo. 256 (*LP*, x. 815).

very personal to the king, was described as truly the concern of the nation assembled in Parliament. As practice proved, this was more than rhetoric: Henry VIII, at least, and Thomas Cromwell treated Parliament as though they believed in this stabilizing function. We need to remember the positive note struck—the ringing assertion that public affairs of real import were the business of Parliament and justified the calling of an unexpectedly sudden one.

Henrician Parliaments unquestionably concerned themselves with affairs of state, and not necessarily only at the Crown's behest; they were freely given information on diplomatic negotiations, like those with France in 1532 which pleased both Houses;[8] in the Cromwell era, as also in the difficult years of Edward VI and Mary, no one attempted to deny (as Elizabeth was to do on occasion) that Parliaments, and indeed the House of Commons, had an active part to play in the high politics of the nation. And even Elizabeth readily conceded a political function to her Parliaments, provided she was allowed to turn the tap off when it suited her. Compelled to use Parliament for the imposition of taxes and the making of laws, Tudor monarchs also thought it necessary and desirable to involve the potentially powerful and potentially difficult in the affairs of the realm by offering the occasions of debate, discussion and support which Parliament represented. For most of the century, so far as we can judge, government certainly saw in Parliament a means of preserving stability and adjusting balances. And despite the occasions of 'conflict' (often no more than a proper exchange of views and arguments), the outcome usually produced consensus and contentment, thus justifying the theory behind the practice.

What, then, of those who came when called? We know at present far too little about the Lords, though work is in progress.[9] That people sought election to the Commons in the reign of Elizabeth has been sufficiently proved by Neale: I need only point to his evidence of new boroughs created by the demand for seats, or of contested elections as demonstrating the desire of rival local individuals and factions to get to the place of power and influence.[10] But similar things evidently happened in the reign of Henry VIII, too. Some of the newly enfranchised boroughs may well have anticipated the sort of purposes well vouched for in the daughter's reign, though most of the new seats were certainly added by Crown policy. Tournai, Calais, Wales and Chester owed the bestowal of the franchise to the king's desire to centralize the realm and demon-

[8] *LP*, v. 1518.
[9] Especially in the hands of Dr Michael Graves.
[10] J. E. Neale, *The Elizabethan House of Commons* (London, 1948), esp. chs. ii–vii.

strate its unity in the visible image of the body politic. However, there are sufficient signs that individuals strove actively, and against other individuals, to get elected: the 'secret labours' made in 1534 when a by-election fell due in Warwickshire, the riotous disputes accompanying the shire election for Shropshire in 1536, the un-called-for ambitions in Norfolk in 1539 of Sir Edmund Knyvet who managed to affront both Cromwell and the duke of Norfolk, the troublesome intervention in 1542 of one Richard Devereux at the first ever election for Carmarthenshire.[11] The beginnings of a systematic use of influence on elections which marked the Parliaments of 1536 and 1539 themselves testify to ambitions to enter the Commons, and the familiar story of the clumsy interference in Kent by Edward's Privy Council in 1547 brings out the real involvement in parliamentary affairs of both gentry and freeholders.[12] There is no reason to doubt that throughout the century the theoretical attachment to the representative institution was matched by a widespread desire to share in its operations. And it would be very rash to suppose that behind this desire was only some mildly pompous wish to enhance one's standing in the eyes of one's fellows. The people who sought election may well be presumed to have wanted to use their place for identifiable ends.

What, then, did people want from Parliament? We may assume, without question, that they were not seeking taxation, though it needs to be pointed out that from 1534 onwards Parliaments came to terms with the fact that peacetime taxation had come to stay.[13] I am not suggesting that the Tudor Commons embraced taxes with the self-sacrificing masochism displayed by twentieth-century Parliaments; but I would suggest that they did not either auto-matically regard all taxation with the bigoted irresponsibility too readily ascribed to them by some historians. They knew as well as we do that government needed to be financed, and when per-suaded that the purposes of government were sound they proved far less difficult about granting money than one might suppose. The only Parliament of the century which made really serious trouble about supply was that of 1523, a Parliament which deliber-ately expressed its grave disquiet about Wolsey's policies. Nor was taxation seen as a bargaining counter: apart from the session of 1566, when fears for the succession produced a real conflict, no Parliament seems ever to have attempted to use supply for the

---

[11] *LP*, vii. 1178; x. 1063; xiv (1) 672, 706, 800, 808; xvii. 48.

[12] *A[cts of the] P[rivy] C[ouncil]*, ii, pp. 516, 518.

[13] *Cf.* G. R. Elton, 'Taxation for War and Peace in Tudor England,' in a forthcoming volume of essays dedicated to the memory of D. M. Joslin, ed. J. M. Winter.

extraction of political concessions, and on that occasion no one doubted that the money grant itself was justified. Tudor Parliaments voted supply soberly and responsibly, and it should be recognized once again that the principle and practice of taxation by consent made a very real contribution to the political stability of the system. We know what happened in the next generation, as soon as serious attempts were made to tax without consent.

Still, it was not the prospect of taking money out of constituents' pockets that lured men into service in the House. Some, of course, did want to pursue political ends. Some men, well aware of the platform which Parliament provided, wished to use it to promote policies or hinder those they thought were likely to be promoted by others. This is as true of the group supporting Catherine of Aragon who organized opposition in the Reformation Parliament,[14] as it is of the 'puritan choir' of 1563 or the brothers Wentworth. But these men, seeking legitimate conflict, clearly formed a small minority of the members of the House. The main part of those who looked beyond the personal gratification and local repute which election to Parliament might bring with it seem to have had one of two ends in view: the obtaining of legislation for themselves or for groups or individuals with whom they were connected, and personal advancement. In other words, to them Parliament offered just that opportunity of fulfilling particular ambitions which are required in an instrument of political stability.

If so far I may well have seemed to be digging over well-tilled ground, I have now to confess that for the rest of this paper I can do little more than suggest lines of enquiry. That all sorts of people —individuals, interests, institutions, companies—wished to use Parliament in order to get their programmes and necessities embodied in legislation is, of course, a familiar point. Very little, however, has been done to see what sort of success they had in this. We need to study acts passed and failed bills, assign them to this or that initiative, and explore local and private records systematically in order to discover who attempted what and who managed to achieve what. The problems of legislative initiative are many and in the past have too often been solved by despair—by simply assuming that all reasonably general acts owed their origin to the Crown or 'the government', while those touching particular interests may safely be ascribed to those interests. This rule of thumb offers an unsafe guide. I have before this attempted to penetrate some of the jungle for the 1530s (and have disconcertingly discovered that even then we cannot be sure that king and minister

[14] G. R. Elton, 'Sir Thomas More and the Opposition to Henry VIII,' *Bulletin of the Institute of Historical Research,* xli (1968), pp. 19 ff.

worked always in mutually informed harmony),[15] while the Parliaments of 1547–57 and of 1589–1610 are being studied with such questions in mind.[16] Miss Miller's revealing study of the manner in which the city of London used Parliament needs to be followed up after 1547.[17] There are other well-organized towns to consider, as well as bodies of gentlemen in the shires. How important was it for a burgess, especially if he was what Neale has termed a carpetbagger, or even for a knight, to serve the purposes and respond to the demands of his constituents? Can we discover anything touching the relations between electors and the man they sent to Westminster? Did re-election have to do with the successful promotion of bills? How many men in the Commons were in fact active about bills? How serious were constituencies about bills they had in the House, and can we find out anything about the cost of obtaining an act of Parliament? There are no answers at present—or only the most tenuous ones—to these and similar questions; and yet we must have answers if we are to understand what went on in Parliament and what men wanted from it. The question is the more obviously important because the existence of private act legislation is peculiar to the English Parliament, distinguishing it, for instance, from those of Scotland and Ireland. We are well advised to seek at least part of the explanation for the political differences between these assemblies in this simple fact.[18]

I cannot on this occasion attempt to fill the gap, but I can offer a few examples from the reign of Henry VIII to show how very real and active this involvement of private interests in the work of the session was. To many men, even the Reformation Parliament signified less a time of revolution in state and church than an opportunity to advance their own business. The sheriffs and escheators of Northumberland, who for years had been paying over the profits in their charge to the chamber, in 1536 found themselves troubled with process out of the Exchequer for some seventy years' arrears; they petitioned the king for a bill of indemnity back to Edward IV, a move which yielded no result.[19] One of the king's chirurgeons did better in 1545 by getting royal approval for a bill to create a profitable monopoly in the appraising of dead men's goods; but

[15] *Reform and Renewal*, ch. 4.

[16] By Professor J. Erikson, Mr A. L. Jenkins, and Miss M. A. Randall.

[17] Helen Miller, 'London and Parliament in the Reign of Henry VIII,' *Bulletin Inst. Hist. Res.*, xxxv (1962), pp. 128 fos.; the unsystematic remarks in Neale, *The Elizabethan House of Commons*—e.g. pp. 336–38, 383–87—are but a beginning.

[18] For Ireland see the remarks by B. Bradshaw in *The Irish Parliamentary Tradition*, ed. B. Farrell (Dublin, 1973), p. 71.

[19] *LP*, x. 1260.

despite the stamped royal signature the bill got nowhere, unlike four others for the settlement of various estates which were similarly approved.[20] The abbot of Conway hoped to introduce a proviso into the Dissolution bill of 1536 with which to save his house, but without success.[21] In 1539, a priest trying to help a couple who had married before learning that the lady's first husband was probably still alive, advised a private act of Parliament to resolve the embarrassment.[22] No act resulted, and it may be doubted whether Parliament would ever have entertained an indemnity bill for bigamy, however inadvertent. In the middle of the 1540 session Thomas Wyat, the poet, could not find time for social courtesies because he was in the thick of preparing his two bills for the Parliament;[23] both, incidentally, passed. The best documented seeker after useful bills in Parliament was Lord Lisle, deputy at Calais—best documented because his correspondence was confiscated and survives, but also because absence from England made statute his best hope for protecting his interests. By 1539, when he was advised that his plan to buy some woods from the earl of Bridgewater could most readily be realized by private bill legislation,[24] he had considerable experience of watching the vagaries of affairs in Parliament. With Sir Richard Whethill, a personal enemy in Calais, he had been at the receiving end: Whethill tried for legislation in 1534 to confirm a patent for a spear's place for his son which he had obtained in the teeth of the deputy's opposition, and two years later he attempted a similar *coup* on his own behalf.[25] On both occasions Lisle's close contacts with Cromwell enabled him to thwart his enemy. In the new Parliament of 1536 he in his turn tried to use statute to do down an opponent. Sir Robert Wingfield held the grant of a marsh in the environs of Calais which the deputy found irksome and wished to see resumed. His agents, talking to Cromwell actually in the Commons' chamber, persuaded the minister that the grant was indeed against the public interest; Cromwell there and then moved the matter in the House, obtained a vote that something be done, and commissioned the drafting of the necessary bill. But despite his repeated promises the bill, produced within twenty-four hours by William Portman of the Middle Temple (later a judge), hung in the House in which Wingfield's friends had evidently also managed to raise some support. In the

---

[20] *LP*, xx (2). 1067, nos 35, 37, 48–49; xxi (2). 770, no. 80.
[21] *LP*, x. 1046.
[22] *LP*, xiv (1). 896.
[23] *LP*, xv. 783.
[24] *LP*, xiv (1). 780, 877.
[25] *LP*, vii. 1492; x. 580.

end it passed, only to be held up in the Lords, but at this point Wingfield voluntarily surrendered the patent into the king's hands, rather than suffer the indignity of an act of Parliament against himself.[26] Even the haphazard evidence of the state papers demonstrates the importance of private bills, and therefore the importance of Parliament to private interests; how much more can we learn from less official archives? They need to be searched.

Though the absence of work done at present prevents a thorough discussion of these important issues, one aspect is more readily accessible and can yield some quite interesting answers even to distinctly preliminary enquiries. The acts passed which dealt with the affairs of individuals—usually but not always property matters —can safely be ascribed to their beneficiaries' initiative, and though the acts themselves are in print only down to 1539 full lists are available in the *Statutes of the Realm*. Though strictly speaking their contents need to be analysed, and though most certainly it would be desirable to consider also failed bills of a like kind, a look at mere numbers of such acts passed has its uses. Private act legislation was a well-established practice in the sixteenth century, but the pattern is far from uniform.[27] Much the biggest number of acts for private persons' concerns was passed in the reign of Henry VII whose first, third and fifth Parliaments yielded 50, 25 and 27 respectively. The average for the reign is 18.7 per session, as compared with 8.3 under Henry VIII, 9.2 under Edward VI, a mere 4.3 under Mary, and a significantly increased 13.4 under Elizabeth. However, the high figures for the first Tudor arise simply from the consequences of the civil wars: the bulk of those private acts dealt with restitutions in blood and resumptions of lands confiscated, being thus necessary products of earlier acts of attainder. This untypical activity apart, private legislation runs around a median of 4 to 5 per session down to the last session of the Reformation Parliament. Meanwhile, acts dealing with the private affairs of the royal family had also come in a steady stream—a total of 24 under the seventh Henry and 81 under the eighth. Strikingly enough, Edward and Mary each used Parliament only once for their private concerns, and Elizabeth not at all.

If one ignores the accident of the post-civil-war settlement, it becomes apparent that it actually was the Crown, under Cromwell's guidance, which first discovered and demonstrated how the machinery of Parliament could be exploited systematically for private

---

[26] *LP*, xi. 34, 61, 94, 108; *Journals of the House of Lords*, i (12 July 1536).

[27] These calculations are based on the tables of contents in *Statutes of the Realm*, vols. ii–iv, counting as private acts those that had not previously been printed or still remained unprinted.

business. The reorganization of the royal estates in the 1530s over which Cromwell and Audley presided necessitated 14, 16 and 13 private acts in the sessions of 27, 28 and 32 Henry VIII. Private interests, possibly somewhat frustrated by the massive public legislation of the Reformation Parliament, immediately picked up the idea, with 18, 16, 13 and 10 acts in the sessions 27–32 Henry VIII. The unexpected Parliament of 1536, called really to deal with the settlement of the succession, was thus very thoroughly used also for the settlement of property matters both royal and private. Detailed research is needed to discover why the Crown came to abandon the method after 1546 and why private bill legislation altogether declined thereafter until 1558, but even this superficial survey shows that in the reign of Elizabeth the landed classes came increasingly to rely on Parliament. At the same time, though public acts declined rather in political and social significance, they remained stable in numbers: the total amount of business transacted in every session—remembering that sessions themselves occurred at longer intervals of time—increased in the second half of the century.[28] The real break-through for private acts, whatever reason may have been behind it, came in the reign of James I whose seven sessions yielded an average of 23.3 private acts, and that despite the fact that two sessions remained totally blank. The average for the productive sessions is thus over 32: we have entered a new era in the use of Parliament. While the import of failed bills needs to be taken into account, and though the crude figures of acts passed need to be refined by further classification, it is manifest that in the course of the sixteenth century Parliament came to be a very important instrument in the management of the political nation's private affairs. Neale's remark that while for the Crown Parliament meant money to the Commons it meant private acts,[29] does indeed, as he says, oversimplify; but the epigram displays real insight, and I could wish that its author had not in his narrative history of the Elizabethan Parliaments told us very little about the first and almost nothing about the second. People wanted Parliaments not only to make laws for church and commonwealth, not only to serve the economic and social needs of particular areas or sectional interests, but also as the major—the most conclusive—means for settling the legal problems involved in their estates policies. Here, then, is a clear way in which the institution acted to promote satisfaction and stability, and the problems caused in James's reign by sessions which failed altogether to serve this purpose need surely

[28] From 1529 to 1601, the average of public acts passed in each session is about 21.

[29] Neale, *House of Commons*, p. 383.

to be taken into account when we consider why the consensus and stability expressed in the work of the Tudor Parliaments began to disappear in the following century.

Lastly, I want to take a look at the question whether election to the House of Commons could be important in serving personal ambition and progress in a man's career. Again, this is much too big a problem to tackle thoroughly here. Some hints are scattered in Neale's book: lawyers found membership a useful way to attract the kind of attention which led to office and promotion, and some individuals actively exploited the parliamentary service they could render to patrons.[30] A systematic study must await the publication of the relevant volumes of the *History of Parliament*, which should supply all the information required. Meanwhile, let me look briefly at the tip of this particular iceberg—at the relationship, if one existed, between election to the Commons and membership of the Privy Council. We have long been familiar with the point that Tudor councillors regularly sat in the Commons and that the failure of the Stuarts to provide such a 'Treasury Bench' played its part in the collapse of co-operation between Crown and Parliament. Here I am concerned with the reverse of all this: could prominence, or even presence, in the House contribute to a man's rise into the Council? Of one man we know not only that it did but also that he deliberately chose Parliament as a place in which to attract the monarch's attention and work his way into power. When Thomas Cromwell told George Cavendish in November 1529 that by his belated entry into the Reformation Parliament he had 'once adventured to put in his foot, where he trusted shortly to be better regarded',[31] he spoke for more than his personal fortune. He prophesied no less than the characteristic way to eminence which was to dominate English politics certainly from the Restoration onwards. Did anyone else in the sixteenth century employ it?[32]

There are, in fact, interesting hints that in this respect, once again, things changed in the 1530s—that Cromwell initiated a later practice. Information, as usual, is difficult to get for the councillors of Henry VII a high proportion of whom, being bishops, peers, doctors of law, judges and serjeants-at-law, do not in any

[30] *E.g. ibid.*, p. 151.

[31] *Two Early Tudor Lives*, ed. R. S. Sylvester and D. P. Harding (New Haven, 1962), p. 116.

[32] For information I rely in part on such obvious sources as *Dict. of National Biography* and the *Official Return of M.P.s*, and in part on the biographies in the files of the History of Parliament Trust. I am grateful to the Trust for permission to use their files, and to Dr Alan Davidson for searching them in reply to my questions.

case come within the range of this question. In 1504 a single
Council meeting included eleven men who could have sat in
Parliament before becoming councillors.[33] Totally deserted by
official returns, we have only the patchiest notion of their possible
presence in the Commons, but the indications are against a notion
that they were parliamentarians before they were councillors. Sir
Thomas Lovell was Speaker in 1485 and Sir Robert Drury in 1495,
but the latter had already had a full career as king's legal counsel,
while the former (in company with Sir Richard Guildford, Sir
Edward Poynings, Sir Gilbert Talbot, Sir Walter Hungerford and
Sir Henry Wyat) had been among Henry's supporters before or at
Bosworth. None of them needed to sit in the Commons to attract
the king's favour, and all them almost certainly were councillors
from the beginning of the reign. Sir Thomas Bourchier probably
belongs to the same category; he attended the Council by 1486.[34]
Nothing useful can be established about Sir Robert Litton and
Sir John Risley. That leaves Edmund Dudley, Speaker in the
Parliament of January 1504. It appears that the first payment to
him of a councillor's fee is recorded for October that year,[35] but as
a member of the Council Learned he was clearly of the Council
before that year. Thus none of Henry VII's councillors can be
thought of as using Parliament as a foundation for their careers;
if they did seek election it was either as established king's men and
leaders of the government, or for private reasons of status and
local importance.

Much the same was true of the first half of Henry VIII's reign.
The reduced Council projected in Wolsey's Eltham Ordinance of
1526 included five men of interest in this context.[36] Sir William
Fitzwilliam the Younger, Sir Henry Guildford and Sir William
Kingston are not known to have sat before 1529; yet the first two
are vouched for as councillors by 1522 and 1516 respectively, while
the last, though possibly not formally a councillor before 1533,
was a well-established courtier by May 1524 when he became constable of the Tower.[37] All three, in fact, were courtiers in terms of
a career-structure. Sir John Gage (vice chamberlain) had been
prominent at court for several years; he is not known ever to have
sat in Parliament. As for Sir Thomas More, though he may have
sat in the Parliament of 1504 (and I am very doubtful of this story

---

[33] *Select Cases in the Council of Henry VII*, ed. C. G. Bayne (Selden Soc.,
London, 1958), p. 40.

[34] *Ibid.*, p. 8.

[35] *The Tree of Commonwealth*, ed. D. M. Brodie (Cambridge, 1948), pp. 2–3.

[36] G. R. Elton, *The Tudor Constitution* (Cambridge, 1960), pp. 93–94.

[37] *LP*, iv. 390(28).

of Roper's, as of some others he tells), he certainly owed neither his entry into the Council in 1517 nor his Speakership in 1523 to any species of parliamentary career.[38]

Biographical study of the first properly-listed Privy Council in August 1540, on the other hand, yields a quite dramatically changed picture.[39] Edward Seymour, never apparently elected to a Parliament, was there as the king's brother-in-law and uncle to the heir apparent. Sir John Russell, Sir Thomas Cheyney, Sir Anthony Wingfield, Sir Richard Riche and Sir John Baker had all sat in 1529 (and probably not before); all of them made it into the Council between 1531 and 1539. It would be wrong to conclude that they all owed their advancement to membership of the Commons; Russell and Cheyney, for instance, were courtiers first. So was Sir Anthony Brown, a burgess in 1539, the same year that (probably) he became a councillor. Still, all these men went through the Commons on their way to the Council Table, and Riche and Baker —professional civil servants—do seem to have followed in the footsteps of Cromwell by making their mark in Parliament. (Cromwell was in effect accompanied by Thomas Audley, lord chancellor by 1540: another veteran of the 1523 Parliament and Speaker in 1529, by which time as chancellor of the Duchy he was a member of the unreformed Council). Thomas Wriothesley and Ralph Sadler, the principal secretaries of 1540, owed their promotion to Cromwell whose private secretaries they had been, but again he got them into Parliament a year before they made it into the Privy Council.[40] Naturally, one must be careful not to assume simply that temporal order (Parliament first, Council after) equals cause and effect, but it does begin to look as though by the 1530s membership of the House of Commons was something that men with political ambition could and would use as a stepping-stone in their careers.

And this situation continued and developed. The privy councillors of November 1551 included seven men who could have done what has here been postulated: all of them did.[41] Sir Robert Bowes first entered Parliament in 1539 but joined the Council only in 1551. Sir John Gates, William Cecil and Sir Edward North sat first in 1542: they were of the Privy Council by 1551, 1550 and 1547 respectively. North, incidentally, was the first clerk of the Parlia-

---

[38] Cf. G. R. Elton, 'Thomas More, Councillor,' in St Thomas More: Action and Contemplation, ed. R. S. Sylvester (New Haven, 1972), pp. 87 ff.

[39] Tudor Constitution, p. 95.

[40] Sadler certainly sat in 1539 (A. J. Slavin, Profit and Power [Cambridge, 1966], p. 40); the History of Parliament Trust suspects a possible election in 1536.   [41] APC, ii, p. 403.

ments ever to sit in the Commons afterwards. Sir John Mason
and Sir Philip Hoby sat in Parliament in 1547, but in Council
only in 1550 and 1551. As for Sir William Petre, that Cromwellian
survival, he had passed through those stages at an earlier date:
Parliament 1536, Council 1545. By this time, therefore, all the
commoners on the Privy Council (and some since promoted to
the peerage, like William Paget) had had a career in the Commons
before they achieved membership of the government. And the
same remained true for new arrivals in Elizabeth's reign when
appointment to the Council often came a long time after a man
had first gone into Parliament and began to attract attention there.
Here are some typical examples, with the date of first election
followed by the date of appointment to the Council: Sir James
Croft, 1542, 1570; Sir Francis Knollys, (?)1533, 1559; Sir Thomas
Mildmay, 1545, 1566; Sir Thomas Smith, 1547, 1571; Sir Francis
Walsingham, 1559, 1573; Sir Christopher Hatton, 1571, 1577;
Thomas Wilson, 1563, 1577; Sir Henry Sidney, 1547, 1575; Robert
Cecil, 1584, 1591; Sir Thomas Egerton, 1584, 1596; Sir John
Fortescue, 1559, 1589; Sir William Knollys, 1571, 1596.

I am not, of course, suggesting that all these men, and others,
reached councillor's status simply because they had served a political apprenticeship in Parliament. But they had indeed served
such an apprenticeship, and the only new recruit to the Council in
the reign who had not was apparently (*quia non potuit*) Archbishop Whitgift. I am not prepared to say that membership of the
Commons had become a necessary prerequisite for elevation to
the Privy Council, but it looks very much as though it had become
a very useful first step. From the 1530s onwards, and not before the
time that Thomas Cromwell showed the way, getting elected to
Parliament was one way—and a prominent way—to get to the top.
Men who wished to reach the Council, men who hoped to help
govern the country, needed other means as well and other connec-
tions, but increasingly they discovered that they could lay sound
foundations by seeking election to Parliament. The queen may
not have consciously chosen her councillors from members of the
Commons (though we do not know that she did not, and we may
suppose that her advisers, a Cecil or Leicester, kept their eyes and
ears open in the Parliament), but in effect she there found the
necessary reservoir of talent. Once again, the point was brought
out more clearly in the reign of her successor because then it ceased
to be so easy to use this particular staircase to the top. Men like
Sir Edwyn Sandys, Sir John Eliot, Sir Thomas Wentworth or
William Noy knew perfectly well that their talents were superior
to those promoted by foolish and incompetent kings dominated by

favourites whose advancement had owed nothing to membership of the House. Men like these, given the opportunity, soon enough proved that their real purposes were to govern, to sit in the Privy Council. Left out in the cold, they could only agitate in a species of opposition, in the hope of attracting attention that way: and Wentworth and Noy achieved the purpose of their disruptive activities.

Thus the ineptitude of early Stuart rule produced a new political sophistication: the ambitious politician who made the life of government so difficult that it seemed best to solve the problem by giving him office. Under Elizabeth, resisters in Parliament were not men who sought high office; those who did found that an active and helpful conformity served the purpose best. So long as trouble in Parliament gathered around natural opposition men like the Wentworth brothers or around men like Norton or Fleetwood who found satisfaction in careers outside the inner rings of government, that trouble was politically insignificant. When men appeared who had hoped to use Parliament for a career leading to the Privy Council and found the road blocked, every sort of warning light went on in Parliament and Council alike. The opposition which mattered was not—then or at any other time—that of irreconcilable principle but that of frustrated political ambition.

Thus Parliament, the premier point of contact between rulers and ruled, between the Crown and the political nation, in the six-teenth century fulfilled its function as a stabilizing mechanism because it was usable and used to satisfy legitimate and potentially powerful aspirations. It mediated in the touchy area of taxation; by producing the required general and particular laws it kept necessary change in decent order; it assisted the rich in the arranging of their affairs; and it helped the ambitious to scale the heights of public power. What more could we ask of the image of the body politic? Only that it should satisfy liberal preconceptions by regularly undoing governments. But that was not a function which sixteenth-century theory ascribed to Parliament, and I can see no reason why it should have done so.

THE ROYAL HISTORICAL SOCIETY

REPORT OF THE COUNCIL, SESSION 1972-73

The Council of the Royal Historical Society has the honour to present the following Report to the Anniversary Meeting.

A conference on 'Urban Civilization' was held at St. John's College, Oxford, from 14 to 16 September 1972. The papers read were:

> 'The Emergence of an Urban Culture in Florence, 1250-1450'. By Dr. George Holmes.
> 'Two Pre-Industrial Cities—Venice and Amsterdam'. By Mr. Peter Burke.
> 'Paris and its Neighbourhood in the Late Eighteenth Century'. By Professor Richard Cobb.
> 'The Role of Religion in the Cultural Structure of a Late Victorian City'. By the Rev. Dr. J. H. S. Kent.
> 'The Forming of an Industrial–Urban Culture in the United States, 1850-1950'. By Professor Eric E. Lampard.

Ninety-four members of the Society and twenty-three guests attended. The President of the Society held a reception for them on 15 September. It was decided to hold the fourth annual conference at the University of York from 17 to 19 September 1973, on the topic 'Government, Propaganda and Public Opinion'.

Council made renewed representations to the Department of Education and Science about the Government's proposed revised regulations for the Export Control of Documents, and to the Department of the Environment concerning its proposals for the reorganization of local government boundaries in so far as they would affect historical documents.

Preliminary notice was received from University College London that plans for the rebuilding of part of the College will involve the demolition about 1976 of the building in which the Society is housed. The College has made an offer of alternative accommodation. Council is considering this and exploring other possibilities.

At the end of 1972 Dr. R. W. Southern retired from the Presidency. Council wishes to record its gratitude to him for his work on the Society's behalf and in particular for his energetic and very successful attempts to increase the membership with a view to making it more fully representative of the historical profession.

The representation of the Society upon various bodies was as follows: Professor G. E. Aylmer and Mr. A. T. Milne on the Joint Anglo-American Committee exercising a general supervision over the production of the *Bibliographies of British History*; the President, Professor C. N. L. Brooke, Professor Sir Goronwy Edwards, Professor J. C. Holt and Professor the Rev. M. D. Knowles on the Advisory Committee of the new edition of Gross, *Sources and Literature of English History*; Professor G. W. S. Barrow, Dr. P. Chaplais and Professor P. H. Sawyer on the Joint Committee of the Society and the British Academy established to prepare an edition of Anglo-Saxon charters; Dr. E. B. Fryde on a committee to regulate British co-operation in the preparation of a new repertory of medieval sources to replace Potthast's *Bibliotheca Historica Medii Aevi*; Professor P. Grierson on the British Academy Committee for the Sylloge of Coins of the British Isles; Professor A. G. Dickens on the Advisory Council on the Export of Works of Art; the President and Professor C. H. Wilson on the British National Committee of the International Historical Congress; Professor Sir Goronwy Edwards on the Council of the British Records Association; Professor A. M. Everitt on the Standing Conference for Local History; Mr. M. R. D. Foot on the Committee to advise the publishers of *The Annual Register*; Professor D. A. Bullough on the Ordnance Survey Archaeological Advisory Committee. Council received reports from these representatives.

The President is *ex officio* a Trustee of the *Spectator*. Professor Medlicott represents the Society on the Court of the University of Exeter.

At the Anniversary Meeting on 24 November 1972 at which the President, Dr. Southern, retired under By-law XV, Professor G. R. Elton was elected to replace him. The Vice-Presidents retiring under By-law XVI were Mr. H. J. Habakkuk and Professor C. H. Philips. Professor M. Roberts and Dr. J. M. Wallace-Hadrill were elected to replace them. The members of Council retiring under By-law XIX were Professor D. A. Bullough, Professor G. R. Elton, Professor H. S. Offler and Professor E. L. G. Stones. Mr. J. P. W. Ehrman, Dr. B. H. Harrison, Mr. A. F. Thompson and Dr. D. E. R. Watt were elected to fill the vacancies. Dr. R. W. Southern and Professor C. R. Cheney were elected Honorary Vice-Presidents under By-law XIV. Messrs. Beeby, Harmar and Co. were appointed auditors for the year 1972-73 under By-law XXXVIII.

Publications, and Papers Read

The following works were published during the session: *Transactions*, Fifth Series, volumes 22 and 23; *Camden*, Fourth Series, volume 10, *Herefordshire Militia Assessments, 1663*, edited by M. A. Faraday for 1971–72; volume 11, *The Early Correspondence of Jabez Bunting, 1820–1829*, edited by W. R. Ward, and volume 12, *The Wentworth Papers, 1597–1628*, edited by J. P. Cooper.

At the ordinary meetings of the Society the following papers were read:

'The New History and the Sense of Social Purpose in American Historical Writing'. By Dr. J. R. Pole. (20 October 1972.)

'The Problem of Papal Power in the Ecclesiology of St. Bernard'. By J. W. Gray. (9 February 1973.)

'New Light on the "Invisible College"; Science and Economic Reform in the Mid-17th Century'. By C. Webster. (9 March 1973.)

'Great Britain and the Coming of the Pacific War, 1939–1941'. By Dr. P. C. Lowe. (11 May 1973.)

At the Anniversary Meeting on 24 November 1972 the President, Dr. R. W. Southern, delivered an address on 'Aspects of the European Tradition of Historical Writing: IV. The Sense of the Past'.

The Alexander Prize was awarded to Dr. C. J. Kitching for his essay on 'The Quest for Concealed Lands in the Reign of Elizabeth I'.

Membership

Council records with regret the death of 14 Fellows since 30 June 1972. Among these Council would mention especially Professor J. C. Beaglehole, O.M., a Corresponding Fellow. The resignation of 10 Fellows, 4 Associates and 4 Subscribing Libraries was received.

Professor L. U. Hanke, a Fellow and President Designate of the American Historical Association, was elected a Corresponding Fellow. 59 Fellows and 16 Associates were elected, 16 Libraries were admitted and 1 Library readmitted. The membership of the Society on 30 June 1973 comprised 1179 Fellows (including 125 Life Fellows), 35 Corresponding Fellows, 154 Associates and 747 Subscribing Libraries (1144, 35, 142 and 734 respectively on 30 June 1972). The Society exchanged publications with 20 societies, British and foreign.

Finance

Despite a substantially higher income, as a result primarily of the increase from 1 July 1972 in the subscription rate of Subscribing Libraries, there was again a deficit on Income and Expenditure Account for the year ended 30 June 1973 of £1,096 (1972: £1,172). This was attributable to sharply rising costs, of which the effect continues to be felt in the current year. At the Anniversary Meeting on 24 November 1972, it was resolved to increase the subscription rate of Fellows to £7 and of Associates to £3 with effect from 1 July 1973. Council is grateful to those Life Fellows who, in recognition of the increases, have since made voluntary contributions to the Society's finances, either as single donations or as promises of a regular annual sum, and to the large number of other Fellows who have signed new covenants for the increased amount of their subscription.

The Andrew Browning Bequest

Last year it was reported briefly that Professor Andrew Browning had bequeathed to the Society his residuary estate. Information has now been received that this comprises assets with a total value, in May 1973, in excess of £75,000.

The immense value to the Society of this bequest, which in its history has been approached only by that of Sir George Prothero, some forty years ago, requires no comment. Council has decided to place the capital in a separate Andrew Browning Fund, and has under consideration the special purposes for which the income of this fund, expected to amount to about £2,500 a year, might appropriately be put.

THE ROYAL HISTORICAL SOCIETY
BALANCE SHEET AS AT 30 JUNE 1973

30.6.72 £	£				
43,495		**ACCUMULATED FUNDS**			
		GENERAL FUND			
		As at 1 July 1972			44,158
	1,594	Royalties from reprints of the Society's publications received in the year and treated as capital . .		2,020	
	15	Royalties from *Essays on Medieval and Modern History* (Macmillan, 1968)		3	
1,609	—	Donations from Life Members		212	
					2,235
45,104					46,393
226		*Add* Profit on Sale of Investments in year . .			—
45,330					46,393
1,172		*Less* Excess of Expenditure and Provisions over Income for year			1,096
44,158					45,297
	13,571	SIR GEORGE W. PROTHERO BEQUEST As at 1 July 1972			13,852
	281	*Add* Profit on Sale of Investments			—
13,852					
5,000		REDDAWAY FUND			5,000
63,010					£64,149
		REPRESENTED BY:			
59,115		INVESTMENTS—at cost			64,401
		Market Value £102,672 (1972: £109,554)			
		SUM DUE ON SURRENDER OF LEASE of 96 Cheyne Walk			
	5,000	As at 1 July 1972		3,750	
	1,250	Paid in year		1,250	
3,750	—	(Payable in annual instalments of £1,250)			2,500
		CURRENT ASSETS			
		Balances at Bank:			
	1,794	Current Accounts		794	
	5,072	Deposit Account		4,909	
	37	Cash in Hand.		29	
	—	Payments in Advance		135	
	6,903			5,867	
		Less CURRENT LIABILITIES			
	506	Subscriptions received in advance .	896		
	94	Conference Fees received in advance .	219		
	108	Sundry Creditors	204		
	6,050	Provision for Publications in Hand .	7,300		
	6,758			8,619	
145					2,752
3,010					£64,149

NOTE: The cost of the Society's Library, Furniture and Office Equipment, and the Stock of its own publications, has been written off to Income and Expenditure Account as and when acquired.

THE ROYAL HISTORICAL SOCIETY

INCOME & EXPENDITURE ACCOUNT FOR THE YEAR ENDED 30 JUNE 1973

30.6.72 £	£		£	£
		INCOME		
198		Subscriptions for 1972/73: Associates	219	
2,227		Libraries	3,121	
3,896		Fellows	4,227	
6,321				7,56?
		(The Society also had 125 Life Fellows at 30 June 1973)		
765		Tax recovered on Covenanted Subscriptions . .		85?
501		Arrears of Subscriptions recovered in year . . .		43?
3,661		Interest and Dividends received and Income Tax recovered		4,49?
86		Prothero Royalties and Reproduction Fees . .		4?
26		Donations and Sundry Receipts		4?
£11,360				£13,42?

		EXPENDITURE		
		SECRETARIAL & ADMINISTRATIVE EXPENSES		
3,940		Salaries, Pension Contributions and National Insurance .	4,541	
266		General Printing and Stationery	506	
347		Postage, Telephone and Sundries.	384	
223		Accountancy and Audit	243	
—		Office Equipment	50	
127		Insurance	118	
96		Meeting and Conference Expenses	183	
4,999			6,025	
900		*Less* Charged to Library and Publications Accounts .	900	
4,099				5,12?
		PUBLICATIONS		
163		Directors' Expenses	200	
		Publishing Costs in the year:		
		Transactions, Fifth Series, Vol. 22 (total cost) 2,460		
		Camden, Fourth Series, Vol. 10 (total cost) 3,118		
		Camden, Fourth Series, Vol. 11 (total cost) . 2,273		
		7,851		
		Less Provision made 30 June 1972 . 6,100	1,751	
2,438				
31		Warehousing, Packing and Postage	—	
		Provision for Publications in Progress:		
		Transactions, Fifth Series, Vol. 23 . . 3,400		
		Camden, Fourth Series, Vol. 12 . . 3,900		
6,050			7,300	
750		Proportion of Secretarial and Administrative Expenses .	750	
9,432			10,001	
1,618		*Less* Sales of Publications	1,368	
7,814				8,6?
£11,913		*Carried forward*		£13,7?

EXPENDITURE (contd.)   £

        Brought forward   13,758

		LIBRARY AND ARCHIVES		
0.6.72	238	Purchase of Books and Publications	290	
1,913	170	Library Assistance and Equipment	243	
	408		533	
	150	Proportion of Secretarial and Administrative Expenses	150	
	558		683	
	23	*Less* Sales of Surplus Books in year	—	
535				683
		OTHER CHARGES		
	19	Alexander Prize and expenses	15	
	15	Subscriptions to other bodies	18	
	50	Prothero Lecture fee and expenses	50	
84				83
2,532		TOTAL EXPENDITURE	14,524	
1,360		INCOME AS ABOVE	13,428	
1,172		EXCESS OF EXPENDITURE AND PROVISIONS OVER INCOME FOR THE YEAR	£1,096	

R. ELTON, *President.*

R. C. DAVIS, *Treasurer.*

We have examined the foregoing Balance Sheet and Income and Expenditure Account with
the books and vouchers of the Society. We have verified the Investments and Bank Balances
appearing in the Balance Sheet. In our opinion the above Balance Sheet and annexed Income
and Expenditure Account are properly drawn up so as to exhibit a true and fair view of the
state of the affairs of the Society according to the best of our information and the explanations
given to us and as shown by the Books of the Society.

             BEEBY, HARMAR & CO.,
             Chartered Accountants, Auditors

FINSBURY COURT,
FINSBURY PAVEMENT,
LONDON EC2A 1HH
8th *August 1973*

THE DAVID BERRY TRUST

Receipts and Payments Account for the Year Ended 30 June 1973

1972			Receipts		
			BALANCE IN HAND 30 June 1972:		
			Cash at Bank:		
	45		Current Account	6	
	56		Deposit Account	38	
531	430		483·63 Shares Charities Official Investment Fund . .	530	574
66			DIVIDEND ON INVESTMENT per Charity Commissioners .		72
2			INTEREST RECEIVED ON DEPOSIT ACCOUNT . . .		5
£599					£651

			Payments		
	—		EXAMINERS' FEES	—	
	—		DAVID BERRY PRIZE	—	
	—		DAVID BERRY MEDAL	—	
	25		POSTAGE AND SUNDRIES	—	
			BALANCE IN HAND 30 June 1973:		
			Cash at Bank:		
	6		Current Account	6	
	38		Deposit Account	115	
			483.63 Shares Charities Official Investment		
599	530		Fund (Market Value 30.6.73 £587)	530	651
£599					£651

We have examined the above account with the books and vouchers of the Trust and find it to ▌ in accordance therewith.

BEEBY, HARMAR & CO.,
Chartered Accountants, Auditors

FINSBURY COURT,
FINSBURY PAVEMENT,
LONDON EC2A 1HH
10th August 1973

The late David Berry, by his Will dated 23rd day of April, 1926, left £1,000 to provide in eve three years a gold medal and prize money for the best essay on the Earl of Bothwell or, at t discretion of the Trustees, on Scottish History of the James Stuarts I to VI in memory of ▌ father, the late Rev. David Berry.

The Trust is regulated by a scheme sanctioned by the Chancery Division of the High Court Justice dated 23rd day of January, 1930, and made in an action 1927 A.1233 David Anders Berry Deceased, Hunter and another *v.* Robertson and another.

The Royal Historical Society is now the Trustee. The Investment held on Capital Accou consists of 634 Charities Official Investment Fund Shares (Market Value £770).

The Trustee will in every second year of the three year period advertise in *The Times* inviti essays.

ALEXANDER PRIZE

The Alexander Prize was established in 1897 by L. C. Alexander, F.R.Hist.S. It consists of a silver medal awarded annually for an essay upon some historical subject. Candidates may select their own subject provided such subject has been previously submitted to and approved by the Literary Director. The essay must be a genuine work of original research, not hitherto published, and one which has not been awarded any other prize. It must not exceed 6,000 words in length and must be sent in on or before 1 November 1974. The detailed regulations should be obtained in advance from the Secretary.

LIST OF ALEXANDER PRIZE ESSAYISTS (1889–1972)[1]

1898. F. Hermia Durham ('The relations of the Crown to trade under James I').
1899. W. F. Lord, BA ('The development of political parties in the reign of Queen Anne').
1901. Laura M. Roberts ('The Peace of Lunéville').
1902. V. B. Redstone ('The social condition of England during the Wars of the Roses').
1903. Rose Graham ('The intellectual influence of English monasticism between the tenth and twelfth centuries').
1904. Enid M. G. Routh ('The balance of power in the seventeenth century').
1905. W. A. P. Mason, MA ('The beginnings of the Cistercian Order').
1906. Rachel R. Reid, MA ('The Rebellion of the Earls, 1569').
1908. Kate Hotblack ('The Peace of Paris, 1763').
1909. Nellie Nield, MA ('The social and economic condition of the unfree classes in England in the twelfth and thirteenth centuries').
1912. H. G. Richardson ('The parish clergy of the thirteenth and fourteenth centuries').
1917. Isobel D. Thornley, BA ('The treason legislation of 1531–1534').
1918. T. F. T. Plucknett, BA ('The place of the Council in the fifteenth century').
1919. Edna F. White, MA ('The jurisdiction of the Privy Council under the Tudors').
1920. J. E. Neale, MA ('The Commons Journals of the Tudor Period').
1922. Eveline C. Martin ('The English establishments on the Gold Coast in the second half of the eighteenth century').

[1] No award was made in 1900, 1907, 1910, 1911, 1913, 1914, 1921, 1946, 1948, 1956, 1969. The prize Essays for 1909 and 1919 were not published in the *Transactions*. No Essays were submitted in 1915, 1916, and 1943.

1923. E. W. Hensman, MA ('The Civil War of 1648 in the east midlands').

1924. Grace Stretton, BA ('Some aspects of mediæval travel').

1925. F. A. Mace, MA ('Devonshire ports in the fourteenth and fifteenth centuries').

1926. Marian J. Tooley, MA ('The authorship of the *Defensor Pacis*').

1927. W. A. Pantin, BA ('Chapters of the English Black Monks, 1215–1540').

1928. Gladys A. Thornton, BA, PhD ('A study in the history of Clare, Suffolk, with special reference to its development as a borough').

1929. F. S. Rodkey, AM, PhD ('Lord Palmerston's policy for the rejuvenation of Turkey, 1839–47').

1930. A. A. Ettinger, DPhil ('The proposed Anglo-Franco-American Treaty of 1852 to guarantee Cuba to Spain').

1931. Kathleen A. Walpole, MA ('The humanitarian movement of the early nineteenth century to remedy abuses on emigrant vessels to America').

1932. Dorothy M. Brodie, BA ('Edmund Dudley, minister of Henry VII').

1933. R. W. Southern, BA ('Ranulf Flambard and early Anglo-Norman administration').

1934. S. B. Chrimes, MA, PhD ('Sir John Fortescue and his theory of dominion').

1935. S. T. Bindoff, MA ('The unreformed diplomatic service, 1812–60').

1936. Rosamond J. Mitchell, MA, BLitt ('English students at Padua, 1460–1475').

1937. C. H. Philips, BA ('The East India Company "Interest", and the English Government, 1783–4').

1938. H. E. I. Phillips, BA ('The last years of the Court of Star Chamber, 1630–41').

1939. Hilda P. Grieve, BA ('The deprived married clergy in Essex, 1553–61').

1940. R. Somerville, MA ('The Duchy of Lancaster Council and Court of Duchy Chamber').

1941. R. A. L. Smith, MA, PhD ('The *Regimen Scaccarii* in English monasteries').

1942. F. L. Carsten, DPhil ('Medieval democracy in the Brandenburg towns and its defeat in the fifteenth century').

1944. Rev. E. W. Kemp, BD ('Pope Alexander III and the canonization of saints').

1945. Helen Suggett, BLitt ('The use of French in England in the later middle ages').

1947. June Milne, BA ('The diplomacy of Dr John Robinson at the court of Charles XII of Sweden, 1697–1709').

1949. Ethel Drus, MA ('The attitude of the Colonial Office to the annexation of Fiji').

1950. Doreen J. Milne, MA, PhD ('The results of the Rye House Plot, and their influence upon the Revolution of 1688').

1951. K. G. Davies, BA ('The origins of the commission system in the West India trade').

1952. G. W. S. Barrow, BLitt ('Scottish rulers and the religious orders, 1070–1153').
1953. W. E. Minchinton, BSc(Econ) ('Bristol—metropolis of the west in the eighteenth century').
1954. Rev. L. Boyle, OP ('The *Oculus Sacerdotis* and some other works of William of Pagula').
1955. G. F. E. Rudé, MA, PhD ('The Gordon riots: a study of the rioters and their victims').
1957. R. F. Hunnisett, MA, DPhil ('The origins of the office of Coroner').
1958. Thomas G. Barnes, AB, DPhil ('County politics and a puritan *cause célèbre*: Somerset churchales, 1633').
1959. Alan Harding, BLitt ('The origins and early history of the Keeper of the Peace').
1960. Gwyn A. Williams, MA, PhD ('London and Edward I').
1961. M. H. Keen, BA ('Treason trials under the law of arms').
1962. G. W. Monger, MA, PhD ('The end of isolation: Britain, Germany and Japan, 1900–1902').
1963. J. S. Moore, BA ('The Domesday teamland: a reconsideration').
1964. M. Kelly, PhD ('The submission of the clergy').
1965. J. J. N. Palmer, BLitt ('Anglo-French negotiations, 1390–1396').
1966. M. T. Clanchy, MA, PhD ('The Franchise of Return of Writs').
1967. R. Lovatt, MA, DPhil ('The *Imitation of Christ* in late medieval England').
1968. M. G. A. Vale, MA, DPhil ('The last years of English Gascony, 1451–1453').
1970. Mrs Margaret Bowker, MA. BLitt ('The Commons Supplication against the Ordinaries in the light of some Archidiaconal Acta').
1971. C. Thompson, MA ('The origins of the politics of the Parliamentary middle group, 1625–1629').
1972. I. d'Alton, BA ('Southern Irish Unionism: A study of Cork City and County Unionists, 1884–1914').
1973. C. J. Kitching, BA, PhD ('The quest for concealed lands in the reign of Elizabeth I').

DAVID BERRY PRIZE

The David Berry Prize was established in 1929 by David Anderson-Berry in memory of his father, the Reverend David Berry. It consists of a gold medal and money prize awarded every three years for Scottish history. Candidates may select any subject dealing with Scottish history within the reigns of James I to James VI inclusive, provided such subject has been previously submitted to and approved by the Council of the Royal Historical Society. The essay must be a genuine work of original research not hitherto published, and one which has not been awarded any other prize. The essay must not exceed 50,000 words. It must be sent in on or sent in on or before 31 October 1976.

LIST OF DAVID BERRY PRIZE ESSAYISTS (1937–1970)[1]

1937. G. Donaldson, MA ('The polity of the Scottish Reformed Church c. 1560–1580, and the rise of the Presbyterian movement').

1943. Rev. Prof. A. F. Scott Pearson, DTh, DLitt ('Anglo-Scottish religious relations, 1400–1600').

1949. T. Bedford Franklin, MA, FRSE ('Monastic agriculture in Scotland, 1440–1600').

1955. W. A. McNeill, MA (' "Estaytt" of the king's rents and pensions, 1621').

1958. Prof. Maurice Lee, PhD ('Maitland of Thirlestane and the foundation of the Stewart despotism in Scotland').

1964. M. H. Merriman ('Scottish collaborators with England during the Anglo-Scottish war, 1543–1550').

1967. Miss M. H. B. Sanderson ('Catholic recusancy in Scotland in the sixteenth century').

1970. Athol L. Murray, MA, LLB, PhD ('The Comptroller, 1425–1610').

[1] No Essays were submitted in 1940. No award was made in 1946, 1952 and 1961.

THE ROYAL HISTORICAL SOCIETY

(INCORPORATED BY ROYAL CHARTER)

OFFICERS AND COUNCIL—1973

STANDING COMMITTEES—1973

Finance Committee

C. E. BLUNT, OBE, FBA, FSA.
PROFESSOR A. G. DICKENS.
PROFESSOR J. A. S. GRENVILLE.
PROFESSOR C. H. PHILIPS.
N. J. WILLIAMS.
PROFESSOR C. H. WILSON.
And the Officers.

Publications Committee

PROFESSOR G. E. AYLMER.
PROFESSOR D. A. BULLOUGH, MA, FSA.
PROFESSOR I. R. CHRISTIE.
M. R. D. FOOT.
B. H. HARRISON.
MISS B. F. HARVEY.
MRS. A. E. B. OWEN.
PROFESSOR P. H. SAWYER.
PROFESSOR F. M. L. THOMPSON.
And the Officers.

Library Committee

T. H. ASTON.
PROFESSOR G. E. AYLMER.
M. R. D. FOOT.
C. J. HOLDSWORTH, MA, PhD.
And the Officers.

LIST OF FELLOWS OF THE
ROYAL HISTORICAL SOCIETY

(CORRECTED TO 31 DECEMBER 1973)

*Names of Officers and Honorary Vice-Presidents are printed in capitals.
Those marked* have compounded for their annual subscriptions.*

Abbott, A. W., CMG, CBE, Frithys Orchard, West Clandon, Surrey.

Adair, J. E., MA, PhD, 1 Crockford Park Road, Addlestone, Surrey.

Adam, R. J., MA, Cromalt, Lade Braes, St Andrews, Fife.

Addison, W. W., FSA, 6 Ravensmere, Epping, Essex.

*Addleshaw, The Very Rev. Canon G. W. O., MA, BD, FSA, The Deanery, Chester.

Ainsworth, Sir John, Bt, MA, c/o National Library, Kildare Street, Dublin 2, Eire.

Akrigg, Professor G. P. V., BA, PhD, Dept of English, University of British Columbia, Vancouver 8, B.C., Canada.

Albion, Rev. Canon Gordon, DSc (Louvain), Sutton Park, Guildford.

Alcock, L., MA, FSA, 15 Beaumont Gate, Glasgow G12 9ED.

Alder, G. J., PhD, Childs Hall, Upper Redlands Road, Reading RG1 5JW.

Alderman, G., MA, DPhil, 43 Walsingham Road, Clapton, London E5.

Alexandrowicz, Professor C. H., LLD, DrJur, 8 Rochester Gardens, Croydon, Surrey.

Allan, D. G. C., MSc(Econ), FSA, 1 Victoria Rise, Clapham Common, London SW4 oPB.

Allen, Professor H. C., MC, MA, School of English and American Studies, University of East Anglia, University Plain, Norwich, NOR 88C.

Allmand, C. T., MA, DPhil, 59 Menlove Avenue, Liverpool L18 2EH.

Altholz, Professor J., PhD, Dept of History, University of Minnesota, 614 Social Sciences Building, Minneapolis, Minn. 55455, USA.

Altschul, Professor M.,PhD, Case Western Reserve University,Cleveland, Ohio, 44106, U.S.A.

Anderson, Professor M. S., MA, PhD, London School of Economics, Houghton Street, WC2A 2AE.

Anderson, Mrs O. R., MA, BLitt, Westfield College, NW3.

*Anderson, R. C., MA, LittD, FSA, 9 Grove Place, Lymington, Hants.

Andrews, K. R., BA, PhD, Dept of History, University of Hull, Cottingham Road, Hull HU6 7RX.

Andrews, Rev. Canon P. J., OBE, DD, Redbourne, De Moulham Road, Swanage, Dorset BH19 1NS.

Anglo, S., BA, PhD, FSA, Dept of History of Ideas, University College, Swansea.

Annan, Lord, OBE, MA, DLitt, DUniv, University College, Gower Street, WC1E 6BT.

Appleby, J. S., Little Pitchbury, Brick Kiln Lane, Great Horkesley, Colchester, Essex CO6 4EU.

Armstrong, Miss A. M., BA, 7 Vale Court, Mallord Street, SW3.

Armstrong, C. A. J., MA, FSA, Hertford College, Oxford.

Armstrong Professor F. H., PhD, University of Western Ontario, London 72, Ontario.

Armstrong, W. A., BA, PhD, Eliot College, The University, Canterbury, Kent.

Arnstein, Professor W. L., PhD, Dept of History, University of Illinois at Urbana–Champaign, 309 Gregory Hall, Urbana, Ill. 61801, U.S.A.

Ashton, Professor R., PhD, The Manor House, Brundall, near Norwich.

Ashworth, Professor W., BSc(Econ), PhD, Dept of Econ. and Soc. History, The University, Bristol.

Aston, Mrs M. E., MA, DPhil, Castle House, Chipping Ongar, Essex.

Aston, T. H., MA, FSA, Corpus Christi College, Oxford.

Auchmuty, Professor J. J., MA, PhD, MRIA, University of Newcastle, N.S.W., Australia.

Avery, D. J., MA, BLitt, 6 St James's Square, London, SW1.

Axelson, Professor E. V., DLitt, University of Cape Town, Rondebosch, S. Africa.

*Aydelotte, Professor W. O., PhD, State University of Iowa, Iowa City, Iowa, U.S.A.

Aylmer, Professor G. E., MA, DPhil, University of York, Heslington, York YO1 5DD.

Bagley, J. J., MA, 10 Beach Priory Gardens, Southport, Lancs.

Bagshawe, T. W., FSA, c/o Luton Museum, Wardown Park, Luton, Bedfordshire.

Bahlman, Dudley W. R., PhD, Dept of History, Williams College, Williamstown, Mass., U.S.A.

Baillie, H. M. G., MBE, MA, FSA, 12B Stanford Road, W8 3QJ.

Baily, L. W. A., 29 Saxon Way, Saffron Walden, Essex.

Bailyn, Professor B., MA, PhD, LittD, LHD, Widener J, Harvard University, Cambridge, Mass. 02138, U.S.A.

Baker, L. G. D., MA, BLitt, Dept of Medieval Hist., The University, Edinburgh.

Baker, T. F. T., BA, Camden Lodge, 50 Hastings Road, Pembury, Kent.

*Bales, P. G., MC, MA, Selwyn House, Fakenham, Norfolk.

Balfour, Professor M. L. G., CBE, MA, 5B Prince Albert Road, NW3.

Ballhatchet, Professor K. A., MA, PhD, 35 Rudall Crescent, Hampstead, London, NW3 6UE.

Banks, Professor J. A., MA, Dept of Sociology, The University, Leicester LE1 7RH.

Barker, E. E., MA, PhD, 60 Marina Road, Little Altcar, Formby, via Liverpool L37 6BP Lancs.

Barker, Professor T. C., MA, PhD, Minsen Dane, Brogdale Road, Faversham, Kent.

Barkley, Professor the Rev. J. M., MA, DD, 2 College Park, Belfast, N. Ireland.

Barley, Professor M. W., MA, FSA, 66 Park Road, Chilwell, Nottingham.

*Barlow, Professor F., MA, DPhil, FBA, Middle Court Hall, Kenton, Exeter.

*Barnes, Professor D. G., MA, PhD, 2300 Overlook Road, Cleveland, Ohio. 44106, U.S.A.

Barnes, Miss P. M., PhD, Public Record Office, Chancery Lane, WC2.

Barnes, Professor T. G., AB, DPhil, University of California, Berkeley, Calif., 94720, U.S.A.

*Barnes, Professor Vida F., MA, PhD, LLD, 16 North Sycamore Street, South Hadley, Mass. 01075, U.S.A.

Barratt, Miss D. M., DPhil, The Corner House, Hampton Poyle, Kidlington, Oxford.

Barron, Mrs C. M., MA, PhD, 35 Rochester Road, NW1.

BARROW, Professor G. W. S., MA, DLitt (*Literary Director*), University of Newcastle, Newcastle upon Tyne.

Bartlett, C. J., PhD, 5 Strathspey Place, West Ferry, Dundee DD5 1QB.

Batho, G. R., MA, The University, Sheffield 10.

Baugh, Professor Daniel A., PhD, Dept of History, McGraw Hall, Cornell University, Ithaca, N.Y. 14850, U.S.A.

Baxter, Professor S. B., PhD, 608 Morgan Creek Road, Chapel Hill, N.C., 27514 U.S.A.

Baylen, Professor J. O., MA, PhD, Georgia State University, 33 Gilmer Street S.E., Atlanta, Georgia, U.S.A.

Beales, D. E. D., MA, PhD, Sidney Sussex College, Cambridge.

Beales, H. L., DLitt, 16 Denman Drive, London, NW11.

Bealey, Professor F., BSc(Econ), Dept of Politics, Taylor Building, Old Aberdeen, AB9 2UB.

Bean, Professor J. M. W., MA, DPhil, 622 Fayerweather Hall, Columbia University, New York, N.Y. 10027, U.S.A.

Beardwood, Miss Alice, BA, BLitt, DPhil, 415 Miller's Lane, Wynnewood, Pa. U.S.A.

Beasley, Professor W. G., PhD, FBA, 172 Hampton Road, Twickenham, Middlesex, TW2 5NJ.

Beattie, Professor J. M., PhD, Dept of History, University of Toronto, Toronto, M5S 1A1, Canada.

Beaumont, H., MA, Silverdale, Severn Bank, Shrewsbury.

Beckett, Professor J. C., MA, 19 Wellington Park Terrace, Belfast 9, N. Ireland.

Beckingsale, B. W., MA, 8 Highbury, Newcastle upon Tyne.

Beddard, R. A., MA, DPhil, Oriel College, Oxford.

Beeler, Professor J. H., PhD, 1302 New Garden Road, Greensboro, N.C. 27410, U.S.A.

*Beer, E. S. de, CBE, MA, DLitt, FBA, FSA, 31 Brompton Square, SW3 2AE.

Beer, Professor Samuel H., PhD, Faculty of Arts & Sciences, Harvard University, Littauer Center G-15, Cambridge, Mass. 02138, U.S.A.

Begley, W. W., 17 St Mary's Gardens, SE11.

Behrens, Miss C. B. A., MA, Dales Barn, Barton, Cambridge.

Bell, P. M. H., BA, BLitt, The School of History, The University, P.O. Box 147, Liverpool.

Beller, E. A., DPhil, Dept of History, Princeton University, N.J., 08540, U.S.A.

Beloff, Professor M., MA, BLitt, All Souls College, Oxford.

Bennett, Captain G. M., RN(ret.) DSC, 33 Argyll Road, W8 7DA.

Bennett, Rev. Canon G. V., MA, DPhil, FSA, New College, Oxford.

Bennett, R. F., MA, Magdalene College, Cambridge.

Bethell, D. L. T., MA, Dept of Medieval History, University College, Belfield, Dublin 4, Ireland.

Bethell, L. M., PhD, University College, Gower Street, WC1E 6BT.

Biddle, M., MA, FSA, Winchester Research Unit, 13 Parchment Street, Winchester.

Bindoff, Professor S. T., MA, 5 Carlton Road, New Malden, Surrey.

*Bing, H. F., MA, 45 Rempstone Road, East Leake, nr Loughborough, Leics.

Binney, J. E. D., DPhil, 6 Pageant Drive, Sherborne, Dorset.

Birch, A., MA, PhD, University of Hong Kong, Hong Kong.

Bishop, A. S., BA, PhD, 254 Leigham Court Road, Streatham, SW16 2RP.

Bishop, T. A. M., MA, The Annexe, Manor House, Hemingford Grey, Hunts.

Black, Professor Eugene C., PhD, Dept of History, Brandeis University, Waltham, Mass. 02154 U.S.A.

Blair, P. Hunter, MA, Emmanuel College, Cambridge.

Blake, E. O., MA, PhD, Roselands, Moorhill Road, Westend, Southampton.

Blake, Professor J. W., CBE, MA, DLitt, Willow Cottage, Mynoe, Limavady, Co. Londonderry, N. Ireland.

Blake, Lord, MA, FBA, The Provost's Lodgings, The Queen's College, Oxford OX1 4AW.

Blakemore, H., PhD, 43 Fitzjohn Avenue, Barnet, Herts.

*Blakey, Professor R. G., PhD, c/o Mr Raymond Shove, Order Dept, Library, University of Minnesota, Minneapolis, Minn., U.S.A.

Blakiston, H. N., BA, 6 Markham Square, SW3.

Blomfield, Mrs K., 8 Elmdene Court, Constitution Hill, Woking, Surrey GU22 7SA.

Blunt, C. E., OBE, FBA, FSA, Ramsbury Hill, Ramsbury, Marlborough, Wilts.

*Boase, T. S. R., MC, MA, FSA, 6 Atherton Drive, SW19 5LB.

*Bolsover, G. H., OBE, MA, PhD, 7 Devonshire Road, Hatch End, Middlesex.

Bolton, Miss Brenda, BA, 21 Steeles Road, London, NW3.

Bolton, Professor G. C., MA, DPhil, 6 Melvista Avenue, Claremont, Western Australia.

Bolton, Professor W. F., AM, PhD, FSA, Douglass College, Rutgers University, New Brunswick, N.J. 08903, U.S.A.

Bond, M. F., OBE, MA, FSA, 19 Bolton Crescent, Windsor, Berks.

Borrie, M. A. F., BA, 14 Lancaster Gate, W2.

Bossy, J. A., MA, PhD, The University, Belfast.

Bottigheimer, Professor Karl S., Dept of History, State University of New York at Stony Brook, Long Island, N.Y., U.S.A.

Boulton, Professor J. T., BLitt, PhD, School of English Studies, The University, Nottingham.

Bowker, Mrs M., MA, BLitt, 5 Spens Avenue, Cambridge.

Bowyer, M. J. F., 32 Netherhall Way, Cambridge.

*Boxer, Professor C. R., DLitt, FBA, Ringshall End, Little Gaddesden, Berkhamsted, Herts.

Boyce, D. G., BA, PhD, Dept of Political Theory and Government, University College, Swansea, SA2 8PP.

Boyle, Professor the Rev. L. E., DPhil, STL, Pontifical Institute of Mediaeval Studies, 59 Queen's Park, Toronto 181, Canada.

Boynton, L. O. J., MA, DPhil, FSA, Westfield College, NW3.
Bramsted, E. K., PhD, DPhil, 41 Daneswood Close, Weybridge, Surrey, KT13 9AY.
Breck, Professor A. D., MA, PhD, University of Denver, Denver, Colorado 80210, U.S.A.
Brentano, Professor R., DPhil, University of California, Berkeley, Calif., U.S.A.
Brett-James, E. A., MA, Royal Military Academy, Sandhurst, Camberley, Surrey.
Bridge, F. R., PhD, The Poplars, Radley Lane, Radley, Leeds.
Briers, Miss P. M., BLitt, 58 Fassett Road, Kingston-on-Thames, Surrey.
Briggs, Professor A., BSc(Econ), MA, DLitt, University of Sussex, Stanmer House, Stanmer, Brighton.
Briggs, R., MA, All Souls College, Oxford OX1 4AL.
Brock, M. G., MA, 31 Linton Road, Oxford OX1 6UL.
Brock, Professor W. R., MA, PhD, Department of History, University of Glasgow, Glasgow 2.
Brodie, Miss D. M., PhD, 137 Roberts Road, Pietermaritzburg, Natal, South Africa.
Brogan, D. H .V., MA, St John's College, Cambridge.
*Bromley, Professor J. S., MA, Merrow, Dene Close, Upper Bassett, Southampton.
*Brooke, Professor C. N. L., MA, LittD, FBA, FSA, 28 Wood Lane, Highgate, N6 5UB.
Brooke, J., BA, 63 Hurst Avenue, Chingford, E4 8DL.
Brooke, Mrs R. B., MA, PhD, 28 Wood Lane, Highgate, N6 5UB.
Brooks, F. W., MA, FSA, The University, Hull.
Brooks, N. P., MA, DPhil, The University, St Andrews, Fife.
Brown, A. L., MA, DPhil, The University, Glasgow G12 8QQ.
Brown, G. S., PhD, 1720 Hanover Road, Ann Arbor, Mich., 48103, U.S.A.
Brown, Judith M., MA, PhD, Dept of History, The University, Manchester M13 9PL.
Brown, Miss L. M., MA, PhD, 93 Church Road, Hanwell, W7.
Brown, Professor M. J., MA, PhD, 333 South Candler Street, Decatur, Georgia 30030, U.S.A.
Brown, P. R. Lamont, MA, FBA, Hillslope, Pullen's Lane, Oxford.
Brown, R. A., MA, DPhil, FSA, King's College, Strand, WC2.
Bruce, J. M., MA, 6 Albany Close, Bushey Heath, Herts, WD2 3SG.
Bruce, Professor M., BA, 22 Chorley Drive, Sheffield, S10 3RR.
Bryant, Sir Arthur W. M., CH, CBE, LLD, 18 Rutland Gate, SW7.
Buckland, P. J., MA, PhD, 6 Rosefield Road, Liverpool L25 8TF.
Bueno de Mesquita, D. M., MA, PhD, Christ Church, Oxford.
Bullock, Sir Alan (L.C.), MA, DLitt, FBA, St Catherine's College, Oxford.
Bullough, Professor D. A., MA, FSA, Dept of Mediaeval History, 71 South Street, St Andrews, Fife.
Burke, U. P., MA, 15 Lower Market Street, Hove, Sussex, BH3 1AT.
Burleigh, The Rev. Principal J. H. S., BD, 4 Braid Avenue, Edinburgh.
Burns, Professor J. H., MA, PhD, 39 Amherst Road, W.13.
Burroughs, P., PhD, Dalhousie University, Halifax, Nova Scotia, Canada.
Burrow, J. W., MA, PhD, Sussex University, Falmer, Brighton.
Bury, J. P. T., MA, Corpus Christi College, Cambridge.

*Butler, Professor Sir James R. M., MVO, OBE, MA, Trinity College, Cambridge CB2 1TQ.
Butler, Professor L. H., MA, DPhil, Principal, Royal Holloway College, Englefield Green, Surrey.
Butler, R. D'O., CMG, MA, All Souls College, Oxford.
BUTTERFIELD, Professor Sir Herbert, MA, LLD, DLitt, DLit, LittD, FBA, 28 High Street, Sawston, Cambridge CB2 4BG.
Bythell, D., MA, DPhil, University College, The Castle, Durham.

Cabaniss, Professor J. A., PhD, University of Mississippi, Box No. 153, University, Mississippi, U.S.A.
Calvert, P. A. R., MA, PhD, AM, Dept of Politics, University of Southampton, Highfield, Southampton SO9 5NH.
Cameron, Professor K., PhD, The University, Nottingham.
Campbell, Professor A. E., MA, PhD, School of History, University of Birmingham, P.O. Box 363, Birmingham B15 2TT.
*Campbell, Miss A. M., AM, PhD, 190 George Street, Brunswick, N.J., U.S.A.
Campbell, Major D. A., FSAScot, An Cladach, Achnacree Bay, Connel, Argyll PA37 1RD.
Campbell, J., MA, FSA, Worcester College, Oxford.
*Campbell, Professor Mildred L., PhD, Vassar College, Poughkeepsie, N.Y., U.S.A.
Campbell, Professor R. H., MA, PhD, University of Stirling, Scotland.
Campbell, Miss Sybil, OBE, MA, Drim-na-Vulun, Lochgilphead, Argyll.
Cant, R. G., MA, The University, St Andrews, Fife.
Cantor, Professor Norman F., PhD, Dept of History, State University of New York at Binghampton, N.Y. 13901, U.S.A.
Capp, B. S., MA, DPhil, Dept of History, University of Warwick, Coventry, Warwickshire CV4 7AL.
Cargill-Thompson, W. D. J., MA, PhD, Dept of Ecclesiastical History, King's College, Strand, WC2.
*Carlson, Professor L. H., PhD, Southern California School of Theology, 1325 College Avenue, Claremont, Calif., U.S.A.
Carman, W. Y., FSA, 94 Mulgrave Road, Sutton, Surrey.
Carr, A. R. M., MA, St Antony's College, Oxford.
Carr, W., PhD, 16 Old Hay Close, Dore, Sheffield.
Carrington, Miss Dorothy, 3 Rue Emmanuel Arene, 20 Ajaccio, Corsica.
Carter, Mrs A. C., MA, 12 Garbrand Walk, Ewell, Epsom, Surrey.
Cartlidge, Rev. J. E. G., Sunnyside House, Snowhill, St George's, Oakengates, Salop.
*Carus-Wilson, Professor E. M., MA, FBA, FSA, 14 Lansdowne Road, W11.
Catto, R. J. A. I., MA, Oriel College, Oxford.
Chadwick, Professor W. O., DD, DLitt, FBA, Selwyn Lodge, Cambridge.
Challis, C. E., MA, PhD, 14 Ashwood Villas, Headingley, Leeds 6.
Chambers, D. S., MA, DPhil, Warburg Institute, Woburn Square, WC1.
Chandaman, Professor C. D., BA, PhD, St David's University College, Lampeter, Cardiganshire.
Chandler, D. G., MA, Hindford, Monteagle Lane, Yately, Camberley, Surrey.

Chandler, G., MA, 23 Dowsefield Lane, Calderstones, Liverpool 18.

Chaplais, P., PhD, FBA, FSA, Wintles Farm House, 36 Mill Street, Eynsham, Oxford.

Charles-Edwards, T. M., DPhil, Corpus Christi College, Oxford.

*Chart, D. A., ISO, LittD, 29 Cambourne Park, Upper Malone, Belfast.

*CHENEY, Professor C. R., MA, DLitt, FBA, 236 Hills Road, Cambridge CB2 2QE.

Chew, Miss H. M., MA, PhD, Seven Hills Nursing Home, St Margaret's Road, St Marychurch, Torquay.

Chibnall, Mrs Marjorie, MA, DPhil, 6 Millington Road, Cambridge.

Child, C. J., OBE, MA, PhM, 94 Westhall Road, Warlingham, Surrey CR3 9HB.

Chorley, The Hon. G. P. H., BA, 40 Castelnau Mansions, London, SW13.

Chrimes, Professor S. B., MA, PhD, LittD, University College, Cathays Park, Cardiff.

*Christie, Mrs, St George's Retreat, Ditchling Common, Burgess Hill, Sussex.

Christie, Professor I. R., MA, 10 Green Lane, Croxley Green, Herts WD3 3HR.

Church, R. A., BA, PhD, The University, Birmingham.

Cirket, A. F., 71 Curlew Crescent, Bedford.

Clanchy, M. T., MA, The University, Glasgow, W2.

Clark, A. E., MA, 32 Durham Avenue, Thornton Cleveleys, Blackpool.

Clark, Professor Dora Mae, PhD, 134 Pennsylvania Ave., Chambersburg, Pa. 17201, U.S.A.   ,

Clark, G. S. R. Kitson, MA, LittD, DLitt, Trinity College, Cambridge CB2 1TQ.

Clarke, P. F., MA, PhD, Dept of History, University College, Gower Street, WC1E 6BT.

*CLAY, Sir Charles T., CB, MA, LittD, FBA, FSA, 30 Queen's Gate Gardens, SW7.

Clementi, Miss D., MA, DPhil, Flat 7, 43 Rutland Gate, SW7.

Clemoes, Professor P. A. M., BA, PhD, Emmanuel College, Cambridge.

Clough, C. H., MA, DPhil, School of History, The University, 8 Abercromby Square, Liverpool 7.

Clover, Mrs V. Helen, MA, PhD, New Hall, Cambridge.

Cobb, H. S., MA, FSA, 1 Child's Way, Hampstead Garden Suburb, NW11.

Cobb, Professor R. C., MA, FBA, Worcester College, Oxford.

Cobban, A. B., MA, PhD, School of History, The University, 8 Abercromby Square, Liverpool 7.

Cocks, E. J., MA, Middle Lodge, Ardingly, Haywards Heath, Sussex.

*Code, Rt Rev. Monsignor Joseph B., MA, STB, ScHistD, DLitt, The Executive House 21E, 4466 West Pine Blvd., St Louis, MO. 63108 U.S.A.

Cohn, H. J., MA, DPhil, University of Warwick, Coventry CV4 7AL.

Cohn, Professor N., MA, DLitt, 61 New End, NW3.

Cole, Lieut-Colonel H. N., OBE, TD, DL, FRSA, 4 Summer Cottages, Guildford Road, Ash, nr Aldershot, Hants.

Coleman, B. I., MA, PhD, Dept of History, The University, Exeter.

Coleman, Professor D. C., BSc, PhD, FBA, Over Hall, Cavendish, Sudbury, Suffolk.

Collier, W. O., MA, FSA, 34 Berwyn Road, Richmond, Surrey.

Collieu, E. G., MA, BLitt, Brasenose College, Oxford.
Collins, Mrs I., MA, BLitt, School of History, 8 Abercromby Square, Liverpool 7.
Collinson, Professor P., MA, PhD, Department of History, University of Sydney, N.S.W. 2006, Australia.
Colvin, H. M., CBE, MA, FBA, St John's College, Oxford.
Conacher, Professor J. B., MA, PhD, 151 Welland Avenue, Toronto 290, Ontario, Canada.
Congreve, A. L., MA, FSA, Orchard Cottage, Cranbrook, Kent.
Connell-Smith, Professor G. E., PhD, 7 Braids Walk, Kirkella, Hull, Yorks.
Constable, G., PhD, 25 Mount Pleasant Street, Cambridge, Mass., U.S.A.
Conway, Professor A. A., MA, University of Canterbury, Christchurch 1, New Zealand.
Cooke, Professor J. J., PhD, Dept of History, College of Liberal Arts, University of Mississippi, University, Miss. 38677, U.S.A.
Coolidge, Professor R. T., MA, BLitt, 27 Rosemount Avenue, Westmount, Quebec, Canada.
Cooper, J. P., MA, Trinity College, Oxford.
Copeland, Professor T. W., PhD, 32 Granville Court, Cheney Lane, Headington, Oxford OX3 OH5.
Cornford, Professor J. P., Dept of Politics, University of Edinburgh, William Robertson Bldg., George Sq., Edinburgh, EH8 9JY.
Cornwall, J. C. K., MA, 1 Orchard Close, Copford Green, Colchester, Essex.
Corson, J. C., MA, PhD, Mossrig, Lilliesleaf, Melrose, Roxburghshire.
Cowan, I. B., MA, PhD, University of Glasgow, Glasgow, G12 8QH.
Cowdrey, Rev. H. E. J., MA, St Edmund Hall, Oxford OX1 4AR.
Cowie, Rev. L. W., MA, PhD, 38 Stratton Road, Merton Park, S.W.19.
Cowley, F. G., PhD, 17 Brookvale Road, West Cross, Swansea.
Cowling, M. J., MA, Peterhouse, Cambridge CB2 1RD.
Cox, A. D. M., MA, University College, Oxford OX1 4BH.
Craig, R. S., BSc(Econ), 99 Muswell Avenue, N10.
Cramp, Professor Rosemary, MA, BLitt, FSA, Department of Archaeology, The Old Fulling Mill, The Banks, Durham.
Cranfield, L. R., 31a Clara Street, South Yarra, Victoria, Australia.
*Crawley, C. W., MA, 1 Madingley Road, Cambridge.
Cremona, The Hon. Mr Justice Professor J. J., DLitt, PhD, LLD, 5 Victoria Gardens, Sliema, Malta.
Crittall, Miss E., MA, FSA, 16 Downside Crescent, NW3.
Crombie, A. C., BSc, MA, PhD, Trinity College, Oxford OX1 3BH.
Crompton, J., MA, BLitt, FSA, Digby Hall, Stoughton Drive South, Leicester LE2 2NB.
Cromwell, Miss V., MA, University of Sussex, Falmer, Brighton, Sussex.
Cross, Miss M. C., MA, PhD, University of York, York YO1 5DD.
Crowder, C. M. D., MA, DPhil, Queen's University, Kingston, Ontario, Canada.
Crowe, Miss S. E., MA, PhD, St Hilda's College, Oxford.
Cruickshank, C. G., MA, DPhil, 15 McKay Road, Wimbledon Common, SW20.
Cumming, Professor I., MEd, PhD, The University, Auckland, New Zealand.

Cummins, J. S., PhD, University College, Gower Street, WC1E 6BT.
Cumpston, Miss I. M., MA, DPhil, Birkbeck College, Malet Street, WC1.
Cunliffe, Professor M. F., MA, BLitt, Dept of American Studies, University of Sussex, Falmer, Brighton.
Cunningham, Professor A. B., MA, PhD, Simon Fraser University, Burnaby 2, B.C., Canada.
Curtis, Professor L. Perry, PhD, Dept of History, Brown University, Providence, R.I. 02912, U.S.A.
Curtis, M. H., PhD, Scripps College, Claremont, Calif., U.S.A.
Cushner, Rev. N. P., SJ, MA, Canisius College, Buffalo, New York 14208, U.S.A.
*Cuttino, Professor G. P., DPhil, Department of History, Emory University, Atlanta, Ga., U.S.A.

Dakin, D., MA, PhD, 7 Langside Avenue, SW15.
Darlington, Professor R. R., BA, PhD, FBA, FSA, Warrenhurst, Twyford, Reading.
Davies, Professor Alun, MA, 46 Eaton Crescent, Swansea.
Davies, C. C., MA, PhD, The Garden House, Church Road, Knighton, Radnor LD7 1EB.
Davies, C. S. L., MA, DPhil, Wadham College, Oxford.
Davies, I. N. R., MA, DPhil, 22 Rowland Close, Wolvercote, Oxford.
Davies, R. R., DPhil, University College, Gower Street, WC1E 6BT.
*DAVIS, G. R. C., MA, DPhil, FSA (*Treasurer*), 214 Somerset Road, SW19 5JE.
Davis, Professor R. H. C., MA, FSA, 56 Fitzroy Avenue, Harborne, Birmingham B17 8RJ.
*Dawe, D. A., 46 Green Lane, Purley, Surrey.
*Day, P. W., MA, 2 Rectory Terrace, Gosforth, Newcastle upon Tyne.
Deane, Miss Phyllis M., MA, Newnham College, Cambridge.
*Deanesly, Professor Margaret, MA, FSA, 196 Clarence Gate Gardens, NW1.
*Deeley, Miss A. P., MA, 41 Linden Road, Bicester, Oxford.
de la Mare, Miss A. C., MA, PhD, Bodleian Library, Oxford.
Denham, E. W., MA, 27 The Drive, Northwood, Middx. HA6 1HW.
Dennis, Professor P. J., MA, PhD, Dept of History, The Royal Military College of Canada, Kingston, Ont. K7L 2W3, Canada.
Denton, J. H., BA, PhD, The University, Manchester M13 9PL.
Dickens, Professor A. G., MA, DLit, FBA, FSA, Institute of Historical Research, University of London, Senate House, WC1E 7HU.
Dickinson, H. T., MA, PhD, Dept of Modern History, The University, Edinburgh.
Dickinson, Rev. J. C., MA, FSA, The University, Birmingham 15.
Dickinson, P. G. M., FSA, The Willows, Wyton, Huntingdon PE17 2AD.
Dickson, P. G. M., MA, DPhil, St Catherine's College, Oxford.
Diké, Professor K. O., MA, PhD, Dept of History, Harvard University, Cambridge, Mass. 02138, U.S.A.
Dilks, Professor D. N., BA, Dept. of International History, The University, Leeds.
Dilworth, Rev. G. M., OSB, PhD, The Abbey, Fort Augustus, Inverness-shire.
Dobson, R. B., MA, DPhil, Department of History, The University, Heslington, York.

Dockery, Rev. J., MA, The Friary, Forest Gate, E7.
*Dodwell, Miss B., MA, The University, Reading.
Dodwell, Professor C. R., MA, PhD, FSA, History of Art Department, The University, Manchester M13 9PL.
Dolley, R. H. M., BA, MRIA, FSA, 48 Malone Avenue, Belfast 9.
Don Peter, The Very Rev. W. L. A., MA, PhD, Aquinas College, Colombo 8, Sri Lanka.
Donald, Professor M. B., MSc, Rabbit Shaw, Stagbury Avenue, Chipstead, Surrey.
*Donaldson, Professor G., MA, PhD, DLitt, 24 East Hermitage Place, Edinburgh EH6 8AD.
*Donaldson-Hudson, Miss R., BA, (address unknown).
Donoughue, B., MA, DPhil, London School of Economics, Houghton Street, London, WC1.
Dore, R. N., MA, Holmrook, 19 Chapel Lane, Hale Barns, Altrincham, Cheshire WA15 0AB.
Douglas, Professor D. C., MA, DLitt, FBA, 4 Henleaze Gardens, Bristol.
Douie, Miss D. L., BA, PhD, FSA, Flat A, 2 Charlbury Road, Oxford.
Doyle, A. I., MA, PhD, University College, The Castle, Durham.
*Drus, Miss E., MA, The University, Southampton.
Du Boulay, Professor F. R. H., MA, Broadmead, Riverhead, Sevenoaks, Kent.
Duckham, B. F., MA, Hillhead Cottage, Balfron, Stirlingshire.
Duggan, C., PhD, King's College, Strand, WC2.
Dugmore, The Rev. Professor C. W., DD, King's College, Strand, WC2.
Duly, Professor L. C., PhD, Dept of History, University of Nebraska, Lincoln, Neb. 68508, U.S.A.
Dunbabin, J. P. D., MA, St Edmund Hall, Oxford.
Duncan, Professor A. A. M., MA, University of Glasgow, 29 Bute Gardens, Glasgow, G12 8QQ.
Dunham, Professor W. H., PhD, 200 Everit Street, New Haven, Conn. 06511, U.S.A.
Dunn, Professor R. S., PhD, Dept of History, The College, University of Pennsylvania, Philadelphia 19104, U.S.A.
Dunning, Rev. Professor P. J., CM, MA, PhD, St Patrick's College, Armagh, Northern Ireland.
Dunning, R. W., BA, PhD, FSA, 16 Comeytrowe Rise, Taunton, Somerset.
Durack, Mrs I. A., MA, PhD, University of Western Australia, Crawley, Western Australia.
Dykes, D. W., MA, Cherry Grove, Welsh St Donats, nr Cowbridge, Glam. CF7 7SS.
Dyos, Professor H. J., BSc(Econ), PhD, 16 Kingsway Road, Leicester.

Eastwood, Rev. C. C., PhD, Heathview, Monks Lane, Audlem, Cheshire.
Eckles, Professor R. B., PhD, P.O. Box 3035, West Lafayette, Indiana, 47906, U.S.A.
Ede, J. R., MA, Public Record Office, Chancery Lane, WC2.
Edmonds, Professor E. L., MA, PhD, Dean of Education, Univ. of Prince Edward Island, Charlottetown, Prince Edward Island, Canada.
Edwards, F. O., SJ, BA, FSA, 114 Mount Street, W1Y 6AH.
EDWARDS, Professor Sir (J.) Goronwy, MA, DLitt, LittD, FBA, FSA, 35 Westmoreland Road, SW13.

Edwards, Miss K., MA, PhD, FSA, Dunbar Cottage, 10 Dunbar Street, Old Aberdeen.

Edwards, Professor R. W. D., MA, PhD, DLitt, 31 Castle Avenue, Clontarf, Dublin.

Ehrman, J. P. W., MA, FBA, FSA, Sloane House, 149 Old Church Street, SW3 6EB.

Elliott, Professor J. H., MA, PhD, FBA, King's College, Strand, WC2.

Ellis, R. H., MA, FSA, Cloth Hill, 6 The Mount, NW3.

Ellul, M., BArch, DipArch, 'Pauline', 55 Old Railway Road, Birkirkara, Malta.

Elrington, C. R., MA, FSA, Institute of Historical Research, Senate House WC1E 7HU.

ELTON, Professor G. R., MA, PhD, LittD, FBA, (*President*), 30 Millington Road, Cambridge CB3 9HP.

Elvin, L., 10 Almond Avenue, Swanpool, Lincoln.

*Emmison, F. G., MBE, PhD, DUniv, FSA, Bibury, Links Drive, Chelmsford.

d'Entrèves, Professor A. P., DPhil, Strada Ai Ronchi 48, Cavoretto, Torino, Italy.

Erickson, Charlotte J., PhD, London School of Economics, Houghton Street, WC2.

*Erith, E. J., Shurlock House, Shurlock Row, Berkshire.

Erskine, Mrs A. M., MA, BLitt, FSA, 44 Birchy Barton Hill, Exeter EX1 3EX.

Evans, Mrs A. K. B., PhD, FSA, White Lodge, 25 Knighton Grange Road, Leicester.

Evans, Sir David (L.), OBE, BA, DLitt, 2 Bay Court, Doctors Commons Road, Berkhamsted, Herts.

Evans, Miss Joan, DLitt, DLit, LLD, LittD, FSA, Thousand Acres, Wootton-under-Edge, Glos.

Evans, R. J. W., MA, PhD, Brasenose College, Oxford.

Evans, The Very Rev. S. J. A., CBE, MA, FSA, The Old Manor, Fulbourne, Cambs.

Everitt, Professor A. M., MA, PhD, The University, Leicester.

Eyck, Professor U. F. J., MA, BLitt, Dept of History, University of Calgary, Alberta T2N IN4, Canada.

Fage, Professor J. D., MA, PhD, Dept of African History, The University, Birmingham.

Fagg, J. E., MA, 47 The Avenue, Durham DH1 4ED.

Farmer, D. F. H., BLitt, FSA, The University, Reading.

Farr, M. W., MA, FSA, 12 Emscote Road, Warwick.

Fearn, Rev. H., MA, PhD, Holy Trinity Vicarage, 6 Wildwood, Northwood, Middlesex.

Fenlon, D. B., BA, PhD, Gonville and Caius College, Cambridge.

Fenn, Rev, R. W. D., MA, BD, FSAScot, Glascwm Vicarage, Llandrindod Wells, Radnorshire.

Ferguson, Professor A. B., PhD, Dept of History, 6727 College Station, Duke University, Durham, N.C. 27708, U.S.A.

Feuchtwanger, E., MA, PhD, Highfield House, Dean, Sparsholt, nr Winchester, Hants.

Fieldhouse, D. K., MA, Nuffield College, Oxford.

Finberg, Professor H. P. R., MA, DLitt, FSA, 151 Park Road, W4 3EX.

Finer, Professor S. E., MA, University of Manchester, Dover Street, Manchester 13.

Fink, Professor Z. S., PhD, 2414 Hartzell Street, Evanston, Ill. 60201, U.S.A.

Finlayson, G. B. A. M., MA, BLitt, 11 Burnhead Road, Glasgow G43 2SU.

Finley, Professor M. I., MA, PhD, 12 Adams Road, Cambridge.

Fisher, D. J. V., MA, Jesus College, Cambridge CB3 9AD.

Fisher, Professor F. J., MA, London School of Economics, Houghton Street, WC2.

Fisher, F. N., Duckpool, Ashleyhay, Wirksworth, Derby DE4 4AJ.

Fisher, Professor S. N., PhD, Box 162, Worthington, Ohio 43085, U.S.A.

Fitch, M. F. B., FSA, c/o Phillimore & Co. Ltd, Shopwyke Hall, Chichester, Sussex.

*Fletcher, The Rt Hon. The Lord, PC, BA, LLD, FSA, 9 Robin Grove, N6 6PA.

Flint, Professor J. E., MA, PhD, Dalhousie University, Halifax, Nova Scotia, Canada.

Foot, M. R. D., MA, BLitt, European Discussion Centre, Wiston House, Wilton Park, Steyning, Sussex BN4 3DZ.

Forbes, D., MA, 89 Gilbert Road, Cambridge.

Ford, W. K., 48 Harlands Road, Haywards Heath, Sussex RH16 1LS.

Forrester, E. G., MA, BLitt, Spring Cottage, Pebble Lane, Brackley, Northants.

Forster, G. C. F., BA, FSA, The University, Leeds 2.

Foster, Professor Elizabeth R., AM, PhD, 205 Stafford Avenue, Wayne, Pa. 19087 U.S.A.

Fowler, K. A., BA, PhD, 2 Nelson Street, Edinburgh 3.

Fox, L., OBE, DL, LHD, MA, FSA, FRSL, Silver Birches, 27 Welcombe Road, Stratford-upon-Avon.

Francis, A. D., CBE, MVO, MA, 21 Cadogan Street, SW3.

Franklin, R. M., BA, Baldwins End, Eton College, Windsor, Berks.

*Fraser, Miss C. M., PhD, 39 King Edward Road, Tynemouth, North Shields NE30 2RW.

Fraser, Miss Maxwell, MA, Crowthorne, 21 Dolphin Road, Slough, Bucks SL1 1TF.

Fraser, P., BA, PhD, Dept of History, Dalhousie University, Halifax, Nova Scotia, Canada.

Frend, Professor W. H. C., TD, MA, DPhil, DD, FSA, Marbrae, Balmaha, Stirlingshire.

Fryde, Professor E. B., DPhil, 1 Plas Danycoed, Aberystwyth, Cards.

*Fryer, Professor C. E., MA, PhD (address unknown).

Fryer, Professor W. R., BLitt, MA., 68 Grove Avenue, Chilwell, Beeston, Notts.

Frykenberg, Professor R. E., MA, PhD, 1840 Chadbourne Avenue, Madison, Wis. 53705, U.S.A.

*Furber, Professor H., MA, PhD, History Department, University of Pennsylvania, Philadelphia, Pa., U.S.A.

Fussell, G. E., DLitt, 55 York Road, Sudbury, Suffolk, CO10 6NF.

Fyrth, H., BSc(Econ.), Dept of Extra Mural Studies, University of London, 7 Ridgemount Street, WC1.

Gabriel, Professor A. L., PhD, FMAA, CFIF, CFBA, Box 578, University of Notre Dame, Notre Dame, Indiana 46556, U.S.A.

*Galbraith, Professor J. S., BS, MA, PhD, University of California, Los Angeles, Calif. 92204, U.S.A.

GALBRAITH, Professor V. H., MA, DLitt, LittD, FBA, 20A Bradmore Road, Oxford.

Gale, Professor H. P. P., OBE, PhD, 6 Nassau Road, London SW13 9QE.

Gale, W. K. V., 19 Ednam Road, Goldthorn Park, Wolverhampton WV4 5BL.

Gann, L. H., MA, BLitt, DPhil, Hoover Institution, Stanford University, Stanford, Calif., U.S.A.

Ganshof, Professor F. L., 12 Rue Jacques Jordaens, Brussels, Belgium.

Gash, Professor N., MA, BLitt, FBA, Gowrie Cottage, 73 Hepburn Gardens, St Andrews.

Gee, E. A., MA, DPhil, FSA, 28 Trentholme Drive, The Mount, York. YO2 2DG.

Gerlach, Professor D. R., MA, PhD, University of Akron, Akron, Ohio 44325, U.S.A.

Gibbs, G. C., MA, Birkbeck College, Malet Street, WC1.

Gibbs, Professor N. H., MA, DPhil, All Souls College, Oxford.

Gibson, Margaret T., MA, DPhil, School of History, The University, Liverpool L69 3BX.

Gifford, Miss D. H., PhD, FSA, Public Record Office, Chancery Lane, WC2.

Gilbert, Professor Bentley B., PhD, Dept of History, University of Ill. at Chicago Circle, Box 4348, Chicago, Ill. 60680, U.S.A.

Gilbert, M., MA, The Map House, Harcourt Hill, Oxford.

Gilley, S., BA, DPhil, Dept of Ecclesiastical History, St Mary's College, University of St Andrew's, St Andrew's, Fife.

Ginter, D. E., AM, PhD, Dept of History, Sir George Williams University, Montreal 107, Canada.

Girtin, T., MA, Butter Field House, Church Street, Old Isleworth, Mddx.

Gleave, Group Capt. T. P., CBE, RAF(Ret.), Willow Bank, River Gardens, Bray-on-Thames, Berks.

*Glover, Professor R. G., MA, PhD, Carleton University, Ottawa 1, Canada.

*Godber, Miss A. J., MA, FSA, Mill Lane Cottage, Willington, Bedford.

Godfrey, Professor J. L., MA, PhD, 231 Hillcrest Circle, Chapel Hill, N.C., U.S.A.

Goldthorp, L. M., MA, Wilcroft House, Pecket Well, Hebden Bridge, Yorks.

Goodman, A. E., MA, BLitt, Dept of Medieval History, The University, Edinburgh.

Goodspeed, Professor D. J., BA, 164 Victoria Street, Niagara-on-the-Lake, Ontario, Canada.

Goodwin, Professor A., MA, Windsor Court, 12 Hound Street, Sherborne, Dorset.

*Gopal, S., MA, DPhil, 30 Edward Elliot Road, Mylapore, Madras, India.

Gordon, Professor D. J., MA, PhD, Wantage Hall, Upper Redlands Road, Reading.

Gordon-Brown, A., Velden, Alexandra Road, Wynberg, C.P., South Africa.

Goring, J. J., MA, PhD, Little Iwood, Rushlake Green, Heathfield, Sussex TW21 9QS.
Gorton, L. J., MA, 41 West Hill Avenue, Epsom, Surrey.
Gosden, P. H. J. H., MA, PhD, The University, Leeds.
Gough, J. W., MA, DLitt, Oriel College, Oxford.
Gowing, Professor Margaret M., BSc(Econ), Linacre College, Oxford.
*Graham, Professor G. S., MA, PhD, Hobbs Cottage, Beckley, Sussex.
Gransden, Mrs A., MA, PhD, FSA, 51 Burlington Road, Sherwood, Nottingham.
Grassby, R. B., MA, Jesus College, Oxford.
Grattan-Kane, P., 12 St John's Close, Helston, Cornwall.
Graves, Professor Edgar B., PhD, LLD, 318 College Hill Road, Clinton, New York 13323, U.S.A.
Gray, J. W., MA, Dept of Medieval History, Queens University, Belfast BT7 1NN.
Greaves, Professor R. W., MA, DPhil, 1920 Hillview Road, Lawrence, Kansas, U.S.A.
Greaves, Mrs R. L., PhD, 1920 Hillview Road, Lawrence, Kansas, U.S.A.
Green, H., BA, Rhinog, Brands Hill Avenue, High Wycombe, Bucks.
Green, Rev. V. H. H., MA, DD, Lincoln College, Oxford.
Greenhill, B. J., CMG, BA, FSA, National Maritime Museum, Greenwich, SE10 9FN.
Greenleaf, Professor W. H., BSc(Econ), PhD, University College, Singleton Park, Swansea, Glam.
Grenville, Professor J. A. S., PhD, University of Birmingham, P.O. Box 363, Birmingham 15.
Gresham, C. A., BA, DLitt, FSA, Bryn-y-deryn, Criccieth, Caerns. LL5 0HR.
Grierson, Professor P., MA, LittD, FBA, FSA, Gonville and Caius College, Cambridge.
Grieve, Miss H. E. P., BA, 153 New London Road, Chelmsford, Essex.
Griffiths, J., MA, Springwood, Stanley Road, New Ferry, Cheshire.
Griffiths, R. A., PhD, University College, Singleton Park, Swansea.
Grimble, I., PhD, 13 Saville Road, Twickenham, Mddx.
Grimm, Professor H. J., PhD, Department of History, 216 North Oval Drive, The Ohio State University, Columbus, Ohio, U.S.A.
Grisbrooke, W. J., MA, 14 The Vale, Edgbaston Park Road, Edgbaston, Birmingham 5.
*Griscom, Rev. Acton, MA, (address unknown).
Gum, Professor E. J., PhD, 5116 Grant Street, Omaha, Nebraska 68104, U.S.A.
Gundersheimer, Professor W. L., MA, PhD, 507 Roumfort Road, Philadelphia, Pa. 19119, U.S.A.
Gurney, Mrs N. K. M., MA, Director, Borthwick Inst. of Historical Research, The University, York, Y01 2PW.

Habakkuk, H. J., MA, FBA, Jesus College, Oxford OX1 3DW.
Haber, Professor F. C., PhD, Dept of History, University of Maryland, College Park, Md. 20742, U.S.A.
*Hadcock, R. N., DLitt, FSA, Winchcombe Farm, Briff Lane, Bucklebury, Reading.
Haffenden, P. S., PhD, 36 The Parkway, Bassett, Southampton.

Haigh, C. A., BA, PhD, Dept of History, The University, Manchester M13 9PL.

Haight, Mrs M. Jackson, PhD, 8 Chemin des Clochettes, Geneva, Switzerland.

Haines, Professor R. M., MA, MLitt, DPhil, FSA, Dalhousie University, Halifax, N.S., Canada.

Hair, P. E. H., MA, DPhil, The School of History, The University, P.O. Box 147, Liverpool.

Halcrow, Miss E. M., MA, BLitt, Achimota School, Achimota, P.B.11, Ghana, West Africa.

Hale, Professor J. R., MA, FSA, University College, Gower Street, WC1E 6BT.

Haley, Professor K. H. D., MA, BLitt, 15 Haugh Lane, Sheffield 11.

Hall, Professor A. R., MA, PhD, 23 Chiswick Staithe, W.4.

Hall, Professor B., MA, PhD, FSA, University of Manchester, M13 9PL.

*Hall, C. S., MA, Flat 16, Petersgath, Moorhead Lane, Shipley, Yorks.

Hall, Professor D. G. E., MA, DLit, 4 Chiltern Road, Hitchin, Herts.

Hall, G. D. G., MA, The President's Lodgings, Corpus Christi College, Oxford OX1 4JF.

Hallam, Professor H. E., MA, PhD, University of Western Australia, Nedlands, Western Australia.

Haller, Professor W., PhD, Rte 2, Southbridge, Holland, Mass. 01550, U.S.A.

Hamer, Professor D., MA, DPhil, History Dept, Victoria University of Wellington, P.O. Box 196, Wellington, New Zealand.

Hamilton, B., BA, PhD, The University, Nottingham NG7 2RD.

Hammersley, G. F., BA, University of Edinburgh, William Robertson Building, George Square, Edinburgh EH8 9JY.

Hampson, Professor N., MA, Ddel'U, The University, Newcastle upon Tyne.

Hand, G. J., MA, DPhil, Woodburn, Sydney Avenue, Blackrock, Co. Dublin, Ireland.

Handover, Miss P. M., MA, 3 Lyon House, 14 Aldersey Road, Guildford, Surrey.

Hanham, Professor H. J., MA, PhD, Harvard University, Cambridge, Mass. 02138, U.S.A.

Hanke, Professor L. U., PhD, University of Massachusetts, Amherst, Mass. 01002, U.S.A.

Harding, A., MA, BLitt, 3 Tantallon Place, Edinburgh.

Harding, F. J. W., MA, BLitt, FSA, Brynrhos, 187 Mayals Road, Swansea SA3 5HQ.

Harding, H. W., BA, LLD, 39 Annunciation Street, Sliema, Malta.

Hargreaves, Professor J. D., MA, 146 Hamilton Place, Aberdeen.

Hargreaves-Mawdsley, Professor W. N., MA, DPhil, FSA, The University, Brandon, Manitoba, Canada.

Harman, Rev. L. W., Hardingstone Vicarage, Northampton.

Harris, Mrs J. F., BA, PhD, Dept of Social Science and Administration, London School of Economics, London, WC2.

Harris, Professor J. R., MA, PhD, The University, P.O. Box 363, Birmingham.

Harrison, B. H., MA, DPhil, Corpus Christi College, Oxford OX1 4JF.

Harrison, C, J., BA, St John's College, Oxford OX1 3JP.

Harrison, Professor Royden, MA, DPhil, 4 Wilton Place, Sheffield S10 2BT.

Harriss, G. L., MA, DPhil, Magdalen College, Oxford.

Hart, C. J. R., MA, MB, BS, Goldthorns, Stilton, Peterborough.

Hart, Mrs J. M., MA, St Anne's College, Oxford.

Hartwell, R. M., MA, DPhil., Nuffield College, Oxford.

Harvey, Miss B. F., MA, BLitt, Somerville College, Oxford OX2 6HD.

Harvey, Margaret M., MA, DPhil, St Aidan's College, Durham.

Harvey, P. D. A., MA, DPhil, FSA, 9 Glen Eyre Close, Bassett, Southampton.

Harvey, Sally P. J., MA, PhD, School of History, The University, Leeds, LS2 9JT.

Haskell, Professor F. J., MA, FBA, Trinity College, Oxford.

Haskins, Professor G. L., AB, LLB, JD, MA, University of Pennsylvania, The Law School, 3400 Chestnut Street, Philadelphia, Pa. 19104 U.S.A.

Haslam, E. B., MA, 5 Pymers Mead, Dulwich, SE21 8NQ.

Hassall, W. O., MA, DPhil, FSA, The Manor House, 26 High Street, Wheatley, Oxford OX9 1XX.

Hastings, Professor Margaret, PhD, Douglass College, Rutgers University, New Brunswick, N.J. 08903, U.S.A.

Hattersley, Professor A. F., MA, DLitt, 1 Sanders Road, Pietermaritzburg, S. Africa.

Hatton, Professor Ragnhild M., PhD, London School of Economics, Houghton Street, WC2.

Havighurst, Professor A. F., PhD, Blake Field, Amherst, Mass. 01002, U.S.A.

*Havinden, Eric, MA, 30 Park Avenue, Solihull, Warwickshire.

Havran, Professor M. J., PhD, Corcoran Dept of History, Randall Hall, University of Virginia, Charlottesville, Va. 22903, U.S.A.

Hay, Professor D., MA, DLitt, FBA, Dept of History, The University, Edinburgh EH8 9JY.

Hazlehurst, G. C. L., BA, DPhil, FRSL, Inst. of Advanced Studies, R.S.S.S., Australian National University, Box 4, P.O. Canberra, ACT, Australia.

Headlam-Morley, Miss A., BLitt, MA, 29 St Mary's Road, Wimbledon, SW19.

Hearder, Professor H., PhD, University College, Cathays Park, Cardiff.

Hembry, Mrs P. M., PhD, Flat 24, Thorncliffe, Lansdown Road, Cheltenham GL51 6PZ.

Hemleben, S. J., MA, DPhil (address unknown).

Henderson, A. J., AB, AM, PhD, 247 North Webster, Jacksonville, Ill. 62650, U.S.A.

Hendy, M. F., MA, The Manor House, Bristol Road, Northfield, Birmingham 31.

Henning, Professor B. D., PhD, Saybrook College, Yale University, New Haven, Conn., U.S.A.

Hennock, P., MA, PhD, School of Cultural and Community Studies, University of Sussex, Falmer, Brighton, Sussex BN1 9QN.

Hexter, Professor J. H., PhD, Dept of History, 237 Hall of Graduate Studies, Yale University, New Haven, Conn. 06520, U.S.A.

Highfield, J. R. L., MA, DPhil, Merton College, Oxford.

HILL, Sir (J. W.) Francis, CBE, MA, LLD, LittD, FSA (*Hon Solicitor*), The Priory, Lincoln.

Hill, J. E. C., MA, DLitt, FBA, The Master's Lodgings, Balliol College, Oxford.

Hill, Professor L. M., MA, PhD, 5066 Berean Lane, Irvine, Calif. 92664, U.S.A.

*Hill, Miss M. C., MA, County Record Office, Shirehall, Shrewsbury.

*Hill, Professor Rosalind M. T., MA, BLitt, FSA, Westfield College, Hampstead, NW3.

Hilton, Professor R. H., DPhil, University of Birmingham, P.O. Box 363, Birmingham 15.

Himmelfarb, Professor Gertrude, PhD, The City of New York Graduate Center, 33 West 42 St, New York, N.Y. 10036.

*Hinsley, Professor F. H., MA, St John's College, Cambridge.

*Hodgett, G. A. J., MA, FSA, King's College, Strand, WC2.

*Hogg, Brigadier O. F. G., CBE, FSA, 1 Hardy Road, Blackheath, SE3.

Holdsworth, C. J., MA, PhD, West End House, Totteridge Lane, N20.

Hollaender, A. E. J., PhD, FSA, 110 Narbonne Avenue, South Side, Clapham Common, SW4 9LQ.

*Hollingsworth, L. W., PhD, Flat 27, Mayfair, 74 Westcliff Road, Bournemouth.

Hollis, Patricia, MA, DPhil, 30 Park Lane, Norwich.

Hollister, Professor C. Warren, MA, PhD, University of California, Santa Barbara, Calif. 93106, U.S.A.

Holmes, G. A., MA, PhD, 431 Banbury Road, Oxford.

Holmes, Professor G. S., MA, BLitt, Tatham House, Burton-in-Lonsdale, Carnforth, Lancs.

Holt, Miss A. D., Fasga-na-Coille, Nethy Bridge, Inverness-shire.

Holt, Professor J. C., MA, DPhil, FSA, University of Reading, White-knights Park, Reading, Berks.

Holt, Professor P. M., MA, DLitt, School of Oriental and African Studies, Malet Street, London WC1E 7HP.

Hook, Mrs. Judith, MA, PhD, Dept of History, Taylor Building, King's College, Old Aberdeen AB9 2UB.

Hope, R. S. H., 25 Hengistbury Road, Southbourne, Bournemouth, Hants.

Horwitz, Professor H. G., BA, DPhil, Dept of History, University of Iowa, Iowa City, Iowa 52240, U.S.A.

*Howard, C. H. D., MA, 15 Sunnydale Gardens, NW7.

*Howard, M. E., MC, MA, FBA, The Homestead, Eastbury, Newbury, Berks.

Howarth, Mrs J. H., MA, St Hilda's College, Oxford.

Howat, G. M. D., MA, BLitt, Old School House, North Moreton, Berks.

Howell, Miss M. E., MA, PhD, 10 Highland Road, Charlton Kings, Cheltenham, Glos. GL53 9LT.

Howell, Professor R., MA, DPhil, Bowdoin College, Brunswick, Maine 04011, U.S.A.

Hudson, G. F., MA, St Antony's College, Oxford OX2 6JF.

Huehns, Miss G., PhD, 35A Sterling Avenue, Edgware, Middlesex HA8 8BP.

Hufton, Miss O. H., PhD, 10 Belmont Drive, Maidenhead, Berks.

Hughes, Professor J. Q., BArch, PhD, Loma Linda, Criccieth, Caernarvons.

Hughes, Miss K. W., MA, PhD, FSA, Newnham College, Cambridge.
Hull, F., BA, PhD, Roundwell Cottage, Bearsted, Maidstone, Kent ME14 4EU.
Hulton, P. H., BA, FSA, 46 St Paul's Road, N1.
HUMPHREYS, Professor R. A., OBE, MA, PhD, DLitt, LittD, DUniv, 13 St Paul's Place, Canonbury, N1 2QE.
Hunnisett, R. F., MA, DPhil, 54 Longdon Wood, Keston, Kent BR2 6EW.
Hurst, M. C., MA, St John's College, Oxford.
Hurstfield, Professor J., DLit, 7 Glenilla Road, NW3.
Hurt, J. S., BA, PhD, BSc(Econ), 14 The Avenue, Barnet, Herts EN5 4EN.
*Hussey, Professor Joan M., MA, BLitt, PhD, FSA, Royal Holloway College, Englefield Green, Surrey.
Hyams, P. R., MA, DPhil, Pembroke College, Oxford.
Hyde, Professor F. E., MA, PhD, Heather Cottage, 41 Village Road, West Kirby, Wirral, Cheshire.
*Hyde, H. Montgomery, MA, DLit, Westwell, Tenterden, Kent.
Hyde, J. K., MA, PhD, The University, Manchester.

Ingham, Professor K., MA, DPhil, The Woodlands, 94 West Town Lane, Bristol 4.
Ives, E. W., PhD, 214 Myton Road, Warwick.

Jack, Professor R. I., MA, PhD, University of Sydney, Sydney, N.S.W., Australia.
Jack, Mrs Sybil M., MA, BLitt, University of Sydney, N.S.W., Australia.
Jackman, Professor S. W., PhD, FSA, 1065 Deal Street, Victoria, British Columbia, Canada.
Jackson, E. D. C., FSA, (address unknown).
Jaffar, Professor S. M., BA, Khudadad Street, Peshawar City, N.W.F. Province, W. Pakistan.
James, M. E., MA, University of Durham, 43-45 North Bailey, Durham.
James, Professor Robert R., MA, FRSL, United Nations, N.Y. 10017, U.S.A.
Jarvis, R. C., ISO, FSA, Shelley, Station Road, Hockley, Essex.
Jasper, Rev. Canon R. C. D., MA, DD, 1 Little Cloister, Westminster Abbey, SW1.
Jeffs, R. M., MA, DPhil, 25 Lawson Road, Sheffield S10 5BU.
Jenkins, D., MA, LLM, Dept of Law, University College of Wales, Aberystwyth, Cards., SY23 2DB.
Jeremy, D. J., BA, MLitt, 16 Britannia Gardens, Westcliff-on-sea, Essex SS0 8BN.
John, Professor A. H., BSc(Econ), PhD, London School of Economics, Houghton Street, WC2.
John, E., MA, The University, Manchester 13.
Johnson, D. J., BA, 41 Cranes Park Avenue, Surbiton, Surrey.
Johnson, Professor D. W. J., BA, BLitt, University College, Gower Street, WC1E 6BT.
*Johnson, J. H., MA, Whitehorns, Cedar Avenue, Chelmsford.
Johnson, W. Branch, FSA, Hope Cottage, 22 Mimram Road, Welwyn, Herts.
Johnston, Miss E. M., MA, PhD, The University, Sheffield 10.

Johnston, Lieut-Colonel G. R., RA, FRSA, Wood Corner, Lankhills Road, Winchester.

Johnston, Professor S. H. F., MA, Fronhyfryd, Llanbadarn Road, Aberystwyth.

Jones, Dwyryd W., MA, DPhil, Dept of History, University of Wales, Aberystwyth.

Jones, G. A., MA, PhD, Dept of History, Faculty of Letters, University of Reading, Whiteknights, Reading, Berks.

Jones, Professor G. Hilton, PhD, Dept of History, Eastern Ill. University, Charleston, Ill. 61920, U.S.A.

Jones, G. J., The Croft, Litchard Bungalows, Bridgend, Glam.

*Jones, Professor G. P., MA, Spa House, Witherstack, via Grange-over-Sands, Lancs.

Jones, H. W., MA, PhD, 32 Leylands Terrace, Bradford BD9 5QR.

Jones, Professor I. G., MA, 12 Laura Place, Aberystwyth, Cards.

Jones, Professor J. R., MA, PhD, School of English and American Studies, University Plain, Norwich.

Jones, Professor M. A., MA, DPhil, Dept of History, University College, Gower Street, WC1E 6BT.

Jones, M. C. E., MA, DPhil, The University, Nottingham.

Jones, The Rev. Canon O. W., MA, The Vicarage, Builth Wells, Breconshire.

Jones, P. E., LLB, FSA, 18 Wansunt Road, Bexley, Kent.

Jones, P. J., DPhil, Brasenose College, Oxford.

Jones, Professor W. J., PhD, Dept of History, The University of Alberta, Edmonton, T6G 2E1, Canada.

Jordan, Professor P. D., PhD, LLD, 26 Cascade Terrace, Burlington, Iowa 52601, U.S.A.

Jordan, Professor W. K., PhD, 3 Conrad Avenue, Cambridge, Mass. 02138, U.S.A.

Judson, Professor Margaret A., PhD, 8 Redcliffe Avenue, Highland Park, N.J. 08904, U.S.A.

Jukes, Rev. H. A. Ll, MA, The Vicarage, Tilney All Saints, nr King's Lynn, Norfolk.

Kamen, H. A. F., MA, DPhil, The University, Warwick, Coventry, CV4 7AL.

*Kay, H., MA, 16 Bourton Drive, Poynton, Stockport, Cheshire.

Kearney, Professor H. F., MA, PhD, Edinburgh University, Old College, South Bridge, Edinburgh 8.

Keeler, Mrs Mary F., PhD, 302 W. 12th Street, Frederick, Md. 21701, U.S.A.

Keen, M. H., MA, Balliol College, Oxford.

Kellaway, C. W., MA, FSA, 2 Grove Terrace, NW5.

Kellett, J. R., MA, PhD, Dept of Economic History, University of Glasgow, G12 8QQ.

Kelly, Professor T., MA, PhD, 55 Freshfield Road, Formby, nr Liverpool.

Kemp, Miss B., MA, FSA, St Hugh's College, Oxford.

Kemp, B. R., BA, PhD, 12 Redhatch Drive, Earley, Reading, Berks.

Kemp, The Very Rev. E. W., DD, The Deanery, Worcester WR1 2LH.

Kemp, Lt-Commander P. K., RN, Malcolm's, 51 Market Hill, Maldon, Essex.

Kendall, Professor P. M., PhD, 928 Holiday Drive, Lawrence, Kansas 66044, U.S.A.

Kennedy, J., MA, 14 Poolfield Avenue, Newcastle-under-Lyme, Staffs. ST5 2NL.

Kent, Rev. J. H. S., MA, PhD, Dept of Theology, University of Bristol, Senate House, Bristol BS8 1TH.

Kenyon, Professor J. P., PhD, Nicholson Hall, Cottingham, Yorks.

Ker, N. R., MA, DLitt, FBA, FSA, Slievemore, Foss, by Pitlochry, Perthshire.

Kerling, Miss N. J. M., PhD, 26 Upper Park Road, NW3.

Kerridge, E. W. J., PhD, Llys Tudur, Myddleton Park, Denbigh LL16 4AL.

Kershaw, Ian, BA, DPhil, 6 Cranston Drive, Sale, Cheshire.

Ketelbey, Miss D. M., MA, 18 Queen's Gardens, St Andrews, Fife.

Khan, M. Siddiq, MA, LLB, The Bougainvilleas, No. 64 North Dhanmondi, Kalabagan, Dacca-5, Bangladesh.

Khanna, Kahan Chand, MA, PhD, 3-B Mathura Road, New Delhi 14, India.

Kiernan, Professor V. G., MA, University of Edinburgh, William Robertson Building, George Square, Edinburgh.

*Kimball, Miss E. G., BLitt, PhD, Drake's Corner Road, Princeton, N.J., U.S.A.

King, E. J., MA, PhD, Dept of History, The University, Sheffield S10 2TN.

King, P. D., BA, PhD, Lancaster View, Bailrigg, Lancaster.

Kingsford, P. W., BSc(Econ), PhD, Hatfield Polytechnic, Bayfordbury, Hertford, Herts.

Kinsley, Professor J., MA, PhD, DLitt, FBA, University of Nottingham, Nottingham NG7 2RD.

Kirby, D. P., MA, PhD, Manoraven, Llanon, Cards.

Kirby, J. L., MA, FSA, 22 Bardwell Court, Bardwell Road, Oxford.

Klibansky, Professor R., MA, PhD, DPhil, FRSC, McGill University, Dept of Philosophy, Montreal, Canada.

Knecht, R. J., MA, 22 Warwick New Road, Leamington Spa, Warwickshire.

*Knight, L. Stanley, MA, Little Claregate, 1 The Drive, Malthouse Lane, Tettenhall, Wolverhampton.

Knowles, C. H., PhD, University College, Cathays Park, Cardiff CF1 1XL.

*KNOWLES, Professor the Rev. M. D., MA, DD, LittD, DLitt, DLit, FBA, FSA, 9 Old House Close, Church Road, SW19.

Kochan, L. E., BA, PhD, 237 Woodstock Road, Oxford.

Koenigsberger, Professor H. G., PhD, Dept of History, Kings College, Strand, London WC2.

Koeppler, Professor H., OBE, DPhil, Wilton Park, Wiston House, Steyning, Sussex.

Kossmann, Professor E. H., DLitt, Rijksuniversiteit te Groningen, Groningen, The Netherlands.

Lambert, M. D., MA, 17 Oakwood Road, Henleaze, Bristol BS9 4NP.

Lamont, W. M., PhD, 9 Bramleys, Kingston, Lewes, Sussex.

Lancaster, Miss J. C., MA, FSA, 43 Craigmair Road, Tulse Hill, SW2.

Landa, Professor L. A., AM, PhD, Princeton University, Princeton, N.J., U.S.A.

Lander, J. R., MA, MLitt, Middlesex College, University of Western Ontario, London, Ont., Canada.

Landes, Professor D. S., PhD, Widener 97, Harvard University, Cambridge, Mass. 02138, U.S.A.

*Langton, Rev. E., DD, Delamere, 43 Glandon Drive, Cheadle Hulme, nr Stockport.

La Page, J., FSA, Craig Lea, 44 Bank Crest, Baildon, Yorkshire.

Laprade, Professor W. T., PhD, 1108 Monmouth Avenue, Durham, N. Carolina, U.S.A.

Larkin, Professor the Rev. J. F., CSV, PhD, University College, De Paul University, 25E Jackson Blvd., Chicago, Ill. 60604, U.S.A.

Larner, J. P., MA, The University, Glasgow, W2.

Latham, Professor R. C., MA, Magdalene College, Cambridge.

Lawrence, Professor C. H., MA, DPhil, Bedford College, Regent's Park, NW1.

*Laws, Lieut-Colonel M. E. S., OBE, MC, Bank Top Cottage, Seal Chart, Sevenoaks, Kent.

Leddy, J. F., MA, BLitt, DPhil, University of Windsor, Windsor, Ontario, Canada.

Lee, J. M., BA, PhD, Birkbeck College, Malet Street, London WC1.

Lee, Professor M. du P., PhD, Douglass College, Rutgers University, New Brunswick, N.J. 08903, U.S.A.

Lees, R. McLachlan, MA, Kent College, Harbridge, Ringwood, Hants.

Legge, Professor M. Dominica, MA, DLitt, 191A Woodstock Road, Oxford OX2 7AB.

Lehmberg, Professor S. E., PhD, Dept of History, University of Minnesota, Minneapolis, Minn. 55455, U.S.A.

Lenanton, Lady, CBE, MA, FSA, Bride Hall, nr Welwyn, Herts.

Le Patourel, Professor J. H., MA, DPhil, Ddel'U, Westcote, Hebers Ghyll Drive, Ilkley, Yorks. LS29 9QH.

Leslie, Professor R. F., BA, PhD, 23 Grove Park Road, W4.

Levine, Professor Mortimer, PhD, 529 Woodhaven Drive, Morgantown, West Va. 26505, U.S.A.

Levy, Professor F. J., PhD, University of Washington, Seattle, Wash. 98195, U.S.A.

Lewis, Professor A. R., MA, PhD, History Dept, University of Massachusetts, Amhurst, Mass. 01003, U.S.A.

Lewis, Professor B., PhD, FBA, 55 Springfield Road, NW8.

Lewis, C. W., BA, FSA, University College, Cathays Park, Cardiff.

Lewis, E. D., MA, DSc, Glamorgan College of Education, Buttrils Road, Barry, Glam.

Lewis, P. S., MA, All Souls College, Oxford.

Lewis, R. A., PhD, University College of North Wales, Bangor.

Leyser, K., MA, Magdalen College, Oxford.

Lhoyd-Owen, Commander J. H., RN, 37 Marlings Park Avenue, Chislehurst, Kent.

Liebeschütz, H., MA, DPhil, Dockenhuden, Marines Road, Liverpool 23.

*Lindsay, Mrs H., MA, PhD, Girton College, Cambridge.

Linehan, P. A., MA, PhD, St John's College, Cambridge.

Lipman, V. D., DPhil, FSA, Flat 14, 33 Kensington Court, W8.

Livermore, Professor H. V., MA, Sandycombe Lodge, Sandycombe Road, St Margarets, Twickenham.

Loades, D. M., MA, PhD, Oatlands, Farnley Mount, Durham.

Lobel, Mrs M. D., BA, FSA, 16 Merton Street, Oxford.

Lockhart, L., MA, PhD, LittD, Cedarwood House, West Green, Barrington, Cambridge CB2 5SA.

Lockie, D. McN., MA, Chemin de la Panouche, Saint-Anne, Grasse, Alpes Maritimes, France.

Loewenberg, Professor B. J., MA, PhD, 15 Center Knolls, Bronxville, New York, U.S.A.

Logan, Rev. F. D., MA, MSD, Emmanuel College, 400 The Fenway, Boston, Mass. 02115, U.S.A.

London, Miss Vera C. M., MA, Underholt, Westwood Road, Bidston, Birkenhead, Cheshire.

Longford, The Right Honble The Countess of, MA, DLitt, Bernhurst, Hurst Green, Sussex.

Longley, D. A., BA, 13 Bournbrook Road, Birmingham 29.

Longrais, Professor F. Joüon des, D-en-droit, LèsL, 4 rue de la Terrasse, Paris XVII, France.

Loomie, Rev. A. J., SJ, MA, PhD, Fordham University, New York, N.Y. 10458, U.S.A.

Lourie, Elena, MA, DPhil, 66 Brandeis Street, Tel-Aviv, Israel.

Lovatt, R. W., MA, DPhil, Peterhouse, Cambridge.

Lovell, J. C., BA, PhD, Eliot College, University of Kent, Canterbury.

Lowe, P. C., BA, PhD, The University, Manchester.

Loyn, H. R., MA, FSA, 196 Fidlas Road, Llanishen, Cardiff.

Luft, The Rev. M., MA, MLitt, Merchant Taylor's School, Crosby, Liverpool 23.

*Lumb, Miss S. V., MA, Flat 309, 112 King's Head Hill, Chingford, E4 7ND.

Luscombe, Professor D. E., MA, PhD, 129 Prospect Road, Totley Rise, Sheffield.

Luttrell, A. T., MA, DPhil, Dept of History, The Royal University of Malta, Msida, Malta.

Lyman, Professor R. W., PhD, Office of the President, Stanford University, Stanford, Calif. 94305, U.S.A.

Lynch, Professor J., MA, PhD, University College, Gower Street, London WC1E 6BT.

Lyon, Professor Bryce D., PhD, Dept of History, Brown University, Providence, Rhode Island 02912, U.S.A.

Lyons, Professor F. S. L., MA, PhD, LittD, Eliot College, University of Kent, Canterbury.

Lyttelton, The Hon. N. A. O., BA, St Antony's College, Oxford.

Mabbs, A. W., Public Record Office, Chancery Lane, WC2.

MacCaffrey, Professor W. T., PhD, 745 Hollyoke Center, Harvard University, Cambridge, Mass. 02138, U.S.A.

McConica, Professor J. K., OSB, MA, DPhil, Pontifical Institute of Medieval Studies, 59 Queen's Park Crescent, Toronto 181, Ont., Canada.

McCord, N., PhD, 7 Hatherton Avenue, Cullercoats, North Shields, Northumberland.

McCracken, Professor J. L., MA, PhD, New University of Ulster, Coleraine, Co. Londonderry, N. Ireland.

McCulloch, Professor S. C., MA, PhD, 2121 Windward Lane, Newport Beach, Calif. 92660, U.S.A.

MacDonagh, Professor O., MA, PhD, RSSS, Australian National University, Box 4 GPO, Canberra, ACT, Australia.
Macdonald, Professor D. F., MA, DPhil, Queen's College, Dundee.
McDonald, Prof. T. H., MA, PhD, Idaho State University, Pocatello, Idaho 83201, U.S.A.
McDowell, Professor R. B., PhD, LittD, Trinity College, Dublin.
Macfarlane, A., MA, DPhil, PhD, King's College, Cambridge CB2 1ST.
Macfarlane, L. J., PhD, FSA, King's College, University of Aberdeen, Aberdeen.
McGrath, P. V., MA, University of Bristol, Bristol.
MacGregor, D. R., BA, 99 Lonsdale Road, SW13.
McGregor, Professor O. R., BSc(Econ), MA, Far End, Wyldes Close, London, N.W.11.
McGurk, J. J. N., BA, MPhil, Conway House, Stanley Avenue, Birkdale, Southport, Lancs.
McGurk, P. M., PhD, Birkbeck College, Malet Street, London WC1E 7HX.
Machin, G. I. T., MA, DPhil, Dept of Modern History, University of Dundee, DD1 4HN.
MacIntyre, A. D., MA, DPhil, Magdalen College, Oxford.
McKenna, Professor J. W., MA, PhD, Haverford College, Haverford, Pa. 19041, U.S.A.
Mackesy, P. G., MA, Pembroke College, Oxford.
*Mackie, Professor J. D., CBE, MC, MA, LLD, FSAScot, 67 Dowanside Road, Glasgow W2.
McKinley, R. A., MA, 42 Boyers Walk, Leicester Forest East, Leics.
Mackintosh, Professor J. P., MA, MP, House of Commons, London SW1A 0AA.
McKisack, Professor May, MA, BLitt, FSA, 59 Parktown, Oxford.
Maclagan, M., MA, FSA, Trinity College, Oxford.
Maclean, J. N. M., BLitt, PhD, 61 Learmonth Court, Edinburgh 4.
MacLeod, R. M., AB, PhD, Dept of History and Social Studies of Science, Physics Bldg., University of Sussex, Falmer, Brighton BN1 9QH.
McManners, Professor J., MA, Christ Church, Oxford OX1 1DP.
MacMichael, N. H., FSA, 2B Little Cloister, Westminster Abbey, SW1.
MacNiocaill, G., PhD, Dept of History, University College, Galway, Ireland.
McNulty, Miss P. A., BA, St George's Hall, Elmhurst Road, Reading.
MacNutt, Professor W. S., MA, University of New Brunswick, Fredericton, N.B., Canada.
Macpherson, Professor C. B., PhD, Dept of Political Economy, University of Toronto, 100 St George Street, Toronto 5, Canada.
McRoberts, Rt Rev. Monsignor David, STL, DLitt, FSA, 16 Drummond Place, Edinburgh EH3 6PL.
Madariaga, Miss Isabel de, PhD, 27 Southwood Lawn Road, N6.
Madden, A. F. McC., D Phil, Nuffield College, Oxford.
Maddicott, J. R., MA, DPhil, Exeter College, Oxford.
Maehl, Professor W. H., PhD, University of Oklahoma, Norman, Oklahoma 73069, U.S.A.
Magnus-Allcroft, Sir Phillip, Bt, CBE, FRSL, Stokesay Court, Craven Arms, Shropshire SY7 9BD.
Mahoney, Professor T. H. D., AM, PhD, MPA, Massachusetts Institute of Technology, Cambridge, Mass. 02138, U.S.A.

*Major, Miss K., MA, BLitt, LittD, FSA, 21 Queensway, Lincoln.
Malone, Professor J. J., PhD, 629 St James Street, Pittsburgh, Pa. 15232, U.S.A.
Mann, Miss J. de L., MA, The Cottage, Bowerhill, Melksham, Wilts.
Manning, B. S., MA, DPhil, The University, Manchester.
Manning, Professor R. B., PhD, 2848 Coleridge Road, Cleveland Heights, Ohio 44118, U.S.A.
Mansergh, Professor P. N. S., OBE, DPhil, DLitt, LittD, FBA, The Master's Lodge, St John's College, Cambridge.
Marchant, Rev. R. A., PhD, BD, Laxfield Vicarage, Woodbridge, Suffolk.
Marder, Professor A. J., PhD, University of California, Irvine, Calif. 92664, U.S.A.
Marett, W. P., BSc(Econ), BCom, MA, PhD, Rutherford Lodge, The University, Loughborough, Leics.
Margetts, J., MA, DipEd, DrPhil, 5 Glenluce Road, Liverpool LI9 9BX.
Markham, F. M. H., MA, Hertford College, Oxford.
Markus, R. A., MA, PhD, The University, 8 Abercromby Square, Liverpool.
Marriner, Sheila, MA, PhD, Social Studies Building, Bedford Street South, Liverpool.
Marsden, A., BA, PhD, 9 Fort Street, Dundee DD2 1BS.
Marshall, Miss D., MA, PhD, 2 The Fold, Old Hutton, Kendall, Westmorland.
Marshall, J. D., PhD, 16 Westgate, Morecambe, Lancs.
Marshall, P. J., MA, DPhil, King's College, Strand, WC2.
Martin, Professor G. H., MA, DPhil, 21 Central Avenue, Leicester LE2 1TB.
Marwick, Professor A. J. B., MA, BLitt, Dept of History, The Open University, Walton Hall, Walton, Bletchley, Bucks.
Mason, F. K., 147 London Road, St Albans, Hertfordshire.
Mason, J. F. A., MA, DPhil, FSA, Christ Church, Oxford OX1 1DP.
Mason, T. W., MA, DPhil, St Peter's College, Oxford OX1 2DL.
Mather, F. C., MA, 69 Ethelburg Avenue, Swaythling, Southampton.
*Mathew, The Most Rev. Archbishop D. J., MA, LittD, FSA, Stonor Park, Henley-on-Thames, Oxon.
Mathias, Professor P., MA, All Souls College, Oxford.
*Mathur-Sherry, Tikait Narain, BA, LLB, 17/254 Chili-Int-Road, Agra (U.P.), India.
Matthew, D. J. A., MA, DPhil, The University, Durham.
Mattingly, Professor H. B., MA, Dept of Ancient History, The University, Leeds.
Mayr-Harting, H. M. R. E., MA, DPhil, St Peter's College, Oxford.
Medlicott, Professor W. N., MA, DLit, DLitt, 2 Cartref, Ellesmere Road, Weybridge, Surrey.
Meekings, C. A. F., MA, 42 Chipstead Street, SW6.
Merson, A. L., MA, The University, Southampton.
Micklewright, F. H. A., MA, 228 South Norwood Hill, SE25.
Midgley, Miss L. M., MA, 84 Wolverhampton Road, Stafford ST17 4AW.
Miller, E., MA, LittD, 36 Almoners Avenue, Cambridge CB1 4PA.
Miller, E. J., BA, 37 Aldbourne Road, W.12.
Miller, Miss H., MA, 32 Abbey Gardens, NW8.
Milne, A. T., MA, 9 Dixon Close, SE21 7BD.

Milne, Miss D. J., MA, PhD, King's College, Aberdeen.
Milsom, Professor S. F. C., MA, FBA, London School of Economics, Houghton Street, WC2.
Milward, Professor A. S., MA, PhD, Inst. of Science and Technology, University of Manchester, PO Box 88, Sackville Street, Manchester M6o 1QD.
Minchinton, Professor W. E., BSc(Econ), The University, Exeter EX4 4PU.
Mingay, Professor G. E., PhD, Mill Field House, Selling Court, Selling, nr Faversham, Kent.
Mitchell, C., MA, BLitt, LittD, Woodhouse Farmhouse, Fyfield, Abingdon, Berks.
Mitchell, L. G., MA, DPhil, University College, Oxford.
Mitchison, Mrs R. M., MA, 6 Dovecot Road, Edinburgh 12.
*Moir, Rev. Prebendary A. L., MA, 55 Mill Street, Hereford.
Momigliano, Professor A. D., DLitt, FBA, University College, Gower Street, WC1E 6BT.
Moody, Professor T. W., MA, PhD, Trinity College, Dublin.
Moore, B. J. S., BA, University of Bristol, 67 Woodland Road, Bristol.
*Moorman, Mrs, MA, Bishop Mount, Ripon, Yorks.
Morey, Rev. Dom R. Adrian, OSB, MA, DPhil, LittD, Benet House, Mount Pleasant, Cambridge.
Morgan, B. G., BArch, PhD, ARIBA, 29 Gerard Road, Wallasey, Cheshire.
Morgan, K. O., MA, DPhil, The Queen's College, Oxford OX1 4BH.
Morgan, Miss P. E., 1A The Cloisters, Hereford, HR1 2NG.
*Morrell, Professor W. P., MA, DPhil, 20 Bedford Street, St Clair, Dunedin SW1, New Zealand.
Morris, The Rev. Professor C., MA, 53 Cobbett Road, Bitterne Park, Southampton SO2 4HJ.
Morris, G. C., MA, King's College, Cambridge.
Morris, J. R., BA, PhD, Little Garth, Ashwell, nr Baldock, Herts.
Morris, Professor R. B., PhD, Dept of History, Colombia University in the City of New York, 605 Fayerweather Hall, New York, N.Y. 10552 U.S.A.
Morton, Miss C. E., MA, MLS, c/o Mrs E. Webster, Powdermill House, Battle, Sussex TN33 0SP.
Morton, Professor W. L., MA, BLitt, LLD, DLitt, Champlain College, Peterborough, Ont., Canada.
Mosse, Professor G. L., PhD, Dept of History, The University of Wisconsin, 3211 Humanities Bldg., 435 N. Park Street, Madison, Wis. 53706 U.S.A.
Mosse, Professor W. E. E., MA, PhD, Dawn Cottage, Ashwellthorpe, Norwich, Norfolk.
MULLINS, E. L. C., OBE, MA (*Librarian*), Institute of Historical Research, University of London, Senate House, WC1E 7HU.
Muntz, Miss I. Hope, FSA, c/o Mrs E. Webster, Powdermill House, Battle, Sussex, TN33 0SP.
Murphy, J., MA, PhD, Fellview, Heathwaite Manor, Windermere, Westmorland.
Murray, A., BA, BPhil, The University, Newcastle upon Tyne.
Murray, Athol L., BA, MA, LLB, PhD, 33 Inverleith Gardens, Edinburgh EH3 5PR.

Murray, Miss K. M. E., BA, BLitt, FSA, Upper Cranmore, Heyshott, Midhurst, Sussex.
Myers, Professor A. R., MA, PhD, FSA, Rosemount, 3 Cholmondeley Road, West Kirby, Wirral, Cheshire.
Myres, J. N. L., CBE, MA, LLD, DLitt, DLit, FBA, PSA, Christ Church, Oxford.

Naidis, Professor M., PhD, 10847 Canby Avenue, Northbridge, California 91324.
Nath, Dwarka, MBE, 30 Crowther Road, South Norwood, SE25.
*NEALE, Professor Sir John (E), MA, DLitt, LittD, LHD, FBA, Adare, Penn Road, Beaconsfield, Bucks.
Nef, Professor J. U., PhD, University of Chicago, Chicago, Ill., U.S.A.
New, Professor J. F. H., Dept of History, Waterloo University, Waterloo, Ontario, Canada.
Newman, A. N., MA, DPhil, 33 Stanley Road, Leicester.
Newsome, D. H., MA, Christ's Hospital, Horsham, Sussex.
Newton, K. C., MA, 82 Dorset Road, Maldon, Essex.
Nicholas, Professor H. G., MA, FBA, New College, Oxford.
Nicholl, D., MA, 2 Church Plantations, Keele, Staffordshire.
Nicol, Professor D. M., MA, PhD, King's College, London WC2R 2LS.
Norman, E. R., MA, PhD, Jesus College, Cambridge.

Oakeshott, W. F., MA, LLD, FBA, FSA, Lincoln College, Oxford.
Obolensky, Prince Dimitri, MA, PhD, FSA, Christ Church, Oxford.
O'Connell, Professor D. P., BA, LLM, PhD, LLD, All Souls College, Oxford.
*Offler, Professor H. S., MA, 28 Old Elvet, Durham.
O'Gorman, F., BA, PhD, The University, Manchester M13 9PL.
*Orr, J. E., MA, ThD, DPhil, 11451 Berwick Street, Los Angeles, Cal. 90049, U.S.A.
Osborn, Professor J. M., PhD, FSA, 1603A Yale Station, New Haven, Conn. Beinecke Library, 06520, U.S.A.
Oschinsky, Dorothea, DPhil, PhD, The University, Liverpool L69 3BX.
Otway-Ruthven, Professor A. J., MA, PhD, 7 Trinity College, Dublin, Eire.
Outhwaite, R. B., BA, PhD, The University, Leicester.
Owen, A. E. B., MA, 79 Whitwell Way, Coton, Cambridge CB3 7PW.
Owen, C. V., The Vicarage, Addlestone, Surrey KT15 1SJ.
Owen, Mrs D. M., MA, FSA, 79 Whitwell Way, Coton, Cambridge CB3 7PW.
Owen, G. D., MA, PhD, Casa Alba, Wray Lane, Reigate, Surrey.
Owen, J. B., BSc, MA, DPhil, The University, Calgary 44, Alberta, Canada.

*Packard, Professor S. R., PhD, 126 Vernon Street, Northampton, Mass., U.S.A.
Pakeman, Professor S. A., MC, MA, 45 Kensington Mansions, Trebovir Road, SW5 9TE.
Pallister, Miss Anne, BA, PhD, Dept of History, University of Reading, Whiteknights, Reading, Berks.
Parker, N. G., MA, PhD, Dept of Modern History, St Salvator's College, The University, St Andrew's, Fife.

Parker, R. A. C., MA, DPhil, The Queen's College, Oxford OX1 4BH.
Parker, The Rev. Dr. T. M., MA, DD, FSA, 36 Chalfont Road, Oxford OX2 6TH.
*Parkinson, Professor C. N., MA, PhD, Les Caches House, St Martins, Guernsey, C.I.
Parris, H., MA, Civil Service College, Sunningdale Park, Ascot, Berks. SL5 0QE.
Parry, E. Jones, MA, PhD, 3 Sussex Mansions, Old Brompton Road, SW7.
Parry, Professor J. H., MA, PhD, Pinnacle Road, Harvard, Mass. 01451, U.S.A.
Parsloe, C. G., BA, 1 Leopold Avenue, SW19.
Patterson, Professor A. T., MA, The Sele, Stoughton, Chichester, Sussex.
Paul, J. E., PhD, 24 Portsdown Avenue, Drayton, nr Portsmouth, Hants.
Pearl, Mrs V. L., MA, DPhil, 70 Holden Road, Woodside Park, N12.
Pearn, B. R., OBE, MA, The White House, Beechwood Avenue, Aylmerton, Norfolk NOR 25Y.
Peaston, Rev. A. E., MA, BLitt, The Manse, Dromore, Co. Down, N. Ireland.
Peek, Miss H. E., MA, FSA, FSAScot, Taintona, Moretonhampstead, Newton Abbot, Devon TQ13 8LG.
Pegues, Professor F. J., PhD, 71 Acton Road, Columbus, Ohio 43214, U.S.A.
Pelham, R. A., MA, PhD, The Court House, West Meon, Hants.
Pennington, D. H., MA, Balliol College, Oxford.
*Percy-Smith, Lieut-Colonel H. K., 13 Beechvale, Hillview Road, Woking, Surrey.
Perkin, Professor H. J., MA, Borwicks, Caton, Lancaster.
Petrie, Sir Charles, Bt, CBE, MA, 190 Coleherne Court, SW5.
Philip, I. G., MA, FSA, 28 Portland Road, Oxford.
Philips, Professor C. H., MA, PhD, DLitt, 3 Winterstoke Gardens, NW7.
Phillips, Sir Henry E. I., CMG, MBE, MA, 34 Ross Court, Putney Hill, SW15.
Phillips, J. R. S., BA, PhD, Dept of Medieval History, University College, Dublin 4, Ireland.
Pitt, H. G., MA, Worcester College, Oxford.
Platt, C. P. S., MA, PhD, FSA, 24 Oakmount Avenue, Highfield, Southampton.
Platt, Professor D. C. St M., MA, DPhil, St Antony's College, Oxford.
Plumb, Professor J. H., PhD, LittD, FBA, FSA, Christ's College, Cambridge.
Pocock, Professor J. G. A., PhD, History Department, Washington University, St Louis, Mo. 63130, U.S.A.
Poirer, Professor Philip P., PhD, Dept of History, The Ohio State University, 216 North Oval Drive, Columbus, Ohio 43210, U.S.A.
Pole, J. R., MA, PhD, 6 Cavendish Avenue, Cambridge.
Pollard, Professor S., BSc(Econ), PhD, Dept of Economic History, The University, Sheffield, S10 2TN.
Porter, B. E., BSc(Econ), PhD, Dept of International Politics, University College of Wales, Aberystwyth SY23 3DB.
Porter, H. C., MA, PhD, Selwyn College, Cambridge.
Postan, Professor M. M., MA, FBA, Peterhouse, Cambridge CB2 1RD.

*Potter, Professor G. R., MA, PhD, FSA, Herongate, Derwent Lane, Hathersage, Sheffield S30 1AS.

Powell, W. R., BLitt, MA, FSA, 2 Glanmead, Shenfield Road, Brentwood, Essex.

Powicke, Professor M. R., MA, University of Toronto, Toronto 5, Ont., Canada.

Prest, J. M., MA, Balliol College, Oxford.

Prest, W. R., MA, DPhil, Dept of History, University of Adelaide, Adelaide, S. Australia 5001.

Preston, Professor A. W., PhD, R.R.3, Bath, Ontario, Canada.

*Preston, Professor R. A., MA, PhD, Duke University, Durham, N.C., U.S.A.

Prestwich, J. O., MA, The Queen's College, Oxford.

Prestwich, Mrs M., MA, St Hilda's College, Oxford.

Prestwich, M. C., MA, DPhil, Dept of Medieval History, The University, St Andrews, Fife.

Price, F. D., MA, BLitt, FSA, Keble College, Oxford.

Price, Professor Jacob M., AM, PhD, University of Michigan, Ann Arbor, Michigan 48104, USA.

Pritchard, Professor D. G., PhD, 11 Coedmor, Sketty, Swansea, Glam. SA2 8BQ.

Proctor, Miss Evelyn E. S., MA, Little Newland, Eynsham, Oxford.

Pronay, N., BA, School of History, The University, Leeds.

Prothero, I. J., BA, PhD, The University, Manchester.

*Pugh, Professor R. B., MA, DLitt, FSA, 67 Southwood Park, N.6.

Pugh, T. B., MA, BLit, 28 Bassett Wood Drive, Southampton.

Pullan, Professor B. S., MA, PhD, The University, Manchester M13 9PL.

Pulzer, P. G. J., MA, PhD, Christ Church, Oxford OX1 1DP.

Quinn, Professor D. B., MA, PhD, DLit, DLitt, 9 Knowsley Road, Cressington Park, Liverpool 19.

Rabb, Professor T. K., MA, PhD, Princeton University, Princeton, N.J. 08540, U.S.A.

Radford, C. A. Ralegh, MA, DLitt, FBA, FSA, Culmcott, Uffculme, Cullompton, Devon EX15 3AT.

*Ramm, Miss A., MA, Somerville College, Oxford.

*Ramsay, G. D., MA, DPhil, St Edmund Hall, Oxford OX1 4AR.

Ramsey, Professor P. H., MA, DPhil, Taylor Building, King's College, Old Aberdeen.

Ranft, Professor B. McL., MA, DPhil, 16 Eliot Vale, SE3.

Ranger, Miss F., MA, 1 Mazoe Close, Bishop's Stortford, Hertfordshire.

Ransome, Miss M. E., MA, 16 Downside Crescent, NW3.

Rathbone, Eleanor, PhD, Flat 5, 24 Morden Road, SE3.

Rawley, Professor J. A., PhD, University of Nebraska, Lincoln, Nebraska 68508, U.S.A.

Read, D., BLitt, MA, Darwin College, University of Kent, Westgate House, Canterbury, Kent.

Reader, W. J., BA, PhD, 67 Wood Vale, N10 3DL.

Rees, Professor W., MA, DSc, DLitt, FSA, 2 Park Road, Penarth, Glam.

Reese, T. R., PhD, Institute of Commonwealth Studies, 27 Russell Square, WC1B 5DS.

Reeves, Miss M. E., MA, PhD, 38 Norham Road, Oxford.

Reid, Professor L. D., MA, PhD, College of Arts and Science, 127 Switzler Hall, University of Missouri, Columbia, Mo. 65201, U.S.A.

Reid, Professor W. S., MA, PhD, University of Guelph, Guelph, Ontario, Canada.

Renold, Miss P., MA, 6 Forest Side, Worcester Park, Surrey.

Reynolds, Miss S. M. G., MA, 26 Lennox Gardens, SW1.

Rich, Professor E. E., MA, St Catharine's College, Cambridge.

Richards, Professor G. M., MA, PhD, FSA, University College of North Wales, Bangor.

Richards, Rev. J. M., MA, BLitt, STL, Heythrop College, 11–13 Cavendish Square, W1M 0AN.

*Richards, R., MA, FSA, Gawsworth Hall, Gawsworth, Macclesfield, Cheshire.

*Richardson, H. G., BSc, MA, FBA, The Grange, Goudhurst, Kent.

Richardson, K. E., MA, PhD, Dept of Politics and History, Lanchester Polytechnic, Priory Street, Coventry.

Richardson, Professor W. C., MA, PhD, Louisiana State University, Baton Rouge, Louisiana, USA.

Richter, M., DrPhil. Institut f. mittelalterliche Geschichte, D355 Marburg, Am Krummbogen 28-CW, West Germany.

Rigold, S. E., MA, FSA, 2 Royal Crescent, W11.

Riley, P. W. J., BA, PhD, The University, Manchester.

Riley-Smith, J. S. C., MA, PhD, 53 Hartington Grove, Cambridge.

Rimmer, Professor W. G., MA, PhD, University of New South Wales, P.O. Box 1, Kensington, N.S.W. 2033, Australia.

Ritcheson, Professor C. R., DPhil, c/o Dept of History, University of Southern California, University Park, Los Angeles 90007 U.S.A.

Roach, Professor J. P. C., MA, PhD, 1 Park Crescent, Sheffield S10 2DY.

Robbins, Professor Caroline, PhD, 815 The Chetwynd, Rosemont, Pa. 19010, U.S.A.

Robbins, Professor K. G., MA, DPhil, University College of North Wales, Bangor.

Roberts, J. M., MA, DPhil, Merton College, Oxford.

Roberts, Professor M., MA, DPhil, FilDr, FBA, 38 Somerset Street, Grahamstown, C.P., South Africa.

Roberts, Brigadier M. R., DSO, Merton Lodge, Nackington, Canterbury, Kent.

Roberts, P. R., MA, PhD, FSA, Eliot College, University of Kent, Canterbury.

Roberts, Professor R. C., PhD, 284 Blenheim Road, Columbus, Ohio 43214, U.S.A.

Roberts, Professor R. S., PhD, University of Rhodesia, Salisbury, P.B. 167H, Rhodesia.

*Robinson, Professor Howard, MA, PhD, LLD, 75 Elmwood Place, Oberlin, Ohio, U.S.A.

Robinson, K. E., CBE, MA, DLitt, LLD, The Old Rectory, Church Westcote, Kingham, Oxford OX7 6SF.

Robinson, R. A. H., BA, PhD, School of History, The University, Birmingham B15 2TT.

Robinton, Professor Madeline R., MA, PhD, 210 Columbia Heights, Brooklyn, New York, U.S.A.

*Rodkey, F. S., AM, PhD, 152 Bradley Drive, Santa Cruz, Calif., U.S.A.

Rodney, Professor W., MA, PhD, 14 Royal Roads Military College, Victoria, B.C., Canada.

Roe, F. Gordon, FSA, 19 Vallance Road, London, N22 4UD.

Rogers, A., MA, PhD, FSA, The Firs, 227 Plains Road, Mapperley, Nottingham.

Rolo, Professor P. J. V., MA, The University, Keele, Staffordshire.

Roots, Professor I. A., MA, University of Exeter, Exeter.

Roper, M., MA, Public Record Office, Chancery Lane, London WC2A 1LR.

Rose, Professor P. L., MA, DenHist (Sorbonne), Dept of History, New York University, 19 University Place, New York, N.Y. 10003, U.S.A.

Roseveare, H. G., PhD, King's College, Strand, WC2.

Roskell, Professor J. S., MA, DPhil, FBA, The University, Manchester M13 9PL.

Roskill, Captain S. W., CBE, DSC, RN(ret), Frostlake Cottage, Malting Lane, Cambridge CB3 9HF.

Ross, C. D., MA, DPhil, Wills Memorial Building, Queens Road, Bristol.

Rothney, Professor G. O., PhD, St John's College, University of Manitoba, Winnipeg, R3T 2N2, Canada.

Rothrock, Professor G. A., MA, PhD, University of Alberta, Edmonton, Alberta, T6G 2E1, Canada.

Rothwell, Professor H., PhD, Hill House, Knapp, Ampfield, nr Romsey, Hants.

*Rowe, Miss B. J. H., MA, BLitt, St Anne's Cottage, Winkton, Christchurch, Hants.

Rowe, W. J., DPhil, 20 Seaview Avenue, Irby, Wirral, Cheshire.

Rowland, Rev. E. C., 233 Tyler Street, Preston, Victoria 3072, Australia.

Rowse, A. L., MA, DLitt, DCL, FBA, All Souls College, Oxford.

Roy, I., MA, DPhil, Dept of History, King's College, Strand, London WC2.

Roy, Professor R. H., MA, PhD, 2841 Tudor Avenue, Victoria, B.C., Canada.

Rubens, A., FRICS, FSA, 16 Grosvenor Place, SW1.

Rubini, D. A., DPhil, Temple University, Philadelphia, Penn., U.S.A.

Rubinstein, N., PhD, Westfield College, Hampstead, NW3.

Ruddock, Miss A. A., PhD, FSA, Birkbeck College, Malet Street, WC1.

Rudé, Professor G. F. E., MA, PhD, Sir George Williams University, Montreal 107, P.Q., Canada.

*RUNCIMAN, The Hon. Sir Steven, MA, DPhil, LLD, DLitt, DLit, LitD, DD, DHL, FBA, FSA, Elshiesfields, Lockerbie, Dumfriesshire.

Rupp, Rev. E. G., MA, DD, FBA, The Principal's Lodge, Wesley House, Cambridge.

Russell, C. S. R., MA, Bedford College, NW1.

Russell, Mrs J. G., MA DPhil, St Hugh's College, Oxford.

Russell, Professor P. E., MA, 23 Belsyre Court, Woodstock Road, Oxford.

Ryan, A. N., MA, University of Liverpool, 8 Abercromby Square, Liverpool 7.

Ryder, A. F. C., MA, DPhil, University of Ibadan, Nigeria.

Sachse, Professor W. L., PhD, Dept of History, University of Wisconsin, Madison, Wis. 53706 U.S.A.

Sainty, J. C., MA, 22 Kelso Place, W8.

*Salmon, Professor E. T., MA PhD, McMaster University, Hamilton, Ontario, Canada L8S 4L9.

Salmon, Professor J. H. M., PhD, Bryn Mawr College, Bryn Mawr, Pa. 19101, U.S.A.

*Saltman, Professor A., MA, PhD, Bar Ilan University, Ramat Gan, Israel.

Saltmarsh, J., MA, FSA, King's College, Cambridge, CB2 1ST.

Sammut, E., LLD, 4 Don Rue Street, Sliema, Malta.

Samuel, E. R., 8 Steynings Way, N12 7LN.

Sanders, I. J., MA, DPhil, Ceri, St Davids Road, Aberystwyth.

Sanderson, Professor G. N., MA, PhD, Dept of Modern History, Royal Holloway College, Englefield Green, Surrey.

Saville, Professor J., BSc(Econ), Dept of Economic and Social History, The University, Hull HU6 7RX.

Sawyer, Professor P. H., MA, The University, Leeds, LS2 9JT.

Sayers, Miss J. E., MA, BLitt, FSA, 17 Sheffield Terrace, Campden Hill, W8.

Scammell, G. V., MA, Pembroke College, Cambridge.

Scammell, Mrs J. M., BA, 137 Huntingdon Road, Cambridge.

Scarisbrick, Professor J. J., MA, PhD, 35 Kenilworth Road, Leamington Spa, Warwickshire.

Schenck, H. G., MA, DPhil, DrJur, University College, Oxford.

Schoeck, Professor R. J., PhD, Folger Shakespeare Library, Washington, D.C., 20003, U.S.A.

Schofield, A. N. E. D., PhD, 15 Westergate, Corfton Road, W5.

Schofield, R. S., MA, PhD, Cambridge Group for History of Population, 20 Silver Street, Cambridge.

Scouloudi, Miss I. C., MSc(Econ), FSA, 67 Victoria Road. W8.

Seaborne, M. V. J., MA, Chester College, Cheyney Road, Chester CH1 4BJ.

Seary, Professor E. R., MA, PhD, LittD, DLitt, FSA, Memorial University of Newfoundland, St John's, Newfoundland, Canada.

Semmel, Professor Bernard, PhD, Dept of History, State University of New York at Stony Brook, Stony Brook, N.Y. 11790, U.S.A.

Seton-Watson, C. I. W., MC, MA, Oriel College, Oxford.

Seton-Watson, Professor G. H. N., MA, FBA, Dept of Russian History, School of Slavonic Studies, London WC1.

Shackleton, R., MA, DLitt, LittD, FBA, FSA, Brasenose College, Oxford.

Shannon, R. T., MA, PhD, 84 Newmarket Road, Norwich, Norfolk.

Sharp, Mrs M., PhD, 59 Southway, NW11 6SB.

Shaw, I. P., MA, 3 Oaks Lane, Shirley, Croydon, Surrey CR0 5HP.

*Shaw, R. C., MSc, FRCS, FSA, Orry's Mount, Kirk Bride, nr Ramsey, Isle of Man.

Shead, N.F., MA, BLitt, 16 Burnside Gardens, Clarkston, Glasgow.

Shennan, J. H., PhD, Glenair, Moorside Road, Brookehouse, Caton, nr Lancaster.

Sheppard, F. H. W., MA, PhD, FSA, 55 New Street, Henley-on-Thames, Oxon.

Sherborne, J. W., MA, 26 Hanbury Road, Bristol.

Sigsworth, Professor E. M., BA, PhD, The University, Heslington, York.

Sillery, A., MA, DPhil, 24 Walton Street, Oxford.

Simmons, Professor J., MA, The University, Leicester.

*Simpson, Rev. F. A., MA, Trinity College, Cambridge.

Simpson, G. G., MA, PhD, FSA, Taylor Building, King's College, Old Aberdeen.
Siney, Professor Marion C., MA, PhD, 2676 Mayfield Road, Cleveland Heights, Ohio 44106, U.S.A.
Singhal, Professor D. P., MA, PhD, University of Queensland, St Lucia, Brisbane, Queensland, Australia 4067.
Skidelsky, Professor R., BA, PhD, Flat 1, 166 Cromwell Road, London SW5 oTJ.
Skinner, Q. R. D., MA, Christ's College, Cambridge.
Slack, P. A., MA, DPhil, Exeter College, Oxford OX1 3DP.
Slade, C. F., PhD, FSA, 28 Holmes Road, Reading.
Slater, A. W., MSc(Econ), 146 Castelnau, SW13 9ET.
Slatter, Miss M. D., MA, 5 Inglewood Court, Liebenrood Road, Bath Road, Reading.
Slavin, Professor A. J., PhD, University of California, Los Angeles, Calif., U.S.A.
Smail, R. C., MBE, MA, PhD, FSA, Sidney Sussex College, Cambridge.
*Smalley, Miss B., MA, PhD, FBA, 50 Rawlinson Road, Oxford OX2 6UE.
Smith, A. G. R., MA, PhD, 40 Stanley Avenue, Paisley, Renfrewshire.
Smith, A. Hassell, BA, PhD, Inst. of East Anglian Studies, University of East Anglia, University Village, Norwich.
Smith, E. A., MA, York House, The Street, Swallowfield, nr Reading.
Smith, Professor F. B., MA, PhD, Dept of History, Australian National University, Canberra, A.C.T., Australia 2000.
Smith, Professor Goldwin A., MA, PhD, DLitt, Wayne State University, Detroit, Michigan, 48202 U.S.A.
Smith, J. Beverley, MA, University College, Aberystwyth SY23 2AX.
Smith, Professor L. Baldwin, PhD, Northwestern University, Evanston, Ill. 60201, U.S.A.
Smith, P., MA, DPhil, 42 Oak Tree Close, Ealing, W5.
Smith, S., BA, PhD, Les Haies, Oatlands Road, Shinfield, Berks.
Smith, W. J., MA, 5 Gravel Hill, Emmer Green, Reading, Berks.
Smout, Professor T. C., MA, PhD, Dept of Econ History, Edinburgh University.
*Smyth, Rev. Canon C. H. E., MA, 12 Manor Court, Pinehurst, Cambridge.
Snell, L. S., MA, FSA, Newman College, Bartley Green, Birmingham 32.
Snow, Professor V. F., MA, PhD, University of Nebraska, Lincoln, Nebraska, U.S.A.
Snyder, Professor H. L., MA, PhD, 1324 Strong Avenue, Lawrence, Kansas 66044, U.S.A.
Soden, G. I., MA, DD, Buck Brigg, Hanworth, Norfolk.
Somers, Rev. H. J., JCB, MA, PhD, St Francis Xavier University, Antigonish, Nova Scotia.
Somerville, Sir Robert, KCVO, MA, FSA, 15 Foxes Dale, Blackheath, London SE3.
Sosin, Professor J. M., PhD, History Dept, University of Nebraska, Lincoln, Nebraska 68508, U.S.A.
SOUTHERN, R. W., MA, DLitt, LittD, FBA, The President's Lodgings, St John's College, Oxford OX1 3JP.
Southgate, D. G., BA, DPhil, 40 Camphill Road, Broughty Ferry, Dundee, Scotland.

Speck, W. A., MA, DPhil, The University, Newcastle upon Tyne.
Spencer, B. W., BA, FSA, 6 Carpenters Wood Drive, Chorleywood, Herts.
Spooner, Professor F. C., MA, PhD, The University, 23 Old Elvet, Durham.
Spufford, P., MA, PhD, The University, Keele, Staffs ST5 5BG.
Stanley, Professor G. F. G., MA, BLitt, DPhil, Library, Mount Alison University, Sackville, New Brunswick, Canada.
Stansky, Professor Peter, PhD, Dept of History, Stanford University, Stanford, Calif. 94305 U.S.A.
Steefel, Professor L. D., MA, PhD, 3549 Irving Avenue South, Minneapolis, Minn. 55408 U.S.A.
Steel, A. B., OBE, MA, LittD, LLD, Wrangbrook, Lisvane Road, Llanishen, Cardiff, CF4 5SE.
Steele, E. D., MA, PhD, The University, Leeds.
Steer, F. W., MA, FSA, 63 Orchard Street, Chichester, Sussex.
Steinberg, J., MA, PhD, Trinity Hall, Cambridge.
Steiner, Mrs Zara S., MA, PhD, New Hall, Cambridge.
Stéphan, Rev. Dom John, OSB, FSA, St Mary's Abbey, Buckfast, Buckfastleigh, Devon.
Stephens, W. B., MA, PhD, FSA, 37 Batcliffe Drive, Leeds 6.
Steven, Miss M. J. E., PhD, University of Western Australia, Perth, W. Australia 6009.
Stone, E., MA, DPhil, FSA, Keble College, Oxford.
Stone, Professor L., MA, Princeton University, Princeton, N.J., U.S.A.
Stones, Professor E. L. G., PhD, FSA, Dept of History, The University, Glasgow G12 8QQ.
*Stones, Professor E. L. G., PhD, FSA, 70 Oakfield Avenue, Glasgow W2.
Storey, Professor R. L., MA, PhD, 19 Elm Avenue, Beeston, Nottingham NG9 1BU.
*Stoye, J. W., MA, DPhil, Magdalen College, Oxford.
Street, J., MA, PhD, 6 Thulborn Close, Teversham, Cambridge.
Strong, R., BA, PhD, FSA, Victoria & Albert Museum, London, SW7.
Stuart C. H., MA, Christ Church, Oxford.
Styles, P., MA, FSA, 21 Castle Lane, Warwick.
Supple, Professor B. E., BSc(Econ), PhD, Dept of Econ and Social History, The University of Sussex, Falmer, Brighton BN1 9QQ.
Surman, Rev. C. E., MA, 4 Holly Lane, Erdington, Birmingham 24.
Sutherland, Professor D. W., DPhil, State University of Iowa, Iowa City, Iowa 52240, U.S.A.
SUTHERLAND, Dame Lucy, DBE, MA, DLitt, LittD, DCL, FBA, 59 Park Town, Oxford.
Sutherland, N. M., MA, PhD, St John's Hall, Bedford College, NW1.
Swart, Professor K. W., PhD, LittD, University College, Gower Street, WC1E 6BT.
Sydenham, M. J., PhD, Carleton University, Ottawa 1, Canada.
Sylvester, Professor R. S., PhD, The Yale Edition of the works of St Thomas More, 1986 Yale Station, New Haven, Conn. U.S.A.
Syrett, Professor D., PhD, 46 Hawthorne Terrace, Leonia, N.J. 07605, U.S.A.

Talbot, C. H., PhD, BD, FSA, 47 Hazlewell Road, SW15.

Tanner, J. I., MA, PhD, Flat One, 57 Drayton Gardens, SW10 9RU.

Tanner, L. E., CVO, MA, DLitt, FSA, 32 Westminster Mansions, Great Smith Street, Westminster SW1P 3BP.

Tarling, Professor P. N., MA, PhD, University of Auckland, Private Bag, Auckland, New Zealand.

Taylor, Arnold J., CBE, MA, DLitt, FSA, 56 Langham Road, Teddington, Middlesex.

Taylor, Professor Arthur J., MA, The University, Leeds LS2 9JT.

Taylor, J., MA, The University, Leeds LS2 9JT.

Taylor, J. W. R., 36 Alexandra Drive, Surbiton, Surrey KT5 9AF.

Taylor, W., MA, PhD, FSAScot, 25 Bingham Terrace, Dundee.

Temple, Nora C., BA, PhD, University College, Cardiff.

Templeman, G., MA, PhD, FSA, 22 Ethelbert Road, Canterbury, Kent.

Thirsk, Mrs I. J., PhD, St Hilda's College, Oxford OX4 1DY.

Thistlethwaite, F., MA, University of East Anglia, Earlham Hall, Norwich NOR 88C.

Thomas, Professor H. S., MA, University of Reading, Reading.

Thomas, Rev. J. A., MA, PhD, 164 Northfield Lane, Brixham, Devon.

THOMAS, K. V., MA, (*Literary Director*), St John's College, Oxford OX1 3JP.

Thomas, P. G. D., MA, PhD, University College, Aberystwyth SY23 2AU.

Thomas, W. E. S., MA, Christ Church, Oxford OX1 1DP.

Thomis, M. I., MA, PhD, 28 Keir Street, Bridge of Allan, Stirlingshire.

Thompson, A. F., MA, Wadham College, Oxford OX1 3PN.

Thompson, Mrs D. K. G., MA, School of History, The University, Birmingham.

Thompson, E. P., MA, Warwick University, Coventry.

Thompson, Professor F. M. L., MA, DPhil, Bedford College, Regent's Park NW1 4NS.

Thompson, P., MA, DPhil, Dept of Sociology, University of Essex, Wivenhoe Park, Colchester, Essex, CO4 3SQ.

Thomson, J. A. F., MA, DPhil, The University, Glasgow, W2.

*Thomson, T. R. F., MA, MD, FSA, Cricklade, Wilts.

Thorne, Professor S. E., MA, LLB, FSA, Harvard Law School, Cambridge, Mass., U.S.A.

Thornton, Professor A. P., MA, DPhil, 11 Highbourne Road, Toronto 7, Canada.

Thorpe, Prof. Lewis, BA, LèsL, PhD, DdeL'U, 26 Parkside, Wollaton Vale, Nottingham.

*Thrupp, Professor S. L., MA, PhD, University of Michigan, Ann Arbor, Mich., 48104, U.S.A.

Thurlow, The Very Rev. A. G. G., MA, FSA, Dean of Gloucester, The Deanery, Gloucester.

Tibbutt, H. G., FSA, 12 Birchdale Avenue, Kempston, Bedford.

Titow, J. Z., PhD, Dept of Economic History, The University, Nottingham.

Titterton, Commander G. A., RN(ret), Flat 4, Clarence House, 8 Granville Road, Eastbourne, Sussex.

Tomkeieff, Mrs O. G., MA, LLB, King's College, Newcastle upon Tyne 2.

Tooley, Miss M. J., MA, The Guest House, St Mary's Convent, Burlington Lane, W4.

Toynbee, Miss M. R., MA, PhD, FSA, 22 Park Town, Oxford OX2 6SH.

Trebilcock, R. C., MA, Pembroke College, Cambridge CB2 1RF.

*Trevor-Roper, Professor H. R., MA, FBA, Oriel College, Oxford.

Trickett, Professor the Rev. A. S., MA, PhD, 509 South 58th Street, Omaha, Nebraska 68106, U.S.A.

Tyacke, N. R. N., MA, DPhil, 1a Spencer Rise, London, NW5.

Tyler, P., BLitt, MA, DPhil, University of Western Australia, Nedlands, Western Australia, 6009.

Ugawa, Professor K., BA, MA, PhD, 1008 Ikebukuco, 2 Chome, Tokyo 171, Japan.

Ullmann, Professor W., MA, LittD, Trinity College, Cambridge.

Underdown, Professor David, PhD, Dept of History, Brown University, Providence, Rhode Island 02912, U.S.A.

Underhill, C. H., The Lodge, Needwood, Burton-upon-Trent, Staffs.

Upton, A. F., MA, 5 West Acres, St Andrews, Fife.

Urry, W. G., PhD, FSA, St Edmund Hall, Oxford.

Vaisey, D. G., MA, FSA, 52 Mill Street, Eynsham, nr Oxford.

Vale, M. G. A., MA, DPhil, Dept of History, The University, Heslington, York.

Van Caenagem, Professor R. C., LLD, Veurestraat 18, 9821 Afsnee, Belgium.

Van Cleve, Professor T. C., MA, PhD, DLitt, Bowdoin College, Brunswick, Maine, U.S.A.

Vann, Professor Richard T., PhD, Dept of History, Wesleyan University, Middletown, Conn. 06457, U.S.A.

*Varley, Mrs J., MA, FSA, 164 Nettleham Road, Lincoln.

Vaughan, Sir (G.) Edgar, KBE, MA, 29 Birch Grove, West Acton, London W3 9SP.

Véliz, Professor C., BSc, PhD, Dept of Sociology, La Trobe University, Melbourne, Victoria, Australia.

Vessey, D. W. T. C., MA, PhD, 10 Uphill Grove, Mill Hill, London NW7.

Villiers, Lady de, MA, BLitt, 4 Church Street, Beckley, Oxford.

Vincent, Professor J. R., MA, PhD, The University, Bristol.

Virgoe, R., BA, PhD, University of East Anglia, Norwich.

Waddell, Professor D. A. G., MA, DPhil, University of Stirling, Stirling FK9 4LA.

*Wagner, Sir Anthony R., KCVO, MA, DLitt, FSA, College of Arms, Queen Victoria Street, EC4.

Waites, B. F., MA, 6 Chater Road, Oakham, Rutland.

*Wake, Miss Joan, CBE, MA, LLD, FSA, 11 Charlbury Road, Oxford.

Walcott, Professor R., MA, PhD, The College of Wooster, Wooster, Ohio 44691 U.S.A.

Waley, D. P., MA, PhD, Dept of Manuscripts, British Museum, WC1B 3DG.

Walford, A. J., MA, PhD, FLA, 45 Parkside Drive, Watford, Herts.

Walker, Rev. Canon D. G., DPhil, FSA, University College, Swansea.

Walker, J., MA, PhD, Ashlynne, 33 Heaton Road, Huddersfield.

Wallace, Professor W. V., MA, New University of Ulster, Coleraine, Northern Ireland.

Wallace-Hadrill, J. M., MA, DLitt, FBA, Merton College, Oxford OX1 4JD.

Wallis, Miss H. M., MA, DPhil, FSA, 96 Lord's View, St John's Wood Road, NW8 7HG.

Wallis, P. J., MA, 27 Westfield Drive, Newcastle upon Tyne 3.

Walne, P., MA, FSA, County Record Office, County Hall, Hertford.

Walters, (W.) E., MA, Burrator, 355 Topsham Road, Exeter.

Wangermann, E., MA, DPhil, The University, Leeds.

*Ward, Mrs G. A., PhD, FSA, Unsted, 51 Hartswood Road, Brentwood, Essex.

Ward, J. T., MA, PhD, Dept of Economic History, McCance Bldg., 16 Richmond Street, Glasgow C1 1XQ.

Ward, Professor W. R., DPhil, University of Durham, 43 North Bailey, Durham.

*Warmington, Professor E. H., MA, 48 Flower Lane, NW7.

Warren, Professor W. L., MA, DPhil, The Queen's University, Belfast, N. Ireland BT7 1NN.

*Waterhouse, Professor E. K., CBE, MA, AM, FBA, Overshot, Badger Lane, Hinksey Hill, Oxford.

*Waters, Lt-Commander D. W., RN, FSA, Jolyons, Bury, nr Pulborough, West Sussex.

Watkin, Rev. Dom Aelred, OSB, MA, FSA, Downside Abbey, Stratton-on-the-Fosse, nr Bath BA3 4RJ.

WATSON, A. G., MA, BLitt, FSA, (*Secretary*), University College, Gower Street, WC1E 6BT.

Watson, J. S., MA, The University, College Gate, North Street, St Andrews, Fife, Scotland.

Watt, Professor D. C., MA, London School of Economics, Houghton Street, WC2.

Watt, D. E. R., MA, DPhil, Dept of Mediaeval History, St Salvator's College, St Andrews, Fife, Scotland.

Watt, J. A., BA, PhD, The University, Hull.

Webb, J. G., MA, 11 Blount Road, Pembroke Park, Old Portsmouth, Hampshire PO1 2TD.

Webb, Professor R. K., PhD, Tanglewood, Whitchurch-on-Thames, nr Reading, Berks.

Webster, (A.) Bruce, MA, FSA, 5 The Terrace, St Stephens, Canterbury.

Webster, C., MA, MSc, Corpus Christi College, Oxford.

Wedgwood, Dame Veronica, OM, DBE, MA, LittD, DLitt, LLD, 22 St Ann's Terrace, St John's Wood, NW8.

Weinbaum, Professor M., PhD, 133–33 Sanford Avenue, Flushing, N.Y. 11355, U.S.A.

Weinstock, Miss M. B., MA, 26 Wey View Crescent, Broadway, Weymouth, Dorset.

Wernham, Professor R. B., MA, Worcester College, Oxford.

*Weske, Mrs Dorothy B., AM, PhD, Oakwood, Sandy Spring, Maryland, U.S.A.

West, Professor F. J., PhD, Dept of History, The University College at Buckingham, Old Bank Building, 2 Bridge Street, Buckingham.

Weston, Professor Corinne C., PhD, 200 Central Park South, New York, N.Y. 10019, U.S.A.

*Whatmore, Rev. L. E., MA, St Wilfred's, South Road, Hailsham, Sussex.

Whelan, Rev. C. B., OSB, MA, Belmont Abbey, Hereford.

White, Professor B. M. I., MA, DLit, FSA, 3 Upper Duke's Drive, Eastbourne, Sussex BN20 7XT.

*Whitelock, Professor D., CBE, MA, LittD, FBA, FSA, 30 Thornton Close, Cambridge.

Whiteman, Miss E. A. O., MA, DPhil, FSA, Lady Margaret Hall, Oxford.

*Whitfield, Professor A. S., BLitt, PhD, Plas Benar, Dyffryn Ardudwy, Merioneth.

Wiener, Professor J. H., BA, PhD, 9 Broadlands Road, London, N6.

Wilkinson, Rev. J. T., MA, DD, Brantwood, Farrington Lane, Knighton, Radnorshire.

Wilks, M. J., MA, PhD, Dept of History, Birkbeck College, Malet Street, WC1.

*Willan, Professor T. S., MA, DPhil, 3 Raynham Avenue, Didsbury, Manchester M20 0BW.

Williams, Professor C. H., MA, 6 Blackfriars, Canterbury.

Williams, D., MA, PhD, DPhil, University of Calgary, Calgary, Alberta, T2N 1N4, Canada.

Williams, Sir Edgar (T.), CB, CBE, DSO, MA, Rhodes House, Oxford.

Williams, Professor Glanmor, MA, DLitt, University College, Swansea.

Williams, Glyndwr, BA, PhD, Queen Mary College, Mile End Road, E1.

Williams, Professor G. A., MA, PhD, Dept of History, The University, York YO1 5DD.

Williams, J. A., BSc(Econ), MA, 44 Pearson Park, Hull, E. Yorks HU5 2TG.

Williams, N. J., MA, DPhil, FSA, 57 Rotherwick Road, NW11 7DD.

Williams, P. H., MA, DPhil, New College, Oxford OX1 3BN.

*Williams, T. G., MA, 63 Eardley Crescent, SW5.

Willson, Professor D. H., PhD, 1881 Fairmount Avenue, St Paul, Minn. 55105 U.S.A.

*Wilson, Professor A. McC, MA, PhD, 1 Brookside, Norwich, Vermont 05055, U.S.A.

Wilson, Professor C. H., MA, FBA, Jesus College, Cambridge.

Wilson, H. S., BA, BLitt, The University, Heslington, York YO1 5DD.

Wilson, Professor T., MA, DPhil, Dept of History, University of Adelaide, Adelaide, South Australia.

Winks, Professor R. W. E., MA, PhD, 648 Berkeley College, Yale University, New Haven, Conn. 06520 U.S.A.

Wiswall, F. L., PhD, 23 Richmond Drive, Darien, Conn. 06820 U.S.A.

Withrington, D. J., MA, BEd, Inst. of Scottish Studies, King's College, Aberdeen, Scotland.

Wolffe, B. P., MA, BLitt, DPhil, Highview, 19 Rosebarn Avenue, Exeter EX4 6DY.

*Wood, Rev. A. Skevington, PhD, Ridgeway, Curbar, Sheffield.

Wood, Mrs S. M., MA, BLitt, St Hugh's College, Oxford.

Woodfill, Professor W. L., PhD, University of California, Davis, Calif. 95616, U.S.A.

Wood-Legh, Miss K. L., BLitt, PhD, DLitt, 49 Owlstone Road, Cambridge.

Woods, J. A., MA, PhD, The University, Leeds 2.

Woolf, S. J., MA, DPhil, The University, Whiteknights, Reading.

Woolrych, Professor A. H., BLitt, MA, Patchetts, Caton, nr Lancaster.
Wormald, B. H. G., MA, Peterhouse, Cambridge CB2 1RD.
Wortley, The Rev. J. T., MA, PhD, History Dept, University of Mani
toba, Winnipeg, Manitoba R3T 2N2, Canada.
Wright, Professor E., MA, Institute of United States Studies, 31 Tavi-
stock Square, London WC1H 9EZ.
Wright, L. B., PhD, 3702 Leland Street, Chevy Chase, Md. 20015, U.S.A.
Wright, Maurice, BA, Dept of Government, Dover Street, Manchester,
M13 9PL.
Wroughton, J. P., MA, 11 Powlett Court, Bath, Somerset BA2 6QJ.

Youings, Professor Joyce A., PhD, The University, Exeter.
Young, Brigadier P., DSO, MC, MA, FSA, Bank House, Ripple, Tewkes-
bury, Glos. GL20 6EP.

Zagorin, Professor P., PhD, 4927 River Road, Scottsville, N.Y. 14546.
Zeeveld, Professor W. Gordon, PhD, Deep Meadow, Woodbine, Md.
21797, U.S.A.
Zeldin, T., MA, DPhil, St Antony's College, Oxford OX2 6JF.

ASSOCIATES OF THE
ROYAL HISTORICAL SOCIETY

Addy, J., MA, PhD, 66 Long Lane, Clayton West, Huddersfield HD8 9PR.

Baird, Rev. E. S., BD, The Vicarage, Harrington, Workington, Cumberland.
Begley, M. R., 119 Tennyson Avenue, King's Lynn, Norfolk.
Bird, E. A., 29 King Edward Evenue, Rainham, Essex RNL3 9RH.
Bratt, C., 65 Moreton Road, Upton, Wirral, Cheshire.
Brigg, Mrs M., The Hollies, Whalley Road, Wilpshire, Blackburn, Lancs.
Brocklesby, R., BA, The Elms, North Eastern Road, Thorne, nr Doncaster, York.
Bryant, W. N., MA, PhD, College of S. Mark and S. John, King's Road, SW10.
Bullivant, C. H., FSA, Sedgemoor House, Warden Road, Minehead, Somerset.
Burton, Commander R. C., RN(ret), Great Streele Oasthouse, Framfield, Sussex.
Butler, Mrs M. C., MA, 4 Castle Street, Warkworth, Morpeth, Northumberland NE65 0UW.

Cairns, Mrs W. N., MA, Alderton House, New Ross, Co. Wexford, Eire.
Carter, F. E. L., CBE, MA, 8 The Leys, London N2 0HE.
Cary, R. H., BA, 23 Bath Road, W4.
Chandra, Shri Suresh, MA, MPhil, 90–36, 155th Street, Jamaica, New York 11432.
Cook, Rev. E. T., 116 Westwood Park, SE23 3QH.
Cooper, Miss J. M., MA, 203B Woodstock Road, Oxford.
Cox, A. H., Winsley, 11A Bagley Close, West Drayton, Middlesex.
Creighton-Williamson, Lt-Col D., 90 Lloyds Bank Ltd, Cox & Kings (F.Sec.), 6 Pall Mall, SW1.

d'Alton, I., BA, 5 Cosin Court, Peterhouse, Cambridge.
Dawson, Mrs, 5 Sinclair Street, Nkana/Kitwe, Zambia.
Dewar, Rev. M. W., MA, PhD, The Rectory, Helen's Bay, Bangor, Co. Down, N. Ireland.
Dowse, Rev. I. R., Y Caplandy (The Cathedral Chaplain's House), Glanrafon, Bangor, Caerns. LL57 1LH.
Draffen of Newington, George, MBE, KLJ, MA, Meadowside, Balmullo, Leuchars, Fife KY16 0AW.
Drew, J. H., 19 Forge Road, Kenilworth, Warwickshire.
Driver, J. T., MA, BLitt, 25 Abbot's Grange, Off Liverpool Road, Chester.

Emberton, W. J., Firs Lodge, 13 Park Lane, Old Basing, Basingstoke, Hants.
Emsden, N., Strathspey, Lansdown, Bourton-on-the-Water, Cheltenham, Glos. GL54 2AR.

Fawcett, Rev. T. J., BD, PhD, 4 The College, Durham DH1 3EH.
Ferguson, J. T., MA, Fayerweather Hall, Columbia University, New York, N.Y., U.S.A.
Field, C. W., The Twenty-Sixth House, Robertsbridge, Sussex.
Fitzwilliam, B. R., ACP, ThA, Rockhampton Grammar School, Archer Street, Rockhampton, Queensland 4700, Australia.
Fryer, J., BA, Greenfields, Whitemore, nr Congleton, Cheshire.

Gardner, W. M., Chequertree, Wittersham, nr Tenterden, Kent.
Granger, E. R., Bluefield, Blofield, Norfolk.
Greatrex, Mrs J. G., MA, Dept of History, St Patrick's College, Carleton University, Colonel By Drive, Ottawa, K1S 1N4, Canada.
Green, P. L., MA, 9 Faulkner Street, Gate Pa, Tauranga, New Zealand.
Griffiths, Rev. G. Ll., MA, BD, Rhiwlas, 10 Brewis Road, Rhos-on-Sea, Colwyn Bay, Denbighs.

Haines, F. D., PhD, Southern Oregon College, Ashland, Oregon, U.S.A.
Hall, P. T., Accrington College of Further Education, Sandy Lane, Accrington, Lancs.
Hannah, L., BA, St John's College, Oxford OX1 3JP.
Harding, Rev. F. A. J., BSc(Econ), 74 Beechwood Avenue, St Albans.
Hardy, Rev. P. E., The Manse, 20 Victoria Road, Hanham, Bristol.
Harte, N. B., BSc(Econ), University College, Gower Street, WC1E 6BT.
Hawtin, Miss G., BA, FSAScot, Honey Cottage, 5 Clifton Road, SW19.
Heath, P., BA, Dept of History, The University, Hull, HU6 7RX.
Henderson-Howat, Mrs A. M. D., 7 Lansdown Crescent, Edinburgh EH12 5EQ.
Henriques, Miss U. R. Q., BA, BLitt, 4 Campden Hill Square, W11.
Hoare, E. T., 70 Addison Road, Enfield, Middx.
Hodge, Mrs G., 85 Hadlow Road, Tonbridge, Kent.
Hope, R. B., MA, MEd, PhD, 5 Partis Way, Newbridge Hill, Bath, Somerset.
Hopewell, S., MA, 133 Barnstaple Road, Thorpe Bay, Essex.
Hughes, R. G., 'Hafod', 92 Main Road, Smalley, Derby DE7 6DS.
Hunt, J. W., MA, 123 Park Road, Chiswick, W4.

Jarvis, L. D., Middlesex Cottage, 86 Mill Road, Stock, Ingatestone, Essex.
Jermy, K. E., MA, 8 Thelwall New Road, Thelwall, Warrington, Lancs WA4 2JF.
Jerram-Burrows, Mrs L. E., Parkanaur House, 88 Sutton Road, Rochford, Essex.
Johnston, F. R., MA, 20 Russell Street, Eccles, Manchester.
Johnstone, H. F. V., 96 Wimborne Road, Poole, Dorset.
Jones, E. W., 54 Walker Road, Blackley Estate, Manchester 9.
Joy, E. T., MA, BSc(Econ), The Rotunda, Ickworth, Bury St Edmunds, Suffolk IP29 5QE.

Keen, Rev. Canon D. A. R., MA, FSA, 6 College Green, Gloucester.
Keen, L. J., 14 Fairfield's Close, Roe Green, NW9.
Keir, Mrs G. I., BA, 21 Raleigh Road, Richmond, Surrey.
Kennedy, M. J., BA, Dept of Medieval History, The University, Glasgow W2.

Kitching, C. J., BA, PhD, 54 Compayne Gardens, NW6.
Knight, G. A., BA, 46 Bold Street, Pemberton, Wigan, Lancs WN5 9E2.
Knowlson, Rev. G. C. V., St John's Vicarage, Knutsford Road, Wilmslow, Cheshire.

Landon, Professor M. de L., MA, PhD, Dept of History, University of Mississippi, University, Miss. 38677, USA.
Laws, Captain W. F., MLitt, University of Otago, P.O. Box 56 Dunedin, New Zealand.
Lea, R. S., MA, 29 Crestway, SW15.
Lewin, Mrs J., MA, 3 Sunnydale Gardens, Mill Hill, NW7.
Lewis, F., 23 Berwick Road, Rainham, Essex.
Lewis, Professor N. B., MA, PhD, 8 Westcombe Park Road SE3 7RB.
Loach, Mrs J., MA, Somerville College, Oxford.

McIntyre, Miss S. C., BA, Lady Margaret Hall, Oxford.
McLeod, D. H., BA, PhD, School of History, Warwick University, Coventry CV4 7AL.
Mansfield, Major A. D., 38 Churchfields, West Mersea, Essex.
Mathews, E. F. J., BSc(Econ), PhD, 2 Park Lake Road, Poole, Dorset.
Meatyard, E., BA, DipEd, Guston, Illtyd Avenue, Llantwit Major, Glam. CF6 9TG.
Metcalf, D. M., MA, DPhil, Ashmolean Museum, Oxford.
Mills, H. J., BSc, MA, Old Timbers, The Square, Wickham, Hants.
Morgan, D. A. L., MA, Dept of History, University College, Gower Street, London WC1E 6 BT.

Newman, L. T., LRIC, CEng, MIGasE, AMInstF, 12 Gay Bowers, Hockley, Essex.
Nicholls, R. E., MA, PhD, Glenholm, Hook Road, Surbiton, Surrey.

Obelkevich, J., MA, (address unknown).
O'Day, Mrs M. R., BA, PhD, Flat 8, 174 Frankley Beeches Road, Birmingham B31 5LW.
Oggins, R. S., PhD, c/o Dept of History SM, State University of New York, Binghampton 13901, U.S.A.
Oldham, C. R., MA, Te Whare, Walkhampton, Yelverton, Devon.
Orme, N. I., MA, DPhil, University of Exeter, Exeter.

Palliser, D. M., MA, DPhil, 30 Sycamore Terrace, Bootham, York.
Parsons, Mrs M. A., MA, 24 Purleybury Close, Purley, Surrey.
Partridge, Miss F. L., BA, 17 Spencer Gardens, SW14 7AH.
Pasmore, H. S., MB, BS, 21 Edwardes Square, W8.
Paton, L. R., 49 Lillian Road, Barnes, SW13.
Paulson, E., BSc(Econ), 11 Darley Avenue, Darley Dale, Matlock, Derbys.
Perry, E., FSAScot, 28 Forest Street, Hathershaw, Oldham, OL8 3ER.
Pitt, B. W. E., Flat 4, Red Roofs, Bath Road, Taplow, Maidenhead, Berks.
Priestley, E. J., MA, 10 Kent Close, Bromborough, Wirral, Cheshire L63 oEF.

Rankin, Colonel R. H., 6203 Beachway Drive, Falls Church, Va. 22041, U.S.A.

Rendall, Miss J., BA, Alcuin College, University of York, Heslington, York.
Richards, N. F., PhD, 376 Maple Avenue, St Lambert, Prov. of Quebec, Canada.
Richmond, C. F., DPhil, 59 The Covert, The University, Keele, Staffs.

Sabben-Clare, E. E., MA, c/o The University Registry, Clarendon Building, Broad Street, Oxford.
Sainsbury, F., 16 Crownfield Avenue, Newbury Park, Ilford, Essex.
Saksena, D. N., First Secretary (Education), Embassy of India, Moscow, USSR.
Sandell, Miss E. M., 12 Avenue Court, 2 Westwood Road, Southampton.
Scannura, C. G., 12/6 Hubbard Flats, Cospicua, Malta.
Scott, The Rev. A. R., MA, BD, PhD, Ahorey Manse, Portadown, Co. Armagh, N. Ireland.
Seddon, P. R., BA, PhD, The University, Nottingham.
Sellers, J. M., MA, 9 Vere Road, Pietermaritzburg, Natal, S. Africa.
Sharpe, F., FSA, Derwen, Launton, Bicester, Oxfordshire OX6 oDP.
Shores, C. F., ARICS, 40 St Mary's Crescent, Hendon, NW4 4LH.
Sibley, Major R. J., 8 Ways End, Beech Avenue, Camberley, Surrey.
Sloan, K., BEd, MPhil, 13 Fernwood, Park Villas, Roundhay, Leeds 8.
Smith, C. D., MA, PhD, 416 Hall of Languages, Syracuse University, Syracuse, N.Y. 13210, U.S.A.
Smith, D. M., Borthwick Institute, St Anthony's Hall, York.
Sorensen, Mrs M. O., MA, 8 Layer Gardens, W3 9PR.
Sparkes, I. G., FLA, 124 Green Hill, High Wycombe, Bucks.
Stafford, D. S., BA, 10 Highfield Close, Wokingham, Berks.
Stitt, F. B., BLitt, William Salt Library, Stafford.

Taylor, R. T., MA, Dept of Political Theory and Government, University College, Swansea SA2 8PP.
Thewlis, J. C., BA, Van Mildert College, Durham.
Thomas, Miss E. J. M., 8 Ravenscroft Road, Northfield End, Henley-on-Thames, Oxon.
Thompson, C. L. F., MA, Orchard House, Stanford Road, Orsett, nr. Grays, Essex RM16 3BX.
Thompson, L. F., Orchard House, Stanford Road, Orsett, nr Grays, Essex RM16 3BX.
Thorold, M. B., 20 Silsoe House, Park Village East, London NW1 4AS.
Tomlinson, H. C., BA, 15 Ivor Street, London NW1.
Tracy, J. N., BA, MPhil, PhD, c/o P. Huth Esq, 6 Chaucer Court, 28 New Dover Road, Canterbury, Kent.
Tristram, B., DipEd, (address unknown).
Tuffs, J. E., 360 Monega Road, Manor Park, E12.

Waldman, T. G., MA, 131 Riverside Drive, New York, N.Y. 10024, U.S.A.
Wall, Rev. J., BD, MA, Ashfield, 45 Middleton Lane, Middleton St George, nr Darlington, Co. Durham.
Wallis, K. W., BA, 48 Berkeley Square, W1.
Warrillow, E. J. D., MBE, FSA, Hill-Cote, Lancaster Road, Newcastle, Staffs.
Westman, Mrs B. H., MA, PhD, 512½ Midvale Avenue, Los Angeles, Calif. 90024, U.S.A.

Whiting, J. R. S., MA, DLitt, 18 College Green, Gloucester.
Wilkinson, F. J., 40 Great James Street, Holborn, London WC1N 3HB.
Williams, A. R., MA, 5 Swanswell Drive, Granley Fields, Cheltenham, Glos.
Williams, H., (address unknown).
Williams, Miss J. M., MA, History Dept, University of Auckland, Private Bag, Auckland, New Zealand.
Windrow, M. C., 40 Zodiac Court, 165 London Road, Croydon, Surrey.
Wood, A. W., 11 Blessington Close, SE13.
Wood, J. O., BA, MEd, Fountains, Monument Gardens, St Peter Port, Guernsey, C.I.
Woodall, R. D., BA, Bethel, 7 Wynthorpe Road, Horbury, nr Wakefield, Yorks, WF4 5BB.
Woodfield, R., BD, MTh, 43 Playfield Crescent, SE22.
Worsley, Miss A. V., BA, (address unknown).
Wright, J. B., BA, White Shutters, Braunston, Rutland LE15 8QT.

Yates, W. N., BA, 29 Ystrad Drive, Johnstown, Carmarthen, S. Wales.

Zerafa, Rev. M. J., St Dominic's Priory, Valletta, Malta.

CORRESPONDING FELLOWS

Andersson, Ingvar, FilDr, Engelbrektsgátan 6A IV, Stockholm, Sweden.

Bartoš, Professor F. M., PhDr, II. Jihozápadní 7, Praha-Spořilov, Czecho-slovakia.

Bischoff, Professor B., DLitt, 8033 Planegg C. München, Ruffini-Allee 27, Germany.

Braudel, Professor F., École Pratique des Hautes Études, 20 rue de la Baume, Paris VIIIᵉ, France.

Cárcano, M. A., Centeno 3131, Buenos Aires, Argentina.

Coolhaas, Professor W. P., Gezichtslaan 71, Bilthoven, Holland.

Creighton, Professor D. G., MA, DLitt, LLD, University of Toronto, Toronto, Canada.

Donoso, R. Presidente de la Sociedad Chilena de Historia y Geografía, Casilla 1386, Santiago, Chile.

Dvornik, Professor the Rev. F., DD, D-ès-Lettres, DLit, Harvard University, Dumbarton Oaks, 1703 32nd Street, Washington, D.C., U.S.A.

Ganshof, Professor F. L., 12 rue Jacques Jordaens, Brussels, Belgium.

Giusti, Rt Rev. Mgr M., JCD, Prefect Archivio Segreto Vaticano, Vatican City, Italy.

Glamann, Professor K., DrPhil, Frederiksberg, Bredegade 13A, 2000 Copenhagen, Denmark.

Gwynn, Professor the Rev. A., SJ, MA, DLitt, Milltown Park, Dublin 6, Eire.

Halicki, Professor O., DrPhil, 35 Baker Avenue, White Plains, New York, USA.

Hancock, Professor Sir Keith, KBE, MA, DLitt, FBA, Australian National University, Box 4, P.O., Canberra, ACT, Australia.

Hanke, Professor L. U., PhD, University of Massachusetts, Amherst, Mass. 01002, USA.

Heimpel, Professor Dr H., DrPhil, Direktor des Max Planck-Instituts für Geschichte, Göttingen, Düstere Eichenweg 28, Germany.

Inalcik, Professor Halil, PhD, The University of Ankara, Ankara, Turkey.

Kuttner, Professor S., MA, JUD, SJD LLD, Institute of Medieval Canon Law, University of California, Berkeley, Calif. 94720, U.S.A.

Langer, Professor W. L., PhD, LLD, DPhil, LHD, LittD, 1 Berkeley Street, Cambridge, Mass. 02138, USA.

Morison, Professor S. E., PhD, LittD, Harvard College Library, 417 Cam-bridge, Mass., U.S.A.

Ostrogorsky, Professor G., The University, Belgrade, Yugoslavia.

Peña y Cámara, J. M. de la, Juan del Castillo 5, 2°, Seville, Spain.
Perkins, Professor D., MA, PhD, LLD, University of Rochester, Rochester, N.Y., U.S.A.
Perroy, Professor E. M. J., D-ès-L, 5 rue Monticelli, Paris XIVe, France.

Rau, Professor Virginia, MA, Universidade de Lisbon, Lisbon, Portugal.
Renouvin, Professor P., D-ès-L, 2 Boulevard Saint Germain, Paris, France.
Rodrígues, Professor José Honório, Rua Paul Redfern, 23, ap. C.O.1, Rio de Janeiro, Gb. ZC—37, Brasil.

Santifaller, Professor L., DrPhil, DrTheol, DrJur, Österreichische Akademie der Wissenschaften, Wien 1, Dr Ignaz Seipel Platz 2, Austria.
Sapori, Professor A., Università Commerciale Luigi Bocconi, Via Sabbatini 8, Milan, Italy.

Van Houtte, Professor J. A., PhD, FBA, Termunkveld, Groeneweg 51, Egenhoven, Heverlee, Belgium.
Verlinden, Professor C., PhD, 8 Via Omero (Valle Giulia), Rome, Italy.

Zavala, S., LLD, Mexican Embassy, 9 rue de Longchamp, Paris XVIe, France.

TRANSACTIONS AND PUBLICATIONS

OF THE

ROYAL HISTORICAL SOCIETY

The annual publications of the Society issued to Fellows and Subscribing Libraries include the *Transactions*, supplemented since 1897 by
a continuation of the publications of the Camden Society (1838–1897) as
the *Camden Series*, and since 1937 by a series of *Guides and handbooks*.
The Society also began in 1937 an annual bibliography of *Writings on
British History*, for the continuation of which the Institute of Historical
Research accepted responsibility in 1965; it publishes, in conjunction
with the American Historical Association, a series of *Bibliographies of
British History*; and from time to time it issues miscellaneous publications. Additional copies of the *Transactions*, the *Camden Series*, the
Guides and handbooks, and the 'Miscellaneous publications' may be
obtained by Fellows and Subscribing Libraries at the prices stated below.
The series of annual bibliographies of *Writings on British history* and
the *Bibliographies of British history* are not included among the volumes
issued to subscribers, but may be obtained by them at the special prices
stated below by ordering from a bookseller or from the publishers. Associates, while receiving only the *Transactions* in return for their subscription, are entitled to purchase at a reduction of 25 per cent one copy
of other volumes issued to Fellows and Subscribing Libraries and one
copy of each of the volumes of the *Writings on British history* and the
Bibliographies of British history at the special price.

N.B. Current volumes of the *Transactions* and *Camden Series* (*i.e.* those
for the current year and two years preceding) are not sold by the Society
to the public, but are available only to members on application to the
Society.

Back issues of both series are obtainable from Wm. Dawson & Sons Ltd,
Cannon House, Folkestone, Kent, and *Guides and handbooks* from Dawsons of Pall Mall at the same address.

TRANSACTIONS

Additional copies of *Transactions* may be had for £2·50. (Special price to
members, who should order from the Society, £1·87.)

Volumes out of print in *Transactions, Old, New and Third Series* may
be obtained from Kraus-Thomson Organisation Ltd.

Old series, 1872–1882. Vols. I to X.
New series, 1884–1906. Vols. I to XX.
Third series, 1907–1917. Vols. I to XI.
Fourth series, 1918–1950. Vols. I to XXXII.
Fifth series, 1951–   . Vols I–XXIII.

MISCELLANEOUS PUBLICATIONS

Copies of the following, which are still in print, may be obtained from
the Society, with the exception of *The Domesday Monachorum of Christ*

Church, Canterbury and *The Royal Historical Society, 1868–1968,* which
can be ordered from Dawsons of Pall Mall, Cannon House, Folkestone,
Kent, and *Essays in Modern History,* which is obtainable from Mac-
millan and Co., Ltd.

Domesday studies. 2 vols. Edited by P. E. Dove. 1886. £3·50. (Vol. 1 out of
    print.)
German opinion and German policy before the War. By G. W. Prothero.
    1916. 75p.
The *Domesday monachorum* of Christ Church, Canterbury. 1944. £15.
Essays in Medieval History, selected from the Transactions of the Royal
    Historical Society. Edited by R. W. Southern. 1968. London, Mac-
    millan. *p.b.,* 50p.
Essays in Modern History, selected from the Transactions of the Royal
    Historical Society. Edited by Ian R. Christie. 1968. London, Mac-
    millan. £2·75, *p.b.,* £1·50.
The Royal Historical Society, 1868–1968. By R. A. Humphreys. 1969.
    £1·25.

BIBLIOGRAPHIES ISSUED IN CONJUNCTION WITH THE AMERICAN HISTORICAL ASSOCIATION

Copies of the following cannot be supplied by the Society, but may be
ordered through a bookseller.

Bibliography of British history: Tudor Period, 1485–1603. Edited by
    Conyers Read. 1st ed. 1933; 2nd ed. 1959. Oxford Univ. Press £3·75.
    (Special price, £2·80.)
Bibliography of British history: Stuart period, 1603–1714. 2nd ed. Edited
    by Mary F. Keeler, 1970. Oxford Univ. Press. £5. (Special price,
    £3·75.)
Bibliography of British history: 1714–1789. Edited by S. M. Pargellis and
    D. J. Medley. 1951. Oxford Univ. Press. (Out of print.) Supplement,
    edited by A. T. Milne and A. N. Newman, *in preparation.*
Bibliography of British history: 1789–1851. Edited by Ian R. Christie and
    Lucy M. Brown, *in preparation.*
Bibliography of British history: 1851–1914. Edited by H. J. Hanham, *in
    preparation.*
Bibliography of English History to 1485. Based on The Sources and
    Literature of English History from earliest times by Charles Gross.
    Revised and expanded by Edgar B. Graves, *in the press.*

ANNUAL BIBLIOGRAPHIES

Copies of the following cannot be supplied by the Society, but may be
ordered from a bookseller or the Institute of Historical Research.

Writings on British history, 1901–1933 (5 vols. in 7); Vol 1–3, 1968, Vol. 4,
    1969, Vol. 5, 1970. London, Jonathan Cape. Vol. 1, £5·25 (special
    price £4·58); Vol. 2, £3·15 (special price £2·75); Vol. 3, £5·25 (special
    price £4·58); Vol. 4 (in two parts), £7·35 (special price £6·40); Vol. 5
    (in two parts), £8·40 (special price £7·35).
Writings on British history, 1934. Compiled by A. T. Milne. 1937. Lon-
    don, Jonathan Cape, £1·75. (Special price, £1·50.)

Writings on British history, 1935. Compiled by A. T. Milne. 1939. London, Jonathan Cape, £1·75. (Special price, £1·50.)
Writings on British history, 1936. Compiled by A. T. Milne. 1940. London, Jonathan Cape, £1·75. (Special price, £1·50.)
Writings on British history, 1937. Compiled by A. T. Milne. 1949. London, Jonathan Cape, £1·75. (Special price, £1·50.)
Writings on British history, 1938. Compiled by A. T. Milne. 1951. London, Jonathan Cape, £1·75. (Special price, £1·50.)
Writings on British history, 1939. Compiled by A. T. Milne. 1953. London, Jonathan Cape. (Out of print.)
Writings on British history, 1940–1945. 2 vols. Compiled by A. T. Milne. 1960. London, Jonathan Cape, £6·30. (Special price, £5·50.)
Writings on British history, 1946–48. Compiled by D. J. Munro. 1973. University of London Inst. of Historical Research, £12·00. (Special price £9·00.)

GUIDES AND HANDBOOKS

Main series

1. Guide to English commercial statistics, 1696–1782. By G. N. Clark, with a catalogue of materials by Barbara M. Franks. 1938. £1·50.
2. Handbook of British chronology. Edited by F. M. Powicke and E. B. Fryde, 1st ed. 1939; 2nd ed. 1961. £4·50.
3. Medieval libraries of Great Britain, a list of surviving books. Edited by N. R. Ker, 1st ed. 1941; 2nd ed. 1964. £4·50.
4. Handbook of dates for students of English history. By C. R. Cheney. 1970. £1·50.
5. Guide to the national and provincial directories of England and Wales, excluding London, published before 1856. By Jane E. Norton. 1950. £2·00.
6. Handbook of Oriental history. Edited by C. H. Philips. 1963. £2·25.
7. Texts and calendars: an analytical guide to serial publications. Edited by E. L. C. Mullins. 1958. £4·50.
8. Anglo-Saxon charters. An annotated list and bibliography. Edited by P. H. Sawyer. 1968. £5·25.
9. A Centenary Guide to the Publications of the Royal Historical Society, 1868–1968. Edited by A. T. Milne. 1968. £3·00.

Supplementary series

1. A Guide to Cabinet Ministers' papers, 1900–1951. Edited by Cameron Hazlehurst and Christine Woodland (*in the press*).

Provisionally accepted for future publication:

A Handbook of British Currency. Edited by P. Grierson and C. E. Blunt.
Texts and calendars: an analytical guide to serial publications. Supplement, 1958–1968. By E. L. C. Mullins.
A Guide to the Local Administrative Units of England and Wales. Edited by F. A. Youngs.
A Register of Parliamentary Poll Books, c. 1700–1870. Edited by E. L. C. Mullins.

THE CAMDEN SERIES

Camdens published before the *Fourth Series* are listed in A. T. Milne's *A Centenary Guide to the Publications of the Royal Historical Society.*

Additional copies of volumes in the *Camden Series* may be had for £3·00. (Special price to members £2·25.)

Volumes out of print in the *Camden Old* and *New Series* may be obtained from Johnson Reprint Co. Ltd. Orders for out-of-print volumes in *Camden Third* and *Fourth Series* should be placed with Wm. Dawson & Sons, Ltd., Cannon House, Folkestone, Kent.

FOURTH SERIES

1. Camden Miscellany, Vol. XXII: 1. Charters of the Earldom of Hereford, 1095–1201. Edited by David Walker. 2. Indentures of Retinue with John of Gaunt, Duke of Lancaster, enrolled in Chancery, 1367–1399. Edited by N. B. Lewis. 3. Autobiographical memoir of Joseph Jewell, 1763–1846. Edited by A. W. Slater. 1964.
2. Documents illustrating the rule of Walter de Wenlock, Abbot of Westminster, 1283–1307. Edited by Barbara Harvey. 1965.
3. The early correspondence of Richard Wood, 1831–1841. Edited by A. B. Cunningham. 1966. (*Out of print.*)
4. Letters from the English abbots to the chapter at Cîteaux, 1442–1521. Edited by C. H. Talbot. 1967.
5. Select writings of George Wyatt. Edited by D. M. Loades. 1968.
6. Records of the trial of Walter Langeton, Bishop of Lichfield and Coventry (1307–1312). Edited by Miss A. Beardwood. 1969.
7. Camden Miscellany, Vol. XXIII: 1. The Account Book of John Balsall of Bristol for a trading voyage to Spain, 1480. Edited by T. F. Reddaway and A. A. Ruddock. 2. A parliamentary diary of Queen Anne's reign. Edited by W. A. Speck. 3. Leicester House politics, 1750–1760, from the papers of John, second Earl of Egmont. Edited by A. N. Newman. 4. The Parliamentary diary of Nathaniel Ryder, 1764–67. Edited by P. D. G. Thomas. 1969.
8. Documents illustrating the British Conquest of Manila, 1762–1763. Edited by Nicholas P. Cushner. 1971.
9. Camden Miscellany, Vol. XXIV: 1. Documents relating to the Breton succession dispute of 1341. Edited by M. Jones. 2. Documents relating to Anglo-French negotiations, 1439. Edited by C. T. Allmand. 3. A 'Fifteenth century chronicle' at Trinity College, Dublin. Edited by G. L. Harriss.
10. Herefordshire Militia Assessments of 1663. Edited by M. A. Faraday.
11. The early correspondence of Jabez Bunting, 1820–1829. Edited by W. R. Ward.
12. Wentworth Papers, 1597–1628. Edited by J. P. Cooper.
13. Camden Miscellany, Vol. XXV: 1. The Letters of William, Lord Paget. Edited by Barrett L. Beer and Sybil Jack. 2. The Parliamentary Diary of John Clementson, 1770–1802. Edited by P. D. G. Thomas. 3. J. B. Pentland's Report on Bolivia, 1827. Edited by J. V. Fifer (*in the press*).

Provisionally accepted for future publication:

The Account Book of Beaulieu Abbey. Edited by S. F. Hockey.

Select documents illustrating the internal crisis of 1296–1298 in England. Edited by Michael Prestwich.
The *Acta* of Archbishop Hugh of Rouen (1130–1164). Edited by T. Waldman.
Cartularies of Reading Abbey. Edited by B. R. Kemp.
A calendar of Western Circuit Assize Orders, 1629–1649. Edited by J. S. Cockburn.
The Letter Book of Thomas Bentham, Bishop of Coventry and Lichfield. Edited by M. Rosemary O'Day and J. A. Berlatsky.
Lawrence Squibb, A Booke of all the Severall Officers of the Court of the Exchequer (1642). Edited by W. H. Bryson.
A Breviat of the Effectes devised for Wales. Edited by P. R. Roberts.
Letters of Henry St John to Charles, Earl of Orrery, 1709–1711. Edited by H. T. Dickinson.
Correspondence of Henry Cromwell, 1655–1659. Edited by Clyve Jones.
Correspondence of William Camden. Edited by Richard DeMolen.
Gervase Markham, The Muster-Master. Edited by Charles L. Hamilton.
Fifteenth-Century Treatises on English Political Ideas. Edited by J.-Ph. Genet.
Sidney Ironworks Accounts, 1541–1573. Edited by D. W. Crossley.
Duchy of Lancaster Ordinances, 1483. Edited by Sir Robert Somerville.
Heresy Trials in the Diocese of Norwich, 1428–31. Edited by N. P. Tanner.